TESTIMONIALS

Our compliments on a fantastic book that touched both my daughters and I in many ways. You put a lot of perspective on both parent and child. So much love within the family structure. Both daughters said, "They would be very proud to have a Mother like you were to Chip."Our greatest respect to you always. M.Michels. 4/96

"Kitty Caley's story on her son was the most profound topic I covered as a jour-nalist. It was very emotional." Linda Stoehr, Editor of Mid Cities News 2/95

Your Book Lifted My Spirit And Touched My Heart!! Judy B. 7/02

"The hard part is making sure people aren't afraid to touch and read the book because it is about AIDS. It will help people to pick it up and read it. She was brave enough to expose everything; her feelings, things she felt were mistakes. She put that aside going with her gut feeling the information would help educate peo-ple." Paul Cobb with AOC in Ft Worth, Texas 2/95

Grandpa Dale, 90, said "Chip was a good boy." Then he reminiscence about Chip. Grandma Dorothy, 88, proudly says "Chip was a real darling! Of my six kids and grandkids Chip was the first to play the piano like I do." Grandma proudly com-pares Chips piano playing to one recital in particular. "Chip was just as refined and beautiful as that million dollar church. Chip did a million dollar perform-ance!" I/03

Just wanted to tell you your book was HEARTWARMING AND SAD! It's people like you that make this a better place to live for all of us! JD Williamson 3/95

Jerry Lynn, Founder of The Caring Friends Center in Dallas said: Kitty is one of the original volunteers and we keep her book available. "ULTIMATE LOVE: A Life of Soul & Searching" is both interesting and educational. An exceptionally good way to inform people in an understandable way. Kitty's concern is not only for the individual with HIV/AIDS, but for everyone. For HIV/AIDS Awareness Kitty's inspiration with the book is a great asset to all cultures. 4/0I

Your book was very tough to read just months after the loss of my loved one, yet very healing and made me feel less alone in my grief. Thank You. Gerald Ediger 6/03

"The book of your sons life was so well done, and like myself I feel it touches many people's life. Your sharing both the good and the bad times was so moving and so real to life! May you be surrounded by Love and Light always." Earl G. Bell I0/03

ULTIMATE
Love

A Life of Soul and Searching

KITTY CALEY

ISBN
978-1-957895-68-0 (Paperback)
978-1-957895-69-7 (eBook)

Dedication

In loving memory I am dedicating "ULTIMATE LOVE: A Life of Soul and Searching" to my son, Brandon Twigg (Emory Dale) "CHIP" Williamson and to EVERYONE WHO HAS BEEN TOUCHED BY THIS TRAUMATIC ILLNESS.

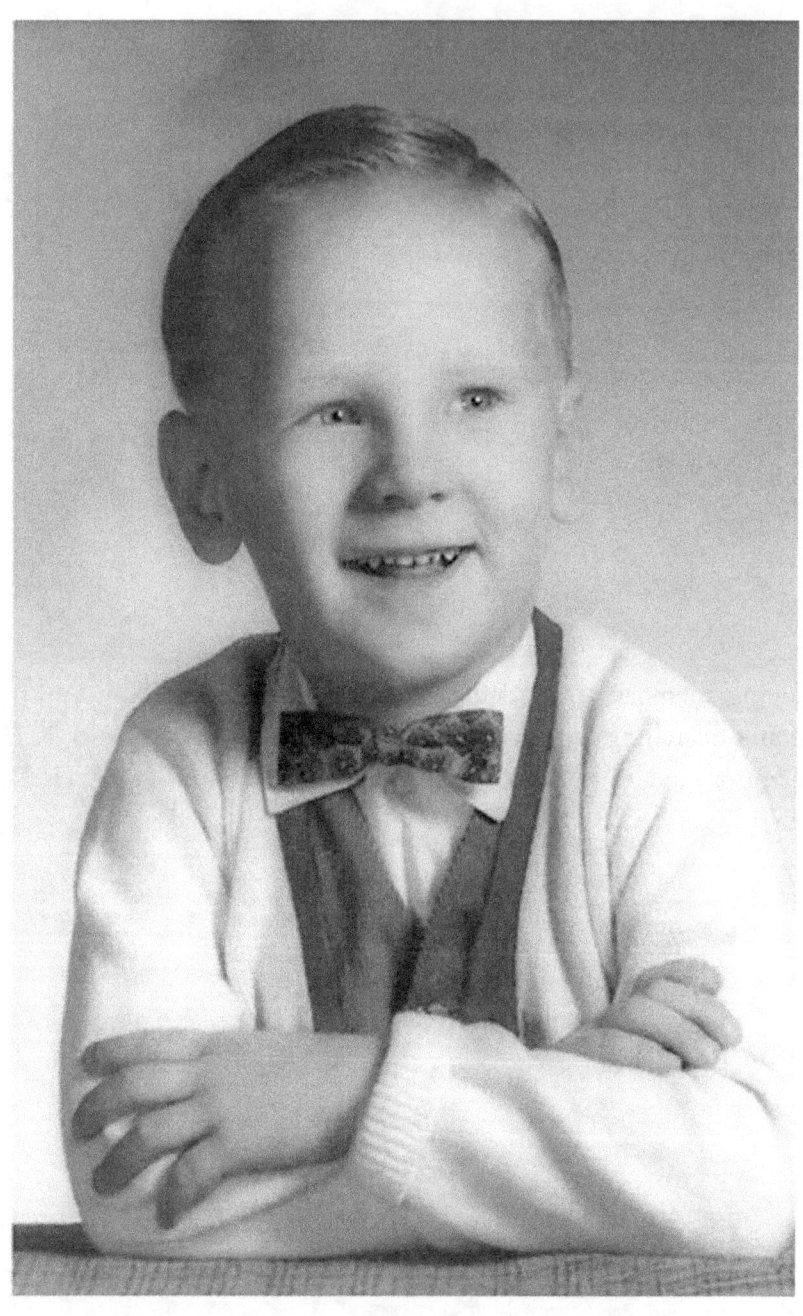

I Lend This Child to You
by Edgar A. Guest

I'll lend you for a little while
A child of mine He said.
For you to love the while he lives
And mourn for when he's dead.

It may be 6 or 7 years or 22 or 3,
But will you till I call him back
Take care of him for me?

He'll bring his charms to gladden you
And should his stay be brief.
You'll have his lovely memories
As solace for your grief.

I cannot promise he will stay
Since all from earth return;
But there are lessons taught down there, I want this child to learn.

I've searched this wide world over In my look for teachers true, And
from the throngs that crowd life's lanes
I have selected you.

Now give him all your love,
Nor think your labor vain,
Nor hate me when I come to call
To take him back again.
I fancied that I heard them say,
"Dear Lord, Thy will be done.
For all the joys this one shall bring,
The risk of grief we'll run.

"We'll shelter him with tenderness
And love him while we may
And for all the happiness he brings
Grateful forever stay.

"And should the angel come to call
Much sooner than we've planned,
We'll brave the bitter grief that comes
And try to understand."

Barbara Shultz, who was MLS Secretary in the office Chip and I were in, was a good friend to us and gave this to me as a special gesture in remembrance of Chip saying it may be too soon at present, but someday I would understand. She was right, and a very thoughtful friend indeed.

Sunday—after church. Chip, his mother, and Scotty,
Ft. Wayne 72.
Inset photos: Small, adorable pictures of Chip in
younger days.

Contents

Foreword

Brandon Twigg Williamson—"CHIP" was a pioneer with AIDS. Be it death because of the 9/11 attack on the United States or the worldwide attack of HIV/AIDS it's a life of love, and in our hearts they remain.

In Chip's days not much was known, nor was there any encouragement. You died with AIDS. Today you live with AIDS due to the great improvement of medicines and knowledge. Yet this often leaves a misconception with people thinking they can just take a pill and that's it! Then it may be too late when people learn of the side effects and what this medicine can do to the body. There is still much pain and suffering. Never knowing what to expect.

The real difference today is that HIV/AIDS can be prevented. Yet the death toll continues to climb. We've come along ways with more understanding and more people wanting to help. Yet in the next breath this may be contradicted with the same stigma and fear still overpowering ones thinking. It's surprising many people still do not understand about AIDS; therefore they do nothing. One may be a carrier of the virus and not know it. Abstinence or Condoms and HIV/AIDS TESTING are the only (sure) way to know you are doing your body justice.

Introduction

One never knows what fate holds in store as life takes its many twists and turns. We are all aware of the sexual revolution in the seventies. This was the younger generation that became more noted for its promiscuity and openness with all lifestyles. It was during this time sex and vices were on the uprise. Today we are paying the price. For many this has or is costing them their lives.

In the beginning society regarded AIDS, Acquired Immune Deficiency Syndrome, as a gay disease. This was not true. It was already among heterosexuals in Africa before it became known in the United States. Haitian immigrants in New York and Miami were having the immune system abnormalities and opportunistic infections.

In the early eighties the AIDS virus was in San Francisco and New York, although then we weren't hearing about it. The rumor is it was kept quiet as a means of gay elimination.

Then AIDS was noted amongst heterosexuals and becoming widely spread. The concern seemed to change. The awareness of AIDS quietly started to surface once it was realized AIDS hadn't any preference as to whom it would attack!

Still, another attack came about by society once the word "AIDS" surfaced. The stigma attached to the disease was on the warpath and overpowered the compassion most needed. Fear was embedded and AIDS misconstrued. Wasn't death, which was without question, already causing enough stress and heartbreak for those infected? It was most devastating for the patient, family, and friends.

To be afraid was understandable. But people need to know where the "needed fear lies." To know and realize what AIDS is all about. AIDS is an incurable disease in which the virus attacks the body's immune system, leaving the individual susceptible to a variety of infections and cancers. Most important, AIDS can be spread only by body fluids, such as blood or semen, that carry the virus. This is where the real fear of this disease lies.

To be afraid of seeing or touching someone with AIDS for fear of getting it is wrong. There isn't any reason to isolate AIDS patients because of mistaken fear. They need the same treatment as the next sick person you're around, taking care of them in your home or visiting them at the hospital. This is all that is necessary and important. They need the same tender love and attention. Maybe more so. That is the best medicine you can give them. Love prevails and is the greatest medicine of all.

That is right. There isn't any reason to treat the person with AIDS any differently. They aren't any different except for an immunodeficiency disease. At the onset of AIDS the sure thing was that you were dying. Yes, this was the real scare. This was their life. This was their concern. They didn't want you to be afraid of them. Had they given you reason to be afraid before? It's no different now. I'm sure all they want is your consideration and understanding. Truly, that's all. Is that asking too much?

Realize stress is one of the worst things for these people to deal with. Haven't they enough to contend with? Why burden them unnecessarily? Death is something we have no control over. When it is to be or how and all the way through and at the end is what's important. The dying person is a loving, caring human being. Enjoy his life with him while you can.

It wasn't easy for my son, or me, living with the unpleasant reality that he was dying without any hope whatsoever, with no cure in sight. To make matters worse, there wasn't any way of knowing what to anticipate next with the vast variety of unknown negative complications. The uncertainty of the medicines or how to care for the patient at this early stage of the disease often was of no avail. This was sad and devastating, leaving the patient to die because of AIDS. One can only imagine the slow torture of constantly being faced with the fear and wonder of what was going to happen next as his young, muscular body slowly, but surely deteriorated, depriving him of his pride and self-esteem.

His life had taken a complete turnabout once he was told he had the reluctant disease, AIDS. His young adult years were about to become completely different and earthshaking, in every respect, from his prior twenty-five years on earth.

Now I can and do want to share with you all that I can. Most of us who are having to deal with this adversity seem to have one major thing in common, which is quite humiliating and possibly the most difficult for us to deal with, let alone the concern for our loved one, and that is this: Why must we be silent?

How do you think this must have made my son feel? Why wasn't I facing reality? He couldn't understand this at first. I had taught him the importance of honesty, and now on his dying bed, "What was happening?"

I don't know if I will ever be able to live down my not being more candid while he was alive. He was honest and up front about this happening to him. We talked, and at first he couldn't understand why I was hesitant about using the word AIDS. He wasn't.

Like my son said, "Honesty is all I have left."

With some friends and dose family, I too was candid. They loved and accepted him for the good person he was.

Then one day he sincerely said, "Mother, I understand and I am sorry. You do what you must."

Today I can still see the empty, sad expression on his face. This was so unfair to him. I repeat, this was so unfair to him.

The disease itself was bad enough, let alone all the distress he had to endure. Never was I ashamed of my son. I was ashamed of the reaction of those who couldn't handle AIDS. That's why it was kept a secret from so many. Not because we want to keep it quiet, but because of society's attitude. However, we cannot accept society's condemnation. Society needs to be educated. AIDS does not discriminate.

I could not and cannot accept the fact that because of AIDS, my son's life or death be judged. Who has the right? Now that he is no longer of this body, now that he has gone across, do you dare to call him unworthy to enter the kingdom of God? What difference does i t make what he died from? Do you dare judge him beyond? Death is death, and in the heavens the spirit is eternal.

Today I understand how anxiety must have taken a toll on my actions, which I hadn't acknowledged during the duration of caring for my son. Now I see how the stress apparently affected both of us, although we never let it take over our love, determination, and concern for each other. This was what kept us going and how we managed within our own capacity and capabilities.

I believe people need to take into consideration what is happening when it comes to AIDS and maybe go about it in a completely different manner than they ordinarily would. In fact, as time goes along, they may realize this is how it needs to be—just like it was for my son and me. For our having such a positive outlook on life and our determination to do our best, we now faced the most negative crisis that life could possibly give us. And so soon in life.

My only regret about writing is the fact that I am now coming forward publicly and my son is gone. Through love and with love to my son, Chip, I am proudly writing this in his memory—a memory of the beautiful person he always was.

Cheryl and Chip on his 11th birthday at our restaurant.
This has always been a favorite picture.

Mermaid made by Chip and friends from shrimp on beach.
(Chapter9)

Chip with Gramma Dorothy. Chipper was always the apple of Gramma's eye, a very- special grandson indeed to each of his Grammas! Today Gramma Dorothy wants to thank Chip for her wonderful trip to Hawaii in 1988, in memory of Chip's thoughtfulness, always. (Chapter 1)

Chip with Grampa Chris when he was learning to walk. Chris was always there to help...or to do some teasing. (Chapter 1)

Chip at 3 years of age. This picture was always one of Gramma's favorites. (Chapter 1)

Chip, Grampa, and Gramma Marge. (Chapter 2)

Chip with patrolman his first day of school in Ft. Wayne, Indiana. (Chapter 2)

Chip in his white sportcoat. Gramma isn't seen, but Chip is opening the car door for her. They are going to his piano recital. Chip's a little younger in lower right comer. (Chapter 2)

Chip and Hank (a.k.a. Hing) are home cleaning oysters. (Chapter2)

Grampa, Chip, and Scotty. (Chapter 2)

When Chip was about eleven years old, he painted the Serenity Prayer for both of his Grammas for Grandmother's Day. (Chapter 2)

God grant me the Serenity to accept the things I cannot change... the Courage to change the things I can ... and the Wisdom to know the difference.

Chip on Mackinaw Island, Michigan, 1972,
always full of fun and frolic with a great sense of humor. (Chapter 2)

Chip and his mother on Mother's Day, 1972.
Kitty is wearing the Chinese ensemble her sister,
Susie, designed and made for her. The jacket is black
with a gold metallic design with exquisite gold trim and
a lightweight wool gaberdine pantsuit to match. Chapter 3.

Chip at the piano. His music and jolly voice made the atmosphere even homier. (Chapter 3)

Chip at sixteen. (Chapter 5)

Chip and Beth on Chip's twenty-first birthday, at the Old San Francisco Steak House in Dallas, Texas. (Chapter 5)

Chip when he received realtor honors in Dallas, Texas (left), in the
familiar stance from his childhood (age six, right). (Chapter 6)

Chip and his cousin Theresa, making a cast of her hand which
turned out to be quite humorous! (Chapter 6)

Chip and his mother when Chip was about eighteen years old. This picture is a favorite of Jerry's. (Chapter 4)

Chip, his mother, and his dad, Jerry celebrating
another birthday. (Chapter 5).

Chip, his mother, and his dad, Jerry at South Fork. Century 2I Pre-Hawaiian
Luau celebration before going to Hawaii that year. (Chapter 6).

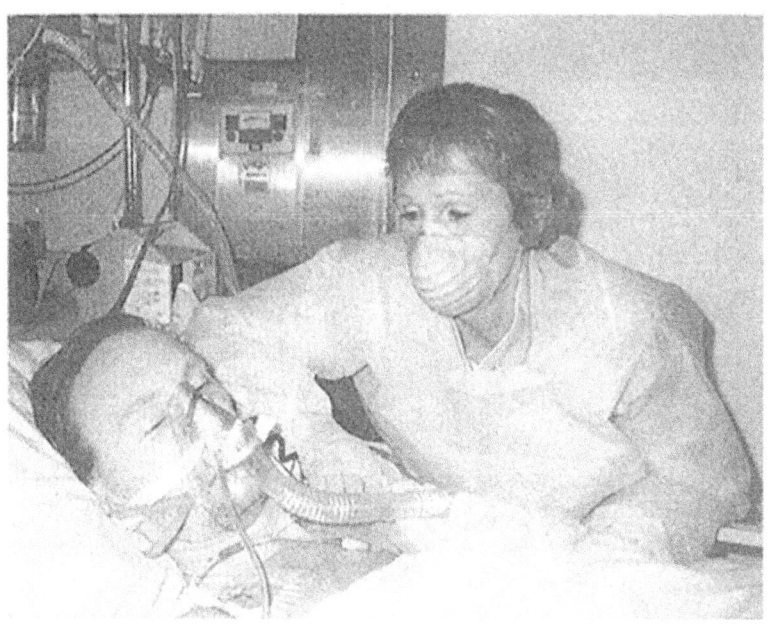

On Chip's second day in the hospital, he stopped breathing and was put on the life machine. His mother is with him. (Chapter 12)

Chip with his snowman back home in Indiana. (Chapter 13)

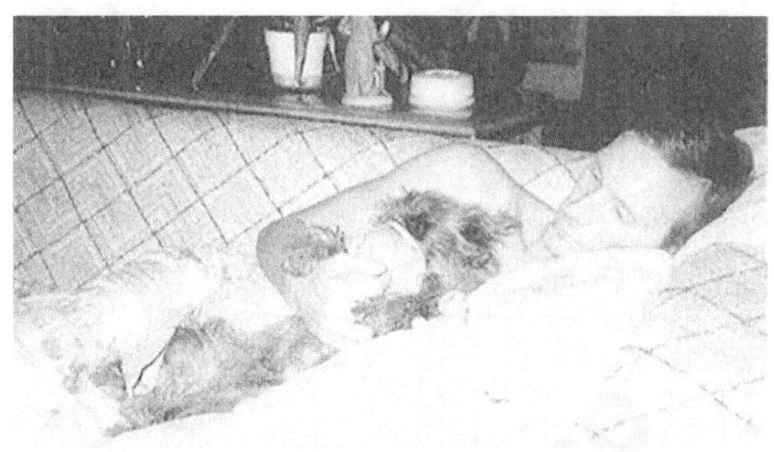

After Chip came home from the hospital. He is humoring his
cairn terrier, Tasha, with a mask from the hospital. Tasha is like
Toto in *The Wizard of Oz.* Shirley Temple and Toto were favorites
Chip enjoyed annually on television. (Chapter 14)

Chip's unique T-shirt, which
he received from Rhonda for his
twenty-sixth birthday. In small
black print it says, "I'M IN NO
SHAPE TO EXERCISE."

In the fall of 1988, Kitty participated in reading names during the first year of the AIDS quilt in Dallas, Texas. Kitty is wearing the Names Cap and holding Chip's pillow and her list of names.

The angels in this symbolic arrangement have watched over Chip for many years, and still remain.

Significant memories of love: Kris Krinkles, Chapter 24; purple bull with red rose in mouth, Chapter 3; blue candle, Chapter 15; doll in lavender lace dress, Chapter 3; bear with red heart on a gold strand in its chest pocket, Chapter 15; *Special Son, Chip pillow,* Chapter 25.

Loyal friend Rhonda admiring Chip's ring for 27th Birthday.
Balloons from her enhanced surprise party that evening with
more friends. (Chapter 22)

Morning of 26th Birthday before his party that eve. Balloons and gifts galore, with
a flower bouquet from Aunt Mary Lou & fm. In Baltimore Md. (Chapter 13)

1

Life and Destiny

Cynthia and I were at the health club. We had gotten acquainted in the previous weeks after our workouts, usually rushing while we prepared for our busy days.

I casually asked, "Cynthia, what ages are your children?"

"My youngest is nine and my oldest is twenty."

A few seconds later, she asked, "Do you have children?"

"I had a son." I paused. Cynthia looked at me, waiting.

In a bleak, soft voice, I added, "I lost him in February."

"Oh, I'm sorry," she said, solemnly.

Thoughts started flashing through my mind, almost as though I were preparing for her next question—and my answer—while she walked toward me.

"How old was your son?"

"Twenty-seven." Thinking of his birth date, I grimly added in dismay, "He would have been twenty-eight this month, two weeks from today."

Remembering this gave me a sad, futile feeling.

"Was he married?"

I looked at her while all the old fears and thoughts came rushing to my mind. Suddenly, through the blur of thoughts, I commented, "No. My son was gay."

Hearing this come out of my mouth surprised me. She seemed only concerned and caring, as though she wanted to listen.

In spite of my fear, I said, "My son passed away because of AIDS."

Cynthia didn't seem shocked, nor did her expression change while she continued to stand there. Even though the openness of my reply was unusual I felt no qualms and a wave of relief washed over me.

I gasped, "You're the first person I've said that to, except, of course, family and friends who knew Chip."

I paused, then smiled and said, "Gosh, that's quite an accomplishment for me! The fact that public opinion is putting such a stigma on AIDS is so wrong. If only they knew what it was doing to the people involved. I cannot cope with the thought of anyone judging or ridiculing my son! I loved him dearly, and it would be so unfair to him. What he went through was more than enough! And, Cynthia, it's definitely apparent AIDS doesn't discriminate."

Cynthia said, "I'm sorry. I can understand how all this must hurt you."

Gravely I replied, "Cynthia, the sad part is that while he was alive I couldn't talk with just anyone about AIDS, except, of course, those I knew could handle the subject. It's been almost nine months since he's been gone. The effort to avoid using the word AIDS was so unfair to him."

I told her how it still bothers me that I wasn't more open. How he couldn't understand at first why I was hesitant to say he had AIDS, especially since he had been raised to feel strongly about the importance of honesty, and then with him on his deathbed.

I told her, too, how he at one point said to me, "Mother, I understand and I am sorry. You do what you feel you must."

"I will never forget the sad, empty expression on his face, nor can I forgive myself."

Shaken a bit, I paused, then continued, "That's why I'm writing about him, his Life and Destiny. When it was suggested I write, my first thought was, Then I can let everyone know what a good son I have. Cynthia, he truly was. I never had to say anything because people were always complimenting me about Chip's character and how pleasant he was. Then people were really surprised to learn he was an only child, always saying he sure didn't act like one. Never was there any reason to defend him, but quite the opposite. And now, if people are going to talk, they need to know what they're talking about. People need to realize the importance of this subject."

Cynthia nodded agreeably and I kept talking. "At the same time, I know there are a lot of others out there like myself, going through some of the same pressures, alone and secluded with the heartbreak of losing loved ones through this horrible, isolated disease."

Looking at the clock, I said, "Goodness, Cynthia, I didn't mean to go on so about that. I realize you need to get to work."

Cynthia replied, "I'm glad you shared with me. It sounds like your experience can benefit and educate many people about AIDS."

Anxiously I said, "Yes, this is one subject that's important to be understood with compassion worldwide!

"Months before we knew anything about AIDS, Chip was going through some puzzling ordeals that were earthshaking. Eventually this was called a nervous breakdown, which was most humiliating to Chip. He had a lot of pride and was always in control, never letting anything get the best of him. It was several months after that 'breakdown' when we learned about the symptoms of AIDS and that it was fatal. The breakdown was never in the picture again.

"Now, Cynthia, since he's been gone, I've learned some things. I believe the temporary, puzzling encounters causing so much confusion were neurological, stemming from his unknown physical condition, definitely not emotional. Since then, they've learned that this often occurs with AIDS, as a first notable symptom. Like I said though, I didn't even know AIDS existed, let alone know anything about the neurological or AIDS Dementia Complex. If only Chip had known! I'm so sorry I did not learn about this until after he passed away."

It hurt just thinking of these things, but I continued.

"Of course, then when the other complications started, I wouldn't accept the fact that my son was going to die, so how could I begin to say it to others, to say he had AIDS? We were always positive, and AIDS was only negative. I would say he had tuberculosis, which was correct, but I would not say anything that implied AIDS might be involved. I couldn't and I wouldn't! It was like a nightmare for Chip and me.

"During Chip's time with the complications, not much was known, and we lived in constant fear."

Cynthia nodded with a sigh and grasped my hand. Now that the dam had broken, words flooded out of my mouth.

"During the later months I was quizzed by someone I had told about his 'breakdown,' in the beginning. Now she crudely asked, 'Just what was it you said Chip had?' Her implication was unexpected and really surprised me. It was enough of a jab to put me on guard."

Cynthia shook her head, sighing. "People can be cruel."

"It did hurt, then later on made me furious when I thought about it. My son was my only concern, and that was enough to make me aware from that day forward!

"In my book I tell about other experiences I had no knowledge of until after Chip was gone—incidents that must have crushed him. If only I had known at the time so I could have comforted him. All his life he took things in stride and never complained."

Cynthia listened while she readied herself for work. I just couldn't seem to stop talking.

"Before he passed away, I had said, 'Chip, I bet one of these days they will learn that your breakdown was not a breakdown, but had something to do with AIDS.' I was speaking from intuition, knowing the sensible, levelheaded person Chip was.

"Today the facts are evident that that's what happened to him spontaneously in the beginning, before AIDS even came into the picture with Chip or before they even knew enough about AIDS to check it out with him. It's just a shame he didn't live long enough to know it was because of the physical over the path his brilliant mind intermittently had taken; the idea of a breakdown really bothered him, to think he had no control. Goodness, Cynthia, I've got to shut up, it's just that one thing leads to another. After he passed away, all I could talk about was the beautiful funeral he had."

I caught myself and said, "I can't get started on that, or I'll really make you late."

I smiled, saying, "Thanks, Cynthia, for listening. It's just that Chip is always on my mind. But I've got to quit talking and let you get to work. Talk with you later."

Cynthia smiled and replied, 'TH hold you to that."

— 3 —

This is why I have come forward now, in loving memory of my son, Chip, to share with you his unique character and his zest for life, which was so short-lived and ended so tragically. I will start with his birth because his life was so phenomenally entwined like deja vu.

On November 19, 1959, at 12:25 P.M. in Orange, California, Chip was born. How could we guess then that this wonderful baby would spend his life searching for love? He was indeed beautiful! I had always feared the possibility of having a red, wrinkly, ugly baby, like some are. Not Chip! He was healthy and truly pretty as a picture with high Indian cheekbones and deep-set, expressive, pretty blue eyes. His skin was so soft and clear. He weighed seven pounds, eleven ounces and was twenty inches long. My brother Duane still says, "He was such a pretty baby! I've seen many newborns, but Chip certainly was the prettiest."

Chip was the most wonderful blessing God could have given us. Just what his dad and I had wanted, a boy! How could we imagine what happiness and sorrow we would experience and how much we would learn through this special child.

It was the wonderful beginning for the three of us. What more could we ask? Our prayers had been answered. My husband and I had been chosen to give this child our love, care, and understanding while he was here on this earth. We were both so happy and proud.

Already Chip's dad had started making all kinds of hunting and fishing plans for them, even though Chip was only a few weeks old.

Once, as he held Chip in his arms, he laughingly said, "I remember when I started fishing and the day I caught my first big fish with my dad."

He was real excited while he talked to Chip about all his plans with him for the future.

He said, "It won't be long until you will be big enough to go fishing with me and you can bai t our hooks. Then we will catch that big ol' fish for you, Chip! We'll be tugging, pulling, and reeling it in together with all our might. Yes siree, Chipper ol' boy. We'll catch lots of fish. You and I!"

The way little Chip looked at his dad, smiling and his eyes sparkling, you would think he already understood every word his dad was saying. Of course, this excited his dad even more while he told Chip more big ol' fish stories about his young days fishing with his dad and sister.

With a big sigh, he hugged Chip close and said, "Yes, son, it won't be long until we'll be having lots of good times together."

Chip's Gramma and Grampa Chris, my mother and stepfather, lived across town from us, in Orange, so Chip and his dad spent a lot of time with them while I worked evenings. When I took Chip in for his six-week checkup, he got a good bill of health from the doctor. I called Chip's Gramma to give her the good report and she invited us for dinner as a little celebration.

Grampa Chris is the one who gave him the nickname "Chip" before he was born.

At the time I had said, "Never, I wouldn't have such a name on my child." Everyone started calling him Chip right away, except me. One day without thinking, I called him Chip.

Grinning, Chip's dad said, "What did you call our son?"

Sure enough, I had called him Chip. It did fit him perfectly. He always was a good "Chip."

After dinner everyone was in the living room talking. Chip was lying on the sofa next to us when I noticed he couldn't seem to catch his breath and started turning pale. Scared, I grabbed him up and Mother rushed over to see what was wrong. While Gramma continued to work with Chip, comforting and turning him, then raising his arm up above his head, I hurried to the telephone and called the doctor. He said to bring Chip to the office immediately. He would meet us there.

I hurriedly wrapped Chip in his blanket, then we rushed out the door and Daddy drove speeding across town. With the anxiety it seemed to be miles farther than usual. As soon as the car stopped, I cuddled Chip up close in my arms, jumped out, and with his dad hurried into the doctor's office.

The doctor was very calm. He lay Chip down on the gurney to examine him while we anxiously watched. The doctor took a long, thin rubber tube and slowly guided it into Chip's nose. Down, down it went into his lungs. The tube was attached to a two-foot glass tank sitting beside the gurney Chip was lying on. While we watched, the doctor slowly and carefully moved the tube around. Then we saw a lot of mucus floating in the tank; it was being suctioned from Chip's lungs. It seemed forever before the doctor finally pulled the tube back out of Chip's nose. Even though Chip hadn't made a sound, I felt such pain just thinking of how this must have felt for him.

After checking Chip more, the doctor finally said, "Now he's going to be okay."

With a sigh of relief, I said, "Thank heavens!"

I leaned over, cuddling and kissing Chip. Then Chip's dad picked him up, giving him a big hug, and I joined in. The doctor told us the problem was caused by the fat in whole milk, and he immediately switched Chip to Sobee Formula. It was damp and foggy outside as Chip's dad slowly drove toward home, turning onto Palmyra Street and into our driveway. Chip looked very content and happy while he lay in my arms wide awake, looking up at me with a big, sweet grin. His pretty blue eyes twinkled and his little lower lip puckered up a little past his top lip as if to say, "Mother, I'm fine now. I didn't mean to scare you and Dad and Cramma and Grampa. I really didn't."

Smiling, I cuddled him close and said, "Chipper, you know how much I love you, and you did give us a scare! Daddy and I are very, very happy that you're okay now. We love you so very much. We truly do."

I cuddled and comforted him with all my might while Daddy parked the car. Then Daddy leaned over and gave us a big, tender, loving kiss, saying, "I sure do love you both." Then he tickled Chip under the chin and joyfully said, "And you, my boy, are super-duper okay now!"

Smiling, I said, "We love you, too, Daddy."

Squeezing Chip, I added, "As soon as we get in the house, we'll call Gramma and Grampa to let them know you are all right. Okay?" I kissed him and thought to myself. This is my world, what more could I want?

I pulled the corner of Chip's blanket down over his face and snuggled him close to my chest to shield him as I got out of the car and ran to the house, his dad following. Then Chip's dad hurried ahead and opened the door, and we rushed into our cozy, warm home. The phone was ringing. Still holding Chip, I hurried to answer, thinking it must be Mother wondering how Chip was. Sure enough, it was her.

"Hi, Mother, we just got home and I'm out of breath from running into the house with Chip. It's really cold out, and we could barely see for the fog."

Mother asked, "How is Chip? What did the doctor say?"

"Chip is fine now. Thank heavens! He sure gave us a big scare. Thank you so much for helping, Mother. It scared me when he couldn't seem to get his breath."

"You did just fine, Kitty. Getting him to the doctor was the important thing to do."

"I told Chip we'd call you soon as we got into the house. He's smiling and cooing now, just as though nothing happened."

Then I explained to her what had taken place at the doctor's office and what the doctor had said.

Mother commented, "Now that we know Chip is doing fine, we will all sleep good tonight. Give him a big hug and kisses for us. We'll see him and his dad tomorrow. Talk with you later."

"Okay, Mother, thanks for calling. Bye."

Gramma and Grampa were naturally getting attached to Chip. When Chip was about six months old and we were at their home one day, I was out on the patio with Chip in his stroller, enjoying the warm sunshine. Before long Chip's dad and Grampa Chris joined us with big, mischievous grins on their faces. Grampa Chris bent down and handed Chipper a big peeled lemon! Chip innocently bit into it and instantly jerked his head and quivered his shoulders while his mouth puckered up from the sour taste. Chip tried again, with all the spasms of funny little faces. He kept trying. Before long he seemed to be enjoying the lemon, even though he still puckered with each sour bite. With his dad and Grampa Chris still laughing, Chip's persistence won over the lemon—and them, too.

Right from the start Chip was always the center of attention and a good sport, even if the joke was being played on him.

He never cried much and I'd heard that crying made for strong lungs. Still, Chipper ended up with a strong, vibrant voice, exactly like his Uncle Duane's, along with the same great personality and enthusiasm.

Chip started standing when he was only seven months old, going from one piece of furniture to the next. Everyone said he would be walking before he was a year old. We encouraged him at first, then realized when the time was right, he'd walk.

Chip was a little past thirteen months old. We had just arrived at Mother's and while I was taking off my coat, I put Chip down, leaning him against my leg for support. Suddenly and unexpectedly, there went Chip, walking away on his own. He didn't stagger, stumble, or fall. Sure enough, and in his own time, he was ready and walking!

Now that Chip had taken the big step and was walking on his own, whenever he was playing and would fall down, I would encourage him by saying, "That's okay. Chip, you'll be all right. Come on, get up!" And up he would come without even a whimper.

Looking back, it's apparent that these early years were the start of Chip's independence. He was taught to do things on his own at an early age, always knowing he had our love and encouragement.

When Chip was ready, he would do whatever had to be done and as need be. Even in these early years. Chip's being strong-minded with a strong will seemed to be natural. In later years this would prove to be the best mold for his survival in life.

Spring was almost here when we moved to my hometown in Indiana, where my dad and stepmother lived with their kids, Debbie and Michael. Chip called them Gramma and Grampa, and the grandparents he had left in California were now Grams and Grampa Chris. Both of Chip's grandparents always loved having him with them. He was always good-natured and livened things up for everyone.

Chip's Uncle Mike and Aunt Debbie were only three and four years older than Chip, and right from the start they were more like brothers and sister. They adored each other and there was never any fussing, but lots of fun and laughter. Maybe I could rephrase that and say Debbie was like a little caring mother like kids play at that age. Even if it was a rainy day and meant staying inside playing with paper doll cutouts or trucks, they all made the best of things together. If it was bright and sunshiny outdoors, they usually had great, adventurous outings, looking for toads, crickets, rabbits, or whatever else they could dream up with the woods and lake nearby, knowing the lake was a restricted area unless adults were present. Then the rolling hills were especially exciting during the winter, with all the snow and ice. They romped and had great times riding their sleds and making snowballs to throw. Making a snowman was always the greatest fun of all for Chip. He loved the snow.

The three of them were fairly close-knit. They were truly good kids and mature for their ages.

Chip's grandparents in Indiana owned a beautiful, big skating rink that Grampa had built not long ago. And now my dad had built a beautiful, large family restaurant, and his invitation for us to participate in this field of his business is what brought my husband and me to Indiana.

While Chip's dad and I worked, Chip spent lots of his time with Gramma while she was working at the rink. Of course, it was more fun than work to the both of them, I believe.

Monitoring the floor was naturally included with the skating rink business, which both of Chip's grandparents shared in. They were both young at heart and it was like one big happy family for everyone. Chip loved all the activity and often was the center of attention while he sat on the counter watching everyone and everything with Gramma. The kids were always coming up to Gramma and Chip, teasing them and often taking Chip out to skate.

When it was closing time, Chip would watch Gramma count the money. When suddenly, zoom! Oops! There'd go some of Gramma's coins! Seems Chip was helping. He'd have a handful and be ready to grab another when Gramma would teasingly yell, "Chipper Demon!"

His speed and dexterity always tickled her. They'd both laugh and giggle up a storm. Chip was such a whiz and so funny and cuddly. He'd always pay her back with a big hug and smooch. This fun and laughter was common ground between them; they were real bosom buddies and a pleasure to see together! His being mischievous won him the pet name Chipper Demon, and he always knew what he was in for when he heard it!

Chip was on roller skates almost as soon as he started walking. Whenever his little legs got too tired. Gramma would pick him up and skate with him in her arms. This didn't interfere with her blowing the whistle and yelling at the kids on skates, "Slow down! You're going too fast!"

Chip loved this! He'd even grab the whistle and give a big blow! It really tickled him to put that big ol' whistle in his mouth and blow as hard and long as he could. If there was a pile-up of skaters on the floor, Gramma would rush over, with Chip still in her arms, to help everyone get untangled. Chip was always thrilled to be right in the middle with all the kids and Gramma, tugging and pulling, bobbing up and down and around until all the kids were up on their skates and skating away. Then away Gramma would skate with Chip still in her arms, like real champs!

Chip liked to fox trot, so whenever I heard the fox-trot music. I'd get him for my partner and away I'd skate with him in my arms onto the floor. Chip always liked this—the faster, the better.

In fact, fox-trot time was the only time anyone could get away with skating fast. Every now and then I'd put Chip down to skate. Sometimes we'd fall, and sure enough, yes. Gramma would see us, it seemed as soon as we hit the floor. It was as though she were watching us all the time! Chip and I would always try to get up in a hurry, but she was swift as lightning and didn't lose any time getting onto the floor. She'd be blowing that loud ol' whistle!

Then teasing. I'd say, "Okay, Chip, next time you've got to catch me if I start to fall or we'll both end up on the floor. Gramma will see us and start blowing her loud whistle at us! And we don't want that, do we?"

Chip would giggle because he knew whether he was on skates or if we'd fallen to the floor Gramma would come to his rescue. Or Grampa if he happened to be monitoring the floor.

Chip's potty training happened about the same as his walking. He hadn't been walking very long when we decided we'd start his potty training. However, we didn't persist because we remembered how he was about walking: once he was ready!

Chip was a little past two years old when, out of the blue, one day he came to me and said, "Mother, I have to potty."

I was surprised since we hadn't been trying to get him out of diapers. I took him to his potty in the bathroom. He even sat there for a little while before he proved that he knew what he was there for. He did it again; he voluntarily potty trained himself. After that, he only wet the bed twice!

Right from the beginning, Chip spoiled me more as a mother than I ever did him as a child.

I always said, "If I ever had another baby, it was sure to be the opposite because Chip was so dam good!"

I once heard we get the children we deserve in life. Upon hearing this, I knew I had to have been blessed. Chip was always happy and content. And all during his life things seemed to come naturally, and he never was a problem.

Chip was a few months past two years old when his dad decided he wanted us to move to Maryland, where most of his family lived. Chip's grandparents in Maryland were Nana and Pappy. We made the move and settled in an apartment in his hometown. We were planning to buy land in the near future to build our home. He had gotten a job in a small town in Maryland bordering West Virginia. Then it wasn't long until he spotted some land in West Virginia where he wanted to build our home. Late summer, Chip's Grams and Grampa Chris moved their family from California to Michigan. Immediately Chip's dad and Chris made plans to go deer hunting in Michigan that fall.

Later, when deer season was nearing, I asked my husband if he would mind if Chip and I went to Mother's a couple of weeks early and he could join us when he got his vacation. We'd never been apart before, and the three of us had always done everything together. He agreed that was fine and he'd drive as planned.

It was a chilly, windy day in October when Chip and I arrived at Chris and Grams' home. Grams was still at work and it would be a big surprise for her because she didn't know we had arrived.

Later that afternoon, Grams drove into the driveway after her day's work at the hospital. She saw a little boy standing in front of the screen door. Naturally she wondered who it was. She didn't recognize Chip because he had outgrown his babyish look. When she had last seen him, as a baby, he was chunky and fat. Now he was tall and slim.

Chip walked out to meet Grams while she was getting out of her car. Was she ever surprised when she realized it was Chip! Grams grabbed Chipper, giving him a big hug and kisses.

She excitedly yelled, "Chip! I didn't know that was you at first. You are growing into a real tall boy! No more of that cuddly baby look!"

They were all smiles, laughing and talking while they walked hand in hand into the house.

A couple of days had gone by and I'd been telling Mother all about the plans we were making, how Chip's dad and Pappy were going to build our new home in the country. Chip and I were both missing his dad.

Then the next day when Mother turned on the television, to our surprise we were seeing U.S. ships at sea positioned near Cuba, awaiting possible orders to go to war! The more we watched, the more worried I became.

"Mother, if war breaks out, what am I going to do? With Chip's dad in Maryland and us here, maybe he won't be able to travel. Then what will I do?"

I was getting all shook up, especially with no phone to make a call. Mother was trying to keep me calm and said, "When Chris gets home he can take you to the phone booth on the comer."

Later, when I called Chip's dad, I told him Mother and I had been watching the ships at sea and how worried I was about war breaking out at any time.

Then I asked him, "What are we going to do if a war does start—with you there and me here?"

He abruptly said, "There isn't going to be any war." He paused, then added, "Anyway, I'm not coming there at all."

I was shocked! I couldn't believe what I was hearing.

Hesitantly, I said, "You're not coming here?"

He said, "No, you can come back here whenever you want and get a separation."

I was stunned. It was as though the world were tumbling down. I felt like a limp rag doll. The next thing I knew, the tears were starting to fall. I couldn't seem to stop them, but I didn't want him to know. It was as though my mind had gone blank. What was I to say? Quietly clearing my throat, I asked, "You want a divorce?"

Defiantly, he said, "No," then clearly stated, "I only want a separation. I have moved out of the apartment. I am staying at Mom and Dad's. I'll send you the money for a bus back and you can go see a lawyer."

I was devastated! I still didn't know what to say or what to do. I didn't understand, and I never suspected this would happen to Chip and me. He loved us, yet why was he talking this way? I was crushed! He told me he wanted me to move back to Indiana or Michigan where I would have work. By now I was crying my heart out. What else could I do?

I didn't realize it at the time, but apparently Chip's dad was shallowly setting me and our son aside for someone who had attracted him for the moment, resulting in his wanting his freedom from being a family man. He seemed to have everything planned and that was that. I limply hung up the telephone.

Earlier that day I had been telling Mother what a good marriage we had, and now this! I had no earthly idea of anything like this happening. How could I tell Mother what he had said? I was so ashamed, so humiliated. I didn't know what to do. What happened to what I thought was a good marriage? What did I do?

Chris was quiet as he drove home and while we got out of the car and went into the house. I didn't say anything. I tried to hold the tears back, but couldn't stop them. Everyone thought I was crying because I missed my husband, and I hated to tell them different. All I could do was cry. I felt so ashamed and miserable. I kept trying to pull myself together, but couldn't.

This was all so sudden and beyond belief. Poor Chip. He came over to me and I pulled him close, then lifted him up on my lap and held him tight. I tried all the more to stop crying, but now he was starting to feel sad, and he didn't even know why. Our precious son, and he was so young. How could I tell him his dad didn't want us with him anymore? This was our little boy whom we had both wanted and whom we loved so very much. We had so many dreams to fulfill, I thought.

Chip was almost three and our fourth anniversary was only two weeks after that, then the holidays. Had his dad forgotten all of this? Oh God, what had happened? And why? I didn't understand, nor did I know what to say. It was difficult, but finally I broke down and told Mother that Chip's dad wanted a separation. Mother was pleasant and tried to comfort me knowing how I felt, but we both knew it was something I would need to deal with. I didn't know what to do, except what my husband had decided.

The day after Halloween, Chip and I went home to do as my husband wanted, although I still couldn't believe this could be happening. I was like a puppet on a string. I was heartbroken and in a state of shock when I started putting things in motion that would eventually dissolve our marriage after a two-year separation.

Chip was exposed to tom and bitter feelings at the very young and tender age of almost three. Naturally he and I became even closer. I needed to make this up to him. From that day forward, without his dad, Chip was my number one responsibility. I only wanted the best for him. I knew this meant I would need to work extra hard to provide for him, but I knew I could and I would. Having only one parent left a large vacuum in his heart and the longing for a father figure that was with him to the very end.

Chip had his third birthday about the same time that his dad and I were granted a separation. Even though it was a sad time for us, we made the best of everything from then on. We arrived back at Grams in Michigan just in time for a surprise birthday party for Chip. His Aunt Janie and Aunt Susie had all kinds of gifts and toys for Chipper, along with lots of balloons.

Almost a month had gone by since Chip and I had moved to Michigan. Being near the family was good for Chip and helped him to adjust to the drastic change that had taken place in his young life. I still hadn't decided if we were going to live in Indiana or Michigan. It was important to me that Chip and I have a place of our own. I felt, now that I had no husband, it was up to me to take care of our child, and the burden was overwhelming at times as I started making plans for us to be in our own place by Christmas. Christmas without a father! The idea of this happening to Chip tore me apart inside.

Then only a month later, just three days before Christmas, an even worse tragedy occurred. I was in a dreadful car accident. Among my many serious injuries were whiplash and a concussion that left me unconscious. I wasn't expected to live,

I can only imagine the thoughts little Chipper must have been thinking that day. It been hard enough without his dad, and now his mother hadn't come home to tuck him in for the night. He must have felt so alone, wondering where I was, knowing I would always be there with him and he'd never be without me. I'm sure he remembered that promise and all the love when I told him. Then when I didn't come home the next day, how could he possibly have felt at his young age, without either his mother or dad, who had always been with him until now? No doubt he was scared and hurting deep inside, especially remembering Mother had said she would always be with him, no matter what. In his little bewildered mind he must have been wondering what to do and what was going to happen next in his big, wide world.

When the family heard about the car accident, Gramma said, it was a sad thing to take Chip in her arms, sit him on her lap, and tell him I wouldn't be coming home for a while. She said she told Chip they would pray for me every night. Chip carefully listened.

Then he seriously said, "I pray every night for Mother, and Dad, and you, Gramma!"

After a brief pause, quickly and sincerely he added, "I will pray more. God'll make my mother well, and she will come home real soon."

Gramma gave Chip a big hug and he whispered softly, "I miss Mother and Dad," and he hugged Gramma real tight.

Chip's Gramma told me how sad his little face had been and how hard it was to see him standing for the longest times at the large sliding-glass door, watching and waiting for me to come up the hill on the long, circular drive at any moment. She said all Chip could see was the snow falling and the drifts getting deeper while he kept watching, leaning against the window with his hands above his head and his little fingers touching the glass, making a fine mist as his warm breath condensed on the cold window.

She said Chip would walk away from the window for a while, leaving his fingerprints in the mist, then he'd go back to the same spot to wait and watch some more. This must have seemed like forever to him. Even then, he was determined for me.

Later I learned from Mother that on Christmas Day, my Aunt Mable and Uncle Gordon had surprised Chip by bringing him to the hospital. Chip had been worrying about me and was lonesome.

As a rule, Chip wasn't allowed in the hospital at his young age, but because my Aunt Mable worked in the hospital, she decided to take it upon herself to bring Chip to see me. Even though I was still unconscious, they thought that if Chip could be there for a little while it would hopefully be good for both of us.

When Mother later told me about this, I could imagine how it must have been. I could picture Aunt Mable and Uncle Gordon, a tall handsome man over six feet tall, with little Chip reaching high above his head to hold his hand while they walked down the long hall with Chip between them. Mother related how Chip was very quiet as they approached my room.

Aunt Mable knelt beside Chip and said, "Chip, your mother may not be able to talk, but you can talk to her, okay? She will be listening, even if she doesn't say a thing. It will make her feel better to hear you talking to her."

With a twinkle in his eyes. Chip smiled and happily said, "I will. I will tell my mother I want her home with me. I miss Mother not with me."

Uncle Gordon opened the door, and Chip hurried in while they followed. He saw me across the room and ran to my bedside. He stood momentarily looking real serious at my face, then he looked down and saw my large, swollen leg and foot. Aunt Mable said his mouth dropped open, then he puckered up as though he was about to cry, but he didn't. Instead, very concerned, he reached his little hand down toward my leg and gently patted my swollen foot. Aunt Mable told Chip my foot was broken and when the swelling went down, the doctor would put it in a cast to make it well.

Chip softly said, "Ohh. Good." Then he slowly edged himself back to the head of my bed, looking and checking me very carefully.

Mother said Aunt Mable and Uncle Gordon said their hearts were breaking while they watched Chip. She said then he spotted a little sore on my wrist, which was from an IV they had removed earlier.

Chip looked puzzled and his little lower lip puckered out while he kept looking at the sore, then he bent his little head down, kissing it, and saying, "There, Mother, that'll make it all better."

Aunt Mable said, "Chip was so sweet and wanted so much to help his mother get well."

It was especially difficult for Aunt Mable and Uncle Gordon to see Chip doing this and neither of them could keep back the tears. Aunt Mable put her arm around

Chip's shoulders and hugged him close. I could imagine how it was for Chip when Mother was telling me.

This was our first Christmas together on our own.

The doctors had said I wouldn't survive the accident or come out of the coma, but the thirteenth day I regained consciousness and a few days later went home.

Looking back, I believe I must have been saved for my son. Chip. Today I understand how we needed each other for life's crises, to face them together.

After I left the hospital, Chip and I continued to stay with his grandparents since I wasn't able to get around very well with my broken leg and the other various complications. However, as soon as I was capable, I located employment at Wabash Magnetics and we moved to a place of our own. The doctor said it was too soon, but still I felt it was my responsibility and important that we be on our own.

Eventually Chip and I settled down in Fort Wayne, Indiana. I devoted my time and energies to Chip and work from then on.

Chip's dad had said he would always care for our son, no matter what. I believed him. I was sure Chip would always come first, with both of us. Our son was number one and we loved him with all our heart. Even so, I was still in a state of shock about our separation and I never questioned his actions.

Before our separation. Chip was always with his dad while I worked and Sunday was our family day together. Chip had been baptized as an Episcopalian when he was an infant in California. Our last time to attend the Episcopal Church was in Cumberland, Maryland. After our divorce, in two years I was excommunicated.

Now that it was only Chip and I, Sunday was a busy workday for me. I'll never forget one particular Sunday when I was taking Chip to the babysitter's.

He touched my hand and solemnly asked, "Mother, why are you working today? It's God's day."

It really got to me, and I was at a loss for words. What could I say? At times like this it was hard to give Chip a correct answer. How could I explain why I was working on God's day? I told him the reason, although it wasn't a right answer: that my job required I work on Sundays. Over the years. Chip and I faced a lot of growing together,

Now that Chip didn't see his dad often, it was good to have Grampa Chris nearby to be the "adult man figure" in Chip's life. He loved Chip and spent a lot of time with him.

Once when Chip was there for the night, late in the evening Chris yawned and said, "I guess I'm going to bed."

Shortly after, Chip decided he'd go on to bed with Grampa Chris. Chip was so small he had to step up on the bed rail, grab hold of the top of the bed, and belly across the pillows to get situated in the middle.

Grampa Chris, always ready for a chance to tease a little, said to Chip, "Get your big butt off the pillow and quiet down."

Chip giggled up a storm at that and didn't want to settle down, but Grampa Chris insisted.

All was quiet when Grams came to bed. Already in her nightie, she quietly slipped into bed and was pulling up the covers when a giggling little voice said, "Grams, get your big butt out of my face and be quiet."

The giggling started all over again.

Grams always said, "This child is as busybody as most, but as the day wears on, most children tire and are ready for bed by early evening. That's when Chip gets all wound up and full of mischief. He's more teasing and hyperactive than at any other time."

There always was a lot of tumbling and playing on the floor with one or both of his grandparents and if his cousins were there, they joined in too.

Chip was cute and mischievous, but never was a nuisance, and everyone enjoyed having him around.

When I wasn't working, he was always with me, even when I went out. He was a little gentleman and never a problem. Starting at his young age and while he was growing up, he stood out in a crowd and seemed to naturally conquer most everyone's heart.

I was always very independent and felt it was my responsibility to provide for Chip and myself with no help from my family. This was important to me, even though it meant working a lot. I was considered the ambitious one, so to speak. I became the target for some teasing by the family for being like this. Chip didn't always understand this razzing and it made him feel bad for me. I honestly believe I was blessed to have a child who was so tender and loving, which seemed to come naturally with him, and he never changed.

One particular day. Chip was excited while we were on our way to Grampa and Gramma's. Ordinarily on a nice hot day like that, he would be going swimming in their lake, but that day Gramma and I were taking him to the VFW (Veterans of Foreign Wars) Street Fair.

All the games and rides didn't wear him out and he didn't give Gramma a chance to notice how tired she was getting. What Chip did, Gramma and Mother did, including all the rides. After a while. Chip had to go to the restroom. We went to a nearby filling station and Gramma waited outside while I went inside with Chip.

When we came out, Chip didn't see Gramma right away. He was wondering where she was. Then he heard a whispering, teasing voice singing, "Demon, Demon."

Chip looked all around and couldn't see Gramma, but he knew that voice. Above all, he knew this had to be Gramma because it was what she called him when she was in a teasing mood, as she often was with Chipper Demon.

She teasingly sang again, "Demon, demon. Chipper Demon."

Then Chip saw Gramma and dashed to her as fast as his little legs would carry him. They grabbed each other, laughing and hugging. She lovingly said, "Chipper Demon, I love you!"

Chip was grinning from ear to ear while returning her hug.

It was nearly supper time when we left the fair. Gramma was busy in the kitchen getting supper and Grampa was tinkering with his bulldozer. Chip was outside with Grampa, knowing that as soon as he finished he would take him for a ride. A little later Grampa was through with the bulldozer. They were about to go for a ride when Chip saw a toad and ran to catch it. It took him awhile, but he finally caught the toad.

With a big grin on his face, he quietly went into the house and softly tiptoed up behind Gramma. Not saying a word, he pulled back at the waist of her britches, just enough to drop that cold, slimy toad down them!

Gramma let out a loud scream and yelled, "Chipper Demon! I'll get you for this!"

They both laughed and out the back door Chip ran.

Two years had gone by since Chip and I were living on our own and his dad and I were granted a divorce. We decided to take a trip to Pensacola, Florida, on the beautiful Atlantic coast. This was our first vacation together. We loaded up the car with all our beach gear and away we went. We stayed in a lovely hotel on the beach, which was perfect since that was where we spent most of our time.

Chip and I were walking on the sandy beach hand in hand. With our free arms we carried all our beach gear to enjoy while in the sun and splashing about in the water. The soft, warm sand began to get hot as it oozed through our toes with every step we took. Our slow pace soon changed into a quick walk, almost running. We made it! We dropped our beach gear and rushed on out to the water's edge to cool our feet.

Chip was giggling and having a great time while he kicked his feet about in the water. He would hike his knees up high and raise his arms as he leaped over the waves with a quick jump and then fell down into the water. He loved the waves—the higher, the better.

After a while, we went back up to the beach and laid out our beach blanket. While I lay soaking up the sun, Chip was having a fantastic time getting acquainted with the other little kids near us on the beach. They stayed busy all afternoon making sand castles, covering each other up with the sand, and making angels in the soft sand by moving their arms back and forth. They were quiet and serious one minute, then excitedly screaming and laughing the next.

Every so often Chip would get me to go back into the water with him. We'd rush out to the edge of the salty water, then wade out a little farther and jump into the waves, laughing and yelling while we fell into the water. Then we'd hurry back to catch the next wave, over and over again. We were like two little kids having the time of our lives.

After two weeks of fun and leisure on the beach, Chip and I headed back to good ol' Hoosier land, Indiana.

Chip would soon be five years old and by now he was a real pro on skates. He'd been skating since he was a little over a year old (including many hours in Gramma's arms or mine while on skates) and had spent lots of times helping Gramma count her money and blow the whistle at all the skaters in the "good ol' days."

Now it was time for his own private party to celebrate with all his skating friends. It was fun and laughter for everyone while they skated around the floor with horns blowing and balloons floating everywhere.

There were lots of presents and fun games for everyone. Centered on his beautiful big cake was a train with locomotive, caboose, and all. Starting in Chip's young years, balloons were of a special significance and were often the highlight of his special events.

2

Fading Memories

It was kindergarten at last and Chip was most anxious to start school. He was a cute little five-year-old with freckles and blond hair. His first day he was wearing blue slacks and a red shirt with blue-and-white etchings, along with his brown-and-tan suede sweater. We were both proud and happy walking to school together his first day. When we arrived I waited while watching him go on up the steps where the patrol boy greeted him at the school door. I'm sure we had similar thoughts about his grand new adventure of stepping out into the world. With a cute little grin on his face, Chip turned around and waved good-bye, then gleefully entered the school building.

He wouldn't be in school long until his birthday in November. I planned a surprise party for him to celebrate with his new classmates. When I arrived at school with cake, ice cream, and mints. Chip was delighted. The highlight of the party was when he proudly gave everyone balloons. Then the teacher let them play games and win prizes that Chip was tickled to give. It was fun and laughter the rest of the school day. This was Chip's day!

Chip's first year in school had gone by quickly.

During the summer Grams and Grampa Chris liked taking Chip on vacation with them. He was a good traveler and never complained about the ride. For a little guy, he was always very attentive and earnestly interested in everything Grams said. Like Grams, he always wanted to see and know about everything. Naturally, this made them good traveling companions.

Grampa Chris was a big man—well over six feet tall—but when it came to him and Chip there was no age gap, nor any lack of communication whatsoever. They played with each other like two little boys and had a mutual respect and admiration.

Chip never had a very big appetite, but ate well. He always ordered for himself like an adult. He was very polite and mannerly. One time when they stopped in Colorado to eat, Chip was very hungry. Grams said Chip very seriously gave his order for his most favorite of all food.

The waitress just stood there and Grampa Chris said to her, "What the hell's the matter, didn't you ever see a kid that didn't want a hamburger?"

Frankly, she probably in all truth could have said no, but she hurriedly started writing the order and Chip was soon eating his favorite food, mashed potatoes and gravy. I could say here that Chip might have taken his lessons in loyalty from his Grampa Chris, because Grampa Chris was always right there to jump to his defense if need be.

Chip's summers were busy with Grams and Grampa and his dad, too. He loved traveling and always looked forward to going to Maryland for a two- week visit with his dad and seeing Nana and Pappy during the summer.

One visit was real special to Chip because his dad took him to the dog pound and said, "Okay, Chip, pick the one you want."

Chip checked all the different dogs, then he finally decided, saying, "That one," and pointing at what must have been the smallest dog in the kennel, a toy fox terrier. Well, that was certainly the best thing his dad could have gotten him. No doubt it meant even more to Chip because it was from his dad. Chip was right at the age when he needed this good memory of his love and the knowledge that his dad cared about him. This little dog naturally won Chip's heart. He named him Scottie.

When Chip came home with Scottie, the dog didn't remain a visitor for long—he became like a little brother to Chip. Everywhere Chip went, Scottie went, even to bed with him. They were inseparable. He seemed to get more teasing about little Scottie. Especially when he and Scottie visited Grams in Michigan, he really got razzed. Grampa Chris would teasingly say, "Here comes Chip with that little mosquito," then laughingly add, "uuh, uuh, uum, ohh... that's Scottie! Huh, Chip?"

Then everyone would join in on the fun.

Scottie's favorite place to lie was on the sofa, all snuggled down under the pillows, and always someone was sitting on him. When Chip would hear him yelping, he'd rush to his rescue. Poor little Scottie! He couldn't seem to keep from getting smashed. Chip's Aunt Susie was his Godmother and she, too, was always there for Chip. She always said when it came to his dog, Scottie, being squashed you better be more careful next time. All Chip had to do was give you that certain look! Then he would cuddle and talk to him for the longest times until he was all soothed and settled. Scottie was so tiny and frail. It seemed he hardly stood a chance, but Chip's love was all he needed and Scottie was soon calm. Then they were both happy and Chip's expression changed to a pleased smile.

Chip seemed to be adjusting fairly well without his dad, although his heart must have been aching. When he was seven years old. Chip clearly expressed his thoughts in a picture he drew for the cover of a letter he had written about attending his class to see what he was learning. In the upper left corner he had neatly drawn a little boy sitting at his desk writing, his feet not reaching the floor. There was a television in front; above and below him were some math problems, and his two-story house was in the lower left comer. In the upper right corner was the sun shining, and below the sun was a large mailbox with the flag up and grass beneath it and the house. In the lower right corner was a chalkboard with all the letters of the alphabet and at the center top was a balloon.

Even though Chip had the one large void in his heart, he was surrounded with love and care, and this had always shown through with good grades and good remarks on his report cards.

Soon after school was out that year Chip's dad would be coming to take him to Maryland to visit. Chip looked forward to being with his dad since they were so far apart and he missed him. But this trip was different from the times before. To start with, Chip had to leave home brokenhearted because his dad wouldn't let him take Scottie with them. Scottie went everywhere with Chip ever since his dad had gotten him for Chip. Now, for the first time, he and Scottie would be separated. Scottie was clean and house broken, but still for unknown reasons his dad said no and never explained why. Just no.

This was difficult for Chip and he didn't understand why his dad was being different. Chip was the innocent child, but he must have wondered what he had done. Until now his dad had always been fair and gracious with him, so why the sudden change? Poor Chip, how would he sleep at night? How would he manage two weeks without Scottie?

It seems this was the beginning of the end for Chip and his dad. Before, his dad had always been proud of him and they had great times together. Suddenly it seemed Chip would need to accept a lot of disappointment and keep a lot of hurt feelings tucked away deep inside.

Ostensibly there was someone in his dad's life and sudden drastic changes occurred pertaining to the time Chip's dad spent with him.

Chip had always been an extrovert and very active. Now it was sad and trying for him to be left with this unsolved puzzle at such an early age. Still, the love of Scottie from his dad helped some.

Chip was young and I never discussed his dad much, not wanting to mention his faults. There were times when we talked, but above all we silently shut out the heartache and loneliness while we went on with our own lives—accepting the fading memories. Looking back I wonder if maybe that was a mistake, that maybe somehow when Chip was little, I didn't allow him to realize that his dad was only human. Of course, I always raised Chip with the idea that "If you don't have something good to say about someone, then don't say anything at all."

Obviously, Chip took that to heart because he grew up to never demean anyone about anything. In fact, quite the opposite. Chip and I accepted life for what it was and made the best of it.

Chip hadn't seen or heard from his dad for quite some time. He wondered why he hadn't been to see him for nearly two years. Remembering the last time was the day when we were both surprised to see his dad arrive at our home unexpectedly. We had a nice visit, probably the most pleasant since our separation years before.

Chip was excited to see him. I imagine the three of us together that day seemed to Chip to be like it was before the separation and he was happy. This was the day I told his dad I was getting married. He spent the afternoon in our home, then left.

After that visit Chip's dad wasn't coming to see him at all, and for unknown reasons Chip wasn't hearing from him anymore because he wouldn't even return Chip's calls. Down deep Chip couldn't help but wonder what he must have done wrong. He didn't understand why his dad was being different. Still, he kept calling his dad every so often on the telephone, but never could reach him. Chip was hurt by this and puzzled about why his dad was doing this to him. What went wrong? He loved his dad and was sure his dad loved him.

Then one day when Chip was ten years old he was missing his dad.

He said, "Mother, Dad hasn't been to see me for a long time. Maybe because we live so far away."

He paused, thinking for a minute, then asked, "May I go live with my dad?"

With that twinkle in his eyes, he excitedly said, "He said when I got older he would take me fishing and hunting with him."

For a few moments he paused and looked down at the floor as though he were thinking about things his dad had told him. Then he looked up at me, smiling, and excitedly added, "And dad said we would build a tree house one of these days."

I smiled. I understood how he was feeling.

Sincerely, he said, "Mother, don't feel bad. I love you."

I knew this talk would come someday, but now that it had, it was sad and hard. I understood and realized this would be good for Chip, especially since he was a boy. He needed his dad, too, but my biggest fear over the years was his dad threatening me, saying Chip would live with him when he was older. He didn't want him while he was young, but said, "When Chip gets older, I'll have him with me. You'll see."

I was thinking to myself, His dad was right. But to hear Chip asking, it was different. He needed his dad's love and missed him.

I kept myself composed and said, "I know, honey. I love you, too."

Then he anxiously asked, "May I go?"

"Yes, Chip, of course, if you're sure that's what you want."

I put my hands on his shoulders and said, "I understand and it's only natural for you to want to live with your dad, too."

By now I was fighting back the tears, but mustn't cry.

Chip was real excited and asked, "Can I call dad now?"

"Sure, honey, go ahead," I answered.

He excitedly ran over to the telephone and dialed his dad's number. Chip stood waiting with a big grin on his face, hoping his dad would hurry up and answer.

Enthusiastically, Chip said, "Hi, Dad. This is Chip."

After a pause, Chip answered, "Fine."

Then he eagerly asked, "Dad, may I come and live with you?" Another pause, then he added, "Mother says I can!"

They talked about it briefly, then Chip hung up. His dad had told him he would talk it over with his wife and call back. That was how Chip learned that his dad had remarried.

Chip could hardly wait for him to call back. Living with his dad would be a big change, but he really needed his dad's love and companionship, too. Chip patiently waited near the telephone the rest of the day. But the telephone never rang. As the evening wore on, his little face grew more and more sad. His dad still hadn't called. Chip was trying not to show his sadness, and at the same time, I too was trying not to let him see that I was afraid of the outcome. We didn't say much. It was as though we were both apprehensive to say anything.

Still, Chip waited, not wanting to give up hope. Surely he would at least call. Soon it was bedtime and still no call from his dad. Climbing into bed that night was heartbreaking for Chip. Not even a call. It was as though his world had fallen apart all around him. All day and all evening he had been waiting for his dad's promised call.

While I was tucking Chip into bed, he sadly asked, "What happened? Dad said he would call back. Why didn't he?"

His little face drooped, then he looked up at me and said, "Mother, it's okay if I stay home."

His eyes were starting to get watery and I reached over, hugging him tightly. I was almost in tears when I cleared my throat and said, "Of course, honey. You know this is always your home and we love you."

I got control of myself, then pulled Chip away from me. I put my hands on his shoulders and held him firmly at arm's length, looking into his sad, tearful blue eyes and said, "You know, I love you very, very much, Chip. You mean everything to me. You always will."

Then I pulled him close to me again and hugged him against my bosom. Pushing his hair back from his forehead and giving him a kiss, I said, "You're a big boy and we'll make it together."

He looked up at me and nodded, attempting a smile, trying not to look unhappy. He hugged me tightly as though he didn't want to let go, then softly said, "I love you so very much. Mother."

After a few minutes of silence, he scooted himself down in bed to rest. His eyes were still watery while he lay silent, but he kept the tears from falling, at least while I remained in his room.

I believe Chip felt he had to be strong. Possibly he even sensed he'd never be dose to his dad again. Naturally he wouldn't want to accept that idea. He loved his dad and knew that his dad must surely love him and really want to be with him. Yet, he hadn't called. Chip didn't understand. He was so sad and vulnerable, and there wasn't anything I could do except try to spare him the agony, giving him the best home possible with all my love and devotion. His dad would need to contend with his actions. I prayed he would come forward for Chip's sake.

I could see and feel the hurt Chip was going through, but why? All he wanted and needed was his dad's love and companionship, like any boy does. Nothing more. It was strange and sad for Chip. His dad didn't seem to be the same anymore. They used to be so close. Even a "no" would not have hurt as much as his total, silent rejection. Chip's dad had told him over the years that he would someday live with him. What happened? How could his dad, also an only boy, although he had older sisters, do this to his only son? What had Chip done that at such a young age he was rejected with no explanation from his dad? That was Chip's first attempt to be with his dad. Why was he rejected?

When Chip was younger and his dad would come to take him for a visit he often boasted, "When Chip gets older, I'll get him. You'll see. He'll live with me when he's fourteen. You wait and see."

Hearing his threat frightened me. Chip was my life and I didn't know what I'd do without him. I loved him with all my heart and wanted to be the parent he could be proud of. I cherished this responsibility. I should have seen the warning when his dad remarried and was behaving differently with Chip, that things would change for him, but I didn't. I couldn't imagine he would deny our son his love or attention. Everyone who knew him said his son would always be first with him, just like he had been with his own dad.

It had taken only one man to mistreat my son and end our relationship. I vowed that was the last time. Chip was my number one responsibility. If anyone wanted my company, it included treating my son with the same care and respect. Apparently Chip's dad didn't feel that way or seem to have control. How did he feel right to shut his child out? I always believed, "If you truly love your spouse, you will naturally love their child. Liking and loving, likewise each have their own space." Because of Chip's good nature and manner, it seems his dad's new wife would have liked him and made their ties even stronger, or at least have accepted him as her husband's child.

One time I called to talk with his dad about Chip's confusion over why he was rejecting him and not giving him his love and consideration anymore. I felt it was necessary and important that we try to help in whatever way we could. His wife let me know I had no business calling and hung up on me! I surmised she couldn't handle the situation, even before I talked with his dad or they knew why I had called. I didn't have time for that sort of rudeness and realized it was up to me.

Before his dad remarried, he'd remember Chip on his birthdays and on holidays. He'd come to take Chip to Maryland for his two-week visit to see Nana and Pappy. Why did that suddenly stop? Chip was never given a reason and neither did I understand. If I didn't understand, how could Chip at his young age? It seemed his dad couldn't be the father he had planned on. If Chip had been a problem or burden I could have understood, but he never was to anyone—quite the opposite.

Chip knew he had my love and I'd do whatever I could for him, even when it came to his mode of dress and possessions. I was thrifty, lived within our means, and wasn't afraid to work. When Chip got older and started earning his own money, he spent much freer than I.

Once when I commented, he reminded me, "Mother, you always took me to the better men's stores when I was little, like Muir's men's store in Fort Wayne."

He was right! What could I say? I wanted him to have the best. His clothes were still like new when his cousins received them. His expensive taste never changed. Always being in the public eye he looked great. Chip never wore jeans, only dress pants, until we moved to Texas. He was always in style with the latest dress trends, including the frayed, tattered jeans with holes.

Since Grampa Chris had died, Grams was coming to our home in Fort Wayne to spend more time with Chip. Grams was proud of Chip and loved taking him to all the "better" places, and they enjoyed anything that was new or different.

Chip had been playing the piano since he was five and played very well. Grams also played the piano and recently got an organ also. She loved to hear Chip play and was his greatest fan, attending all of his recitals and always marveling over how well he performed.

I asked Mother to choose a piano for Chip's thirteenth birthday. I had been working many extra long hours and had set up a special savings for Chip so I could surprise him with his first big gift, which I was sure he would love. At that time Chip was still playing on his old upright piano, which was about fifty years old. He enjoyed playing and was good about practicing. I knew he would enjoy having a new piano. I also knew I could trust Mother's judgment when it came to choosing the right piano for the money. And too, I didn't have the time. Mother found him a piano at Grinnell Piano Salon in Battle Creek, Michigan, and had it delivered to our home in Fort Wayne. Chipper sure was surprised and pleased when he saw his new piano.

Hank, the man I married, was exceptionally good with Chip and they always got along great together. In fact, he was so good to Chip that there was never a need for discipline, only guidance.

Whenever people teamed Chip was my only child, they were surprised. He didn't have the "bratty, spoiled" nature of an only child. I don't believe he had a selfish or mean bone in his body. In fact. I'm sure he didn't. Neither Chip, nor Hank.

My husband, Hank, and I became the owners of a fine Chinese restaurant during Chip's elementary and junior high school years.

Chip enjoyed the Chinese cuisine and the restaurant with its unique Chinese decor and pleasant atmosphere. He would come to the restaurant after school to do his homework.

We hadn't had the restaurant long, when one evening while Chip was there we had gotten quite busy and he voluntarily started working the cash register. Until then I hadn't even given thought to his knowing how to make change, but he seemed to know what he was doing, and that evening there weren't any mistakes. Working with the public seemed to come naturally to Chip.

As a rule, when his homework was done, he didn't waste any time checking to see how everything was with the customers. He beamed from head to toe, going from one table to the next, asking if everything was okay. If they needed anything—more rice, rolls, tea, or whatever else he could offer—he would hurry and get it for them.

Then Chip would help bus and set tables or fold napkins. He was a big help to the waitresses, and they loved it—and Chip, too. He was like a little brother to them. Especially Melody, whom he always cheerfully greeted as "My Lady." Oftentimes on weekends there seemed to be an extra rush getting the side work done to go out for fun times with "My Lady, Melody," either to the movies or for pizza after work.

Working with people is what Chip liked most, and his genuine graciousness never changed. He understood that the customers always came first. This would prove to be a big benefit to him professionally in the future also as a realtor.

Eventually Chip started waiting tables. The trays were almost as big as he was, at twelve years old, but he managed to carry them without any problem. Chip gave excellent service and always kept close tabs on his customers. It wasn't long until the clientele started asking, "Where's Chip?" if they didn't see him.

Customers were always complimenting him, saying, "For such a little guy, he sure works hard," "He's so polite and always smiling," "He always has something pleasant to say," "He really makes you feel good," "He's such a little gentleman," etc., etc.

These compliments came as often as Chip's natural politeness.

It was apparent Chip was greatly influenced by Hank's humbleness during his young years growing up. Chipper even seemed to have inherited his hearty chuckle and great sense of humor, which enhanced his (their) great personalities. They were two of a kind when it came to their kind treatment of people and the way people thought the world of them, with respect and admiration.

Before we knew it, Chip naturally worked himself into the restaurant business. There were no plans or intentions for him to start working at his young age, but it seemed to have happened automatically. It was a great business for the three of us to be doing something we all enjoyed while being together.

Chip did most everything, but he didn't care for working in the kitchen. He didn't like doing dishes, the preparation work, or cooking. However, he liked watching all the preparation of the many foods. Once in a while he would get busy and help with something such as wrapping egg rolls or making won tons, mainly because of the fascination, I believe, and wanting to be near Hank. Years later Chip always made sweet-and-sour pork as his specialty at home.

Sometimes Chip would bring his friends to the restaurant. He liked treating them to egg rolls, fortune cookies and almond cookies, and of course, oolong tea. Chip would proudly say, "We could buy the almond cookies, but Mother makes them much better."

Then Chip would please them with more cookies.

Chip and I both learned more about Chinese cooking than we realized at the time. Chinese food is always individually prepared to order and because of our excellent Chinese cuisine, people would come from miles around, plus many from our church, to enjoy dinner. Hank had a great reputation for his Chinese cooking wherever he cooked. He had grown up working in his uncle's Chinese restaurant and had a knack, it seemed. I met him at the elegant Golden Dragon Restaurant in Fort Wayne. Even before our restaurant opened, people would come from miles around for certain dishes they preferred him to cook. Before we started our business. Hank had become a computer programmer, but having his own restaurant was his dream. Therefore he was successful in both fields.

Chip's observation of and participation in the restaurant while young seemed to make many things more natural to him throughout his life. That was how, at a very young age, Chip earned and planned for what he desired. No doubt the good start early in years enhanced his charisma and charm, making him the person he was throughout life.

Although Mother's Day was often just another workday, it had always been a very special day to me. Now that Chip was earning his own money, he was anxious to make it extra special in his own way. He had been gone awhile. When he returned, he entered by pushing the restaurant door open with his back. Once inside he turned around and was all smiles, holding out a beautiful, large bouquet of all white flowers. They truly looked like a wedding bouquet! He walked up to me and sat them on the table saying, "Happy Mother's Day!"

In the bouquet were tulips, daisies, carnations, lilies, and little bitty sweetheart roses enhanced with dainty baby's breath. The baby blue, satin lace bow with the leather lee and commodore greenery served as the only color.

My eyes were watery as I smiled and gave Chip a big hug, saying, "Thank you, honey. This is the prettiest bouquet I've ever seen! You make me the proudest mother in the whole wide world, all the time!"

Hank came out and was all smiles, admiring the flowers. Chip was grinning and blushing while I hugged him again, thanking him more.

Chipper had a special fondness for elderly people, and two of our neighbors were elderly widow ladies, Betsy and Martha. He knew they were often lonely and he enjoyed their company too, so he spent treasured time with them. He especially liked going to Martha's home because of the beautiful oriental decor. Martha had lived in China, and her stories always fascinated Chip. This Mother's Day he surprised both Betsy and Martha with lovely bouquets also. As soon as we arrived home, they were so delighted that they both brought them over to show Hank and me.

For Grams and Gramma he also had a special Mother's Day gift, which he had spent many days working on with oil paints. This was the serenity prayer, which says: God grant me he serenity to accept the things I cannot change. The courage to change the things I can, and the wisdom to know the difference. Then he placed these in large eleven-by-fourteen-inch picture frames. Grams displays hers above her fireplace today in memory of Chip.

We had been making plans to spend our vacation in Canada at the world's expo. It had been several years since Chip had been to Maryland to see Nana and Pappy. And his dad still wasn't visiting or returning his calls. We told Chip we would stop in Maryland so he could visit his grandparents if he'd like. Of course, he was delighted! I called to let them know when we would be coming and that we'd leave Chip with them for the day if they would like. Everything seemed fine, and Chip was anxious.

We didn't mind going out of our way so Chip could see Nana and Pappy, but suddenly it was an inconvenience to them. We received a surprise letter from Nana saying,

"You said you were planning on coming on the 30th. I'm sorry but we won't be here. We are going to Baltimore. I need special care for my blood pressure, but I certainly hope Chip will understand. I thought I would let you know so you would not come out of your way."

Chip understood, but was disappointed. I almost called to tell them we could go to Baltimore, but after giving it careful thought and not wanting Chip's hopes built up for another letdown, I decided to drop it. We'd make it up to Chip. That was how it had been the past few years for unknown reasons. We never knew why. Chip went with the flow and enjoyed his own good times. We had a good life and were busy, busy, busy.

Hank and I wanted to have a baby, and I had gone to the doctor to get a fertility shot after having gone through a series of tests. Then to my surprise I was told I would never have another baby. This bothered me and I became obsessed with my inability to give my husband a child of his own. Even though Hank loved Chip and treated him like his own, saying he was all that mattered, my obsession still drove a wedge between us. Our marriage then ended in sadness for us.

Again, it was just Chip and I and his dog, Scottie.

One day disaster hit and Chip had to make a heartbreaking decision. His little dog, Scottie, who had been like a brother to him, got distemper. Chip had always babied Scottie and given him all the love and care possible. Whatever the veterinarian told him to do for Scottie, he did. Yet Scottie didn't get any better. The veterinarian told Chip he could continue like he had been with Scottie and maybe he would recover, although it wasn't likely, or he could have Scottie put to sleep.

Chip didn't know what to do. He didn't want to lose Scottie, but Scottie was suffering. We had a heart-to-heart talk. Then Chip called Nana. She said she'd call his dad, since he had gotten Chip the dog and knew what Scottie meant to him.

Chip hadn't heard from his dad since the day he had asked to live with him, over three years ago, except for a Christmas card. Poor Chip, what a big decision he had to make on his own. Nana advised him to have Scottie put to sleep. But he waited and waited, hoping his dad would call, but was afraid since he wasn't hearing from him anymore.

Chip was crushed; he needed his dad especially now. He didn't want to leave Scottie's side. The writing was all over his sad face: "Please Dad. Please call. Why don't you call?"

This was no doubt the saddest time in Chip's young life. Surely his dad cared about Scottie, and Chip needed his comfort, too. If only he'd call, maybe Chip wouldn't feel so lost. Still the call never came. It almost broke his heart.

Finally, after much hesitation, much thinking, and much dreading, Chip decided.

With a long, solemn expression, he said, "Okay. I'd better have Scottie put to sleep. He won't eat and I can't get him well."

The heartbreak of losing his dog, his constant companion, and his dad's rejection created emotions so strong that they were tearing him apart. Chip had been doing well until now, he hadn't shed a tear, but going to bed that night was like a nightmare and the tears wouldn't stop.

I went into Chip's room and sat on his bed beside him. While I struggled to keep my own emotions in check, I softly said, "That's okay, Chip. I understand."

I wiped the tears from his eyes. He looked at me with his lips pressed together, gulping, trying to stop the tears. This broke my heart. I closed my eyes and the tears streamed down my cheeks. The pillow beneath Chip's head was soaked. At first I couldn't talk while I fought the tears. I bent over, reaching my hands under his shoulders and pulling him to me. He put his arms around me and held tight.

Sobbing, "I don't wa-wa-want to lose you, Mother. I don't wa-want to lose you."

His little heart was breaking. Having to have Scottie put to sleep, knowing he wouldn't be there with him anymore, the same as his dad wasn't with him anymore was the most staggering, the most terrifying realization to Chip. He was heartbroken, feeling the double loss of his dad and Scottie.

I felt his tears dropping on my arm while he squeezed me even more. Stammering through his tears, he sobbed, "I d-d-don't want to I-I-lose Nana."

I caressed him gently, yet firmly. "Chipper, you aren't going to lose Nana or me. We will always be with you," I cried.

This was breaking my heart. I knew what Chip was feeling. He had never cried this much ever before. He was devastated!

As soon as I could pull myself together, half crying, I said, "Oh, Chip, you know I love you. I truly love you very, very much. I love you with all of my heart! I am so sorry you had to have Scottie put to sleep. Honey, this is so unfair to you. I wish I could do something."

Now I couldn't stop the tears. I sat with Chip, thinking, crying, and trying to comfort him, knowing his heart was breaking more and more. If only I could do something to ease his pain and loss.

I'm sure Nana came to Chip's mind because he had gotten Scottie while he was with her and his dad years before. Now his dad wasn't at his side anymore, nor was he seeing Nana, and apparently he was afraid he never would again. This torturous crisis was caving in on him. It was as though his world had completely tumbled, as though he knew and felt it. If those were Chip's thoughts, he was right.

For some cruel, heartless, selfish reason, the tie with Chip's dad had apparently been broken without a word being said to Chip. The son Chip's dad had always wanted he apparently had deserted even before now, when Chip was only ten years old! His very own number one responsibility. He still wasn't coming to Chip's rescue—the son he was going to do so much with. Where was he now when Chip so desperately needed him? How could he let this happen? This was his son! A son who was all give, all love, not the least bit selfish or spiteful. A son who listened, had good manners, was polite and kind.

Still, Chip never gave up. He only wanted a dad he could love and be loved by, and to have a mutual proudness. Chip wrote many letters to his dad. Some he sent, some he didn't.

Chipper was doing okay, considering all the rejections he had had over the past few years. His dad wasn't coming forward to help, not even to offer his love. To know Chip you wouldn't have had any idea of the effect his dad's apparent rejections had on him; he quietly tucked his feelings away deep inside at the start of his early years.

Chip was a proud person, although secretly lonely without his dad's love. I believe this is what made Chip strong over the years. This was just how it always seemed to be when it came to dealing with his dad. Then too, during his time of tears while losing Scottie, it was as though he intuitively knew and felt the loss of Nana.

This was earthshaking at such an early age, for him to learn that life could be very uncertain and unfair at times. So early in life to learn that surviving is within. Nevertheless, Chip took everything in stride and went on with his own life.

3

Why, Dad, What Have I Done?

"Wake up, Mother," Chip shouted excitedly, "we're coming into Dallas!" "Oh, okay," I replied. "I didn't really sleep much. You and Jerry have kept me awake with all your laughing and talking."

I had been lying in the back seat of the car trying to sleep for the last two or three hours. At least it seemed like it had been, although when traveling it's sometimes hard to keep track of time. It was a good feeling lying there listening to them, thinking how close they were already, even though Jerry and I had only been married about three months.

I was thinking. Isn't it amazing the strange twists and turns life often takes? Jerry had been my first boyfriend. We met at the roller skating rink, where we skated together every chance we got.

Heavens, the thought crossed my mind, it doesn't seem possible. I was fourteen then, the same age Chip is now.

A few years later Jerry joined the Army, and the last time I saw him was the night before he went overseas. After that, I moved to California to live with my mother. Twenty years had gone by and now we were together. Seeing him again after all those years seemed like it had to be fate that brought us back together. He was single and had children from a previous marriage, so that helped me some to overcome my obsession. Chip and Jerry had a good relationship right from the start. That meant a lot to me for Chip's happiness and peace of mind, since at the time he couldn't seem to communicate with his own dad.

I had just put our home on the market before leaving on vacation. After two weeks in Texas, the three of us agreed this was where we would like to live once our house sold. To our surprise, when we got back home our house already had a buyer. It was only a matter of weeks until we returned to Texas.

Since Chip was familiar with the restaurant business and enjoyed working with people, he went to work almost immediately in a nice family restaurant. With his experience and manner he was always able to do quite well.

In the fall Chip started his freshman year at Mesquite High School. He liked his new school and living in Texas, but after about six weeks, the desire to be with his dad was overwhelming him again. Chip was remembering his dad's promises that once Chip was fourteen he would be living with him. Between father and son this was no doubt a natural way to inspire Chip and made him proud. But then, to hear his dad continually direct this as a threat at me was terrifying. He knew I was a good mother and how much his threat hurt, knowing Chip meant everything to me. The thought of not raising my son was devastating. Then, the thought annoyed me that he didn't want the responsibility while Chip was little, but when he was older and could fend for himself, then his dad wanted him.

The tide seemed to have changed with Chip's trauma tic, heartbreaking experience, when ten years old, with his dad. Still, Chip trusted his dad to keep his word. I understood because throughout life we grow up being impressed with certain things from when we were little, especially by people we love. Chip and I were a lot alike, and we had both grown up trusting that people would do exactly what they had promised. I realized he had held onto his dad's vow all these years, remembering how much his dad loved him.

Jerry and I sat down with Chip to discuss the important decision he was contemplating. I really didn't want him to go, but realized I must say okay for Chip's sake. My main concern was that he wouldn't be rejected and hurt again. Hopefully by now his dad could accept the responsibility and give Chip the love and care he deserved as his first-born child. His son.

Since Chip still wasn't hearing from his dad, he thought that maybe the many miles between them made a difference, the way it had seemed when his dad suddenly stopped taking him for their summer times together. Whatever the reason, Chip wanted to get it resolved so they could be together. While we talked, it was apparent his mind was made up. It wasn't that he was unhappy, but he trusted his dad to keep his word and as he remembered his dad's plans it was what he wanted too. Chip was sure his dad would be happy that he was finally coming to live with him.

Our discussion was brief, and we agreed that in all fairness it should be good for them both. There didn't seem to be any reason it shouldn't work out. Chip was at that age when things were changing and I believe there were topics he would want to discuss only with his dad, along with having the fatherly assurance that was needed during those adolescent years.

Chip only wanted to hear our okay and to assure us he knew this was his home, but he wanted to be with his dad also. We understood and Chip was right; he had always been level-headed and had reasoned things out before pursuing them.

I knew Chip wouldn't be a problem for them, and I couldn't help but feel that they were actually the lucky ones. There would be some adjustments, living in a different environment, but he had a natural way of fitting in. Chip was mannerly, minded his own business, and was always particular about himself and his surroundings. I was sure he wouldn't be any bother to them because he did everything for himself. If anything, he would be a big help. I was confident he would be fine, and too, being near Nana and Pappy would be good for him. He had missed Nana and was anxious to see her.

Chip matured quickly, I believe, because I always treated him like an adult and took him everywhere with me when not working. He had been around adults more than children, starting in his young years. Like in the restaurant business, people always praised him and he was the typical little gentleman everyone loved. I worked a lot and it wasn't fair to Chip, yet I needed to work so I could still give him the kind of life I felt he deserved. Being deprived of his dad was enough missing in his life, and I needed to make everything, within my power, up to him. Having the restaurant had been an ideal situation since he was there primarily when not in school or swimming. In the future we would see that this was good experience for both of us.

This time when Chip called his dad he had himself checked out of school and arranged everything, including his flight reservation. The only request he made of his dad was that he meet him at the airport in Baltimore, which was the nearest airport to him. Chip felt that if he did everything himself, including using his own money, then his dad and his dad's wife would see that he wouldn't be a burden to them and hopefully would welcome him into their home. Chip was elated when his dad assured him that he would be at the airport when he arrived.

I was proud of the way Chip had taken charge and how thorough he was in doing everything on his own. Even though young, he was responsible and independent, leaving nothing to question.

The thought of Chip's leaving made me sad. What would I do without him? Even though I worked, we had always been there for each other. Now a major part of my life would be gone. Still, I wanted only the best for Chip, and he needed to have some of those promises fulfilled that were long past due.

Jerry announced, "Okay, Chip, you name the place. We'll go out to dinner before going to the airport."

I chimed in, "Sure Chip, we'll have a going-away party for you."

Chip was excited about going as he sorted and packed, "Sure! he cheerfully announced. "How about pizza?"

"Sounds good to me," Jerry replied.

"Me too," I added.

"Pizza it is!" Jerry exclaimed.

A few minutes later Chip left the house for a while. When he came back, he motioned for Jerry to follow him into his bedroom. After a while they came out with mischievous grins on their faces, not saying a word.

"Okay, what are you two up to?" I quizzed.

They looked at each other, grinning, and didn't comment.

A little later, with his luggage all stowed in the trunk of the car, Chip came back in, took a final look around the house, and said, "I'll sure miss this place," then out the door he went.

I smiled while my heart was sobbing. Chip was still my baby, must I let him go? It sure was hard, but I dare not let him know. I'm sure he felt the same, although it was important he go. He seemed happy to finally be fulfilling a lifetime dream.

On the way to the pizza parlor, we stopped at the motel where we had stayed when we first came to Texas. Jerry and I waited in the car while Chip went into the gift shop. Then Jerry distracted me when Chip came out, and the next thing I knew Chip was closing the trunk lid and getting back into the car, and we were on our way. I was puzzled and wondered what was happening, but since neither of them made any comment, I didn't either.

The pizza tasted great, but I was having a hard time trying not to let Chip see how his leaving was affecting me. When we were almost finished eating, Chip excused himself. He was soon back, and then I saw what all the commotion and secrecy was about.

All smiles, Chip stood a beautiful petite doll down on the table in front of me. She was absolutely gorgeous! She stood about twenty inches tall and was wearing an extravagant dress of lavender lace over satin, with a bouffant skirt that was thirty-six inches in diameter and flowed to the floor. In her tiny hands she was carrying lilacs with lavender streamers flowing to one side of her skirt from her tiny waist. She had very petite features, with dark eyes and long dark hair, and was wearing a wide-brimmed lace hat that matched her dress. Her only jewelry was a single strand of pearls, and she wore a white mink stole over her shoulders. Absolutely beautiful! That did it. The tears tumbled down my cheeks. It was just like Chip to do something like this!

Smiling, he gave me a big hug and said, "Just for you, Mother. I'll miss you."

This was a going-away party for Chip, but he reversed roles and bought this lovely doll for me! I'll never know, but I'm sure he paid dearly for that doll. Price was no object; if it was what he wanted, he bought it. Chip always wanted me to have the best. He had put me on a pedestal and kept me there.

All too soon it was time to take Chip to the Dallas-Fort Worth Airport. I really hated to say good-bye. I missed him already and he wasn't even gone yet. I tried to keep smiling so he wouldn't know how sad I felt. Gosh, how I love him!

We waited until the plane departed, then started home.

Once Jerry and I were home and inside, I stopped in the foyer and looked all around, thinking how empty the whole house seemed. I stood there a few moments with Jerry's arm around me, quietly holding my doll. Then I walked over to Chip's bedroom and stood in the doorway scanning his room. All that was left was his exquisite western design, king-size waterbed. My heart felt as empty as the room, and a tear slowly escaped down my cheek while thinking about Chip. Our first time apart, and for how long? It didn't seem right. I wandered on down the hall and into our bedroom. Then I slowly sat down on the bed holding the doll on my lap, thinking,

God bless you. Chipper. You are such a sweetheart. Your dad sure is lucky. I wonder what you are doing now. I miss you so very much. Already, so very, very much, Chip.

My thoughts were random while my eyes wandered over to the dresser, where my attention was drawn to the statue of a little purple velvet bull with a red rose hanging from its mouth. I thought. That's the bull Chip got me since I stayed home when he and Jerry went to their first rodeo in Mesquite. Thinking about that and knowing Chip wouldn't be home only brought more tears.

My mind raced. I knew Chip was excited about living with his dad. He had told Jerry that he didn't want to upset me, knowing his leaving would be hard for me, but it was something he had to do. Jerry assured him I'd understand.

Chip never said, but apparently his concern for me was why he took care of all the arrangements. Jerry was good with Chip and already treated him like his own son, but Chip needed his natural dad's love and care also.

One day I overheard Jerry say, "If you're happy, it makes your Mother happy. She only wants the best for you."

I saw Chip smile. He knew, but liked hearing Jerry say it.

My feelings about his being with his dad were mixed. I was happy because I understood his wanting to share all those big dreams and plans with his dad, and I knew it would be good if they could finally have a good father/son relationship, which was long past due.

I, too, had always wanted Chip to share those hunting and fishing dreams with his dad, knowing what they meant to him. Although they never interested me, I knew Chip was still looking forward to them. One of his dad's biggest dreams was for the two of them to build a car together, and since it wouldn't be long before Chip could start driving it was an ideal project for the near future. Chip was saving for a new car, but building a car with his dad would be fun, he had said.

Hopefully, it would turn out well this time for both Chip and his dad. Still, I had a feeling, or was it hope, that Chip would come back home in a year or so.

I wouldn't need to wait, not even a year, more like a week! What a surprise, and how sad for Chip! To learn of the heartbreak, humiliation, and disappointment for Chip was almost more than I could bear when I finally heard the whole story.

Nana had called Chip's Gramma in Indiana to tell her that Chip had been staying with her and Pappy the past week. Chip was not welcome in his dad's house. Why? I was shocked when I heard this! I felt terrible realizing the devastation and hurt Chip must be feeling. After all he had done just so he could be with his dad! I couldn't believe what I was hearing.

Nana had told Chip's Gramma she didn't like the way he was being treated at his dad's place. She said she loved Chip so very much and he was no problem, but at her age and with Pappy's cancer she didn't feel she could take care of Chip, too. Since she hadn't seen Chip for some time, I realized that she couldn't have known he was independent and could take care of himself. Actually, he could have been a big help to Nana if she had let him. Nana asked Chip's Gramma if he could come there and stay.

This caught Gramma by surprise, but she answered, "Well, yes, he can come here or go home, whichever he wants! He's always welcome in our home. He's never a problem, and we enjoy having him."

I'm sure Gramma felt the same as I did when she told me about Nana calling her instead of me. Gramma didn't even know Chip had gone to his dad's. My family was always great with Chip, but his own home was where he belonged. After what had just happened, it would definitely be our home.

Chip came home crushed after all his high hopes. He didn't say much, but it was understandable how he must have felt after all he had gone through to make it possible to be with his dad, only to learn that his dad had led him on all those years with empty promises. Chip had tried so hard. And now he faced the humiliation of knowing that his dad didn't want him in, or near, his home. Chip was never told why he had to leave so suddenly and so soon. His only alternative was to swallow his pride and tuck this heartbreak away deep inside. Still, he must have been devastated about not being given a fair chance or reason, wondering, Why, Dad, what have I done?

If Chip had done something wrong I would have understood, but how could a rightful decision have been made in only one day and with a clear conscience about his innocent son?

Chip didn't dwell on his unpleasant experience with his dad, but it was sad to learn what he had gone through.

First of all, his dad wasn't at the airport to meet him as he expected. In his place was Chip's cousin, Debbie, and her husband. Chip appreciated her being there, but was disappointed and surprised since his dad had assured him he'd be there.

How confusing the long trip to West Virginia must have seemed to Chip, with so many thoughts running through his mind, wondering where his dad was or what happened. Wondering if his dad surely wasn't as anxious to see him as he'd sounded, or said on the phone. Wasn't he? It had been a long time since they had been together. There was so much he wanted to share and things to hear from his dad.

When they arrived at his dad's place the reception was cool. Chip learned he had a half sister who was a little past a year old. It seems natural they would have wanted them to get acquainted. Regardless of their uncanny treatment, Chip thought of her while in Hawaii four years later and sent her a Hawaiian T-shirt for a souvenir. I'm sure he would have treated her like a little princess, if he'd only been given the chance. Chip could have brightened all their lives and brought a lot of happiness, the same as he did with everyone he was around. It's a shame they didn't take advantage of the opportunity. It was actually their loss and our gain, but an unfair foul for which Chip would be penalized for life.

The second day Nana came to the rescue and took Chip home with her. The rest of the week while Chip was at Nana's, his dad came for him one evening and took him bowling during his team night.

At first Chip was excited, but while there he was disappointed to only sit and watch. He knew how to bowl and would have enjoyed it much more if his dad had taken him bowling or if only they'd had more time together. Chip was brokenhearted and angry.

He said his dad did offer to buy him a Coke, but he refused. Chip flared, "I wasn't about to take anything from him!"

Knowing Chip, even though he was hurt, he would be polite and try not to let it show. Still, his thoughts no doubt must have been written all over his face: if only this evening could have been for just you and me, Dad.

Chip wanted to talk with his dad. He was still the same innocent, caring son as the last time he saw his dad, only now he was at an age when he needed his dad to discuss things that were on his mind. Instead he felt deserted in a strange place with no one to turn to.

Couldn't his dad sense or see the way Chip felt and realize Chip had needs that only he could give his son? It could have been so different. Couldn't he see the sadness in his son's face? And like Chip, didn't he still want the same father/son relationship that they could naturally share?

I had thought Chip's dad had character. Why couldn't he be the father he wanted and had promised his son? Had he allowed his own bitterness to creep in and deprive his son of his attention? Could he justify neglecting his son like this? Couldn't he see what this was doing to them? Surely he knew where the fault lay.

Chip was not one to cause problems, nor was he used to being around them. He no doubt felt the tension and animosity. Yet, out of respect, he said nothing.

Again, in Chip's young adolescent years, he was reaching out to his dad. Didn't his dad realize that this was a cry for help to the dad he trusted and desperately needed? Why else would his son have gone to all the expense on his own and made the arrangements to be with him? Couldn't he appreciate the sacrifices his son had apparently made to be with him at long last as he had planned? Wasn't he proud of everything his son had done to be a part of his life? Or had he even taken the time to know? Why wouldn't he take the time to realize what an extra fine son he had and now make his (their) dream real?

Why was he denying Chip his love, care, and understanding? How did he think this made his son feel? Didn't he know what this crude torment was doing to Chip? How could he not be thinking of his young son's life then and in the future? Only a few words of concern from his dad may have made all the difference in Chip's life and possibly all the difference in Chip's future, and his life may not have ended at only twenty-seven.

Chip saw his dad one more time, when he took Chip to the airport to send him home. Hurt and angry, Chip said, "He would not come and get me, but sure could make the drive to send me back!"

Under the circumstances, I believe Chip's anger was understandable. What was he to think? How was he to feel? He was definitely affected by the short visit and left to contend with the realization that his dad had let him down when he needed him. Silently Chip put that part of his life behind him and went on, without his dad, no doubt wondering, Why, Dad, what have I done?

Chip used to be the number one grandson with Nana and was given all the love and closeness that every grandchild cherishes, but now that apparently had perished for reasons never revealed. What more cruel growing pains could he have been given by those he loved?

My stepchildren had always been welcome in our home as long as they showed respect and didn't cause problems, and that was the way I raised Chip. These young years are most important for future years once they venture out in life. That is why I could never understand his dad's rejection of him. Yes, hadn't his dad rejected him again from being in his home? First at ten years old, and now again at fourteen, Chip wasn't welcome with his own dad.

If Chip had been a demanding child or if he had gone to his dad's to cause problems or be disrespectful to his stepmother or half sister, then I would have understood. Chip did not have any hale, animosity, or jealousy in him. That was not his style, not even with their callous treatment of him. That's why I never worried about Chip. I knew the kind of person he was and was confident of his behavior, knowing he wasn't disrespectful, regardless!

Chip buried the bad experiences with his dad. First, it had been an unpleasant experience and he didn't want to think about his dad as being that way. Second, he didn't want me to be upset or for me to feel I must do something that he knew would be of no avail.

I believe it was at this time that Chip got the idea that it was his responsibility to protect me. He felt certain things were up to him, not me, to contend with. He didn't want the fact that he was hurt to hurt me, which he knew it would.

Chip's genuine consideration was amazing. We were a close team over the years, knowing we could rely on each other. We had a strong bond and were the best of friends. As for his dad. Chip was hurt and disappointed. Still, he was his dad, and Chip didn't want to give up hope for the "someday." I believe Chip and I were both strong deep down inside and could carry the extra load for others.

After the first rejection years before, we had sought counseling for Chip for a short time, but it hadn't resolved the deep-rooted problem. How could it, knowing the basic solution was love and care, which was continually denied him by his dad?

Back home to the positive foundation. Chip plowed right in at school and did fine, making above-average grades. He majored in journalism and was on the newspaper staff. He was very creative and always doing some sort of clever writing. He was very witty and had a great sense of humor that carried right into his writing. In a few words he could say so much and get his point across, usually with a chuckle. He no doubt could have pursued a successful career in journalism or writing. This is what his Gramma in Indiana knew he would be great in. She always got tickled reading things he'd write or just a good ol' letter telling her what was happening in the Texas lives and the world today. Then at one time he entertained being a pianist. Chip had lots of enthusiasm and energy that played right into the keyboard with great rhythm. The faster, the better; and then to top it all off, the fun really began when he hyped it up with his jolly, deep, resonant voice singing to his heart's content! He was great! A show within himself that was always so much fun, or fun for everyone to join in! He loved the boogie-woogie! Then at other times he played so gently and with such ease that you could feel it in your heart or whatever the mood might be while the lovely music echoed throughout the house. His piano playing was especially festive during the holidays. Just like Grams' Christmas music on the piano or organ was for the family back home. Chip consoled us and made our Christmases complete, too.

It was like Grand Central Station having Chip home. The previous week had been quiet without him and all his friends. Chip was always having a pool party with lots of dancing inside and out on the deck. All the music and laughter was a lot better than the quietness. We were glad Chip entertained his friends at home where they often felt it was their home away from home. They were a good bunch of kids and Jerry and I got along great with them. Chip was proud of the way his friends often talked with me about their personal problems or things that were on their mind, whether they wanted an opinion or just someone to talk with.

They would tell Chip, "You're sure lucky to have a mother like that. I wish I did."

Chipper kept himself busy going to school and working. He didn't dwell on the past and kept his feelings tucked deep down inside. He kept his good attitude and held his head high while he went on with his own life

4

New Orleans

"Chip, are you going to the spa today?"

"I am, Mother, after I stop at the library and return a book. Then I'm going to the club in Dallas. Want to go with me? After our workouts we can go up on the roof and lay out in the sun."

"That sounds like a good idea! I was planning on laying out today, and I've never laid out at the club in Turtle Creek."

"Then why don't you go with me and we can lay out together?"

"Okay, that sounds like fun. Chip, I know the swimming pool's upstairs at that club, but how do I get to the sunning area?"

"It's on the roof by the apartments. You'll see a door near the pool that leads out to the roof; go out it and there will be people laying out there. I'm not sure if that area belongs to them or to the club. Whichever, they both share."

"Sounds great! Give me a few minutes to get my things together. Okay?"

"Sure. Whenever you're ready, we'll go."

"Are you swimming today, Chipper?"

"No, later on Beth and I are playing tennis, so I'll pass on swimming this time and only work out. You go ahead and swim. I'll see you on the roof when you're done."

"Okay. Sounds good. I'll be swimming a mile, then see you out there. I'm almost ready to go. Give me another minute."

When Chip was younger, he was on the swimming team, but now tennis had priority. He and Beth played almost every day. Chip, Jerry, and I joined Presidents Health Club when Chip was almost sixteen.

While we were getting in the car, Chip said, "Mother, I'm sure glad you got us a membership at the club. I always thought that was a great idea."

"I'm glad you use it, Chipper. It's a good way to keep you in shape." I grinned and added, "What could be better timing? Renewing it every birthday when you're a year older."

Chip proudly smiled. "Thanks, Mother."

"At times I wish I'd let you learn karate when you were little and wanted to, but I wasn't sure about it then. I guess that's how people felt about the spa when we joined.

Not many seemed to go then either, but now it seems like most everyone goes. At least at one time or another."

Smiling, I slightly nudged him on the shoulder, "I'm glad you've kept going. It's well worth it, and it shows."

Chip was a clean-cut, good-looking young man with light hair and piercing blue eyes. He was glad his freckles were almost all gone because of the teasing over the years. He had a sleek, slim body, with a small waist and a little derriere, and nice broad shoulders. Chip would like to have weighed a little more, but seemed to stay around 130 pounds. He was muscular and had neat ripples, which he worked out to maintain. He was five foot ten and dressed very sharp with class. Chip's style and character never changed, nor did his youthful zest for life. He had a magnanimous personality, a low, resonant voice, and a fabulous sense of humor. He had a dynamic, positive attitude, was spontaneous and always on the go. He definitely enjoyed the good life, traveling, dining, and entertainment. Chip had high standards and a lot of pride, and lived life to its fullest. He was a delight to be with and you knew you were in for a good time.

One day I came home and found a note Chip had left on the kitchen table. Dear Mother & Jerry,

"We'll, I know this will hurt, but I've gotta get away for awhile. I figure now is a good time 'cause we are getting along pretty good. Nothing will happen to me, but if it does at least this way you won't blame yourselves. I love ya both very much, but I've been told I've gotta 'get out of my mother's apron strings.' I'm 17, & maybe just leaving like this is immature but at the same time I've always dreamed of being on my own and this way I'll be able to get everything out of my system (running). I'll be back, maybe soon or maybe later on. But I will keep in touch, I promise. And lean take care of myself. Mother,! love you very much, maybe too much. I've always not wanted to hurt ya, but talking with my counselor & others, I've gotta start thinking of myself more. She said I have to live for me, no one else. I know that's maybe wrong, and it's tearing me up inside & I've decided io go. Please understand. I will keep in touch with ya, often." Love ya, "Chip XO"

I was surprised and sad when I read the note. I didn't know what to think. I had no idea anything was bothering him so much that he'd leave home, and so suddenly. What happened? Why? Where did Chip go? What should I do? What could I do? All these questions and more kept going through my mind. I knew Chip was good at concealing any thing he thought might upset me, but what could this be that would cause him to leave home? He mentioned this as being our good time for getting along. He never was a problem, outside of the growing-up pains kids go through.

I closed my eyes tightly and took a deep breath. As I let it out, I prayed, "Oh, God, please, don't let anything happen to Chip. Please, please keep him safe and take care of him. Thank you, God. Thank you."

Chip was still young and this was the first time he'd ever done anything so unexpected. What was wrong? What had or hadn't I done? From the letter he left, it was even harder to figure out, or was it? The note was like Chip. He was sincere and made it clear why he left, at least to a degree. All through it, he was loving and caring, trying not to hurt us any more than necessary, while telling his reasons. I wasn't angry with him. I was worried and afraid. I didn't want anything to happen to him.

We had always talked out problems, but now his note left me wondering what we hadn't talked about and why we hadn't, if something was bothering him so much. It was clear that he felt he needed to leave us, and he had a mind of his own. He always did pretty much what he wanted, when he wanted. So why and who would say to him, "You're tied to your mother's apron strings." He certainly wasn't. Never! Quite the opposite. Was talking and giving him my time whenever I could tying him to my apron strings? Who had said that to him and why? I couldn't imagine. I realized some kids could be cruel and say things to intentionally hurt others, but I knew Chip's friends and they weren't of that caliber. His friends were decent and respected him. They knew Chip and how independent he was. They certainly knew I didn't control him, that I only gave him guidance. They knew Chip! So who? I could understand how hearing such a remark would no doubt bother him, just like it did me when I thought about it! Chip had a lot of pride. No way on earth would he ever be tied to my apron strings. If anything, at times I felt as though I may have shoved him, so to speak, out of the nest too soon.

While he was growing up, I was strict and stern, but Chip understood. I knew he had to be his own person and I didn't want it said that he was a "mama's boy," any more than I knew he would. That remark alone would give him the inclination to leave home. Maybe we were both overly cautious about this since I was raising him without his own dad, and it gave Chip more reason to be on guard—even more than he should have been at times. But I could always trust him and his judgment. He had always been my main concern, with "no strings" attached, and just the thought of someone saying such a thing was aggravating. I wondered how anyone could say something like that to Chip, knowing it would be like putting a knife in him and turning it.

I naturally worried and wondered about Chip's being gone, but he said he'd call and I trusted he would. I understood that when he felt that the time was right, we would hear from him. The remark about my apron strings seemed to have cinched it that Chip would run away. How unfair!

Within a week Chip called to let us know he was in New Orleans.

From that time on. Chipper was pretty much on his own. Occasionally he would come home, but never for long. He always took responsibility for himself, whether or not he was home. Jerry and I were happy to make ourselves available to Chip when he needed us, which was seldom. He took great pride in being his own person and we, too, were proud of the way he took care of things. Even when times got rough, he'd somehow master things, knowing it was all a part of life. I had always told him, "We're only given what we can handle. The rough times make you stronger."

A couple of weeks after Chip left home, the father of one of Chip's friends stopped by. While we were talking he asked, "Where's Chip?"

I replied, "He went to New Orleans."

With a tone of dismay in his voice, he said, "Ooh, he must have gone with Ron." Then he let out a big sigh. "I had plans for him to marry my little girl and take care of her one of these days."

I smiled, but didn't comment. I remember thinking that was a nice remark and I could understand why he would want Chip for a son-in-law, but I didn't think any more of it. Actually, I hadn't given thought of Chip in relation to marriage yet. He was much too young and could wait at least until he was twenty-six. I knew Chip and Rhonda saw a lot of each other, but I also knew he was spending time with some other cute girls. Chip was definitely a ladies' man. He had a great personality and the gentlemanly, charming manner that girls liked.

Chip definitely liked New Orleans and the nightlife. He kept his promise and called every so often to see how we were and to let us know how he was doing.

One day he excitedly called and was anxious for us to visit him. It was almost time for Mardi Gras! He had already started making plans. Mardi Gras did sound like a great idea, and of course we were anxious to see Chip. Too, the timing was perfect for our vacation. It was Chip's first time to be away from home so long and already it seemed like forever. Of course, I couldn't let on to Chip that it seemed that long.

Not any too soon we were on our way to New Orleans. It was great seeing Chip. There he stood with those beautiful, piercing blue eyes and a big heartwarming smile. He had on his tight faded jeans and a tailored white T-shirt that neatly emphasized his broad, muscular shoulders and chest. He had such a neat physique and carried himself well. He looked just as clean- cut and refreshing as ever.

Chip was full of enthusiasm and excited about showing us New Orleans. Mardi Gras was every bit as festive as Chip had claimed it would be. Everybody seemed to be having a ball—yelling, laughing, and carrying on. The parades were fabulous— so colorful and exciting with all of the unique, exquisite costumes!

While die beautiful floats went by, everyone, including us, was jumping up into the air to catch the Mardi Gras coins and beads that were being thrown by the entertainers from the floats. It was hilarious! You would think that you couldn't help but catch a certain coin or string of beads. They would be coming right at you, but as you jumped to grab them, oops, there they would go, right into the hands of someone next to you. Then there would be more beads and lots of coins all at once, coming right at you!

I'd yell, "Hurry, Jerry, get me that one! Ooh, thank you, I like this, even better than the other one. Here come some more! Ooh, thank you, sweetheart."

It was exciting! I don't know if it was the coins and beads or all the commotion, or both.

Chipper yelled, "Just a minute, Mother, I'll get you that real pretty one," then he jumped up to grab more beads.

There were so many different kinds and colors. Everyone was scurrying to catch more. Chip and Jerry were having great fun grabbing all they could for me. I slowed down, laughing while I watched them. We had so much fun watching the parade and catching trinkets for at least a couple of hours. I really didn't know for sure how long. Who keeps track of time at a place like that! It was all fun and gaiety while we tried to catch our breath in between floats.

The streets were more crowded than usual because of Mardi Gras. We went up one street and down the next, visiting all the different tourist shops. Of course, we saw lots of exciting and entertaining floor shows with Chip taking us to many of the places he liked in particular, showing us a fantastic time!

Bourbon Street in the French Quarter, New Orleans! I believe everyone who goes to New Orleans visits Bourbon Street. It is one of those areas you want to see and never forget once you do. I could certainly see why Chip or any young man would enjoy it here. Lots of partying and great fun! So it seemed. Everything was splendid and quite unique with all the different nightclubs and floor shows.

On one occasion while we walked down the middle of the crowded streets we began to notice all the balconies above the clubs. Then one particular balcony caught our eyes. In fact, many people noticed and were looking up. All the attention seemed to be going to the same balcony while we passed below. While we kept looking up I couldn't believe what I was seeing. A group of young people were up there on the one balcony and a girl was in the process of stripping! Completely naked! Wow, a free show! I knew Chip and Jerry were also watching me, waiting for my reaction. I believe they were trying not to grin or make much of what was happening; apparently they were curious to see my response. I didn't know what to say or do, I was flabbergasted! I was embarrassed, yet I didn't want to appear naive. I hadn't expected to see anything like that.

Chip spoke up and said, "That goes on all the time here in the French Quarter. You get used to it."

Chip grinned and so did Jerry and I as we walked on.

I thought, Well, that's life. To each his own. After all, this is Bourbon Street.

Later on Chip said, "I'll see y'all after a while. I'm going on down to the other end of Bourbon Street."

New Orleans and being with Chip was an adventurous pleasure.

A few more months went by with Chip still in New Orleans.

One day he called asking us to come and get him, saying he was sick. He said he hadn't planned on bothering us, but had been too sick to work the past few days and still wasn't any better. Naturally we were soon on our way. I was glad he called and was coming home, sick or not sick. It hadn't been the same with him gone.

When we got to New Orleans, Chip still wasn't feeling any better. He seemed to have the flu. Soon we were on our way home with Jerry driving. Even though Chip didn't feel like talking much, the subject of the past few months came up. He attempted to do the best he could, even though he was worn-out. After a short lull in the conversation I casually asked, "Chip, are you gay?"

Hesitant, he answered with a question, "Why do you ask?"

I told him it crossed my mind (later) going to shows of female impersonators during Mardi Gras. I paused, then added, "I started thinking about things." Smiling, I patted his leg, saying, "No offense to the performers. They were the greatest!"

Chip nodded. We talked and I assured him I understood. I told him that I had thought about this happening since I raised him without his own dad, especially when his dad suddenly stopped communicating with him and then the rejections when he was so young. Chip and I never talked much about his dad, nor dwelled on the subject. We took care of our own wellbeing without him.

At this time, though, I commented, "It was always so sad seeing you come a way from the empty mailbox, which at one time often had something for you from your dad. Remember? It was during that time when we sought counseling for you. I was concerned then, and asked the counselor about gay life. He assured me I needn't worry. Maybe I shouldn't have taken him at his word. But I never thought any more about it, until now."

Chip wasn't feeling well, as it was, so we didn't say much more. Soon he was sound asleep, leaning his head over on my shoulder. I smiled, but my heart saddened, thinking what lay ahead for him with his new lifestyle, let alone this sickness he was now feeling.

I lay my head back and dosed my eyes with my thoughts to God. God, he is so decent and good. Please take care of him and may everything be okay. I love him so very much. He gives me every reason to be proud of him. Thank you, God, that he's coming home. Even though he's never been sick much and is now, home is where he belongs. I know he didn't want to call, but I'm glad he did. Thank you, God. Just so he'll be okay, soon. That's what counts. Thank you, God. Thank you.

It was later when I remembered Chip telling me his friend, Ron, wanted to talk to me. In fact, that was shortly before Chip had gone to New Orleans. Ron and I had sat down to talk, but he never seemed to say much. He kept looking at the floor and I remember asking him to look at me so we could talk, but he never did. That was the first time one of Chip's friends wanted to talk with me and couldn't. Later I learned he was the first person Chip had been intimate with. This had bothered Chip, and Ron said he'd talk with me. Evidently Chip couldn't tell me either and it troubled him so much he left home.

Chip was always popular with the girls. When he wasn't working or in school, he was usually with the girls at our home or on a date. So, no, I never suspected anything. And too, there apparently wasn't any reason to because Chip hadn't known it himself until just before going to New Orleans.

I couldn't stress my concern enough about how important it was that he not get any ideas about destroying himself because of what his life had become. He was my son whom Jerry and I loved dearly. He was a part of me and nothing could stop my love and concern for him. Sitting beside me was the same good person I had raised for seven teen years. He didn't act or seem any different because he wasn't. The only difference was that now I knew about his personal lifestyle. Truly it was no one's business, except his.

I could imagine how hard it had been to tell us, when it was hard to accept the fact himself. No wonder he left home. I'm sure it would have been different if I had known what was bothering him. I'm sure he knew, down deep, that I would still love him. Yet, knowing Chip I realized that he had left because he didn't want to disappoint me. And too, I'm sure he needed to come to grips with this within himself. I assured him our relationship was still the same. If anything, it may have made us even closer, if that were possible.

I was always there, the same as before. I told Chip that he was all that really mattered, and Jerry agreed.

Chip was still very young and it was great to have him home.

We assured him, "Nothing's changed. This is your home. It always has been and always will be."

I was beginning to understand. Apparently he left without saying anything because of the adjustment he had to make himself and with the idea his life now wasn't what we had anticipated. The part that bothered me was knowing how difficult it would be for him. We weren't disappointed in him. Things happen unexpectedly throughout life.

I realized that in order for him to go on with his life he must accept that he was gay; otherwise, chances were he could end his own life.

"What kind of parent would I be if I couldn't love and care about you regardless?" I asked Chip. "Especially when you need me the most."

I'm sure Chip knew life was not going to be easy. It was a new kind of life. He had his own personal adjustments to make. First accepting himself as gay would take time with a lot of trials, maybe the rest of his life. I imagine it was almost like starting over, or was it? How much more difficult could life be than it had already been all these years, trying to get the love and consideration he needed and wanted from his dad, long before he became gay. It seems Chip had to go on with his endless, lonely search, searching in vain for love.

I had every reason to be proud of Chip, and I never gave thought to his being any different from anyone else we were ever around, straight or gay. I was Chip's mother, and I still valued his opinions, the same as always. Out of respect to the family, friends, and his own self-esteem, Chip never flaunted his lifestyle. Even though in his generation promiscuity was at its peak, Chip was decent and respectable. He kept a low profile on his intimate friendships. Most of all. Chip did not ever want to embarrass Jerry or me, and he never did.

I always told Chip, "You come first, don't worry about us. You have your life to live, so live it and always know we're your family and we care. That's what is most important."

This never caused problems between Chip and me. I respected and admired my son, knowing his reputable character. I never harped at him to change or see a doctor because I understood the situation, realizing it was apparently meant to be. The only reason to seek counseling would be to help him accept it himself and to help end the confusion of his life over the years.

It is believed there is a strong possibility that being gay is in the genes. Possibly a combination of that and the overall situation while a child is growing up. Just because he was a boy, instead of a girl, didn't mean that he didn't have the same feelings and needs to be met. Starting when Chip was three, his dad was never there when he needed him and eventually not at all. Was his dad ever concerned with his son's attempts to be with him? It didn't matter how hard Chip tried to reach his dad, his pleas fell on deaf ears. So doesn't it stand to reason? Chip's life, to a degree, never changed. He kept on searching for love. It may not make sense or seem right, but isn't love what life is all about? Doesn't everyone want love? What won't we do for love?

If one is confused and rejected when still a child, what is to be expected? Doesn't that responsibility belong to the parents while that young child is growing up?

One day, years later. Chip said to me, "Mother, it's strange, but you know, I seem to be seeking guys about the same age as my dad. I hadn't realized it until I got to thinking about it."

Then we talked about whether or not it was a coincidence. It was true, he still wanted his dad's love.

If his search for a father's love continued on into adulthood, couldn't it be because of what he was denied in childhood? It wasn't as though Chip withdrew from his dad, but quite the opposite. I'm sure I loved Chip enough for both his dad and myself, but he still needed his dad, too. Being gay isn't a choice, but rejecting your own son is a choice. Therefore, could the rejection and lack of a father's love possibly have had a bearing on his lifestyle?

I was afraid the gay life would be a lonely, hard struggle. I don't believe anyone can know this as much as the individual who experiences it and needs to adjust. I could only imagine, and my heart ached for Chip whenever I thought about this. I knew it was beyond his control. Being gay isn't something any human being desires, let alone the negative attitudes of others that they may need to deal with.

It's clear that all the reasons have not been pinpointed. Gay lifestyle is not caused by force or influence by a gay person. This seems to be the main fear of this lifestyle, but once this fear is overcome by understanding, it will be realized the fear was for naught. Gays keep with their kind the same as straights keep with their kind when it comes to intimacy.

People from all walks of life may be gay. It doesn't seem to matter who you are or what you are; chances are, you will be gay if it's meant to be. I do believe it is beyond a person's control and definitely it is not a choice.

To suddenly realize you are gay changes your whole life. It would definitely take courage and common sense to overcome and make the best of it. What can a person do? Is he to end his life because of the stigma surrounding homosexuality? I would think not! I can only imagine how learning you're gay must seem. No doubt wondering why. Why am I this way? Or, why did this happen to me?

Possibly the day may come when we'll understand this lifestyle more and why it happens as it does or to whom it does, along with how to cope with it fairly, without there being such an unfair turmoil for those concerned. At this time I don't have the answers any more than the next person, it seems. Although, someday when the time is right, we'll learn the answers. Understanding and compassion seem to be the key elements, whether it be now or once we know more.

I did know my son's new lifestyle wasn't any reason to shun him or make him feel any worse about himself. He was still the same decent, respectable young man, and the last thing he ever wanted was to hurt me. I am thankful he was the man he was, a man with a lot of backbone who made the best of things.

Until we understand life as it is, we can only look for truth and not be judgmental, never knowing what life holds in store for us or those we love.

On earth being gay isn't a choice, it needs to be an acceptance.

5

Bahama Persuasion

"Chip, do you feel like answering the telephone? I'm up to my elbows in pie dough for apple pies."

"Sure, Mother. It's probably Beth, calling to let me know what time she will be over this evening."

"Great! The pies will be ready to eat by then. I sure wish you felt up to having some. You may by then."

"That sounds good," Chip agreed as he answered the phone.

It was Beth. She was a neighbor who lived down the street from us when we first bought our home in Texas. Chip and Beth seemed to have clicked right from the start and were together most of the time. Beth was an adorable girl, a little younger than Chip. She was like a petite baby doll with long dark hair and dark eyes. Very sharp! Definitely Chip's kind of girl, and they made a great couple. Often it seemed they were up to some mischief or teasing someone or each other.

When Chip hung up, he said, "Mother, would you make a French creme pie?"

"Umm, sure!" I agreed. "We haven't had any for a while."

"I mentioned the French creme to Beth; she said it sounded good. I told her it was, and you'd make one so she could try it."

"I'm glad you did. I've got enough dough, so I'll make a couple of them." I grinned and added, "Once you're feeling better, knowing you and Jerry, they won't last long."

"Especially the French creme," Chip agreed with a mere grin, while he gradually crept back to the sofa to lie down.

Chip was feeling much better now, but still hadn't gotten his vim and vigor back.

When we had arrived home from New Orleans about two weeks ago, Chip was glad to be home in his own bed. Still, after a couple of days, he seemed to be feeling worse and agreed he needed to see a doctor.

After the doctor gave Chip a thorough examination, we were surprised when he suggested Chip go directly to the hospital, and not even go home first. He had hepatitis. Chip hadn't been in the hospital since he was five years old when he had his tonsils taken out. In fact, he never missed school because he was never sick and had only been to a doctor for shots when needed while growing up. The doctor said this was A-Hepatitis, which was airborne and he could have gotten it anywhere, such as in a restaurant or even by the mere touch of someone passing on the street. The doctor explained B-Hepatitis to us, which was communicated by sexual relations, and assured us this wasn't that, even though both kinds could be quite serious.

There were different times the doctor mentioned to me, during our visits, that this could be fatal. I wondered why he was mentioning this so often, but with Chip being in the hospital and sick, this was already unusual and a scare. Still, I couldn't imagine his not getting well. I'm not sure if the doctor kept repeating the word "fatal" because I wasn't accepting the fact, or because maybe I wasn't comprehending what he was saying. With medicines today, treatment has improved greatly and one's not as likely to be put in the hospital for hepatitis.

Chip was in the hospital for about a week when he was finally well enough to return home where he could rest a few more days, then be himself again, feeling great!

When Chip's friends learned about his trip and new lifestyle, it didn't make their friendship any different. They liked Chip for who he was and said that he was still the same good friend to them.

Then Chip returned to school with plans of graduating with his class. All the teachers would cooperate on his catching up except for his typing teacher. With the crisis of his new lifestyle, this added snag (by one teacher only) was like the final blow, which was enough to discourage him from continuing his desired education. This was only a fraction of the adjustments he would need to make, although a major one. I'm sure this was one of the most difficult knocks for Chip to accept because he was never a quitter!

Chip didn't stop there. He immediately took the negative and made it into a positive by submitting to the GED Test, which he easily passed without prior study. After that he took classes at the junior colleges.

It was a few years later when Chip was quite surprised to learn that there had been several more kids he knew while in the same school who were also homosexuals. And to think, during that vulnerable time he was taking it even harder, thinking he was the only one and knowing it was something you didn't share with just anyone.

Chip and Jerry had been checking at different car lots to be sure Chip still wanted the little MGB convertible sports car he had first mentioned. Sure enough, that was still his choice! He ordered exactly what he wanted and it was ready to be picked up.

Chip looked proud in his new MGB, pulling into the driveway. Smiling and blowing the horn, he yelled, "I'm home!"

I'd been watching for him, knowing Jerry had taken him to get his car. When I ran out the door, he excitedly yelled, "Come on, Mother, I'll take you for a ride! Just a minute, though, I want to take the top off first."

While Chip was unsnapping the top, Jerry pulled into the driveway. Jerry looked at me with a wink and teasingly said, "Chip said we could drive his car to California."

Chip grinned and replied, "Well, maybe later."

"Only teasing," Jerry joked.

Knowing Chip, he probably would let us take his car most anywhere. That is, if we could get him out of it long enough.

I said, "Well, I can imagine the miles you'll be putting on this little jewel."

Chip grinned. He knew what I meant. I was real happy for him as we drove along. He looked sharp behind the wheel with the top off and the wind lightly blowing his hair in the breeze. The MGB was perfect for him!

We were proud he was able to buy his own new car when he was so young. He deserved it after his hard work and saving for it. Then Chip decided to only invest an adequate amount down in order to give him sufficient payments to establish his credit for the future. He always seemed to be a step ahead and did well with his choice of payments.

Chip hadn't had his car long when he decided to try his dad one more time. He thought he'd take a friend to help with the driving since it would be about a three-day drive. Chip wanted to talk and try to clear the air about his life over the years. Either his dad cared or he didn't. Chip would soon be eighteen, but naturally he still wanted that father/son relationship.

Chip never had told me who made the comment to him that he was "tied to his mother's apron strings." That is, not until the subject had come up some time later and I asked. He was reluctant to say, but finally confessed it was his dad. I hadn't thought of his dad talking that way to him, but then understood more why Chip had left home. To hear such an accusation from his dad had to have crushed him, and apparently it had been preying on his mind ever since that brief visit.

It hurt me, for Chip, to know how needlessly cruel he was to our son. Why? I hadn't seen his dad for years, but remembered his unnecessarily cruel remarks being made to me; but then, after all those years, why to Chip? For what reason? That's an example of how Chip and I trust certain people. Neither of us wanted to think of his own father as being deliberately cruel. It's a shame he didn't know his son any better than that or he would have known differently. And to think, that was when Chip was only fourteen and he made the trip, at his own expense, to be with his father. Didn't that tell him he wanted to be dad's boy? Why was it necessary to misconstrue something that important?

This gave Chip all the more reason to want to see his dad. He wasn't the little boy now and maybe things could be different. He wanted his dad to be proud of him and to know how well he was doing.

When he called to check on the visit, his dad said, "Only you, if you're coming, not anyone else."

Chip hadn't expected his dad to cut him short and the remark caught him off guard. He dreaded telling his friend his dad said he couldn't go to his house with him. Hadn't his dad considered the distance for Chip's first time and his drive alone? Chip dreaded the idea of no company and seriously considered not going. I wanted to call his dad, but Chip wouldn't allow it. I respected Chip's word and said nothing more.

Still, Chip needed to talk with him and get all those "tucked in" aches and pains out in the open. After a few angry words to let off steam, he decided to make the long haul alone.

When Chip arrived at his dad's, his reception was cool, same as before, although this time it was a little different since Chip had his own transportation. He said his dad enjoyed driving his new car around town, showing it off.

Even though his visit was brief, they seemed to have more time together than before. He and his dad talked some, but Chip never was able to actually talk about the important things that were on his mind. Chip said they briefly touched on the subject of gays. He felt that his dad surmised what he was aiming at and no doubt was aware what Chip wanted to talk about because his dad told him about a good friend he'd had for years who was gay.

When Chip told me, I said, "Really, it's more common than people may admit. Some know that their friends are gay and some don't. Being gay shouldn't change a true friendship. It never did with you."

Well, so far. Chip's trip hadn't been much different from prior attempts to see his dad. However, since he had his own transportation and after driving so far, he was determined to make his trip worthwhile, and a few more miles would be worth a welcoming face. Soon he was on his way to Baltimore to visit a couple of aunts on his dad's side and their families. Visiting with them had always been a pleasure. Chip was family and that was exactly how they treated him, which was all he needed. That's all he had ever wanted from his dad.

After his pleasant visit in Baltimore and some fabulous pictures, a few days later Chip was on his way to Indiana and Michigan to see more relatives. He went to Indiana first to see Cindy, his stepsister, who was exactly nine months older than he was. He thought maybe she could go with him to Michigan. He knew Grams would welcome both of them and it would be fun.

When Chip and Cindy arrived at Grams, there were other family members visiting who lived nearby. After cheerfully greeting everyone and introducing Cindy, Grams commenced to prepare dinner so they could eat before starting back that evening.

Grams always prepared a feast for anyone who came to her home and she sure wanted to "do it up right" for Chip and Cindy. It had always been Grams' policy to be especially nice to the friends of her grandchildren. She had met Cindy previously, on our wedding day.

Shortly after dinner, Chip and Cindy prepared to leave. When Grams went into the bedroom for something, Chip followed. He hugged her and said very sincerely, "Thanks, Grams."

"For what?"

"For being nice to my sister."

Grams was a bit overwhelmed, thinking. Isn't everyone supposed to be nice and mannerly to the friends and family of grandchildren?

When Mother told me about that, she said, "That thought lingered and returned many, many times in the years following that visit of Chip's. Thinking how sensitive he was to kindness, not only to himself, but to others."

Mother wasn't aware that Chip's dad had recently refused to let his friend come to their house.

Chip brought Cindy home to Texas to stay with us for a while. He was always especially good and thoughtful with Cindy whenever he had the opportunity.

Days later Chip said, "Mother, while visiting Martha in Ft. Wayne she told me something that in one way will make you happy, and in another way may make you sad" he paused, then said, "Hank's married and has a little boy." Chip knew what was in my heart and phrased that perfectly.

Not long after his trip, Chip wrote a letter to his dad:

Dad,

Just wanted to write and let ya know that I really appreciate your concern about my car. I waited home all day Thanksgiving, hoping you would call, and of course, you never did. I guess I should have known. Couldn't you find a few minutes to give me a ring? Well, I suppose you were out deer hunting all day Thanksgiving, right?

This is one example of your different ways, which I was trying to explain to you when I was back there. You obviously don't care about me. I could use some money if you would be able to go a little out of your way to help me. I zoos also short about sixty-five dollars from what you said when I was back there. (I'm talkin' about the traveling money... in case you've forgotten.)

You are also expected to help pay expenses for a shrink. Ya see, thanks to a good many people... mainly myself, I suppose I'm gay.

Chip

P.S. Merry X-mas!

Seems that letter was to let off steam. It was years later when I found it tucked away in a drawer, apparently just like he tucked his hurt and anger away down deep inside.

Chip never really gave up on his dad completely, but held on to that little glimmer of hope for the elusive "someday." Over the years following that fateful trip, their only contact was an occasional telephone call.

One day months later, Chipper came home in tears. He tried to conceal his hurt, hurrying into his bedroom. Possibly it was instinct that made me notice, and I stopped what I was doing for the moment and followed him to his bedroom. There I stopped momentarily, then softly knocked on his door as I entered. I asked, "Chip, what's wrong?"

He quickly turned his head away. He hesitated, then said his love affair had ended. Seeing him unhappy over his first love made me sad. What could I do? Before I knew it, I found myself crying with him. I loved Chip and all I wanted was for him to be happy. Love and happiness were my greatest desires for Chip, although a real love in the gay lifestyle seemed to be rare. Chip felt he was close to it a couple of times, but later realized, or felt, that there could only be that real love between a man and a woman. To be gay, one often seems to be sentenced to a life of searching and loneliness.

Not long after we learned of Chip's lifestyle, Jerry and I spent a couple of enjoyable evenings out with him at gay nightclubs in Dallas. He wanted to share his social life, and what better way than to let us see for ourselves? Too, I believe he wanted us to know how it was, rather than only hearing malicious gossip about the gay lifestyle. Even though he knew this wasn't a problem for us, in consideration of others for us, he no doubt felt better to be able to share the assurance.

Chip proudly introduced us to his friends, and the floor shows were superb. Everyone seemed to be having a good time and there was never anything out of line. The girls were dancing together and so were the guys, and sometimes there were mixed couples. We had always been open- minded and shared things over the years, so why change it now? It was great that Chip could be at ease with us and his friends with his new lifestyle. Chip's unique character had an aura of distinction when it came to people and his zest for life.

Being gay had difficulties and it took a lot of adjustments, I'm sure. Now that my question or thought about this happening at one time had become a reality, I felt that I must learn to live with this just like Chip must. With Chip's decency and respect it was never a problem. He kept his two lives separate. It seems the serenity prayer Chip liked so much when young was now "fruit for thought" while he faced his life.

People need to understand, a gay person is the same as anyone else, except for his sexual life, and that's only the individual's business. As long as this is kept private, and gay people conduct themselves like anyone else while in your presence, why not let life be? Why interfere? There isn't any reason to discuss their sexual activities any more than you would care to have yours discussed, is there?

Chip grew to love Jerry very much and soon took his surname as his own. Out of respect to his dad, he also kept his last name, but decided to change his first name to Brandon. There was a young neighbor couple who had a little boy, born on Chip's tenth birthday. Chip had been good friends with Kim and he always liked her son's name, Brandon. So he became Brandon T. Williamson (using his dad's initial with Jerry's surname), which we agreed sounded professional.

His name reflected his love for the family and a feeling of belonging. Of course, he would always be a good "Chip."

Chip moved into his own apartment in Dallas when he was eighteen. Everything seemed to be going well for him.

Then one day several months later, the telephone rang about ten o'clock at night. Jerry was at work and my brother Duane was visiting from Indiana. We were reminiscing about our days growing up. When I answered the phone, it was Chipper.

Very slowly and calmly, he said, "Hi, Mother, this is Chip. My oven blew up on me when I lit it," and quickly added, "but everything's okay now."

"What?" I gasped. "Chipper, are you okay? Are you sure?"

"Yes, Mother, I am now. It only singed my eyebrows and hair. My bums aren't too bad. Just a little red."

In shock, I exclaimed, "Chip! Duane and I will be right over! Just sit still, we'll be right there."

"Mother, I'm okay! It's late and you can wait until tomorrow. I called so it wouldn't scare you when you saw me."

"That's alright, Chip, we'll be right there."

I knew Chip, and I had a feeling it was a lot worse than he said. He was acting very calm, and I was too shook up to say much. I hung up the phone, telling Duane what had happened. We rushed out of the house and into the car, and went speeding into Dallas to Chip's apartment, which was about fifteen miles away.

I couldn't believe my eyes when Chip opened the door. His shirt was off and his face, chest, and arms were an angry red. I don't know how he had remained as calm as he was.

I was frightened when I saw him, but tried to remain calm and not say anything to scare him. His eyebrows and hair were singed; his hair in front was almost completely burned away.

"Chip, I'm sure glad you called! We need to take you to the hospital."

Chip was remaining calm so we wouldn't see the pain he must have been in or else he was in shock. Duane wrapped a sheet around him and we rushed to the hospital. He had third-degree bums! They treated his burns with Silvadine and wrapped his head, chest, and arms in gauze, almost completely covering his upper body. The doctor warned him not to break any blisters for fear of infection. Chip hadn't realized the extent of his bums. He was surprised and definitely thankful we had come over. This was the first time he had ever experienced anything this painful.

Chip had been wanting to call his dad to ask if his half sister had gotten the T-shirt he sent her from Hawaii since he had never heard from them. Now with his burns it gave him more reason to call, especially since his condition was much worse than he realized and he wouldn't be able to work for a while. He also needed to know if his dad had insurance on him. Chip had been doing fine on his own with no help, but now possibly his dad could help this one time.

It was a mistake to think his dad might help, but by calling he did learn some important information. Since he had last been there, the year before, Pappy had died. Chip had been very close to him at one time. He also learned that his dad had been in a serious accident on his job a few weeks earlier. Chip couldn't help but wonder why no one had let him know. What if his own dad had died? Would anyone have notified him? The shock of learning all this at this late date, with the misery and pain he was already feeling, had to be devastating, and hurt even more.

His dad did file a claim with his insurance company for Chip's hospital bills. Chip learned from the insurance company several weeks later that the money had been sent to his dad. Then some time later, after a phone call, his dad finally sent the insurance money to the hospital.

Chip feared his bums would scar, but I kept putting fresh aloe vera from our plants on his sensitive sores until they healed. Chip was thankful there wasn't any trace of a scar.

"Thanks to you, Mother, for using the aloe vera." He smiled.

One day I was thinking about all the things that were happening to Chip. It seemed so unfair and had to be tearing him up inside. It never seemed to be something small, but astronomical and unjust without due cause. I sat down and wrote Chip's dad a long letter.

In the letter, referring to his accident, I asked Chip's dad why he hadn't let Chip know or gotten someone else to call if he couldn't. I asked him if he didn't know that Chip cared about him and would have wanted to be with him if he were hurt. I asked him if maybe that was why no one had contacted Chip. I also wanted to know why Chip had not been told when Pappy died. I suggested that it was long past time for him to open up his mind and heart and be a proper father to Chip, as he had wanted to be when Chip was very young—the kind of father he surely was to his daughter. "I pray, before it's too late, you'll treat Chip like you once wanted to."

I didn't mail the letter. I tucked it away in a drawer.

Several years later, Chip said to me, "Mother, I read that letter you wrote to Dad."

"What letter?"

He went into another room, took the letter from a drawer, came back, and handed it to me.

"Oh, that one. I wrote it a few months after your bad bums, but never mailed it."

"You should have. It's a good letter."

I reread it. Chip was right. It was amazing that the letter still wasn't outdated. Maybe I just needed that little nudge from Chip. Every word still held true. I should have mailed it when I wrote it, but it wasn't too late.

It was about Chip and his dad. I was trying to reach him, for his sake and his son's. It was almost as though I knew how things were going to end between Chip and his dad. If only I'd listened to my intuition. His dad still didn't respond when he received the letter years later. Even then he didn't think about his son or what was at stake.

I'm thankful Chip didn't let his dad's irrational manner get the best of him. Instead, he pursued his life to the best of his ability and did just fine on his own, somehow always keeping that special brightness about himself.

Chip and Jerry were always good about leaving me telephone messages and notes, usually thoughtful or funny notes. One day I came home and found an interesting note from Chip. It read:

> *Mother, gone to Bahamas for awhile w/Beth. If you can, would you go by my apt. & get the waterbed & phone equip.? Please.*
> *Love you, Brandon*

I was surprised when I read the note. But on second thought, Chip and Beth were always up to something on the spur of the moment, and the Bahamas did sound like fun. My next thought was, Wouldn't you know he didn't forget Mother, although the moving part didn't strike me as so much fun. It had to be done and he knew I'd do it. I was cost-conscious enough to know that if I didn't do it, Chip would need to pay another month's rent unnecessarily. I called Jerry about the note and to tell him I would be needing the pickup.

Jerry wanted me to wait and he would help, but I said, "No, I'll go ahead and get it done while you're at work. I'll be out to get the truck, okay?"

I'll never forget that afternoon's job. I checked with the landlord and learned Chip had taken care of everything with him.

To reach Chip's second-floor apartment I had to go up about seven or eight steps to a landing, turn left ninety degrees and ascend five more steps, then turn right down the hallway to the third door. Once I had the door unlocked, I thought, Why didn't I wait for Jerry? This may be tricky getting the bed down those twisting stairs. This may take a little longer than I planned!

I opened the door and went in. Chip had emptied and dismantled the waterbed, which was a big help. Then there was the telephone equipment and some small kitchen necessities. I'd forgotten how many parts there were to a waterbed. I could see there would be many trips up and down those stairs. Then I was thinking. Chip, I'm sure you're having a good time, but this would have been a lot easier doing this together. I picked up one of the long side boards of the waterbed and started down the hall.

When I reached the stairs, I had to hold the board up lengthwise and angle to the left. Holding the board at that angle I couldn't see past it, so I felt my way down while I counted the steps. One, two, three, four, five, now the landing, angle back to the right, down seven more steps. I counted the steps while I shuffled along, slowly and awkwardly feeling my way since I couldn't see over the board. At times like that I wished I were taller. It took a lot of twisting and turning to carry the board around the turns and down the steps. After I reached the bottom of the stairs the going got easier.

Carrying the side board out and loading it into the pickup was no problem from there. The side board wasn't so heavy and I seemed to handle it all without too much trouble. I figured if there was a problem it would be the big bulky head board, but I managed. I don't know how many trips I made, it seemed like dozens, and I had to do a lot of maneuvering to negotiate the stairs with the two sharp turns.

Finally everything was loaded, and I took a final look around to make sure I hadn't missed anything.

I laughed to myself, thinking, Just wait, Chipper, next time I have some moving, or better yet, next time you go to Nassau, I'm going with you. Well, at last it was all taken care of, thank heavens. It really wasn't so bad. I guess there are things you wouldn't think about doing, such as this, until they come up. Isn't that what being a parent is all about?

Looking back, it's just one of those things you don't forget, remembering how spontaneous he and Beth were. I really loved that little guy, including all those parts of his contrary teenage years such as this.

I laughed, thinking of Chip, Beth, and the Bahamas.

I had a feeling Beth was in love with Chip almost from the beginning. Later I learned that was the reason for the trip to Nassau, in the Bahamas. More than anything she was hoping to come home as Brandon's wife. She thought the romantic setting with the *Bahama Persuasion* would soften him up and she'd somehow sway him over. The two of them were a great match, with a lot of charisma. Even though she realized there wasn't any way to win him over with his lifestyle, this was sad for both of them. Still, they were close and good for each other, and remained the best of friends.

Later Beth moved away, but whenever she was back in town she always got in touch with Chip. Different times on his birthdays she'd just show up. She was almost as spontaneous as Chip. There was always a special attachment between them. If anyone could have won Chip over, it would have been her.

Chip graduated from Commercial College and became a realtor in Dallas in 1979. I became a real estate broker in January. Living in different areas, we worked out of different offices. Later, in '84, I changed companies and sold real estate with the same Century 21 office as Chip. It was great working with him again. Eventually we planned on having our own company.

Chip's professional manner was serious and quite congenial. Having grown up working with the public, he was a natural with his customers and easily built a good rapport with them. At the office, agents loved having (opportunity) phone time with Chip. His speed and dexterity were amazing! Just like when he was a little boy with Gramma at the rink. With his low, resonant voice he sounded very professional. He was always pleasant and quick to answer the phone, route their call, get their message, or take care of whatever need they had. No sooner would he take care of one call and another would come in. Before you knew it, he was also handling that call! Truly, the agents loved it.

They'd say, "There goes Chip, he's got it!"

His speed took a lot of pressure off the other agents, and they liked that too. They liked listening to how professionally Chip took care of the calls, with lots of enthusiasm. Even with hearing only one side of the conversation, he was intriguing, so positive and eager to please. Just like when he was little, but now a young man venturing out in life.

Chip seemed to always conquer everyone's heart, whether a co-worker or customer. Everyone, especially the women and girls, enjoyed his company—his charm and gentlemanly manner, along with his great sense of humor.

6

California Bound

"Go ahead, Chip, go get your boarding pass. We'll be right in as soon as we get the car parked."

That was the usual routine we went through when Chip took a flight out of Dallas/Fort Worth International Airport. It made no difference if he were only going to Houston or as far as Hawaii, there always seemed to be the last-minute rush getting to the airport before departure time. All the while Chip remained calm. I was never sure which deserved the credit, our living near DFW or the rushing, but we always seemed to arrive in time.

Jerry parked the car, then we hurried into the terminal. Assuredly, there stood Chip grinning, with ticket and boarding pass in hand. He was California Bound! Once he boarded, we waited until his flight departed, then left for home.

We would be seeing Chip in about a week. Jerry and I had planned a trip to Las Vegas and California in hopes that Chip would go with us. He had been very busy listing and selling houses in real estate, so we were trying to convince him that a break would do him good. We hadn't been on a trip together since going to Galveston in '77 and one other trip when Grams and Bill, her new husband, visited us and we showed them all over Texas.

Here it was already the start of '85. Still, Chip didn't want to take time off at the office, but he pleasantly surprised us by having everything set for his customers. Until his return, Zane, our team leader and a good friend, would oversee things for him. Chip planned to go on to California and we were to meet him in Hollywood after Jerry and I enjoyed a few days in Las Vegas. The rest of the trip we would spend with relatives in San Diego, then the three of us would drive home together.

Shortly after Chip and I started working in the same office, I had suggested he move back home since it would be closer, and re-establishing his business would no doubt take extra effort.

Chip was hesitant about moving. Several months passed by, then I tried to reason with him that he would still pay his own living expenses and be his own responsibility. So why not, with our home as large as it was with a split bedroom floor plan? And it would be like separate living quarters at one end of the house.

"It's only you. Chip. You'll still be your own person." Smiling, I added, "I know better than to try and mother you."

Finally he said, "I'll think about it and let you know."

Chip still drove the long distance for quite some time, then finally agreed to move back home. But he seemed to put undue pressure on himself, believing he should be out on his own like he had been for years. Too, he had always lived in Dallas and our present location was "out of the way," so to speak, so his move was only to be temporary.

California always seemed to draw Chip. Maybe it was because he was a native and still had some roots there. He often said, "California is the place to be."

Chip liked city life and felt at home in the delightful cities of Los Angeles and Hollywood where he had many friends. To him that was the "real life." He loved it. The people, the excitement of meeting new friends and new places induced him to go there, like most young men with a zest for good times.

When Jerry and I arrived in Hollywood, Chip introduced us to his friend Neil. Chip and Neil had been friends in Dallas prior to Neil's moving to California. We had a pleasant visit after touring his immaculate home.

While we were there, Chip showed us his favorite places. He had discovered one place in particular that he was excited for us to see. He waited until just before dark when the sun was starting to set so we could enjoy the full beauty. Then he drove through a lovely, luxurious residential area and on up a steep, winding road. It wasn't much farther when a big smile covered Chip's face as he approached a quiet, isolated spot at the top of the mountain.

Excited, he stopped the car, threw up his arms, and exclaimed, "This is it!"

When we got out of the car we could see why Chip was anxious to bring us here! The location was splendid and truly breathtaking! We agreed it was an ideal location with just enough space for a lovely home overlooking the entire Hollywood and Los Angeles area. It was such a spectacular sight with the vast expanse of lights below.

Then Chip took us to an enchanting restaurant in Hollywood with dinner out on the terrace. It was like old times with Chip's delightful temperament in this wonderful atmosphere. At heart, he truly was a romanticist and enjoyed the more exquisite luxuries in life.

The next day Jerry and I went to San Diego where Chip planned to join us. We were visiting with my sister, Ruth; her daughter, Theresa; and Theresa's family. Theresa was a year older than Chip and had a little boy, Joshua, who was three years old.

When Chip arrived he was still in great spirits. He glowed with happiness, the same as we noticed while with him in Hollywood. His contentment and joy were exhilarating. His determination was definitely on fire. He was anxious to go back home to list and sell houses!

He said, "Mother, you name it and that's what we'll do. We'll sell as many as you want."

With his positive attitude and inspiration, there was no doubt we'd do exactly that!

Later that day he said, "Mother, let's go to the coffee shop this evening where we can talk."

I was happy about the way Chip was feeling and he truly had me curious.

That evening in the coffee shop I learned why Chip was in such good spirits. He had stayed another day in Hollywood to attend a cult meeting with Neil, who introduced him to the group. He wanted to share what had transpired. Naturally I was interested and had been impressed with his high spirits, although now that he mentioned "cult" I was skeptical, but listened.

We both had negative viewpoints about cults when a group attempted to invade the Dallas area years before. Knowing the rumor and facts was how they tried to get the younger generation to turn against their parents so they could gain control.

Some organizations have been known to come into focus that aren't always of the cult nature, although what isn't of common belief may often be misconstrued. Still, one needs to be cautious and aware.

Chip was excited as he talked. I'm sure the cult must have been responsible for the way he was feeling, happy and content as though he were at complete peace. He had renewed enthusiasm, with great desires and expectations for his life, both present and future. He was definitely eager to get everything in order. He knew there were things in Texas he needed to take care of first, and after that he would be moving to California as he had always wanted. I'm sure the California move was most motivating to him, and he was feeling good about himself, knowing he would be moving there.

Somehow, Chip's life was different. He had his usual positive attitude, but his priorities had changed. I couldn't deny that he was a genuinely happy person. I was sure Chip was fine, but I was dubious about a cult. He was impressed with the people involved and his friend Neil. They had all been helped in some persona l way, and to a degree I could understand when he told me things. Still, I talked very little and mostly listened, wondering about the religious encounter he was experiencing.

Chip was sure he had found what he wanted. I believe he found a peacefulness that made him feel good and a feeling of togetherness, something everyone wants. I liked his sharing with me and felt confident, knowing he was sensible and would make the right decisions. It was wonderful to see how happy he truly was. Chip had an intelligent mind and no matter what he did, he had to be in control. Even now while talking, he was reasoning things out; he seemed to be on the right track. Chip wasn't rushing anything while he let time take its course. He was pretty sharp and seemed to have a knack about certain things. I don't believe anyone could ever pull the wool over his eyes.

Joshua had Chip's undivided attention and they were instant buddies.

Chipper later commented, "Joshua's the kind of boy I wish I could give you for a grandchild."

He was a very special little three-year-old whom Jerry and I grew quite fond of, also, in the short time we were there. We knew how much Chip would love to have a child someday. I assured him it was okay if he didn't give us a grandchild. Having him was all that mattered. I hadn't even given thought to Chip's having a child because he was still young himself.

I told him, "Your cousins have kids and they're family, which is like having grandchildren of my own."

Jerry and I both felt this way because anytime we were around them, they were like our own. The part that was sad was the fact that Chip would have made such a good dad.

A couple of times he said, "I wish you hadn't put all your eggs in one basket."

He was genuinely sincere, but I assured him my one egg was fine. All Joking aside, he knew what I meant.

After a day of shopping, Chip and Theresa came home laughing and cutting up. They sorted through their packages until they came to one particular box. Still laughing they opened it and poured the contents into a bowl, then began adding water according to directions. The box contained a powdery substance, which began to thicken while they stirred. When it reached the texture of a thick paste, Theresa sat down on the sofa, placed some newspaper on the coffee table in front of her, then leaned forward, laying her hand on the newspaper. Chip came over and poured the paste like texture over her hand.

They giggled and announced they were making a plaster cast of her hand. They sat laughing and talking while ten minutes, fifteen minutes, and finally thirty minutes had gone by. All that time Theresa had sat in the same position with her hand on the coffee table, patiently waiting for the plaster to set.

Chip was starting to wonder why the paste wasn't setting and becoming firm like it should have by now. He picked up the box and was again reading the directions when a grin came to his face.

Jerry walked over, took one look at the box, and laughed. "This is patching plaster, not plaster of paris."

Theresa was a good sport. Even though they didn't get a cast of her hand, we all had a good laugh.

The evening before we were to start home for Texas, Chip came in just as we were sitting down to dinner. He said he wasn't hungry and went into the bedroom and began packing his things.

After dinner I noticed that Chip had become very quiet and wasn't talking to me. When I said something to him, he just looked at me and didn't comment. He was shunning me. A little later, he got his bag and headed out the door, saying he was going to the bus station.

Jerry said, "Wait a minute, we'll take you."

Chip hesitated, then said, "Okay. I'm taking a bus to L.A. and flying home."

All the way to the bus station he was distant and still not talking to me. I couldn't imagine what had come over him. He had never acted this way toward me. Why was he acting this way, and why was he mainly treating me differently? When we arrived at the bus station, Chip started to get out of the car. His Aunt Ruth, who was sitting beside him, pulled him back toward her and gave him a hug, saying, "We love you. Chip."

He bleakly smiled, said thanks, and went inside the terminal without looking my way. Jerry drove off. I didn't know what was wrong or what had come over him. He had smiled at Ruth and talked to Jerry, but obviously didn't want anything to do with me. I was puzzled with his extreme, sudden change toward me.

The next day Jerry and I started to Texas without Chip. His deciding to fly home didn't surprise me because I knew he didn't want to make the drive, although he had planned to and would have, I'm sure, until his last trip to Hollywood the day before. Then what happened?

Chip arrived home from California the day after us. He was still distant with me and didn't say too much to Jerry.

He was back to his usual busy routine with all his real estate transactions, some of which were about to close. One was what we call a double bubble in real estate, selling his listing and also locating a new home for his customers.

Then we would soon be closing a transaction together in which he had sold one of my listings in a nice, prestigious neighborhood.

When I had first put the house on the market, after Chip saw it he said, "Mother, I'll sell this house for you. I believe it's exactly what my customers are looking for."

Sure enough. Chip was right! He had his customers on contract and did a great job getting it sold and everything in top shape for both parties involved within a week.

Clients liked Chip, realizing he was always willing to go that extra mile in helping with their needs and important questions in listing and selling their homes. They appreciated his honesty and sincerity.

Just before Chip left the Dallas area he was realtor of the month. The way things were starting to open up for him because of his hard work, it wouldn't be long until he would be receiving various recognitions in the Northeast Tarrant County area. And what would make this special was the fact that Chip was doing this strictly on his own, not dependent on Mother or expecting handouts from her or anyone. This was the way Chip wanted it, although there were certain areas we worked together as a team, and we were about to list a home on the market that bordered a golf course in a prestigious area.

I had been a top producer and had received other various recognitions over the years, and I was sure Chip would soon be in the ranks also. I was real proud of him.

Of course, I was a fortunate mother. Chip was always one to make me proud over the years.

One day I was lying in the sun when Chip came home. He seemed to be in a good mood and frame of mind, more like himself, when he came into the backyard. For the first time since California it was like old times.

"Hi, Chip, are you going to lie in the sun?"

"No, Mother, I just wanted to talk."

"Good, Chipper. I know real estate's been keeping you busy, and it's about time I get some of your attention," I teased.

We talked about real estate, then before long the topic of the cult came up.

Chip spoke sincerely from his heart. "It was different. Mother. I attended lectures where all they did was sit around and chant. Really, Mother, it was the most serene, the most calm, most wonderful couple of weeks I ever had. They played wonderful, special flute music, which most people can't deal with."

"Did they serve anything to eat?"

"After the lecture, they passed around fresh fruit. Once in a while someone may bake something and bring it."

"Do you think they would put something in the food they baked? I don't know much about them, but I heard that they may do things like that in cults. Or had you thought about their using such devious means to gain control?"

"No, Mother, it was usually fresh fruit. They really were a good group." Then he showed me a picture of some of them, telling me a little about each one and what their jobs and professions were.

"They do look like a fine group of people. Chipper."

"They are." Then he told me about some of them before they joined the group, how they had drug, drinking, or family problems.

It was understandable, the seeking, reaching, and love. Unity.

"Do these people pass out flowers?"

"No, Mother, they don't do that. I guess they handle it in a little classier way. They get the kids to fall in love with them. Then when the kids' parents die or they get endowments, it all goes to the gurus. They believe that the fewer material and financial things you have, the closer you can get to the supreme being."

"Oh well, Chip, just don't let them get the best of you."

I realized Chip wasn't being as extreme as I thought and that made me feel better, along with our good discussion that seemed to clear the air. This was more like Chip to make things right.

I felt one reason he may have been attracted was because it helped fill in the one gap created over the years for him. He was still searching and wanting that special love he had been denied. However, I couldn't shake the feeling that they may somehow have been responsible for his sudden change of attitude toward me. Could I have been a target? If so, what could they possibly have said or done? I wondered, what else could it be? Still, we had a strong bond between us that was sure to see us through, somehow it would. It always had.

About two weeks later, around six o'clock in the morning I was doing aerobics with Joanie Greggains during her "Morning Stretch" TV show. I had just finished aerobics with Charlene Prickett on her "Getting Fit." The front door was suddenly flung open. Hooked up in time to see Chip burst into the house and rush down the hall to his bedroom, yelling, 'They're after me!"

I stopped and went to the door and looked out. There was no one in sight and Chip's car was parked at the curb. It looked okay. I called to remind him he had a ten o'clock appointment to complete the closing transaction on the house he had sold for my people. His customers only had one small detail to complete today. I didn't hear an answer, so I assumed he had gone to bed. He didn't seem to be getting much rest lately.

I started my aerobics again. Chip must have fallen asleep immediately. I hadn't heard any sounds and it was almost time for him to be getting up to go to the title company. I waited awhile longer. Finally I thought I'd better wake him.

I knocked on his bedroom door. There wasn't any answer. Usually he would be awake by now or yell out not to bother him, that he was getting up. But not this time. So I opened the door while I called him. He was sound asleep and hadn't budged.

As a rule his alarm woke him. He never liked my intruding, so I seldom went in his room. I knew he hadn't had much rest and he looked peaceful, but I had to wake him. Again I yelled, "Chip, it's time to get up! Remember your appointment?"

He was lying on his back and didn't answer. So I walked over and started to touch his shoulder, saying, "Chip, are you getting up?"

He immediately raised up on his elbows, then instantly drew his shoulders back and stared at me as if to say, "Hey, wait a minute, don't touch me. Who are you?"

His stare startled me. He stayed in that position staring at me for a long time, his expression unchanged! He didn't move or speak, only stared! I tried to talk to him about the time and his appointment, but couldn't get a response, only that blank stare. I didn't know what to think or do. I was puzzled. I was overwhelmed! What on earth was the matter? He knew who I was, but why was he looking at me as though he weren't sure?

"Chip, what is it?" I questioned.

He didn't answer. And I didn't understand. I persisted, trying to get a response.

"Chip, speak to me." He wouldn't.

"Chip, what is it? Will you speak to me?"

He only stared. I reached to touch him on the shoulder, but he pulled his shoulders back even further as though he were afraid of my touching him. His eyes seemed to ask, "Who are you? What do you want?" I couldn't seem to reach him through whatever fog was clouding his mind. I was puzzled and didn't know what to do. I kept repeating my questions over and over, but didn't get a reply.

Then the telephone rang. As a rule I always answer within the first couple of rings; this time I didn't. I figured it was probably his purchasers for the house we had sold. I left his room, and soon the telephone rang again. I went back into his room and Chip was up and sitting at his desk. Still he wouldn't answer.

I raised my voice, "Chip, pick up that telephone!"

He didn't budge. This wasn't like Chip. Again I yelled, "Pick up that phone or I will. I'll tell them you're right here!"

I never would have done that to him, but I was furious and he still hadn't said a word. I angrily glared at him.

He picked up the receiver, but didn't speak.

Questioningly, I watched him. He kept gazing at me. Suddenly he looked like he was about to cry! It broke my heart to see this! What was wrong? Was he going to cry? Not Chip! He wasn't one to cry. I was stunned and a wave of sadness washed over me, bringing me to the brink of tears. I didn't know what to think as I felt a deep pain for him in his silent dilemma. I reached over and grabbed the telephone out of his hand in a hurry.

Sure enough it was his customers. I told them Chip had been out all night with a tragic incident and I would be right there. They said that's why they were calling, to save him the trip. Everything was closed and fine, and they wanted to thank him.

To think Chip could have slept. They hadn't expected him there since all but the one detail hadn't been completed yesterday and now it was. Just the same Chip ordinarily would have gone as a common courtesy.

I told him I was taking the extra keys to the purchasers and would be right back. He made no comment, so I left.

I kept the meeting with his customers as brief as possible because I was concerned about him. I didn't know what to think. I was completely baffled, What could I do? Maybe, just maybe, when I got back he'd be okay and we could talk. I sure hoped so.

He seemed to be just as terrified as I was about what was happening, yet he wouldn't talk to me and let me know what I could do. I didn't understand or know how to react to his being this way. It wasn't like him to keep something like this up. Never in all his life! Why wouldn't he talk?

I was anxious to get home and felt I needed to hurry so I drove fast. "God, please may Chip be okay. Please may he talk to me."

When I returned home, Chip was in the living room. He looked at me, his face expressionless. He started staring at me as though he were still wondering about me. I kept trying to talk to him. Still he wouldn't utter a word. This silence continued for a long time, with neither of us speaking.

Finally, I asked, "Chipper, do you want to talk now?"

Without answering he continued to gaze at me with the same puzzled expression. I kept myself busy, hoping he'd soon say something.

After awhile I asked, "Chipper, what are your plans for today?"

He didn't say anything. I remained calm and kept trying to break the ice, but the more I tried, the more he seemed to pull away. I had hoped to make conversation or nonchalantly catch him off guard and try to sway him into talking, but he never would answer.

After awhile he went into his bedroom. A few minutes later I went to check on him and he was coming back down the hall. I spoke to him, but he still didn't speak.

This time, before I knew it I was yelling and screaming at him, "Chip, will you talk to me? Please? Why are you doing this to me?"

Eventually I started losing control emotionally. This was not like Chip and I didn't know how to handle what was happening. I spent the next several hours begging, pleading, and demanding that he talk to me. At one point I put my hands on his shoulders and shook him, then pounded on his chest. I shocked myself to do such a thing, even though as weary and weak as I was it couldn't have fazed him. I felt helpless and began to cry. Never in all his life had I ever treated him in such a manner as this! I was at my wit's end. What was happening to me?

I continued receiving his blank stares and silence. Everything seemed to be in such turmoil. He was always the one I could rely on for sensible advice.

Finally I pulled myself together. After awhile I asked Chip for an address. He picked up a piece of paper and began looking around as if looking for a pen or pencil. Then he turned to me and made motions over the paper like he was writing. I found him a pencil and he wrote down the address. Still he didn't speak.

I felt like he wanted to talk, yet he didn't or couldn't, it seemed. I didn't know what was happening and knew he wouldn't intentionally be doing anything like this, yet I didn't know what to do. I had never yelled or raised my voice to him the way I was. I was bewildered as to why this was happening. I seemed to be the one to go into a rage while he remained calm and looked at me as though he couldn't understand what was wrong or why I was so shook up.

His continued silence enraged me more and before I realized what I was doing, I ordered him out of the house! To emphasize my point, I opened the door and waited while he walked out carrying his religious book.

I closed the door and locked it! Now I was in tears. I had walked across the foyer and into the living room before it actually hit me what I'd done. I ran back and unlocked the door. Sure, he had his own key, but what was I doing locking my son out of his home? How could I do that? I felt terrible. I was upset, furious and frustrated. Chip and I never, ever had such a lack of communication. Why? Why weren't we communicating?

A little later Chip came back home, went into his bedroom, got his keys, then walked quietly out to his car and drove away.

In retrospect, Chip evidently couldn't talk because of aphasia. The changes in him were apparently the start of the neurological, ADC symptoms, which weren't yet known. Still not knowing it at this time. Chip was about to become a pioneer of many unknown facts while he ventured into the unfamiliar.

His unusual behavior may have had nothing to do with his brief involvement with the cult. And he no doubt wouldn't have been involved if it hadn't been for his trying complications that had started during that time, which we were not to know about for many months to come.

Chip still hadn't returned when Jerry came home from work. So I told him what had been going on all day and how worried I was.

He said, "Don't worry. You know Chip, he will probably be home tonight or tomorrow. Then he will tell you all about it."

7

Theresa to the Rescue

About eight-thirty that evening the telephone rang. I hurried to answer, hoping it would be Chip.

"Hi, Mother, can I come home?"

"Of course, Chipper! I've been wondering when you'd be back. You know you don't need to ask. I wasn't thinking. I never should have ordered you to leave."

Remembering how I had acted caused tears to well up inside me. It had been such a traumatic day for both of us—probably worse for Chip, sending him away. Still, he knew there wasn't any reason to be asking if he could come home. Of course, we'd never been in such a dilemma as today either. I cleared my throat, trying to hold back the tears so he wouldn't hear how hurt I felt.

"I know I talked terrible to you, Chip, but I was just shook up with your not talking to me. I was telling Jerry what happened and wondered where you were. He said you'd be home or call. I'm sure glad you did! We'll see you in a little while."

Then he told me what he'd been doing. "I started to Houston and turned around. I thought I'd go there or to California. I'm in Fort Worth at a Texaco station and they're checking my car to make sure everything's okay."

"Good, then we'll see you in a little while. Chip."

"Okay, soon as they finish with the car."

I felt better knowing he was coming home. I thought he sounded okay, but he knew he didn't need to ask to come home. I only hoped he wasn't feeling bad after the way I had told him to leave. He was always good at concealing his feelings, and that's why I felt even worse about what had happened. That whole day was so difficult for both of us.

Chip wasn't one to pull pranks or intentionally try to upset me and I couldn't understand what was happening. I was at a loss without his response.

I waited expectantly for Chip, thinking he'd be home soon. I knew it might take half an hour or perhaps an hour—whichever, I wanted to be up when he arrived. It was getting late. I waited and waited and waited. Where was he? He said he wouldn't be long. That was almost eleven-thirty. And now it was more than three hours since he had called. As a rule, when Chip said he was going to do something, he did it. I could not imagine what had happened. About three o'clock, I decided to go to bed. I didn't understand; maybe he went somewhere else first.

I thought for sure Chip would be home sometime in the morning, but he didn't show up. I didn't know what to think.

It was Saturday morning and a couple of days had gone by with still no word from Chip. I had left the house to attend to some business. When I returned, I heard Jerry talking on the phone. From his end of the conversation I could tell he must be talking to Chip. I was so glad he finally called. Hearing only one side, I couldn't seem to understand what they were talking about while I eagerly waited. I gestured to Jerry that I wanted to talk. After awhile he handed the telephone to me.

"Chip?"

"Hi, Mother!

"Where you at, Chip?"

"California."

Surprised by his answer, I repeated, "California! Uh, why didn't you come home after we talked? I waited up, thinking you'd be right home. It was almost three o'clock when I went to bed. I thought you'd surely be here in the morning."

Chip sounded cheerful while he talked about his trip. Suddenly he changed the subject. I wasn't sure what he meant He was confusing me and I looked at Jerry, puzzled. Jerry shrugged his shoulders, indicating that he didn't understand either. Still holding the telephone, I said in surprise, "He must have hung up on me. Why? He said he's in California, but why did he hang up?"

Reluctantly, I hung up.

"He said he's in a motel on the beach. We've been talking for about fifteen minutes," Jerry replied.

"What motel?"

"He didn't say. All he said was he's paying seventy dollars a night." "Seventy dollars!" I exclaimed. "What's he doing?"

"I don't know. I wasn't sure what he meant at times."

"Me either. I hope he's okay."

"This was the third time he called. He called twice while you were gone. He wanted to talk to you." Jerry paused, then added, "Before this last call from Chip, I got an unusual call from a man who said he rode all the way to California with Chip."

"How did that happen?"

"He was hitchhiking and Chip picked him up. He got our telephone number from the business card Chip gave him. He said he was calling to tell us there was something wrong. He didn't know what it was, but at times Chip seemed to be 'out of it.' He was beginning to wonder if they'd make it to California."

After the calls from Chip and the call from the hitchhiker, I wasn't sure what was happening.

"Sweetheart, what are we going to do? Do we even know the name of the motel?"

"No, honey. All I know is, it's on the beach in San Diego."

"What can we do? I just hope he'll call back."

I didn't know what to do or what to think. Chip wasn't like this, at least he never had been before. I was worried and not sure what to do. I prayed God would keep him safe and Chip would call us back and let us know where he was. I kept wondering when and if he would call and how he was. I didn't know what was wrong, especially since Jerry had told me about the call from the hitchhiker. I wouldn't have questioned his being in California if I didn't think something wasn't right. I never should have yelled at him. If only I had handled it differently. I didn't understand, and later I thought about the cult and wondered if they may have influenced him. Could they have been trying to turn Chip against me? Why was he in such a different frame of mind at times? I didn't know much about cults, but in the beginning I knew Chip was in a good frame of mind, really peaceful and beautiful. It was amazing the way he handled himself, as if he had finally found what he had been searching for. Suddenly it had become a nightmare. I was totally baffled. The waiting was hard, but there wasn't anything we could do since we didn't know exactly where he was.

I wishfully said to Jerry, "Surely he will call back."

Jerry figured he would be calling at any minute, the same as he had been. Yet I was worried and skeptical since we weren't sure of anything.

Later that day. Chip finally called. He said his car had been broken into and he wasn't going near it. He was afraid someone may have put something in it.

Jerry tried to reason with him, but Chip said, "No, I'm not driving it. It has a bomb in it."

I tried talking to Chip, and he started telling me about the bomb. He suddenly changed the subject and was talking about his motel. Then he abruptly said he had to go and hung up.

The next day about midmorning, Chip called. He seemed fine and in a good frame of mind. I asked if he was going to come home, and he said maybe later. He had called the police about his car, and security at the beach was checking it for him. He said security had been trying to locate him because his car had been vandalized. The side window and sunroof were smashed in and evidently someone had taken all his tapes.

I could imagine how alarmed Chip must have been since he was already afraid of his car, thinking it had a bomb in it. Security wanted to go with him to the car, but Chip said he was afraid to go near it. A few minutes later he hung up so he could talk to the police, saying he would call us back.

It was evening when Chip called again for the fourth time that day. He said he could only talk a few minutes because they would be serving him a lovely gourmet dinner in a little while.

He described the lavish motel on the beach where he was having all his meals served in his room.

He said, "Mother, you'd love it. I'll bring you and Jerry with me next time."

I could imagine his extravagance, living like a king. It was the good life, the way Chip liked things. No worries and not a care in the world! If only the other things weren't happening. In a few minutes Chip said, "Dinner's here. Talk with you later."

Click! He was gone even more abruptly than before.

Chip called unexpectedly, as though he were only across town. We never knew what to expect, but needed to keep in touch. One time he would sound okay and another time he would be incoherent. We never knew what to expect, and he didn't seem to think anything of it! Other times you would not have thought there were complications.

Finally, during one conversation he mentioned the name of the motel where he was staying. From the beginning this is what we were hoping to hear. Until then all we could do was be patient and wait. We certainly didn't want to lose complete contact with him.

As soon as we hung up, I called his Aunt Ruth and cousin Theresa. I told them what had transpired since Chip's last day at home and how he had ended up in San Diego.

I said, "At least he's talking to me now, and that's some progress. I'm not really sure what to think or do at this time, though. I don't want to upset our progress, yet I'm not sure."

Theresa said Chip had called her while she was gone and had left his telephone number. She was about to call him when she received our call. Theresa gave me the number and I asked if she would try to contact him as soon as we hung up. I told her he might open up to her more. We needed to know what was happening and someone needed to get through to him, somehow. Hopefully, all would go well with Theresa to the rescue.

When Theresa called, he asked her to come to the motel. She agreed, and he gave her directions where she could meet him. When Theresa got there she didn't see any sign of him and couldn't find him anywhere, so she went back home.

Chip called again and gave her more detailed directions, so she returned to Mission Bayagain, a forty-five-minute drive each way from where she lived. When she arrived she still didn't see any sign of him. Her patience was wearing thin.

She said to herself, I give up, and she returned home again.

A little later, Chip called again. By then Theresa was really getting exasperated. They were acting more like brother and sister than cousins. When she answered she said, "Why weren't you standing out front where you were supposed to be?"

Chip said, "I was and I didn't see you anywhere."

Then he told her he was staying in a motel across the street from where she had gone to meet him.

She said, "Oh, great! And what's the name of the motel?"

Chip told her and gave her his room number. So Theresa drove back to the other motel where he said he was. When she got there, she saw him dancing in front of the window in his room.

When recounting it to me, Theresa said, "I saw him and he must have seen me, but he wasn't paying any attention to me at all. He seemed to look right through me, and kept dancing, I thought, Uh oh, what's wrong with him?

"I started to turn around and leave because I had had it with him, going back and forth and stuff, but I thought, No, I'm going to get Chip to look at me and I'll say, 'Hey, I'm here. Open the damn door!'

"Finally, I got him to look at me and when he saw me, I said, 'Are you going to let me in or what?'"

"No, I have a bomb on this door," Chip said.

"Like, who you trying to kid," Theresa said. "Yeah, right. You have a bomb on the door."

"Sure, there's a bomb on the door. It's going to blow up if you try to open it."

She persisted, "Yeah, uh huh. Unlock the door!"

"You can't unlock the door from the inside. You need to get the keys from the office and unlock it from the outside," Chip insisted.

Theresa said to me, "I couldn't believe what was going on and I thought, You've got to be kidding." So she said to Chip, "Open the damn door!"

She said it took her ten or fifteen minutes to get Chip to open the door. Then he must have snapped back to being himself because once he let her in the room they had a good, sensible conversation. He told her all about leaving Texas and what he had been doing. He said he had gone to Los Angeles first before coming to San Diego. After awhile he ordered dinner for them.

Then Chip told Theresa he couldn't find his car. He said he had left it on the Sea World parking lot. Theresa took him in her car to look for it. They cruised around looking everywhere.

Theresa said, "He knew damn well where his car was, but he didn't want to get it. We passed right by it many times and he didn't say one word to me. I saw a security guard and told him, 'We're looking for this guy's car.' I looked at Chip and told him, Tell this security guard what kind of car you have.'"

Chip told the security guard the kind of car he had. The guard said, "Oh, yes, we put a note on your car. Your car was broken into."

When Theresa told me about this, I remembered Chip telling us his car had been broken into. Evidently he was afraid to go near it. In retrospect, knowing his complications, I could imagine how it must have been terrifying for him, and with good reason.

Theresa said that after talking to the security guard and locating Chip's car, she realized she had driven past it several times and Chip hadn't said a word. She said the side window was completely broken out and the sunroof was all smashed in.

Theresa looked inside because Chip still refused to go near it. She tried to get him to clean out the glass, but he wouldn't because he was afraid it would blow up. He suggested that Theresa drive his car and he would drive hers. She refused and insisted Chip get in his car and follow her. He told her the car might blow up, so she carefully checked it for him. Opening the hood she checked the engine, the wiring, and everything so he could see there wasn't a bomb in it. Then she firmly insisted, "Chip start it up," and he did.

Chip told Theresa he would follow her home.

She said, "Okay, follow me."

They started toward her house driving about forty-five miles per hour, then Chip started slowing down. Theresa looked back and wondered what he was doing, so she slowed down too. When Chip started catching up, they got on the freeway and Theresa started back up to fifty miles per hour, slow enough so Chip could stay right behind her.

She said, "Once again Chip started slowing down. He was driving slower and slower, and I was really getting aggravated. I was only going fifty and Chip kept dropping his speed. He was getting farther and farther away. Finally I said, 'Okay, I've had it! I'm leaving,' and I took off and left him behind. I was tired of his games. I thought. I'm going home!"

Apparently Chip went back to his motel.

We hadn't heard from him for a couple of days. Then we got a telephone call from my dad in Indiana. They wanted to know about Chip and what was happening.

Dad said, "Chip called us and was wanting a thousand dollars. He said that he was in California and needed money to go to Texas. I told him I would send him two hundred dollars, that it should be enough to get him home. We've already wired him the money, but I wanted to call you and see what you thought."

"Yes, Dad, he's been gone several days now. I'm surprised he called you for money, though."

Dad said, "That's all right. I told him if he really needed a thousand dollars, I would send it."

"That's fine, Dad. I'm sure what you sent will be enough."

Apparently Chip was okay when he called them because Dad didn't mention anything about Chip's not making sense.

I said, "Chip's been calling us regularly since he arrived in California and he hasn't said anything to us about needing money. In fact, I was sure he had plenty. From the way it sounds, he's spending much freer than usual. He's had some good real estate closings and seems to be living it up. I don't understand his calling you for money. Maybe he's out of checks."

"We were just wondering and wanted to make sure everything was okay."

I hesitated, then asked, "How did he sound to you, Dad? We're not really sure what's wrong, but..." and I briefed Dad on what had been happening.

Dad said, "Keep in touch and if we can do anything, be sure to call us. We love you all. Tell Jerry hello."

"Okay, Dad, and thanks. Talk with you later. Love y'all."

A little later, Chip called. He said he was a at travel agency. Then he told us about his conversation with Grampa, and that he had asked him to send him some money to fly home. I asked Chip what he was going to do with his car. He said he didn't want it anymore. I tried to reason with him, but could tell I wasn't getting through to him. I asked him to give the receiver to the lady at the agency, which he did.

This was my first opportunity to talk to someone else about how Chip was acting while in their presence. I first briefed her on my reason for talking with her and asked her not to sell Chip any tickets. Then I asked how he appeared to her. She seemed to verify what I had related. She was understanding and said she would try to reason with him. She assured me he wasn't being a problem, in fact, he was very nice and congenial. I told her he was always like that and I was only concerned about the sudden changes and explained what I meant.

After I hung up I took three deep breaths and tried to calm myself down, I was shaking so much. Never before had I ever had to defend Chip or give explanations, and the crushing part is that he was still thoughtful as usual, yet this confusion must have been tough on him too.

I was getting even more concerned. I knew I had to do something. I had to get to Chip. Even though he may not think so, I felt I needed to get to him as soon as possible. I called to check on flights to San Diego. Things were happening so fast. I did not know what to do or what not to do, or even what I could do, but I knew I had to do something and quick! It had already been long enough with his questionable state and for him to be alone. This seemed like such an unfair predicament for him to be in. It wasn't like Chip to borrow money and want to fly home when he had his car. Surely he wouldn't leave his car, I wondered.

As soon as Jerry got home from work I told him everything that had been happening: about Dad calling, about Chip's call and my conversation with the lady at the agency.

Jerry said, "We need to go out there and see what's going on."

"I've already called and checked on flights. Since we just got back from vacation, shall I go alone?"

"I hate for you to go alone." Thinking for a moment, Jerry then said, "But like you said, I just got back to work and it would probably be best. It sounds like Chip definitely needs at least one of us with him. Are you sure you'll be okay? You need to bring him home, then we can work it out."

"That's what I think. I only hope he will talk with me. I've got to get through to him. Can you imagine how this must be for him? I don't understand."

I made reservations on the very next flight, which was almost immediately. I didn't have time to call San Diego to ask if Ruth or Theresa had anything to tell me about Chip. I made one quick call to let Chip know I was coming, but he wasn't at the motel. So I left a message with the clerk. Jerry said he would call Ruth and Theresa to let them know I was coming.

I didn't know what was happening or what I could do. All I knew was that I needed to be with Chip. I had to get to him because something just wasn't right. I wasn't sure how he would react to my being there, but I felt I must go. Remembering the day he left home, I wondered if he would even talk to me. Still, somehow I would get through to him. I must get through!

Arriving in San Diego I felt like a stranger in a strange place. San Diego was so big and I had never been there alone or without a car. I had no idea how to get to Ruth's or Theresa's from the airport, and I wasn't too sure what I was going to do. I intended to contact Ruth and Theresa, but was intent on contacting Chip first. I located a telephone and called Chip's motel. They told me Chip had checked out.

Shocked, I said, "What? When did he check out?"

"He just left in a cab," the clerk answered.

"He checked out of the motel and left in a cab," I repeated, then asked, "Are you sure? Do you know where he was going?"

"No."

"What cab was he in?" I asked.

He didn't know that either. I could hear him asking the other clerk, then he replied, "They saw him get into a Yellow Cab."

I was frantic! I wondered. Now what am I going to do? Where did he go? He knew I was coming. Or had he even received the message I left? Surely he didn't leave because I was coming. Chip wouldn't do that, or would he? I was worried, knowing how quickly he could change. Why did he take a cab and where was his car?

I got the number of the cab company and called them. I was appalled by what was happening, although I soon learned it was only the beginning. The cab company couldn't or wouldn't help me. Iwas told they couldn't tell me where they had taken a customer because it would be infringing upon personal rights. I tried to reason with them, telling them Chip was my son and why I needed to know where he was. I wasn't getting anywhere and their answers were annoying me. They refused to disclose any information. I needed help and they couldn't cooperate. At the same time I was trying to stay calm. With the tears welled up inside, I was forced to hang up. My plan was to come to San Diego and get Chip, and then the two of us would go home together. It didn't work that way.

I was in the big city of San Diego with no earthly idea where Chip was. I was so humiliated and frustrated that I wanted to be alone and cry. Tears threatened to spill over onto my cheeks while I struggled to maintain control. Where was Chip?

I called Ruth and told her I was at the airport. While I waited for her it gave me a little time to collect my thoughts. I didn't dream I would be back so soon only a few weeks after vacation, but it would be good seeing Ruth and family again. She and

Theresa certainly were a big help.

After Ruth arrived at the airport we drove around looking for Chip, stopping anywhere we could think of that he may have gone. We were constantly on the lookout for his car and often stopped at convenience stores to see if he had been there. We drove from San Diego to Vista and Escondido, still searching for his car or any trace of him.

While looking, Ruth and I filled each other in on what had been happening concerning Chip. I told her how he had checked out and left the motel before I got there and about the cab company's refusal to help me. While I listened to Ruth, it seemed as though everything kept going from bad to worse and we still weren't finding him. By now I was feeling real sad for Chip.

Ruth said, "I never knew when he was going to be himself again. At first I thought he was acting, but he kept it up for so long and I knew he couldn't be that good an actor. Then I felt that I had to get help for him before he got hurt or hurt himself. I could see he was trying to hold onto reality, and he would be fine at times, but it would slip away from him."

I told Ruth I knew what she meant, that she was describing how it was for me the day he left home, except he wasn't talking. Still, he was calm, cool, and collected like himself. I'm sure he wanted to talk at one time in particular. Yet there was some kind of dark cloud that neither of us understood and we couldn't seem to communicate whatsoever.

I said, "This just doesn't seem right. He's not one to cause problems and I don't understand what's happening to him."

Ruth said a couple of days earlier her boyfriend and another guy were talking with Chip outdoors while she and Theresa were in the house. While they were talking, the two guys took Chip by the arm. Chip jerked away from them and ran directly into traffic.

I said, "Taking Chip's arm was a mistake. He may have been afraid and thought they were the people he was imagining were after him with a bomb, and he wanted to get away. And too, no one ever takes Chip by the arm."

I continued, "It's things like this that I don't understand. Why do they keep happening to him in his condition? Any other time, nothing like this ever happened. It seems like when he's down and out, he's being kicked even more. Know what I mean?"

Ruth agreed and told me what happened next. She said they thought for sure he was going to get hit by a car. There were some police officers who witnessed Chip's flight, and when they approached Chip, he talked to them very logically and sincerely.

When the policemen told him they were taking him in, he said, "Sure, I'd be happy to go with you," and he got into the police car and went peacefully with them.

I'm sure Chip felt they had saved him from the two men who earlier had tried to hold him. (Later Chip told me he had known what he was doing.)

Ruth said, "When he ran out into traffic, it really gave us a scare. We thought for sure he was going to get hit by a car."

Ruth went on to say she was glad that at last they had him in custody and would be able to see for themselves that he needed help. When she called the police station, to her dismay they told her they had let Chip go. Ruth couldn't believe her ears.

She said to them, "You let him go in a strange city? For heaven's sake, why would you do that with the condition he's in?"

She was furious because they didn't want to be bothered when Chip's life was at stake! Chip wasn't mean or vicious, or in any way harmful to anyone else, but was in danger of harming himself! During Ruth's dispute with the police, she informed them that she didn't like their alibis. When she asked to talk to Chip, they advised her to call back on another line.

She called back and told Chip to stay there and she would be right down to get him. When she got to the police station, Chip wasn't there. He had disappeared.

Ruth drove slowly looking for Chip. She finally found him walking down the street. She pulled over and he got in.

Ruth said she definitely felt that he needed help, but had been unable to get it for him. She attempted to take Chip in for observation at the Hillcrest Mental Health Department, thinking they would help. They did talk with Chip and agreed that he needed to stay there, except they didn't have a bed available. So they weren't able to help either. Ruth was getting real upset. The police wouldn't help and the mental health institution wouldn't help. And now, where was he? While she was telling me all this, I could just imagine what Chip must have been going through.

We still hadn't found him, and hearing all Ruth had to tell caused me to be even more apprehensive. This was tearing me up to know all he was going through while I listened and quietly cried on the inside. We looked until almost dark, then decided to call it a day.

We went to Theresa's home in hopes he might be there, but he wasn't. Thinking he still might show up, Ruth and I decided to spend the night with Theresa. After talking more, Ruth came up with an idea for Chip's sake. She still felt that the police were theories who would need to take him into get help once they saw he needed it. This would mean calling the police on Chip if he came to Theresa's. I really hated the idea of the police and Chip. Nothing like this had ever happened before. Yet after what I'd been hearing I didn't know what else to do. As we had hoped, Chip showed up later that evening.

It seems the plan backfired because when the police came, they saw no apparent reason to take Chip. I was happy to see him and felt even worse knowing what we had tried. I was so glad they didn't take him. He sounded and acted perfectly normal.

After the police left, he said, "Mother, let's go to the coffee shop where we can talk and have something to eat."

Before going to the coffee shop, Ruth cautioned me not to let Chip manipulate me. I was already feeling sad because of the police and wasn't too sure how she thought he might try to manipulate me. I halfway took her advice and felt very bad, thinking he needed comfort rather than my being on guard. Regardless, he was alright and we had a fair talk. Chip was himself all the time and it seemed so wrong trying to keep up my defenses. We didn't make any definite plans about going home. I didn't want to push Chip, even though he was in a good frame of mind. I knew Chip wasn't one to be pushed, especially by his mother. Too, I felt he had been under enough pressure and I could wait.

Later we went back to Theresa's and Chip left. When he got into his car, I noticed the broken window he had told us about. I could understand how he would have thought someone was after him with a bomb. So many of the things he feared made sense because of other things that were actually happening to him. It would be enough to make anyone paranoid, I thought.

In spite of all the negative occurrences, Chip seemed to go with the flow, not letting anything completely pull him down. Considering everything that was happening, he seemed to do well and still held his own.

I have to admire Chip when I look back on those mystifying phases, knowing what he went through must have been pure hell and an awkward situation for him. Apparently his common sense was with him frequently enough that it helped to see him through all that was happening. I wasn't sure how to handle things myself, but had to keep my bearings. I wanted him to know I was there and he could count on me.

8

The Penalty for Waiting

I stayed with Theresa in Escondido the following week, hoping Chip would soon return to Texas with me. It was a couple of days after Chip and I had gone to the coffee shop when I saw him again. I was lying in the sun by the pool when he walked up.

"Hi, Mother! Getting a California tan?" he teased.

"Hi, Chipper! I am." I laughed. "I've been wondering when you'd be back. It's good seeing you."

Chip seemed fine, same as when I'd last seen him. We had only talked a few minutes when I asked if he was ready to start home. That was a mistake. I should have bit my tongue. Suddenly, without saying another word, he started to walk away.

I immediately knew I'd said the wrong thing or mentioned it too soon. There wasn't any way Chip would be pressured. I continued to lie silent, although something told me I should have taken the initiative and talked more with him, especially when I sensed he wanted me to call him back. But I didn't say another word, and away he went.

In retrospect, I believe Chip saw me as the mother image coming to take him home, and this may have caused a resentment because this was something I had promised I wouldn't do. I didn't want him to think that, but this was the beginning of what seemed to be many sporadic loose ends between us for some time to come. Perhaps it was a personality conflict in disguise, with neither of us understanding the overall situation or knowing how to cope with it,

Although circumstances were different, I don't believe Chip realized his personality changes with occasional spurts of paranoia, or as Ruth said, he was trying his best to hold onto reality when they did try to takeover. He certainly didn't think anything was wrong with himself. After all, neither the police nor the doctors would keep him. I understood Chip's reasoning because so much of the time he was in control and was fine, but I also knew he still needed professional help. I was sure that when he saw a doctor everything would be worked out. It wasn't as though he had gone off the deep end and there was no hope, but quite the opposite. We were both strong-headed. Where there was a will, there was a way.

A few days later, his friend Neil called Theresa's home to let me know Chip had been arrested for disturbing the peace and was in the Orange County Jail. Neil didn't know much, but Chip had asked him to call. He said Chip had been in jail two or three days. Then I realized why I hadn't heard from him. I was surprised to hear Neil mention Chip's money and his moving to Hollywood the short time we talked, although that was the least of my concerns and I didn't think any more of it at the time.

After talking to Neil, I immediately called the Orange County Jail, which was at least one hundred miles away. I was informed Chip would need to call me.

While I waited for his call I spent the entire afternoon repeatedly calling long distance everywhere, trying to find out exactly what I needed to do to get him out. Also, I was hoping to get his car as soon as possible, but soon found out that it had been impounded and was about fifteen miles farther away.

Both Chip and his car were locked up for the weekend. I hated the idea of his being in jail all that time. He wasn't that caliber of person, but there wasn't a thing I could do! I was afraid we were both in for a long wait.

I continued making call after call, trying to convey to someone Chip's sudden and sporadic disorientation. I hoped to reach someone who would be of help. After many dead-end calls that directed me first to one person then another, each giving me very little cooperation, I finally reached the jail psychologist. From our conversation I realized they must have observed what I was trying to tell them, although it was apparent the psychologist wasn't going to tell me much. I was afraid of what might happen in those hostile surroundings.

Later Chip called. Was I ever glad to hear his voice!

"Mother, would you come and get me now?"

"I'd like to. Chip, but they told me it's too late. I've been on the phone all afternoon, calling everywhere and trying to do something, but they said I had to wait until Monday. I hate it too, but I will be there first thing."

"No, Mother. You won't need to come. I'll go to court and they' II let me out. They only keep you a week, then let you go."

"Hang in there, Chip, and I'll see you as soon as I can."

Chip said he was arrested while waiting for me in front of the Hilton Inn near Disneyland because he wouldn't leave when they asked him to. Then he said he couldn't talk long because others wanted to use the phone, and said he'd tell me about it later.

Monday morning I was up at five o'clock and soon on my way to the Orange County Jail, driving my sister's car. Dawn was breaking and the traffic wasn't too heavy. I wanted to leave in plenty of time since I wasn't familiar with the area and didn't know exactly where I was going. By the time I reached the courthouse, traffic was heavy, but there weren't many people around.

I was anxious to talk to the prosecuting attorney before court. When I was directed to his office, I found only his secretary. She said I would need to wait and see him in court. I understood, but was desperate to see him before, if possible. I wanted him to understand how things were for Chip. I don't know if it was the embarrassment and humiliation of what was happening to Chip and me, or what, but suddenly I was almost in tears. I needed to get hold of myself. I didn't want to break down in front of the secretary, but my voice started to weaken when I asked, "Please, would you at least let Mr. Logan know I need to talk with him?"

I could hardly wait for her answer when the tears smothered my eyes. I quickly turned my head in the opposite direction and took a deep breath. Not wanting her to think I was being rude, I managed to hold back the tears as I turned toward her again, and with a weak smile, I softly said, "I'll be in the courtroom. Thank you."

I felt so alone in that big ol' courthouse when I walked out into the hallway. I poked along, knowing I still had a long wait. I wondered how Chip was doing. All I had to do was think about him, and there wasn't any stopping the tears as they cascaded down my cheeks. I was sure he must be feeling strange, like I was, in an utterly awkward predicament. Such a terrible hassle to go through and why? All because he was innocently waiting for me.

I talked to God, as I often do. "Oh God, please, please help us. Please may Chip be okay and want to come home. Please, God, let me talk with Mr. Logan, the assistant city attorney, so he will understand. Thank you, God. Thank you so very much for listening to me."

I prayed quietly to myself through my tears while! sat waiting, all alone in the courtroom. The tears had been building up inside of me for a long time, and I couldn't seem to stop them. To think I was in a courtroom, of all places, with Chip in jail, of all places. Why did this happen to him? He didn't belong in jail. Ever! At least the courtroom was empty, and that's exactly how I felt. I thought, I must stop the tears, clear my eyes, and pull myself together before anyone comes in.

After a few minutes the tears subsided, just in time, as people filed into the courtroom.

A few minutes later, to my surprise I heard my name called. I looked up and the bailiff in the front of the courtroom motioned me to come forward.

When I approached, he said, "Mark Logan would like to see you. He is in his office."

For a moment the name didn't register, in my state of mind, then it suddenly dawned on me who he meant. I was so happy, at last maybe someone was going to listen and hopefully help! I felt a big smile come to my face when I thanked the bailiff and hurried to Mr. Logan's office as fast as my legs would carry me.

Mr. Logan was on the telephone. While I waited I felt nervous, happy, and anxious all at the same time. In a few minutes he welcomed me into his office. He was a pleasant young man and before long I felt completely at ease and comfortable talking with him. I told him briefly about Chip's actions over the past few weeks and about coming to California in hopes of getting him to return to Texas with me. I wanted him to understand that Chip wasn't a bad person and never in his life was he a troublemaker. I explained that from what Chip had related to me and our experiences lately, I believed he was disoriented at the time of his arrest. I assured him that it was the first time he had ever been in this kind of predicament.

Mr. Logan listened intently and when I concluded, he said in a cordial, business manner that he would speak with the judge and possibly the judge might want to talk with me before court convened. I said that would be fine with me. I left his office feeling much better than I had in days. I felt that finally there was hope for Chip. At last someone was interested enough to care and to understand there was an extraordinary problem. I went back to the courtroom and waited.

Shortly thereafter, Mr. Logan motioned for me to come forward. Together we went into the judge's chambers, where I proceeded to repeat things that were happening to Chipper. The judge listened carefully, then agreed he would let Chip return to Texas with me and drop all charges. I was most thankful to the judge and Mr. Logan. At long last someone had taken the time to listen with compassion.

I went back into the courtroom and waited for the inmates who would be arraigned that day to arrive from the jail. It hurt to know Chip would be among them. I could imagine how it must have mortified him when he filed in, handcuffed and linked to the others by one long chain. I never wanted anything to be wrong with Chip, but since he didn't seem to be fully aware of what was going on at various times, I was wishing this could be one of those times, to save him the humiliation; but when he came into the room he seemed to be fully aware of everything. Once they were in the courtroom inside the holding cell (a metal, cage-like enclosure surrounding their seats), the handcuffs and chain were dropped off onto the floor.

Seeing Chip so solemn made me want to be near, to touch him and let him know I understood, and to assure him he was okay and I knew it was no true fault of his own. God, why did this happen to him? I cried to myself. He wasn't really doing anything wrong, only innocently parked in the wrong place. He hadn't intended harm. Yet look at him now. He's never been in such a degrading predicament. It's so unfair. He doesn't deserve this! If only he had been able to get help when he sought it, he could have been spared this terrible ordeal.

There were about twenty cases to be heard. When Chip's name was called, he stood up and the judge came right to the point. He issued an order that Chip go to Texas with his mother and seek help there. After Chip agreed, his case was dismissed.

Court adjourned about noon. Chip was returned to the jail to wait for the final paperwork before he could be released. When I got to the jail they told me there would be a delay. So I decided to get his car from the pound.

After I got Chip's car I wanted to get his window replaced if it wouldn't take too long. Fortunately the glass company was able to fix it right then. While waiting I was getting anxious to get back to the jail for fear Chip might be ready and I wouldn't be there. After all he had already been through, I didn't want to prolong things any more than necessary. He had already paid the penalty for waiting.

It was late afternoon when I returned, and to my astonishment he would still be awhile longer. I had been hurrying and worrying for nothing. I couldn't believe it was almost dark when Chip finally walked out! It had been a long, aggravating wait, but it sure was good to finally see him on the outside.

We were both glad that was finally behind us. From my experiences, I felt the attitudes of some of the clerks and workers at the jail were a bit unjustified. To some extent I could understand because of what they were dealing with most of the time. Yet their rudeness didn't help anyone. Surely they could show a little respect and kindness for their fellowman, regardless.

I had gotten Chip a nice new jacket while in Las Vegas that he liked very much. He was wearing it the last time I saw him, but when I had gotten his belongings while waiting they didn't give me the jacket. Then I had asked for it. The person in charge denied having it. Chip definitely had been wearing it when arrested. It was his only means to keep warm on the cool nights with the window broken out. I regretted that the late hour and the long drive to Escondido prevented me from pursuing it further or I would have.

It sure was good that Chip was finally out of jail and such a relief that all that was behind us. It had been a terrible, long tiring episode for both of us, especially Chip. Since we had two cars, I followed him. After driving a few miles, we stopped at a coffee shop.

When Chip had finished his sandwich, he asked, "Mother, how about a banana split?"

"No, thank you, Chipper. You go ahead and have one."

"I was going to, but I think I'll get a brownie with chocolate ice cream and hot fudge, instead."

Chip loved ice cream. I often wondered how he stayed so slim with all he ate. It was great being with him and knowing we would soon be going home.

At a much later date, after Chip had passed away, I teamed about his experience while in jail from a tape that he left me. This is what he had said:

"I was at Disneyland at the Hilton Inn. I was in my car out front in the main parking area. They came out and asked me what I was doing. I told them I was waiting on my family. They asked, "Who is your family?' I told them and then they asked me when you were to be here. I told them I didn't know, that you were supposed to be here sometime. They told me, Leave, you'll have to leave.' I told them, I can't leave. I'll miss my mother.' I tended up the police came, so I locked the doors. Somehow they got the doors unlocked and threw my checkbook, my wallet, and all my stuff in the trunk of my car. I guess they parked it in the garage."

Shocked, Chip exclaimed, "They arrested me, and took my ass to jail! You know, I was tripping out. I didn't know what was happening. They handcuffed me and I could swear those handcuffs had automatic remotes on them that kept getting tighter on me."

He had a good sense of humor, for what he had gone through, while recalling this. He was laughing while telling about the handcuffs.

He said, "I would scream, 'You're making them too tight. Stop it!' And it seemed they'd loosen them up a little bit. Then they took me to jail."

Chip continued, "The first thing they did was park me in the parking garage. They all rushed out and shut everything down. I thought, Oh, God, they're going to gas me. They're gassing me. They're going to gas me." Laughing, he said, "I thought, What did I ever do to deserve to be gassed like this? Well, fifteen minutes later, they come walking back out—yanked me out of the G. Damn sink. And I wasn't fighting them. I don't fight—especially police officers! Well, they yanked me out and took me inside and threw me on the ground. They took my favorite coat, the one you got me, Mother. It was reversible. It was a nice coat! They kept that. I never got it back."

Chip coughed, then said, "Then they put me in this solitary tank. There's this one little hole. I guess, now I guess, it's where you pee." He chuckled. "Or you're supposed to pee in, but I thought that was the gas tank." He chuckled again. "I thought they were going to do it again. I sort of was feeling in my mind, like, there's a movie, I think it's Joan Crawford, Don't Let Me Die, something like that. Well, I thought they were gassing me again!

"Then they took me down with everybody else. I had to clean up. They make sure you wash up, wash your hair, and make sure you don't have any lice. But they don't make sure that much. The shower felt good, needless to say. Needless to say, everybody was staring at me."

Still, with his good sense of humor, he chuckled while he continued with the next part, "But needless to say I was real proud."

"Why?"

He laughed. "If I had to tell you why, you have no sense of..." he chuckled, "no sense of imagination, can't think of a better word."

He went on to say, "How ironic it was, the only thing I was blessed with. I swear to God."

Chip proudly laughed, saying, "To be blessed with such a piece of equipment only to have it turn you around and knock your lights out for the world!"

He continued, "While I was eating one day, they put me on the outside row. Two people came up from behind. One smashed my head and the other smashed my side. If I'd been smart, I would have rolled on the floor and made all kinds of scenes, saying, 'Oohh, these people are hurting me. Oohh, my God. Get me to the medical unit.' But I didn't. I didn't do anything and nobody else did either. They had security guards everywhere and there were four other people sitting at the table, and all these people, including myself, knew what happened. Nobody said a word about it. They did not say a damn word about it! Not one person. I was furious! I caught my breath and everything. It got to the point where I would not eat my prison food because I just knew they were feeding us rat poison. I gave nobody an attitude. I did not. You know, I was petrified! I was scared to death being in the Orange County Jail!"

Listening to what Chip was saying was tearing me up and made me furious. At both them and myself! To think for some strange reason I set this tape aside and didn't listen to it when I should have. Damn! What was wrong with me? I love Chip so much and he must have felt I let him down when he asked me one day, "Mother, did you listen to the tape?"

Ordinarily I would have listened to the tape immediately, and under ordinary circumstances we would have discussed it. I didn't even give him a fair answer.

I said something like, "No, Chip, I started to, but stopped. I will listen to it later."

I can't believe I did that to my son when I think back. We always talked about things, yet for some unknown reason I never listened to the tape until after he was gone, except for maybe a sentence. Chip accepted my word and said nothing more, but how must this have made him feel? Judging from his words on this tape, he needed his mother's comfort then. It even hurts me now to say, it must have been the unknown stress I was going through, because I've never been one to make excuses; but facts are facts. And the fact was it hurt to know I was losing my son at that time. But I mustn't get ahead of myself. Back to the rest of Chip's tape about his jail experience.

Chip continued, "I had to sleep 'left over' because they were real crowded. One night I was sleeping on the floor. I don't know why, but they leave the bars open. I guess so people can walk up the hall. I don't know. These three guys chose me. This is gross. I don't know if he peed on my mouth or they just had a napkin and dribbled water or what. That made me sick! That really bothered me. Whatever, it woke me up, fast! So they couldn't have done much. But still the thought's just been making me real sick the last couple of days."

Chip kept talking, "Then three guys decided that they wanted to hassle me and I thought, Oh, damn it! So I sat there and tried to read the paper. What did they do? They got these towels and they would get them wet and start flinging them at me. I thought, G. Damn them! If I just ignore it, they'll stop. If I get up and push one of them back, whatever, then the three of them will jump on me and we're all going to get in trouble. So I figured. Be cool and let them get it out of their system. Well, after about an hour—it probably wasn't that long—well, after awhile, it was making me berserk! They left. They finally left me alone.

"Mother, I hadn't been able to reach you. I believed after five days when I signed a paper, they would let me go. But then you came up there and the judge said, 'As long as you promise to get your mother back to Texas you can get out of this place.'

"I said, 'Okay, I promise.' So, late, late, late, almost dark, I got out of there." After a pause, Chip said, "I was freaking all the way about that." To learn of this cruelty at a later date when there was nothing I could do, not even talk with Chip, was devastating! If only I'd listened to his tape when he asked me. Then was when I should have been comforting him, that was the least I could have done.

I knew Chip hadn't felt like making the tape, but still he made the attempt, knowing I wanted it for our book. To bring up all these earthshaking facts of what he'd been going through hadn't been easy, I'm sure. But these are Chip's words and this is a prime example of how Chip was... telling it like it is, going with it and doing the best he could with his nightmare.

Chip and I had driven on to Escondido to stay at Theresa's another night before starting to Texas. Ruth and Theresa were glad to see us and happy Chip was taking me home. I called Jerry and he was glad we'd finally be on our way.

He said, "Be careful and take it easy."

The next morning after we had been up awhile, Chip made a phone call. I was sitting across the room and realized whom he had called when he nonchalantly asked, "Are you my dad?"

There was a pause and Chip responded, "I was just wondering if you were my dad."

I was shocked, but didn't make any comment. Whether Chip was disoriented or not, he wasn't being smart. He was placid and to the point. I knew how alone Chip was when it came to his dad, even though he was a rare subject. No matter how Chip felt, he never spoke wrong of his dad. He respected him as his father.

9

Coastal Vacations

We thanked Ruth and Theresa, then started home. Chip stopped for gas and to have his car checked. Actually I believe Chip was procrastinating while at the station, not wanting to leave California. He made no comment and eventually drove on.

When he left town I thought he might be going the wrong way, yet I knew he had a good sense of direction and I didn't. So I kept quiet. After awhile I noticed that we were on the back roads in the foothills of San Diego rather than the freeway. I kept watching for a sign of where we were. After awhile Chip let me know he was taking me to a place where he'd been the other day and wanted me to see it. He knew I'd like how the town was nestled amongst the rolling hills and bordering the cove.

At last, a big smile covered Chip's face and he said, "This is it. Mother! La Jolla Cove!"

"Chipper, I see what you mean. This is beautiful!"

I gazed and marveled at the beauty while he cruised up and over the hills and all around this lovely city. When I spotted the water, I exclaimed, "Chipper, there's the ocean!"

He drove a little closer to the cove when I marveled, "It looks so inviting!"

"Mother, when I was here the other day, I knew you'd like it here. I'll park the car so we can go to the beach. Want to? There's a park nearby with a shower room where you can change."

"Sounds great. Chip! I can get some more California sun before we start home," J teased. Then I remembered, "Chip, talk about coincidence! This is just like our first vacation together when you were five years old. Remember? We went to Florida on the Atlantic Coast, and now you've brought me to the Pacific." After pausing, I added with a joyful laugh, "How 'bout that, twenty years ago and you're now the age I was when I took you there! What a unique twenty-year coastal coincidence."

"I remember. You have some good pictures of that trip. Turnabout's fair play, wouldn't you say?"

"Leave it up to you. Chip. I'm sure lucky to have you." My happiness with Chip glowed while I continued, "I sure do remember those pictures. Some real cute ones of you." Then I teased, "Your beach ball was almost as big as you back then."

"Mother, we've done a lot over the years."

"We sure have, Chip, and you've always made me proud. People have always said we look alike, and now that you're older, more like brother and sister." I smiled and nudged Chip, "Probably because we've been through so much together."

Chip and I reminisced more, then he paused and said, "Jerry would like it here too."

"I'm sure. He almost came with me." I looked at Chip's happy face and added, "Maybe next time. Here or Galveston, like before when we first moved to Texas."

Chip parked the car. We got out and went into the separate shower rooms. As soon as we had our bathing suits on, we met on the outside. Then we walked over to the stairs leading to the beach in the cove and walked down the steps along the sea wall. I was astonished to see the beach almost completely covered with shrimp, which must have washed ashore with the high tides. Watching the big, rolling waves was fascinating, as they surged briskly onto the beach, but seeing all those shrimp going to waste seemed such a shame. There wasn't a shrimp-less spot to lie on, but it didn't seem to make any difference. The beach was crowded with people.

The shrimp mingled in the sand was a bit prickling, poking me through the towel and making the sandy texture somewhat uncomfortable. Still the hot sun felt great.

It must have been uncomfortable for Chip too. Before long he jumped up and began to wander along the beach and then went up on the sea wall overlooking the ocean. After a while he met a man with two little girls. They talked awhile and then they tossed a beach ball back and forth. Soon they all began to pile up the shrimp. I had no idea what they were up to until I noticed that all that shrimp was taking on the shape of a mermaid. It was interesting watching them. I was remembering Chip with the other little kids during our Florida vacation and their creativeness on the beach; he had gone from sand castle sand angels to the present mermaid. It tickled me and I thought, Twenty years later and Chip and this other guy are still young at heart, like kids with kids. That's great! After awhile they were done; the mermaid was unique.

Chip came over to me and asked, "Mother, do you have your camera with you?"

"No, Chip, I didn't bring it."

"Maybe I have one in the car. Hand me my keys, I'll check in the trunk." I handed him his keys and he headed off in the direction of the car. When Chip didn't return after what seemed like about an hour, I began to wonder where he was and what was taking him so long. I didn't have a watch to check the time, so I lay there awhile longer, thinking he would surely be back soon. I believe the man and his little girls were waiting for him too, but after awhile they left.

I waited a little longer, then thought, Maybe I should go up to the car and see what's happened.

I left our things on the beach so Chip would see them if he came back while I was gone, so he would know I hadn't gone far. I walked up the steps and through the park to where the car was parked. The car was gone! I was shocked! Looking about,

— 94 —

I knew the car had been there, but where did Chip go? Now I was really worried. Surely he didn't leave me. What was I going to do? My purse was in the car, and Chip had the keys. I didn't have anything! I didn't know anyone around there, and I wasn't even sure where I was. All my money was in my purse. All these thoughts kept running through my mind. What is Theresa's phone number? Oh no, I don't have it memorized and it's unlisted! How am I going to contact anyone? I was getting frantic. I walked back and forth, trying to think what to do. Before I knew it I was in tears. I couldn't go anywhere wearing only my bikini. Of course, there was the beach towel down on the beach, but I had to leave it so Chip would know I was here. Oh, God, what am I going to do? Where is Chip? Could he have parked some place else and gone back to the beach by now?

I went back through the park and down the steps to our beach towel. Still no Chip. I looked over toward the mermaid. It was still there, but where was Chip? I sat down on the towel for a few more minutes. I didn't know what to do. I needed to find Chip.

I went back up the steps, keeping an eye on the towel while I climbed to be sure I wouldn't miss him if he came from the other direction. Surely he didn't leave me. He wouldn't leave me on the beach. He must know everything I have is in his car.

I couldn't seem to stop all the scary notions. I was all alone and afraid of what might have happened to him. The thought of Chip's leaving me would never have crossed my mind if it weren't for his sudden changes or whatever it was that was causing him to act erratically at times. It's strange that I was uncertain of him now, because whenever we were together I wasn't. His changes hadn't been too extreme or often. He had been doing fine when we arrived here. When I wasn't sure of him or his actions I would snap at him and that's about all i t took, and he would be alright or snap back at me. Then we'd both be alright.

Still worrying and fretting, I happened to look across the street and down about a block where I saw a hotel with a large, circular drive in front. I couldn't believe my eyes; there was a car that looked like Chip's parked in the driveway. I stood a minute, wanting to be sure, then I rushed across the street and over to it. I peeked in the windows and breathed a sigh of relief to see it was his car.

I didn't see Chip, so I hurried inside the hotel and across the lobby to the registration desk. I asked, "Is there a young man in here by the name of Brandon, or Chip, Williamson?"

They looked at me quizzingly, so I added, "I'm his mother."

The girl spoke up, "Yes, he was going to get a room. He went upstairs to check on one."

The man behind the desk interrupted. "No, I believe he left. I saw him go out the door."

The girl clerk added, "Yes, he said he was going to check with his mother and tell her he was getting a room."

"That's me," I said. "Just a minute, I'll be back."

I went out the door, across the street, and back to the park steps. When I started down the stairs I looked down, and there was Chip at the bottom. Was I ever glad to see him! He saw me about the same time and yelled frantically, "Where have you been?"

I looked at him in surprise while he continued, "I've been looking for you! You were leaving me! You were taking off and deserting me, weren't you?"

I was shocked at his words.

I exclaimed, "Chipper, no, look! Right there on the beach you can see where I left our towels. I left them there so you would know I hadn't gone far."

When I reached the bottom of the stairs I pointed toward our towels while we walked to where I'd left them, and I said, "See, right there they are. I left them so you would know I was still here."

He just looked at me and I added, "You know better. I wouldn't leave you. I didn't want you to think I had left. And what about you? Heavens, you had me worried. Where have you been?"

He repeated, "You were leaving me, weren't you? You were deserting me! I know. Because you weren't here when I came back." "Chip, I left the towel there!" Then I noticed he had a camera.

"Oh, you got a camera. Did you get a picture of your mermaid?"

While we walked toward the mermaid, I said, "I think that man with the two little girls was waiting for you, but then I guess they couldn't stay any longer and left."

Chip and I stood a few minutes looking at the mermaid.

"Y'all really put a lot of work and time into making that mermaid. It's really neat and almost looks real."

All of a sudden Chip kicked the mermaid real hard with his foot and made a big indentation in her side.

"Chip, why did you do that? You messed it up!"

He screamed, "There's something in it! Something evil! I had to get it out! Get the evil out!"

I exclaimed, "Chipper, there's nothing in there! That's the shrimp that washed onto the shore. You, that man, and his two little girls made the mermaid with them. That's why you went and got your camera." I paused a moment before asking, "Aren't you going to take a picture?"

All the time I was talking, Chip stood staring at the mermaid as though something were wrong. Finally, although hesitant, he snapped the camera. We went over to our beach towels and sat there a few minutes. It was getting late, so I asked Chip if he'd like to go back to Theresa's and start fresh the next day.

He said, "No, I want to go to Hollywood and see Neil before we start back."

"Okay, there's a store I would like to go to in Los Angeles too. It will be almost on our way. So we can go there before heading home once you see Neil. Okay?"

"Sure," he answered.

"Chip, you really had me worried."

"I didn't have a camera, so I bought one at the camera shop. You can have it."

"That's okay, Chip, you keep it. Looks like a nice one."

To my surprise, when I received our credit card statement the next month there was the charge for that camera Chi p had purchased! Was I ever shocked! Still, I could only laugh. This was the first time he had ever used my charge card.

After we left La Jolla Cove, on the way to Hollywood Chip drove through Orange, the town where he was born. He wanted me to show him the house we lived in when he was a baby. When we got to Palmyra Street, we were disappointed to find our house was no longer there and was now a commercial area.

Another thirty-five miles and we would be in Los Angeles. Unfortunately, leaving La Jolla Cove when we did put us right at the peak rush hour. Traffic was stop and go.

Chip suggested, "Mother, let's go to Venice. I'd like to show you a real pretty park. You'll love it, with everyone on skates."

"No, Chipper, it's getting late and we need to get started home after we see Neil."

I believe that was one "no" that should have been a "yes." I didn't say anything more and thought he would surprise me and we'd end up in Venice just like we did in La Jolla. I believe the "no" crushed him, just like his sincerity crushed me, realizing I'd hurt him, when he later said, "I just wanted to show you a good time in Venice. That could have been such a wonderful trip."

Chip was being his usual thoughtful self, and looking back it's obvious he was wanting to do all the things we enjoyed. I hadn't thought of that then, and at that time traffic was wearing on my nerves, even though Chip was driving and the traffic never bothered him. He was a good driver.

We finally arrived in Hollywood, where Chip stopped for a brief visit with Neil. After we left I remembered what Chip had told me the cult philosophy was: "The less you have financially and materially, the closer you'll be to attainment with the supreme being in Guru."

I thought, That's probably why Neil was concerned about Chip's finances when he called to let us know Chip was in jail. Until now I'd forgotten.

Chip had gone through thousands of dollars in a short time, but evidently he hadn't given any to the cult. Fortunately he didn't have any more dealings with the cult.

Finally we left the city and the heavy traffic behind us and were on our way. I must have fallen asleep. I woke up the next morning and found that Chip had been driving all night. Instead of taking the interstate, he had taken highway 80 so we could enjoy the scenery.

Every time he saw a tourist shop he'd stop and go inside to browse. It seemed Chip was trying to annoy me, and possibly he felt I was doing the same to him. We were not our usual selves with one another. It could have been Chip's mood swings with the personality change that I couldn't seem to cope with or understand. Also, I believe I was still wanting to rely on Chip more than was fair, considering what he was coping with. I hadn't yet comprehended what was happening or the extent of his confusion at times; I was expecting him to be his usual self and therefore was treating him likewise.

At one souvenir shop he stayed so long that I became very irritated.

I said, "Chipper, let's go!"

He seemed to be deliberately wasting time, looking and poking around. I couldn't persuade him to leave.

I angrily asked, "Are you coming or not?"

Chip looked at me calmly and didn't say a word. I couldn't believe he was doing this. I finally went out to the car. I was surprised to see the keys were in the ignition switch. I took the keys and went back inside. I again asked Chip to leave. Still he didn't speak to me.

"Chip, let's go. I have the keys and I'm leaving without you if you don't come on."

I went out and he followed, but he didn't get in the car.

"Come on, Chip. I'll drive."

He wouldn't get in so I drove away. I didn't go far, only to the ramp leading onto the highway. I pulled the car over to the side and stopped. I knew under normal circumstances he wouldn't act this way, and I would never leave him regardless. I was nervous and frustrated, just the opposite of what he seemed to be. Yet why was he being so obstinate with me? All I knew was that things weren't like they usually were between us and this was tough on both of us. I wanted to get home, and I don't think Chip liked leaving California.

Slowly and carefully I backed the car to where I had left Chip, but he wasn't there. I knew he had to be nearby and might have gone back inside, so I waited. A few minutes later he came out of the store and over to the driver's side of the car. I got out and went around to the rider's side and he drove off.

He told me he had called Jerry and told Jerry I was giving him a hard time and that I'd left him; Jerry assured him I'd be back.

Chip asked Jerry, "Well, what am I supposed to do with her?"

Jerry told him, "Just be calm and don't say anything to her."

I believe his talking to Jerry helped. At least he quit stopping every time something caught his attention.

Chip had a small paper sack that he had twisted shut about two inches from the top. Ever since we'd left California, from time to time he'd grab the sack and blow into it fast and consistent, never saying a word. This was starting to bother me.

I asked, "Chip, why are you doing that?"

I thought he was trying to aggravate me because he didn't answer, but kept the sack near and occasionally continued blowing into it. Even though it was bothering me, I finally decided it was useless to say anything. I hadn't given thought to his being short of breath and not wanting to say anything to scare me.

Even though Chip seemed distant at times, it was apparent he was trying to work out whatever was on his mind. He may have had some confusion at times, but I felt he was in deep thought many times and doing his best. It brought to mind what his Aunt Ruth had said about his trying to hold onto reality.

Also what Chip's good friend, Beth, always claimed, "I never knew anyone like Chip. No, not ever. Things might not be right at the time or something might start to get the best of him, when he'd suddenly say, 'To hell with this,' and spontaneously he'd bounce right back and be even more determined!" She laughed and repeated, "No, I never knew anyone like Chip!"

Thinking about what Ruth and Beth said made sense as to what I was now observing. His overpowering determination was what always saw him through and on his own. He wasn't about to let anything get him down for long if he could help it.

At one time when he was driving along he started thinking out loud. He said, "Oh, I know. I know who my dad is, and could my mother be...."

I hadn't thought any more about his asking his dad on the phone if he were his dad until I heard this. I was horrified at his insinuating words. "Chip, you know better! Why are you saying that? You know who your mother and dad are!"

I don't know whether my anger fazed him, but he didn't say another word. His calm, annoying changes occurring every so often baffled me. This was the opposite of his usual self and it was hard for me not to snap at him. I thought it had to be the cult. And I imagine he couldn't understand why I seemed to be different with him at times. How was he to know in his confusion? Neither of us knew what was actually happening, only that it caused waves between us, which we didn't like and weren't used to.

I wore my jacket, like the one Chip used to have, to keep warm because Chip kept the air-conditioning cold. I don't know how long I had been asleep when Chip roused me, frantic and yelling, "Mother! Mother! Hurry, hurry, quick! You're on fire!"

I woke up while Chip was driving the car overt© the side of the road and yelling, "Hurry, hurry, get out! Get out!"

He reached over me, opened the car door, and was helping me out when I noticed the sleeve of my jacket was on fire. Chi p was out of the car and over to my side smothering the spot, which hadn't begun to flame yet. The breeze from the air-conditioning had apparently blown an ash from his cigarette onto my sleeve. Chip was all shook up and I was too, once I realized what was happening. When I checked it, everything was okay and I assured him it could be mended, that the sleeve was a little too long anyway and the edge is all that was damaged. Chipper wouldn't smoke anymore all the way home and apologized over and over, assuring me he would be careful.

We were arriving in El Paso, about halfway home, when Chip decided to stop. I thought he might want to get a motel since we had been three days on the road, including the first day at the beach, and he hadn't rested yet. He didn't seem tired, but I felt sure he must have been. Chip usually made the trip in twenty-four hours or so, but this trip he didn't seem concerned about the time or resting. More than likely we would have been home by now if it hadn't been for the endless procrastination.

He drove off the freeway. Then after driving a short distance he spotted a mall, pulled in, and parked the car. He didn't say a word when he got out, so I hurried and got out, then ran to join him, even though I had the feeling he didn't want to be bothered. Chip hadn't said much, but that whole trip his actions seemed to speak louder than words.

I don't believe he would have made the trip if the judge hadn't ordered him to take me home. Never had we had such a controversial time with each other. Once inside the mall, before I knew it Chip had slipped away from me and I didn't know where he had gone. After looking at length, I went back to the car to wait. I knew he would need to come back sooner or later. I was starting to worry when he finally returned.

"Mother, you're to call Jerry."

"Did you call him again?"

"He wants to talk with you," Chip seriously said.

"Chipper, why did you call him? What have I done?"

"He said he would talk with you when you call him."

"Okay, I'll call. You come with me, though. Okay?"

Chip agreed and went with me to call.

"Hi, Chip said you wanted me to call."

"Yes, he called earlier. He wanted me to tell you to let him do the driving and to stop giving him a hard time."

"Okay, but sometimes I don't know what to do. I'll talk with you when we get home. Love you. Bye."

Hanging up the phone, I said to Chip, "Okay, let's go. I promise I won't bother you. We're about halfway home now."

On our way back to the car Chip said, "I'm selling my car."

I didn't comment, but was thinking, He's not serious.

While getting into the car Chip said, "The salesman said to bring my car in and he'd buy it after he looked at it."

Chip had a Prelude sports car and I didn't think he wanted to sell it. However, I was a little concerned because he sounded serious and had been gone awhile before returning, although he hadn't taken his car with him. After he'd driven about a mile, he pulled into a car lot where there were both new and used cars, which made me wonder.

I sat in the car waiting while he went inside. Shortly Chip came back with a salesman, who walked around the car looking at it Chip followed while he was checking it over.

Then I heard Chip ask, "Do I have enough air in my tires?"

The salesman said, "Yes, they look fine to me."

"Great! Thank you," Chip cheerfully said as he shook hands with the salesman, got into his car, and drove away.

Chip was still blowing into the sack from time to time. I didn't know anything about hyperventilation or that he was having a problem breathing. Later I learned he had a good reason and was wise to be blowing into the paper sack because it did help him breathe.

Finally on the fifth day we arrived home that morning.

Chip announced, "We're home."

"Yes, we're home at last, and Chip, you must be exhausted! I don't know how you drove for five days without any sleep."

It was amazing. Chip didn't even seem tired.

A little later I asked, "Are you going to call the counseling center?" He said, "Not now," and went to his bedroom.

I knew better than to push him, but more than anything I wanted to see what his reaction would be and encourage him to call for his own wellbeing.

10

Oh No, Not Again

Chip woke early the next morning after our exhausting trip and left the house saying very little. While he was gone, I called the counseling center and several other places trying to find out what needed to be done to get help for him. Everyone I talked to said the same thing, "Chip will need to call."

I understood the law was to protect him, but this worried me because I wasn't sure when or if he would call.

When Chip came home I let him know what I was told when I called about counseling for him. I asked if he would call, but he didn't seem interested in pursuing the idea.

"Chip, remember you told the judge you would seek help once you got home."

"Mother, if I needed to, I would. I'm okay."

"I know you're okay right now, but sometimes you aren't."

"Mother..." His tone seemed to say, Are you sure?

"Chip, why don't you call and just talk briefly with the lady I talked to. That's all I'm asking. If you don't agree with what she says, you won't need to pursue it any further. Okay? It would be up to you. If you wanted to set up a time and talk with them, you could decide together. Will you?"

Chip wasn't in any hurry. He went to his room to lie down. He needed to rest, so I didn't say any more for the time being. Somehow I had to get help for him, but he would need to talk with a counselor. How was I ever going to persuade him when he didn't think it necessary? I needed to be careful, hoping he would soon pursue it himself. I assured him I only wanted him to get counseling so he could understand what was happening and work it out.

Again that evening I called the counselor, Ann. I told her Chip was still hesitant about talking to anyone.

"Ann, if I call you after Chip wakes up, maybe he would come to the telephone. Would that be alright with you?"

"Yes, that would be fine."

Later that night when Chip woke up, I asked, "If I call Ann, the counselor, would you talk with her?"

To my surprise, Chip said, "Okay, I'll call her."

He picked up the telephone and rang the number I gave him. Chip and Ann talked awhile, and then I heard him setting up an appointment for the next day. From this end of the conversation, it sounded encouraging.

I thought, Thank heavens, at last we're getting somewhere.

The next day when it came time for Chip's appointment, he decided he didn't need to go. I tried to reason with him, but his mind was made up. He wasn't going! At least he had talked with the counselor, that was something. I knew it was necessary that he see her, but how was I going to get him to her? He had almost taken that step and I mustn't give up hope.

Chip hadn't liked his Aunt Ruth trying to make him an appointment in California and I believe he thought that since she hadn't succeeded after trying three different times, it proved he didn't need to see anyone.

A couple of weeks later Chip and a friend decided to go to Austin. While he was gone, we learned of another generous gesture Chip had made while in California. A gas station attendant called to ask, "Is the hundred-dollar check I got from a Brandon any good?"

I asked, "What check are you referring to?"

"He purchased ten dollars' worth of gas, then wrote this check and said I could keep the change. Is the check good?"

"Well, I'm sure it is. Why?"

"I wanted to be sure before cashing it," he answered, then quickly hung up.

When Chip came home, I confronted him about the call concerning the check. He said he had done that a couple of times when he didn't have change. Another thing Chip said he had done was to take a taxi and go for a ride. He would tell the driver to slop at a convenience store, then say to him, "Okay, go on in and get anything you want. I'll pay for it."

Chip said most of the time, the drivers would only get a pack of cigarettes or maybe a newspaper. He'd tell them, "Go ahead, get a carton or whatever else you want."

He had always been generous, but not quite like that.

Suddenly Chip seemed skeptical of his food. When he sat down to dinner after he put food on his plate, he would pick at it with his fork as though he were checking the contents close while sorting it on his plate. He might eat only two or three bites, then comment, "This doesn't look right," and ask, "Is there something in this?"

Other times after his inspection he might only say, "I'm not hungry," then shove his plate aside.

I couldn't get him to eat, not even his favorite foods. I was astounded with his insinuations, thinking I was putting something in his food. I didn't understand why he suspected this. I'm sure he knew better, yet he was afraid.

I could see that he was losing weight and I was concerned. He didn't act tired, but he looked drained from not eating or sleeping. How could he go for days without rest? He had never let himself go and had always been particular about the way he looked, but what was happening now? This wasn't like Chip. Why was he so afraid of me, and how on earth could he think I would do anything to harm him? This didn't make sense! But then the way Chip was at times didn't make sense. Still, much of the time he was himself and doing well as usual.

Thoughts of the cult flashed briefly through my mind, although I knew he wasn't involved with it anymore. But since his strange behavior had begun about the time I knew he was involved with them, some bizarre influence from them seemed to be about the only logical explanation. Why else would he be afraid of me?

One day I decided to lie in the sun for about an hour. After going outdoors,! remembered some business papers in my car that I could work on while tanning. I went through the house to the garage. While I was getting the papers. Chip came to the door I had gone through. When I tried, but couldn't open it I thought I had locked it automatically when I went out, which I often did.

I called for Chip and was surprised to hear him instantly say, "You can stay in there."

"Chipper, will you unlock this door?" I asked.

It was evident he was standing on the other side of the door and apparently locked it when he answered.

"No. I'm not going to unlock the door. You're going to shoot me."

I was stunned, "What? Chip, you know better! Unlock this door!"

He was silent and wouldn't open the door. I shook on it and pounded, but he still wouldn't open it. He was standing just inside, not saying or doing anything. I was becoming frustrated.

"Open this door! And stop this!" I yelled.

"No, you've got a gun!" Chip sounded serious and sincere.

"Chip, I don't have a gun. You know better! Why are you doing this?" I pleaded.

I couldn't imagine where he had gotten the idea I had a gun.

"You can go out the garage door," he suggested.

"No, I can't. I'm in my bikini!" I yelled.

I was trying to think of a way to get him to open the door. I was becoming nervous and frustrated as the anger welled up in me. Banking on his concern for me, I thought of a ruse to get him to open the door.

"Chip, would you get me a glass of water? It's hot in here/' I thought he would naturally open the door and I could go in, but it didn't quite happen that way. He got the water, okay, but he went out and around to the garage door, then called, "Mother, I'm sitting the water on the fender of my car. You can open the garage door and it will be here for you."

I was surprised and thought, Oh no, then yelled, "Chipper, no, I'm in my bikini! I can't come out there. You go back around and open the inside door for me!"

Almost in tears from all the chaos, I whimpered, "Oh, Chipper, why are you doing this to me? I'm in my bikini and you know I can't come out there. Chip, please, you know better. Why are you doing this?"

I pounded on the door again. What had given him the idea I had a gun and was going to shoot him? I didn't have a gun and I wondered how he could think I would do such a thing. I couldn't understand his reasoning. I could always count on him to be sensible and reason things out. Yet he really sounded frightened! This wasn't like Chip and I didn't know how to handle the situation. Possibly I depended on him more than I realized because I was at a loss as to what to do next.

While I was contemplating what to do, I heard Chip talking. He was telling someone that his mother was in the garage. Without thinking of the consequence, I pressed the button to open the garage door. I hadn't realized that my actions might frighten Chip until I heard him say as he hurried into the house, "I'm going to call the police."

By then I recognized the person Chip had been talking to was the Chem Lawn man, who had come to service our lawn. Oh, no, here I was clad only in my bikini. I was embarrassed. How could everything have become so chaotic in such a short time?

Anxious I said, "Hurry, would you do me a favor? Would you cup your hands and help me over the fence? I must get into the house and I know...I know the back door is open."

We rushed over to the fence. He bent down, cupped his hands and I put one foot into them using them as a step. Up and over I went. I hadn't done anything like this in years! I ran to the back door and hurried into the house to the telephone. I called Jerry in a hurry to explain what had happened.

He said, "This is exactly what you've been needing. Call the police. They will take him in for you."

"Well, yes." I hesitated. "I guess I need to," I whimpered and hung up the phone, hating the idea of calling the police.

I was all shook up and felt terrible. To call the police on Chip didn't seem right. I'd never dreamed of doing anything like this, certainly not before his complications, and it was hard to think about doing such a thing to my own son now. I hated the idea of the police taking Chip. I knew it had been terrible for him in California when the police had arrested him and I didn't want that to happen again. What was I to do? Trying to sort my thoughts, I knew I must do it not to him, but for him.

Still hating the idea, but making up my mind, I got the portable telephone and took it out to the lawn chair. My heart was going ninety miles an hour, it seemed. I felt I must calm down. God, I hate to do this to Chip. It's not fair. I really don't want io call. But I must get help, Well, here goes. Then I happened to look up and there stood three police officers in the backyard! Was I ever shocked!

I stammered, "Ooh, goodness. I...I'm glad you're here! I was getting ready to call you."

There I was caught in my bikini! Laughing nervously from the embarrassment, I felt my face flush as I said, "Oh, please excuse the way I look." I hurried to grab a towel to wrap around me as I repeated, 'I'm so glad you're here.'"

By then I was starting to calm down and get myself together. I hadn't expected them to be here before I called, but I was glad I didn't need to call them.

I said, "You have got to take my son! I have been trying to get some help to get him to the hospital for weeks now. I've got to get help for him as soon as possible."

I was talking fast. They sure caught me off-guard and I was a nervous wreck from everything that was happening. And now the thought of the police and Chip made me feel miserable. We went into the house and I directed them to Chipper's bedroom. I was already feeling unhappy for Chip and I didn't like doing this to him. It was so unfair, but what else could I do?

He was sitting up in bed when they entered his room. One policeman left the room to call the station while the other two officers stayed with Chip, trying to talk him into getting up and getting dressed to go with them. Hearing this was tearing me up.

Chip said innocently, "No, I'm fine. I can stay here. I'll just stay in bed. I don't need to go anywhere. I'm okay."

Even though he was polite, it was apparent something was wrong. The longer I stood there listening, the worse the contrition was, knowing he would need to go with them. I hated this for Chip, thinking, Oh no, not again!

It seemed so wrong for him to be going through such a hassle and I was torn emotionally. Never had he done anything to involve the police, and why now? Why, God, why? I could hardly bear this happening, but there was no choice since Chip needed help. Somehow, and hopefully, this would bring an end to all the turmoil for Chip's sake.

In due time one officer said, "Come on, get up and get your clothes on. You're going with us!"

Hearing this broke my heart. I couldn't take any more and quickly left the room. I hurried to the other officer using the telephone.

When he hung up I pleaded, "Please, if you take him in, don't hurt him or be rough with him. Okay? He's really very good and won't cause any problems. It's just that he had a rough time with the police in California and he's afraid it might happen again, I'm sure. I believe he's having a problem and needs to go to the hospital. Okay? Will you be able to take him to the hospital?"

The police officer told me someone would call me in about three hours to let me know.

I continued, "Please, don't keep him in jail. He doesn't need that." Then I asked, "Surely they won't keep him there, will they? He needs help and I don't want him mistreated because of a misunderstanding about his actions. He isn't a difficult person, whether he's himself or not."

The policeman listened politely. Still I was petrified thinking what could happen. In the back of my mind I was worried they would put handcuffs on him. The thought was so unbearable, yet I understood they probably had to. I knew Chip would hate handcuffs and I couldn't bear the thought of seeing them on him.

Soon the other officers came out with Chip. Darn! They had handcuffs on him! I quickly turned a way while they were walking out the door. I hated such a degrading defeat for Chip! Then I hated that I had turned away. This was wrong to be happening to him! Why must this be complicated? I was so sorry. I felt weak and drained. I couldn't stop crying, thinking what all Chip was going through and what this must be doing to him.

It seemed like an eternity while I waited the three hours for the call concerning Chip's fate. Finally they called and said they were taking him to the hospital. Was I ever thankful! Hopefully they would help him get over whatever was wrong and he would soon be home as though nothing had ever happened.

"Hi, sweetheart, am I ever glad to see you," I said when Jerry came home from work. Adding, after he kissed me, "They called from the police station a few minutes ago and said they would be taking Chip to the hospital."

"Finally! They'll check him over and find out what's happening," Jerry commented.

I started crying again. "Yes. I'm glad for that reason, but it doesn't seem right for this to be happening to him."

"Call the hospital and see when visiting hours are. We'll go see him."

"I did, but they said we can't visit until tomorrow."

Jerry took a shower before dinner. Meanwhile I noticed a black metal tube, about a foot long, lying on the counter. I looked at it, wondering what it was, but didn't think any more about it. During dinner I told Jerry what had transpired.

"I don't understand why he thought I had a gun and was going to shoot him. But for some reason he was afraid of me."

"He knows better," Jerry said, "but you know how he's been lately."

"I know, but where would he get such an idea? I don't know why he keeps thinking I want to hurt him."

When I got up to get something from the refrigerator, I noticed the piece of pipe again. Curious I asked, "What's that?"

"What?" asked Jerry.

"That black pipe," I said as I pointed at it.

"That's a scope."

"A scope?" I quizzed.

"Yes. It's a rifle scope. Chip found it in the garage and laid it there."

"He did? I never noticed it until awhile ago."

"He found it yesterday."

"Is it off a gun?" I asked.

"Yes. There wasn't any gun, but it was with some of those things you brought home the other day to get rid of for those people."

"Oh, I forgot about that. I didn't even know there was anything like that among those things."

Then it dawned on me. "That's why Chip thought I had a gun! I had no idea where he had gotten such an idea until now. If he found that scope in the garage, that must be why he thought I was out there. Gosh, that's terrible! In his confused state of mind, lean imagine his thoughts. If only I'd known. This makes me feel even worse."

I was bewildered and said, "That's what I don't understand. Chip's sensible enough to know that where there's a gun scope, it would seem only natural for the gun to be in the garage where he found the scope. But then somehow, he seems to get all confused and tends to have thoughts that aren't realistic. He would never think that I would harm him if he weren't confused."

"I know," Jerry agreed.

"Now I understand why he locked me in the garage. Still, he got me a glass of water, even though he was afraid. It all makes sense now. Yet look at all the incidents. Things that keep happening to Chip seem to have a connection and make sense in that respect, when you think about them."

Jerry held my hand and squeezed it while I talked and wept.

"Coming home from California, no matter what, he was always thoughtful and good to me regardless of how I was. Sometimes we had a terrible time communicating. Yet it's strange how he could still keep his love and concern when all those terrible notions about me seemed to haunt him. Why is this happening to him? Chip, of all people. He wouldn't hurt anyone no matter what, and he's never been a troublemaker! Never.

"He doesn't deserve this!" I wailed.

"I know," Jerry calmly replied.

We did not understand what was happening to Chip at the time. Maybe, had we known, we could have taken steps to avoid some of these unfortunate situations. Not understanding or realizing his condition at the time made us fear for him, yet we were angry at some of the things that went through his mind. Not until much later would we know why this had occurred.

11

A Time of Unknown Answers

The next day Jerry and I went to see Chip in the hospital. He was fine, but certainly wasn't happy being in the psychiatric ward. I understood, but was relieved that at long last he was being treated.

The psychiatrist said he had suffered a nervous breakdown.

As soon as Chip's friends Darlene and Rhonda learned that he was in the hospital they made the long trips from Dallas almost daily to visit him in Fort Worth. Chip and Rhonda had been good friends since high school and he had met Darlene in Houston several years ago.

After Chip had been in the hospital a couple of days, he told us about calling his real estate customers who had been there to see him earlier that day. He said that they had a nice visit and prayed with him. At first we weren't sure, even though he seemed sincere. Then the next day his customers called our home to ask how Chip was doing. They let us know that they thought the world of Chip, were anxious for him to get well, and were looking forward to working with him as soon as he came home.

I was grateful for their concern and felt bad I had doubted Chip. I should have known better and believed my intuition instead of circumstances. He was already more like himself, and doubting him the times I had must have seemed unfair to him. I never had before and prayed it wasn't obvious I was dubious. If he was aware, he played it cool and didn't comment. Of course, he wouldn't. He wasn't one to be critical, but understanding. His friends kept in contact about his progress.

Another time Chip told us he had been tied to the bed and couldn't get up. He was so serious and in full control of all his faculties when he told us that it made me wonder. I'd heard of this happening and not being disclosed, so I decided to ask.

The nurses assured me he hadn't been restrained, which led me to wonder if he was right. Or possibly the medication may have had some bearing, although that didn't seem likely in light of how he seemed with us. He often seemed in control and to have a grip more than would seem likely for a nervous breakdown, provided he wasn't heavily medicated. Yet, I wasn't too familiar and could only observe and go by what the psychiatrist was saying, plus what I had been experiencing with him the past few months.

When we visited Chip he always joined us. However, one visit we found him in bed shivering under several blankets. He had been alternating between chills and sweats. The doctors were treating him for the flu, yet they hadn't been able to control the symptoms.

We wanted him to stay in bed, but as soon as he was a little more comfortable he insisted on getting up, saying he felt better and would be okay. I knew that no matter how he felt, if he had company he must be hospitable. It was a couple more days before the flu symptoms subsided.

When Chip's psychiatrist told us he had a nervous breakdown, I didn't question it. Today I do. As time progresses, I believe in retrospect, it will be apparent that Chip didn't have a breakdown, but had something much more serious—something the medical profession in the United States knew little about and something the general public knew even less about.

I believe that his unusual state of mind and erratic behavior had to have been AIDS Dementia Complex (ADC), although during the time Chip had these complications not much was known about the virus nor its symptoms. *It was a time of unknown answers.*

In time to come, after Chip passed away, I learned about ADC and how it had been discovered to oftentimes take place in the beginning with acquired immune deficiency syndrome. This is an organic disease of the neurological system that is usually caused by the AIDS virus itself. Some patients may die of brain damage within a few months, and in some it may only alter the brain's metabolism. Some of the effects of ADC are hyperactivity, delusional thinking, apathy, depression, and suicidal thoughts. A person's genetic makeup or history of disease may influence susceptibility. And, looking back, much of this was exactly how Chip seemed to be at various times.

Not realizing it at the time, I was witness to many of Chip's traumatic experiences that apparently were symptoms of ADC. It is believed that 90 percent of AIDS victims may have these symptoms at one time or another. Research suggests that very often this is an early, unnoticed effect.

Evidently the causes of Chip's confusion, complications, and depression were physical. If only he'd known it. Apparently Chip was a pioneer of AIDS.

At the time I knew little about AIDS. Eventually these particular, earthshaking symptoms subsided, but at a later date chills and sweats were documented as symptoms of AIDS. Apparently Chip had faced the various trials of ADC primarily on his own, before dementia was realized or related to AIDS. Or before it was even taken into account with Chip because AIDS wasn't in the picture for several months to come.

After Chip had been in the hospital a week, I talked with his psychiatrist again, hoping Chip could come home. She said he needed to stay longer and could either stay where he was or could go to the state hospital in Wichita Falls. I wasn't familiar with Wichita Falls and I couldn't know what it was like, so I talked with Chip, asking him which he'd rather do.

He said, "I want to come home. I am all right and there isn't any reason to keep me here or anywhere."

"Chip, your doctor says you need to stay a little longer."

"Mother, I don't belong here. I'm not like the people here who really have problems."

"Chip, I understand what you're saying. I wondered about that myself, yet I want you well and safe. Do you know what I mean? Most of the time you are fine, but at times you are irrational and I want to be sure you don't have future complications. That's most important, don't you think?"

"No. There's nothing wrong with me."

I could imagine how he must have felt being with patients who had real bad chronic problems, and I wondered why they didn't keep them separated. At times their actions were enough to upset anyone.

Chip had become friends with a lady who had a nervous breakdown due to marital problems. She too was obviously a person with class, yet needed help. It was good to know he had someone compatible to talk with. I tried to reason with him by pointing out that anyone could get sick and find themselves in the same place he was. It didn't matter who you were.

I'm sure he couldn't accept the idea of a nervous breakdown, so it stood even more to reason why he didn't like being there. Mental problems are more frustrating and harder to accept than physical problems for most everyone, no doubt due to society. Chip had a brilliant mind and high IQ. Even now he was often in control and sensible, like himself before the complications. Yet I had to be sure, for his sake, with all that had been happening.

I asked the doctor what the difference would be for Chip if he transferred to Wichita Falls. She said he would have more space and be allowed to go outside and play tennis. Here he must stay inside.

I immediately thought. Chip wouldn't like being cooped up in here for long, but he would love outdoors and tennis! It's about time something goes in his favor.

Chip didn't want to go to Wichita Falls and I was about to make an important decision, which I wanted to be in his best interest. I was very explicit with the doctor, asking for all the facts. Ordinarily I never went against Chip's wishes, but I thought he didn't realize how much better it would be having more space and being able to go outdoors. I decided it would be best.

Within a couple of days, Chip was transferred. Knowing he wasn't satisfied with the decision and wanting to assure him we hadn't deserted him after sending him so far away, we immediately made the three-hour drive to visit. The following weekend we took the camper and he was allowed to spend time with us. He was fine and it was obvious I had made a mistake sending him there.

Although he resented being at Wichita Falls and let me know, his attitude was better than could be expected. As usual, he made the best of the situation.

Then we discovered that the doctor had unfortunately been mistaken about his being allowed to go outdoors. Being allowed outside on the grounds was a privilege for which he must qualify by being there a certain length of time. Surely the doctor knew Chip wouldn't be hospitalized much longer when she spoke with me. He was only there almost three weeks, which wasn't enough time to earn outdoor time. Of course, I'm glad it wasn't longer, but since I based my decision on the outdoor activity I resented even three weeks of my son's life being spent in a place where he did not need to be nor want to be.

Even the psychiatrists at Wichita Falls couldn't understand why he was there. They confronted Jerry and me about it during our first and only conference. The following week while we were there the psychiatrists said they were sending Chip home. Of course, we were all delighted. I certainly wouldn't have gone through all the red tape, humiliation, and heartache of sending him to Wichita Falls if the doctor had told the true facts of how it was! It was wrong for Chip! It was only a matter of time in revising the paperwork for Chip to return home.

Although it was a four-hour drive each way for Darlene and Rhonda, they still visited Chip. Rhonda's visits were only the beginning. It's ironic. Her dad was the one who told me that he had plans for Chip to take care of her someday; in turn, she was the one who stood by him throughout his sickness.

While Chip was at Wichita Falls he had another bout with the "flu." As before, he alternated between chills and sweats. These became so severe that he was sent to the infirmary. After several days of continual misery he recovered.

Chip wrote a letter to his Aunt Ruth letting her know where he was:

"Hi! *Of course, you should know you are and always will be my favorite aunt. I love you (even though you tried to have me locked up 3 times)*" and drew a smiley face. *"It's really not so bad here in the funny farm & the men don't wear white, but they did come to take me away, in handcuffs! Talk about disgrace! Lots of love, Brandon*

"Please keep writing."

Chip used his real name, Brandon, all the time.

Chip was in Wichita Falls not quite three weeks when we brought him home. No more erratic behavior!

The good that came out of going to Wichita Falls was the psychiatrist, Dr. Gravelee, who became a good friend to Chip and me.

Dr. Gravelee told me, "When I first met Chip he seemed special. I'll never forget it. I was sitting at the other end of the table during staffing, not saying anything, only observing. Chip was being very assertive and open. Of course, he was angry and that showed, which was okay."

"I know, he didn't want to be there," I replied.

"Right," she continued. "I listened while the psychiatrist talked with him, watching his responses. He was frustrating the living daylights out of him. Suddenly

I realized I was grinning. I found myself thinking, Yes, I know what you mean." She laughed and continued, "From the first I thought, He has no reason being here. There is something going on with him, but it isn't something that's going to be resolved here."

"And it wasn't," I stated, then said, "I really couldn't blame him for being upset with me for sending him there. That truly was the first time in his life I felt he was angry at me or disappointed I had failed him. Never before had I gone against his wishes. I was sorry and saddened even more when I learned; it wasn't like I was told. And to go against his wishes. So often he was always right, sick or not sick."

She said, "Well, I think he understood why. When he was talking he knew there was the need for something to be done and no one was sure what. He didn't even understand himself, maybe. It wasn't something that we could fix for him. I think he understood your helplessness, your need to try to help, to try to do something. I really do believe he understood that."

"Later he told me he understood. At first, he just let me know he didn't like what I had done, but he wasn't mean or hateful."

"No, he never was mean or destructive! He had to put his anger, his frustration somewhere, and where is it safer to put than on the one you feel most safe with and most loved by? With Mom."

"Yes, that's true," I agreed.

"There was something about Chip. I will never forget him. I got such a kick out of him. He was so open and honest, so bright and charming! Utterly charming! He was so interesting to talk to. He had an openness like he invited people to come in, to be comfortable. He was so real. You know, psychologically, Kitty, he was pretty healthy. He needed to talk about some things and somebody needed to hear."

"He did. He liked you, and obviously he was like his usual self," I agreed.

We talked a little longer and she said, "I could see between y'all, the feelings you must have been through, feelings you and he shared. You had a good relationship."

"Yes, we always did. It meant a lot to both of us."

While Chip was in Wichita Falls, Dr. Gravelee was great for him. Then, months later, we had a friendly visit. I was thankful Chip had come in contact with a good psychiatrist who took an interest and cared enough to understand and know him. She and Chip were both good, down-to-earth people with a lot of potential. She understood and knew Chip.

It was months later, after Chip had passed away, when I talked with Dr. Gravelee about Chip and related all he had gone through before being admitted to the hospital. We discussed the research I'd been doing about ADC symptoms being related to the AIDS complications. Before I ever read about ADC I mentioned to her that I suspected that in time they would learn what Chip had gone through in the beginning had to do with AIDS.

Dr. Gravelee said, "Knowing him as a patient and as a person, I would be inclined to believe, even not having done all the appropriate examinations at the time. But from what you're telling me and what I'm hearing about symptoms and history, it sounds more to me like a brain dysfunction. There are all sorts of brain dysfunctions that can occur from physical illness. Some of them have neurological-type symptoms, such as dementia and other behavior disorders. Some of them affect thinking, memory, speech, or any part of the brain can be affected. Of course, this is an opinion after the fact, but I think certainly we were dealing with some organic, as opposed to emotional, dysfunction that resulted from damaged brain tissue or something going on in the brain. You have enough evidence to speculate that there was brain dysfunction going on because of the behavior that was occurring and given the knowledge you're getting later that there may indeed be some neurological-type syndromes as AIDS advances."

I commented, "Dr. Hope, what I don't understand, while all this was happening he was always so good to me, no matter what frame of mind he was in. Sometimes I find this hard to relate without confusing others."

Dr. Gravelee stated, "What you're saying is, besides the fear and confusion and everything that was happening with him, he was able to maintain his love and his relationship with you."

"Yes, how could he have done that?" I asked.

Dr. Gravelee related to me, "Because it was very important to him, I imagine. It was so important to him that it could override anything else that was happening. He may have been terrified and frightened and felt alienated or out of touch with reality, but it sort of helped him hold onto his reality."

When I told her about what happened in California while he was waiting for me, Dr. Gravelee gave a sigh of amazement and said he was retrograding. I am thankful Dr. Gravelee was there for Chip as a psychiatrist and his friend.

The day after we brought Chip home from Wichita Falls we called Gramma. While he was talking to her I was on the extension. It was hilarious listening to them, especially when he told her about Wichita Falls.

"They told me to sign some papers and I could get out in three days. I told them, 'I don't want out in three days, I want out now. What are these papers? I don't understand them.' And I wouldn't work with them. So, they decided to screw me to the wall." Chip heartily laughed.

Gramma teased, "I know, they wouldn't even let you mop floors, would they?"

"They would not let me do anything! It was really wild, and all those crazy people. I could handle them. None of them really bothered me, except the first day I got there. Some Mexican spit on the floor and I said, Don't be doing that crap!' He got up and knocked the hell out of me." Chip chuckled.

"That was an experience and a half, wasn't it?" Gramma laughed.

"Ohh, that was a trip, it was, it sure was!" Chip laughed.

Chip and Gramma talked awhile longer. I didn't say much, only laughed. It was like when he was little, always laughing.

Chip was under doctor's care on an outpatient basis when he came home, even though he wasn't having any more confused behavior. Yet he wasn't able to communicate with the new counselor. Once, upon her suggestion, Chip took me to one of the meetings. I immediately saw that she wasn't doing him any good.

Soon after that Chip decided he would go to the Oak Lawn Counseling Center in Dallas where his lifestyle was understood. I agreed that was a wise choice, especially under the circumstances.

Chip was sleeping a lot and wanted to be left alone. Occasionally he would make comments indicating that he didn't want to live. I reasoned with him that it was understandable with all he had gone through, but reminded him of the long way he had come.

I said, "Remember Chip, you're a survivor. You don't give up. You've been through some bad times over the years and you've always pulled through. And you will this time too. You know Jerry and I are with you and we want you up and on your feet. That's what counts."

"I know, Mother. I hate putting you through this hassle."

"Nonsense, you know better than to think that!"

Chip had a downcast expression while I reasoned with him, trying to do away with any negative ideas.

"This past episode has just been toying with you, Chip, keeping you a little more on your toes." I laughed and added, "Even me. We've both been to California and back a couple of times recently. Then you were gallivanting all over Texas."

"Yes, I know," he said with a slight chuckle as a smile crept over his face. "It has been wild!"

With Chip feeling the way he was, I didn't like leaving him for long. I continued working, but not like before. In my profession I set my own pace, which normally meant many hours. I would leave the house with several things to do some days, but I couldn't stay away for long, wondering how Chip was. Before I knew it, I was home again making sure he was all right. Even though he insisted on being alone, I felt I must be with him more than he may have wanted. He needed to know I cared how he was and to know I was available to listen.

I didn't believe Chip would attempt anything. Yet these past months had taken a terrible toll on him with all he had been through. I lived with the constant worry and fear of never knowing. I wanted to be near, even more, with all the humiliation and hard times he was facing. Just the thought of him thinking about taking his life was terrifying and constantly on my mind.

Another time I reasoned with him, "Chip, I understand how and why you could feel that way at times, but I also know you, and you could never do that."

"I know. I really couldn't."

"Suicide is something people don't want to do, even those who succeed. Somehow, someway they will always try to get a message across to be stopped. It's only if the message isn't received that they succeed."

A few weeks had gone by with Chip keeping to himself and sleeping more. He just didn't want to be disturbed. He seemed to be about the way he was shortly before he moved home with us. For several weeks he had completely withdrawn from everything and everyone, kept himself in the dark with his shades drawn and the door locked. When anyone came he didn't go to the door, nor answer the telephone when it rang. Even though I hadn't implied it, this was all the more reason I had wanted him to move back home, although as soon as he did he snapped right back and was fine.

One day when Chip was feeling under the weather and sounded like he was mad at the world during his withdrawal, he blurted out, "Maybe I have AIDS."

It didn't faze me until he explained what he was saying.

He said, "Not too many people know about AIDS because it's basically among gays in the States. They're hoping to eliminate them with it."

I was surprised, but it made sense because of the animosity there seemed to be about one's personal lifestyle. What he was saying hadn't made me think that that was what was wrong with him. Possibly he was wondering about it himself. If he was, he didn't say any more. If it had ever entered my mind, I must have unknowingly blocked it out because I later learned that denial plays a big part in any life-threatening situation.

Although Chip always tried to spare me any heartache, he shared both the good and the bad. He was the normal, average teenager who grew into a fine young man, enjoying life.

Several days later Chip came out of his withdrawal. He started moving around the house more. Then one day I asked if he would help me move a dresser. We hadn't carried it far when he suddenly turned pale, and I was afraid he was going to pass out. He never had before, but looked like he might, and it frightened me. I told him we'd better stop, but he insisted he was okay and we got it moved. I'm sure that must have scared him as much as it did me, even though he didn't comment.

It was great that Chipper had overcome his other personality and was himself again with his great sense of humor. Walking into his room and hearing his cheerful voice was enough to ease anyone's mind. We had a strong bond between us and enjoyed each other's company. You name it, we talked about it—health, dress style, drugs, sex, and life in general. We were friends as well as mother and son with a mutual respect and admiration, both willing to listen with understanding and optimism.

Chip was sensible and kept me abreast of his generation. During many of our talks I learned about things in the past, things he hadn't told me when they happened, such as the night he was going down the freeway and the wheel came off his motorcycle. Three years later, since he was driving his car, there wouldn't be any reason to worry me and he could lift the protective shield and let me know.

It didn't seem possible the summer of '85 was gone. Chip was becoming restless and bored, so he decided to go back to work since he had been feeling good for a few weeks. He felt fine until about the fourth day, then he began feeling terrible again. Still he insisted on completing the day's work. By the time he came home he was running a high fever and went straight to bed. It seemed the flu-like symptoms were with him again. Either he'd be having violent chills or was perspiring profusely. When he still wasn't feeling better after a few days, he decided to see the family doctor in Irving.

Dr. Tyska ran a series of tests, gave him a shot for the flu, and wrote a prescription.

When Chip returned for his test results, the doctor said his white blood cell count was extremely low. Chip asked about the possibility of AIDS. Dr. Tyska told him he would need to go to the Dallas Health Clinic for that particular test because it was the only facility doing the Human T-cell Lymphotropic Virus, HTLV III, test. There was a variation of names for the virus test, but today it's been given one name, which is the HIV test, Human Immunodeficiency Virus.

When Chip came home he told me he had gone to Dallas to take the HTLV III test. He said it was done anonymously, and he would need to return in one week for the results. If I had any idea of the seriousness of the test I must have blocked it out and refused to think about it. I believe all I was thinking about was getting Chip over the flu. No doubt Chip was terrified, wondering about the test results, but he didn't let Jerry or me know.

Looking back, I can imagine how he must have felt lying there already miserable, wondering if he was going to be the next gay cancellation. Why hadn't I realized what must have been on his mind? Hadn't he told me what AIDS was all about, getting rid of his sort? The only possible answer is that I canceled out the idea when Chip told me. Not that I hadn't listened, I understood what he had said, but I apparently didn't let it register. I don't have any other logical explanation.

It was about the same when Chip came home with the results. He said, "The HTLV III test was positive, which means that I have come in contact with the virus, but not that I have AIDS."

I wasn't sure what that meant even after Chip explained, but I didn't question him. The word "positive" scared me, but hearing the words "not that I have AIDS" relieved me, and I chose to believe that he didn't have it and would be okay. As open-minded as we were and the way we discussed things, I don't know what happened that time, or possibly from the start in California. These unknown complications seemed to put a devastating damper on our communication, long before we knew anything about them.

I remember Chip saying, "I wasn't going to tell you."

I replied, "I needed to know," and I believe we both lapsed into silence without realizing it, awestruck even though it was not AIDS. I didn't give it any more thought.

AIDS or death was not consciously on my mind. Still, Chip's getting well from the flu was my concern.

I knew Chip didn't want to worry me, yet he knew it was important for me to know about something as serious as AIDS. It wasn't something he could take care of himself, then tell me about when he knew I wouldn't be upset. If he could have concealed something that important without being unfair he would have, just to save me the heartache of knowing. I don't believe Chip would have mentioned AIDS to me the first time, if he hadn't been feeling so down and out and defeated about what was happening to him. Apparently AIDS was a new topic he must have been concealing from me, knowing the only outcome was death. No doubt AIDS was a fear he had been living with, knowing his lifestyle put him at high risk.

About a year earlier Chip had gotten shingles and probably would have kept it to himself if it hadn't become so unbearably painful. And wouldn't you know chicken pox was the only childhood virus he had besides the measles when a baby.

Shingles was a chicken pox virus that lay dormant. Apparently that is why he later suffered with shingles, from the nerve ends that were related to chicken pox he had when he was an infant.

Chip was a healthy child, full of vim and vigor. Still, in his young adult years, for some reason when an illness did pursue him it always seemed to be one of the more painful or of a rarer nature, such as kidney stones when he was only eighteen, which was rare at such an early age. The stones were so large he had to have surgery to remove the first one, and two other times a short time later, he passed the stones after much more pain and suffering.

Occasionally there was another frustrating, unbearable incident that had been happening to Chip the prior year that was never solved. Unexpectedly he would start having this terrible itching all over his chest, arms, and neck. His body would breakout in red welts while the pain and aggravating itching became even more intense and torturous. His natural reaction was to scratch himself for relief, but there wasn't any help while the nerve- racking itching continued for at least forty-five minutes to an hour. Chip was afflicted with no letup whatsoever until this perplexing battle finally ceased on its own.

In the beginning this happened while he was at the dermatologist's. The doctor had no idea what it was or what to do. Then Chip went to several other doctors, but no one seemed to know the answer or a cure for this unbearable, chronic itching. This happened at its leisure and subsided when it was ready after great length.

Of course, AIDS wasn't in our vocabulary at the time this happened. It was to be in the distant future years while I was talking with an AIDS patient that I learned this had possibly (or likely)been another part of the unknown AIDS plot.

When Chip returned to Dr. Tyska he told him the results of the HTLV III test, but the doctor didn't seem overly concerned. Chip and Jerry had gone to Dr. Tyska over the years the few times they needed a doctor, and we thought surely he would have said something and not been so casual if there was reason, after he heard the results. Instead he continued to treat him for the flu.

Chip was making repeated trips and paying a small fortune each visit. Jerry and I began to wonder why Chip was going to the doctor so often and still feeling worse. Jerry decided to call the doctor rather than upset Chip with how he already felt.

Jerry frankly asked Dr. Tyska what he was doing for Chip, then said, "If you can't do anything for him, get us a specialist who can! He keeps getting worse and needs taken care of now!"

Dr. Tyska said he would contact a specialist and call back.

Jerry said, "Fine, if that's what it takes. He needs someone who can do something for him."

Within the week Dr. Tyska called and referred Chip to Dr. Blais, an infectious disease specialist in Fort Worth. I called and scheduled an appointment for the next day. Chip was extremely weak and the twenty-mile drive was a long ride in his weakened condition, but Dr. Blais was good and concerned. He also had an excellent black nurse, Alyce, who showed an interest in Chip's care and monitored his condition with great sincerity.

Dr. Blais ran many tests and took the time to check Chip thoroughly. He talked to him about his condition, then asked me to join him in his office. Until then I hadn't thought any more about the test Chip had taken in Dallas. What Dr. Blais told us was not good news, but his kind, thoughtful attitude helped greatly to soften the blow. He said Chip had ARC. He did not say AIDS, and he never mentioned death.

I honestly don't know if what Dr. Blais said actually got through to us or if we realized how gravely ill Chip was. Neither Chip nor I had heard of ARC, so naturally we didn't know what he was talking about until he explained it was AIDS-Related Complex.

Yet today my mind is still blank about that day. The doctor talked to me about Chip, but for some reason I didn't grasp what he was saying. While I sat in the lobby waiting for Chip, I didn't dream that he might have something this terrible. I thought a specialist would diagnose Chip's condition and restore him to health from what I thought was some sort of flu. I didn't realize it at the time, but apparently both Chip and I must have gone into shock, denial, or whatever else it could be called. I don't know. I don't know. I do know we were both exceptionally quiet during the long drive home. Even though AIDS or death was not mentioned, something must have happened to Chip and me that we didn't understand ourselves.

Looking back, we were both taking everything in stride as much as possible, yet there must have been an undercurrent that we were unknowingly left to struggle with.

In time, I came to understand that ARC could develop into AIDS and usually did. I learned that even i f i t didn't become AIDS, a person may still die with ARC. But I don't believe it registered with either of us that day. I remember that I was glad he only had ARC and not AIDS. I was sure he would pull through, no matter what, and eventually would be able to go on with his life and a career that had been developing so beautifully through his hard work and determination.

Chip's days were unpredictable. Many times all he did was sleep. Often when he woke up his entire body was soaking wet and his bed drenched with perspiration. Then he would be gripped by violent chills while his entire body trembled. I would stack the blankets three or four deep on top of his heavy bedspread.

Chip felt hot and feverish to the touch, yet he continued to tremble from the chill. There didn't seem to be any middle ground. It was either the chronic chills or chronic sweats. I was afraid to put so many blankets on since he had such a high fever, but he insisted.

I'd say, "But, Chip, you know all these blankets aren't helping your fever." "Mother, I'm cold!"

At first this often led to an argument. Yet what could I do to get him warm? There were times he trembled so hard that his whole body shook. When it was at its worst I would put my arms around him, pulling him close, trying to give some of my body heat. It would help, but never enough. God, what were we to do?

It was terrible and miserable for Chip. He would sit on a chair while I completely changed his bedding, removing the wet sheets and many times blankets to be washed. I'd hurry as fast as I could for fear that he'd freeze. This was a constant race. The trembling never seemed to cease. At times he shook so bad with chills he couldn't even light a cigarette.

Chip's whole life seemed to be drastically changing. He decided to go to the Oak Lawn Counseling Center in Dallas. He needed to talk with a professional whom he could communicate with and who would understand his disillusionment.

12

If It Hadn't Been for Gramma

Early the next morning I heard the shower water running. Chip must have been getting ready for his first appointment, which was in a couple of hours, at the Oak Lawn Counseling Center. He had been looking forward to this meeting ever since he'd spoken with them about his complications. He knew this would be someone professional he could confide in and be able to relate what he was up against with his recent staggering traumas.

Later when I went into his room he was sitting quietly at his desk, clean and refreshed, but he looked utterly exhausted as though the task of showering and dressing had completely drained him of all his energy.

"Mother, I thought after a shower I'd feel better, but..."

I could see the weariness in his face and hear the overwhelming fatigue in his voice.

"Chipper, if you don't feel like going, why don't you cancel your appointment? They'll understand."

As a rule, Chip kept his appointments, but he definitely looked as though he shouldn't be going anywhere. He sat silently, seeming too weak to move.

"Chip, you don't look like you should go. Why don't you call and cancel?" I encouraged.

He looked as though he were being pulled in several different directions all at once. I knew his attitude about commitments made it hard for him to break an appointment, and too, he wanted to go. After a few more minutes, although reluctant, he slowly picked up the telephone as if it required all his strength while he pressed the number. His downhearted expression lightened to one of relief. Then he called and canceled his appointment with the counselor he'd been seeing. He had such a drained look that I didn't want to leave him. I thought he'd be going back to bed.

Moments later he said, "Mother, take me to the hospital."

Stunned, I asked, "Do you want to go now?"

"Please."

Evidently Chip was debating this when he made his somber cancellations. I had no idea he felt this extreme, even though he didn't sound or look well. I hadn't even given thought of his going to the hospital and his announcement caught me off guard. For him to ask I felt there wasn't time to waste and I didn't even take time to get his things together. I knew the last few days had been like a nightmare. Then to cancel his appointment and suddenly mention the hospital cinched everything, making me realize how much worse he must have felt.

When he rose to his feet he could hardly stand up. I rushed to his side, putting my arm around his waist.

I said, "Chipper, put your arm around my shoulder and lean your weight on me. I will keep ahold of you around the middle while we walk. Okay?"

"Okay, Mother."

While we walked down the hall I asked, "There, how's that?"

"Fine," said Chip.

"With your height and my shortness, it makes my shoulders about the right height to lean on without difficulty, doesn't it?"

"Yes, but am I getting too heavy?"

"No, Chip, you're fine. You could lean even more. I know you're trying not to."

"That's okay, Mother."

Slowly we moved down the hall, out the door, and into the garage to the car. After getting Chip settled, I hurried back into the house and called Dr. Blais to let him know I was taking Chip to the hospital. He told me to stop by his office and get Chip's records to be admitted.

While driving down the freeway I glanced at Chip, saying, "I need to stop by the doctor's office to get your records. To save time and so you won't need to wait long, why don't I drop you off at the hospital on our way? Maybe they'll get you in quicker. Would you be okay by yourself until I get back?"

"I will." He nodded.

I knew the sooner he go t to bed the better. He looked so somber and tired as he stared straight ahead not saying a word. All of a sudden a terrifying thought flashed through my mind when I glanced toward him, He's not planning on coming home.

The idea scared me. I thought to myself, Oh God, please help.

I didn't understand why such a terrible notion had flashed through my mind. When we arrived at the hospital's emergency entrance, Chip seemed a little stronger.

When he reached for the car door, I asked, "Do you want me to help you go inside?"

"No, Mother, I'm okay," he said while getting out. Then I watched him move slowly toward the entrance.

I rushed to the doctor's office, where I was met by his nurse, Alyce, as soon as I entered. She handed me Chip's records and told me that Chip was probably eligible for Social Security benefits. Then she said I could have him admitted to the hospital across the street, where he could remain under his doctor's care. If only it had dawned on me what she was trying to say, but Chip's going to the hospital was so unexpected, and evidently I wasn't comprehending what she was saying, any more than I was familiar with the procedures and what was happening. I told her I had already dropped him off at the hospital because he was feeling so bad. If only I had waited.

She suggested I call Social Security and I might get things in motion. It seemed time was of the essence, so I used the doctor's telephone to make what I thought was going to be one quick call. Before I realized it I had been on the phone over two hours, being put on hold and repeating some of the calls I had already made. I felt like I had talked to everyone in Fort Worth by the time I discovered the necessary proceedings to put things in motion. I was worried about Chip, but felt I couldn't stop in the middle of the calls.

Looking back, I realize I should have taken Chip to the hospital Alyce mentioned, but everything happening was new to me and nothing seemed to register with me during that time. I imagine it was the confusion and scare of things happening suddenly and in such a turmoil. Still, I was thankful to Alyce for her kindness and making me aware of Social Security. Chip had worked for years and this would help.

I rushed back to the hospital and found Chip lying on a gurney, still waiting to be seen by a doctor. I was surprised he hadn't been given a room or that his temperature hadn't even been taken yet! There wasn't any way he could have sat up, and I was grateful he was lying down. Still, I wondered how they could keep him waiting on a hard gurney when it was obvious how worn out and exhausted he must be.

I stayed with Chip, waiting and waiting. The minutes turned into hours with no apparent concern. This was most perturbing. I tried to remain calm, knowing Chip was already miserable.

I told Chip how Alyce had told me about Social Security and the many calls I had made.

In his misery a smile crept over his face. "She's the greatest!"

I agreed with Chip. "Yes, Alyce was great with you from the start. She was so sweet and concerned, wanting you to have the best care. If it weren't for her, I wouldn't have given thought to your Social Security. Alyce is the best of nurses and a fine person."

Chip and I were both worried and wondering why he felt so bad and what was going to be done. My being there may have been harder on Chip, with him worrying about my comfort and the time it was taking. I assured him I was okay. But it was ridiculous and aggravating the way the resident doctors were messing around, wasting time in the emergency area.

Finally they got around to Chipper—slowly, but surely, and more slowly than surely. A doctor appeared, but then he was gone again and didn't return for a long time.

Finally I walked out into the hall to see what was happening. To my astonishment there sat the doctor who was supposed to be taking care of Chip! I stood only a few feet away watching him for a long time as he cut up and laughed with another doctor while the blank paperwork lay waiting on the desk in front of him. I didn't take my eyes off him and almost bit my tongue to keep from saying anything. At last he apparently got the message and started filling in the paperwork.

Would you believe the clock was nearing midnight when Chip was given a room? He had spent over thirteen hours on a hard gurney with me standing, leaning over him for a little support. If I was miserable and weak, how must Chip have felt?

Could all the wasted time have been because his papers said he had ARC? Was that reason to treat him like a victim rather than a patient? If so, what happened to doctors' oaths?

I hadn't known Chip was going to be under constant supervision until he was given a room in intensive care. It scared me to learn he was much more serious than I realized. I believe it was a double shock, after the long wait in emergency with no apparent concern or care for his well-being all that time. Now I was pleased to know he would be under close observation.

Regardless, I was happy he finally got a room and could get a good night's rest, although he would need to make an adjustment in intensive care with the lights on all the time.

Then I was crushed to learn the dreadful part about the visiting hours in intensive care. Chip could only have visitors for fifteen minutes every three hours. I wanted to be with him longer and more often. I stayed awhile to make sure he was okay before I started home.

After that night there were many trips back and forth, as many as five times in one day since the visiting time was so short and stretched out. Other times I stayed at the hospital and waited in the lobby about two-and-a-half hours between fifteen-minute visits. It was either drive the forty miles round-trip every couple of hours or stay all day in between short fifteen-minute visits. It didn't matter as long as I could be with Chip. I wanted him to know I was always there.

Jerry and I went to the hospital first thing the next morning. We had to wait outside of ICU a few minutes because of an emergency. The door was kept locked so no one could enter for that very reason.

ICU was a large room with the nurses' station in the center. Each room was almost all glass on the side toward the nurses' station so they could easily view the rooms. Chip's room was in the far corner from the entrance. He saw us when we approached and forced a bit of a smile. Outside his room I seemed to be all thumbs while I hurried to put on the gown, mask, and gloves.

Jerry said, "Calm down," as he tied my gown.

We hadn't been told anything yet, but I sensed time was important with Chip. It was as though I were living on pins and needles from that time on.

I hurried on in while Jerry was putting on his garments. Chip looked a little more rested. I leaned over the bed rail, giving him a hug and kiss.

"I love you. How you doing. Chipper?"

"Okay."

"We came as soon as we could. You know, they have a fifteen-minute limit on our visits and only every three hours. I will come every time though. Fifteen minutes isn't very long, but you can rest that way. Okay?"

When Jerry came in he commented, "It sure is bright in here. Did you sleep okay?"

"Some," Chip said. "It's like being in a fishbowl, not knowing whether it's day or night with the lights always on. It was hard on Mother yesterday! She stood all the time I was waiting to get in. The assholes were so slow!"

I didn't want Chip to be upset, so I chimed in, "It's okay, Chip, at least we got you in here and that's the main thing. Now you have to get well and come home."

Then I told Chip, "We have to wear these gowns, gloves, and masks when we're with you so we don't give you any of our germs. You can't give us anything, but if we're not careful, the slightest thing would be bad for you." I added, "And we sure don't want to make you any worse!" I clenched his hand a little tighter, giving him a great big smile and added, "I love you."

Chip smiled and said, "I love you, too."

Fifteen minutes sure wasn't long. It seemed as though it was just enough time to get all covered up with the garments we had to wear and then time to get them all undone and off again.

On our way out we stopped at the nurses' station to talk with Chip's new doctor, Dr. Douglas, who was an attractive, young female intern. She was very pleasant and seemed to be thorough and good with Chip. I was surprised when she told us Chip had pneumonia and they were running more tests. I told her to be sure and call us any time Chip needed us.

I called my sister Ruth to let her know Chip was in ICU and she called Mother and Dad to let them know. After telling my family what was happening, I felt I needed to call Maryland. I hadn't spoken to Chip's dad in years and at the time I didn't care to. From past performances he hadn't been the father Chip needed. Still, that was no excuse for me to neglect my responsibility. I must make the call for Chip's sake. Chip hadn't said anything, but I thought it would make him feel good. So I prepared to call.

I called his dad's sister in Baltimore and her husband answered the telephone. I told him everything about Chip and his being in the hospital. This was Chip's aunt and uncle who had always been great with him and made his trips to Maryland worthwhile, even when the efforts failed with his father. Then they gave me the oldest sister's number in Cumberland, who lived closer to Chip's dad. I called and told her Chip's condition and let it up to her discretion if she wanted to tell his dad because I wasn't sure of anything with him anymore. But he was his dad.

Chip's dad called later and asked, "What's with Chip?"

When I told him about Chip's being in the hospital and what had been happening, he seemed concerned. I told him Chip was in ICU and I felt his contacting Chip would make him feel good. Our conversation was brief and he said he would call the hospital.

I mentioned, "He may not be able to talk since he's in ICU, but I'm sure they will tell him you called, and that will no doubt help."

A couple of days later, Chip's aunt (his dad's sister in Houston) called the hospital. She was a nurse and I imagine she was making the call for her brother to assure him of the situation, along with letting Chip know she was thinking of him. Chip hadn't seen her since he and Beth last visited in their home for a few days, years ago.

Chip was still weak. I continually prayed and talked to God. Daily, Jerry visited Chip with me, then while he was at work I went alone. I was there every visit, as I told him I would be.

The second evening while I was with Chip I noticed the monitoring screen was going wild. His temperature had jumped to 1045! It scared me. I didn't want to alarm Chip so I calmly told him I was going out for a minute and would be right back. I rushed to the nurse and told her. She went into Chip's room and immediately covered him with an electric ice blanket. The room was already kept extra cold because of his steady fever. The ice blanket looked like a heavy padded piece of insulation about five feet long and two feet wide with a cord going to a refrigeration unit.

I waited, keeping an eye on both Chip and the monitor, watching for his temperature to go down. I waited for what seemed like forever, until finally the numbers started slowly lowering. Once they started dropping more, I thought they would continue. Then the nurse said it would take awhile for his fever to go lower.

Minutes later I suddenly felt what a long day it had been or maybe the previous day was starting to catch up with me. Whichever, I was astounded to feel complete exhaustion all at once!

I hated to leave Chip, but I felt sure he would be alright. I gave him a hug and kiss, telling him Jerry and I would be up to see him early in the morning. Then I took off my gown, gloves, and mask as I wearily headed toward the door.

Jerry and I went to the hospital first thing the next morning. As we approached Chip's room we were shocked to see a mask on his face with all kinds of tubes and wires attached to him, many of which were coming from a big machine by his bed. And still more tubes were going down his nose and throat. Seeing the monstrous machine with his nose and mouth covered scared me.

I hadn't expected anything like this! My first thought was, Why does Chip have on a mask? I thought we were the only ones who needed to wear them. This was new to me and I was astounded, not sure of what to think or expect.

Dr. Douglas came over about that time and let us know Chip's temperature had soared to 106.2! And he had stopped breathing!

I was terrified to think a false security had come over me and I'd left believing his temperature was going down. Instead his temperature had gone back up again! It hurt knowing he had stopped breathing, and I wasn't there. Too, it was shocking to know they had put the respirator on Chip to do his breathing. To know he was now on a life machine was frightening.

Dr. Douglas told us Chip had been very short of breath prior to his high temperature. Chip said he couldn't breathe and was wearing out. Hearing this I thought back to Chip with the paper sack on our trip home from California; now I understood. Chip was wise to have known what he was doing.

Thank heavens they were able to bring him back. What if he hadn't come to the hospital when he had? Oh God, what was going on? I could only be grateful he was here. Yet this was a life machine and it was only his second day in the hospital. All the tubes and the mask on his face scared me, but it wasn't as bad as we thought. Then again it was! Oh God, am I ever thankful Chip asked to come to the hospital when he did.

Jerry and I talked to Chip even though he wasn't able to answer. He was obviously miserable as he lay helpless looking up at us. He'd gag and choke every now and then as he fought the discomfort of the tube in his throat. We were devastated, not being sure of anything, except the awareness of his discomfort.

I held Chip's hand saying, "Chipper, if you hear me, shake your head." But his head didn't move.

So I said, "If you hear me, squeeze my hand."

I waited, but no squeeze. I tried again and again, but didn't get a response. Chip looked so lifeless and not getting any reaction frightened me. It was frightening to see him lying there, knowing I couldn't do anything to help. This visit they let us stay longer.

Still I was afraid and hated to leave him when our time was up, but I knew we were tiring him out more.

Smiling bravely, I gave him a kiss and said, "I love you, Chip. I'll see you in a little bit. We need to go now so you can get some rest."

After taking off my gown and gloves, I went back to Chip's bedside and took his hand in my bare hand, raising it to my lips and kissing it. Then I bent over the bed rail as I stretched to reach him with another kiss on his forehead. Gently touching his cheek with a reassuring smile, I softly whispered, "I love you, Chipper," and backed away almost at the brink of tears.

Ruth called us at the hospital to tell us Mother had made flight reservations and we were to pick her up at the airport later that day. Meanwhile my brother Duane and our stepmother were driving Mother's car. Ruth had called and told them how critical Chip had gotten and they immediately decided to come and be with him. I hadn't expected Ruth to tell them the seriousness of Chip's condition, yet I hadn't called anyone because I was concentrating solely on Chip. I appreciated her taking care of everything and was glad Chip's Uncle Duane and both his grammas, from Indiana and Michigan, were coming. Even though Chip wouldn't be able to go gallivanting around town with them as usual, he'd love the wonderful surprise.

Neither of Chip's grammas had seen him for several years, but he had always been the "apple of their eye," so to speak. It was dreadfully heartbreaking for them to suddenly learn of his illness. Of course, Uncle Duane was always there when needed.

Again, Rhonda and Darlene were coming to see Chip almost every evening.

Jerry and I went to the DFW Airport to get Mother when her flight arrived. I felt relief that Mother, who was my greatest ally, had come to be with us. On our way to the hospital I told her Chip was on the respirator.

I said, "Mother, I keep trying to get Chip to squeeze my hand or blink his eyes, but he doesn't seem to be able to."

I clued Mother in on how we must wear masks, gowns, and gloves when we're with Chip to protect him because his immune system is so low and he doesn't have any resistance. While I was telling Mother, she fought to hold back the tears and every so often turned her head away with a painful, sad look in her eyes. Talking about Chip and seeing her sadness and the tears about to drop at any moment made it more difficult to control my own emotions. Before I knew it we were both crying our hearts out.

Between sobs, Mother said, "It's a good thing you have Jerry. He's a good man." Wiping her tears, she laughingly said, "Now he'll have to put up with two cry babies for awhile."

Half crying and half laughing, I said, "Yes, but he keeps getting pains in his side. I think Chip may be getting to him more than our crying could."

Mother exclaimed, "Oh, really?"

"Yes, his pains just started since Chip went into the hospital this time. I have a feeling it's nerves because it didn't bother him until then, but he won't go to the doctor now. He said we need to take care of Chipper first."

Jerry tried to change the subject by telling how upset Chip was when I took him to the emergency and had to wait so long.

"Yes, Mother, I'm pretty lucky to have them. They're good at spoiling me."

"Yes, Kitty, you sure are! They are both so good to you. And Jerry, you take care of yourself. You don't want to wait too long and maybe end up with an ulcer," Mother said.

We arrived at the hospital just when visiting time started. Chip was only allowed two visitors, but since Mother had come from out of state and with Chip so sick, we were all allowed to go in. While we put on our gowns, masks, and gloves, I reminded Mother that Chip wasn't responding, because I knew it was going to be hard on her. Mother was like me, rushing to get everything on so she could get in to see Chip. He was lying there watching us, with no expression or movement whatsoever.

When Mother walked in and cheerfully greeted him, Chip's eyes opened wide, like big balloons! Grams went over to Chip and took his hand, giving him a kiss. Smiling, she started asking him questions, which he surprisingly answered by moving his head up and down or back and forth!

Jerry and I couldn't believe our eyes! We looked at each other and he squeezed my hand while we happily smiled, watching the two of them. Seeing Chip and Mother together "talking" was definitely a blessing. Chip was responding to Grams with big, exaggerated movements of his head. It was as though he remembered what I had been trying to get him to do and what he couldn't seem to do for me, he was doing for Grams! Such big, fast movements! Oh, what a blessing. Her coming was the best thing that could have happened, exactly what he needed!

Grams hadn't been with Chip long when she removed her gloves, saying, "I want to touch you, Chip," and she took his hand and squeezed it. Smiling at him, she said, "Okay, Chip? Hove you very much, and loving you means touching you too."

Chip blinked his eyes. That blink of love was a wonderful expression from the bottom of his heart. I'm sure. God bless him! He hadn't seen Grams for almost eight years, and here she was! If it hadn't been for Gramma I truly believe he would have passed on.

The next day his other gramma and Uncle Duane arrived. That made Chip's day! It was almost unbearable for them to see him suffering, knowing there was no way to relieve his discomfort. But their love prevailed and I'm sure they were the best medicine in the world for him. Both of Chip's grammas and Uncle Duane had always had a strong bond with Chip and a great admiration for each other.

Chip's dad had contacted the hospital again during the time Chip was critical, and the doctor reported his condition and suggested he visit Chip now. Still, Chip's dad would not come. It was upsetting Chip to know that he'd only call. For Chip's sake, it was agreed that he wouldn't be told about his dad's calls anymore; but it wasn't necessary because he didn't call the hospital again while Chip was there.

The next day the specialist in infectious disease came in while Mother and I were with Chip. He said it wasn't necessary for us to wear the gowns, masks, and gloves. I was surprised, but glad. Even though I wondered, Why not for Chip's sake? We soon discovered that it depended on who was on duty during our visit.

In the beginning of the AIDS epidemic, people wore the gowns, masks, and gloves for their own protection. When they realized it wasn't spread by casual contact, only by blood and other body fluids, they felt it was necessary to wear gowns, gloves, and masks for the protection of the patient whose immune system was at high risk from the slightest germ that the individual visiting him or her might transmit. I didn't understand, but apparently Chip wasn't at risk since he recovered from pneumonia.

The doctors didn't seem to know anything definite about Chip's complications. Nor could they seem to grow a culture from any of the many attempts. Still, Chip was continually undergoing test after test.

The thermostat in Chipper's room was purposely set at 60 degrees in an attempt to help regulate his body temperature. He only had a light sheet over him and the thermal ice blanket on most of the time to help keep his fever down. Still he continued with a high fever up to 104 and 105 degrees. His body shook uncontrollably while the disease ravaged his young body. During my short visits, I was extremely cold and numb. I wondered how Chip's body was able to withstand this. It didn't seem fair, but the doctors must know best.

It was almost a week before Chip was relieved of the tube in his throat, and on the eleventh day he was taken completely off the respirator. It had been such a scare to see him hooked up to that big piece of equipment while it monitored his vital signs and breathed for him.

Chip didn't have much of an appetite. Often I found his tray ice-cold and untouched, the food still covered and wrapped. Since the doctor stressed it was imperative that he eat, I felt if the nurse had been doing an adequate job she would have attempted to feed him or at least unwrap his food. He didn't have the strength and at times he had a tendency to eat on the spur of the moment. Even though his appetite was usually null. I'd try to feed him and sometimes he'd take a couple bites.

Chip's two grammas drove home together after being here a week. Duane decided to stay a little longer to help with Chip when he would come home from the hospital. Later I learned they were also concerned about me. Really, I did fine as long as Chip was okay, which was unpredictable. Still, I felt sure he was going to be okay in time.

A couple of times while I was at the hospital late at night the nurses were concerned about how I was doing. I appreciated their concern, yet inside I resented the fact my son was dying and they were asking about me. I thought, My son's lying there dying why are you asking about me? It really hurt and once I confronted them, saying that it was Chip I was concerned about, that I would be fine. I honestly felt that way.

Chip wasn't progressing as fast as I was hoping so I decided to surprise him with a visitor I was sure he would be happy to see. I called his friend Ray in Houston. They hadn't seen each other in a couple of years, but at one time he had been a special person to Chip and that's what he needed. If he could perk Chip up it was worth a try. On second thought, Ray was whom Chip had gone to see before going to California the last time.

Ray said he would leave immediately and should be at the hospital in about five hours. I wanted to surprise Chip, so I didn't tell him. I arrived after Ray's visit, just as he was entering the lounge, where we greeted each other. Ray said Chip was asleep when he arrived. When he woke up, Ray already had his mask on and was in the process of putting on his gown and gloves. Ray said Chip hadn't recognized him until he walked into his room and started talking. He immediately recognized his voice and tears came to Chip's eyes, and his, Ray confessed.

Ray said, "We had a good cry together, and then we talked."

While Ray was telling me, tears smothered my eyes. I was happy that Chip had finally been able to let go of some of the long pent-up emotions.

"That's the best thing that could have happened to Chip. He hasn't been able to cry. He needed that," I told Ray.

Outside of visits from Chip's family and good friends, his days in the hospital proved to be fairly miserable and unpleasant. It was a mixture of many things, no doubt worse than necessary because his lifestyle had become common knowledge since he had gone into the hospital with ARC. Before this his life was a private, personal matter and never a problem. People always respected Chip and admired him, knowing the good, decent person he was. This is what was important, whether he be sick or up and walking.

Dr. Douglas and most of the nurses were great and treated Chip as he was accustomed to. They were professional without indifference and saw Chip for the gentle, sick person he was.

While in the hospital Chip wasn't in any condition to tell what was happening to him, but later it was heartbreaking to learn how unfair he had been treated by two of the nurses chained with his care. It was crude and unnecessary torment for him to suffer the prejudice added to the agony produced by the loathsome disease. This is what I was saddened to learn later

Chip said, "One of the nurses put my bed pan where I could not possibly reach it, making it necessary for me to call her when I needed to use it."

He said, "I would say, 'Come, come now. I have to go.' She knew I was having diarrhea and when I had to go, I had to go. There wasn't any stopping it! So, of course, she wouldn't make it in time and I dirtied all over myself and the bed. I hated that. I felt so bad and humiliated. While she would be cleaning up, I would say to her, 'Sit the bedpan right here so I can reach it and it won't happen.' Then where did she sit it? At the other end of the bed. Why did she put it where I couldn't reach it? It happened again. By now the nurse was getting angry and taking it out on me because she had to clean up the mess again. I don't think she cleaned me very well. She said she did, but it didn't feel like it to me. It happened again. Needless to say, I couldn't reach the bedpan at the other end of the bed and by now I was crying. I was mad. That happened several times.

"I kept telling her, 'Leave the damn bedpan right here where I can reach it! I won't bother you and you won't have to clean me up and I won't have to be humiliated!' She and I never got along."

It seems common sense the nurse would have understood, or was she intentionally being vindictive? Wasn't it obvious Chip had no control over the diarrhea and his suggestion was made to help both of them?

They ran many tests daily on Chip. One of the most painful was when they did a bone marrow biopsy.

Chip said, "That was miserable and I wasn't given anything to help with the pain."

They had taken blood from Chip so many times that eventually they couldn't get it any place except in his groin! The nurse told me earlier how much more painful it would be taking blood from his groin.

Chip agreed, "That was horribly painful. Even before that, taking blood from my arm was painful the way the nurses kept poking and poking, trying to find a vein."

"Chip, I'm so sorry. You've always had large veins; and to think much of this is being done for future resources to help others. Then to think a nurse can be that crude is a shame," I replied and excused myself in a hurry so Chip wouldn't see how upset I was becoming.

I returned a few minutes later after I had cried my heart out thinking of Chip and people being vindictive.

I could only imagine the discomfort he was going through and didn't understand why it was necessary to continue. The human body can only take so much. It seemed they were bleeding him dry.

Another atrocious experience Chip went through was when a nurse, without warning, woke him in the middle of the night.

Chip said, "She didn't tell me what she was going to do or any thing, which naturally made it worse. She started putting lemon juice down my throat and at about the same time, she started shoving tubes down my nose. She kept jabbing all the way down to my stomach. I couldn't believe it! I cried, it hurt so badly. Then she pulled it back out and said, 'Oh, I didn't get anything.' I said, 'Oh, great, what does that mean?' Thinking, Here it goes again. Oh, damn it! Sure enough, there she went sticking her tubes down me—all the way down to my stomach again! I couldn't believe it was hurting so bad. She pulled it back out and said, 'Oh, I didn't get any.' I asked, What does that mean?' There she went again with those tubes. By that time, I was bleeding—really bleeding bad! tasked the nurse for a towel or something. She gave me one lousy little Kleenex! Then she pulled the tubes out of my nose and ran out of the room hysterical. I can't do it, I can't do it. Ooh, I'm sorry, I can't do it.' I thought to myself, Damn bitch, I know you can't, but don't get upset on my account.' Needless to say, I didn't see her again."

Chip said, "Apparently she was trying to get stomach juices. Evidently I hadn't processed much at the time."

I was furious, sad, and heartbroken to later learn of their insensitivity. To think I had put trust in their profession.

Chip said, "A life machine ruins everything—your mind and your mobility. I did remember you and Jerry, though. Remember when you gave me the pencil and paper?"

I smiled, saying, "Yes, you remembered. It was hard, but you wrote those three important words, I LOVE YOU.'"

Chip heartily chuckled. "Barely."

Our talking about the respirator brought back all the memories of how hard it was for him to respond, let alone write, the day he motioned for a pencil and paper. It was awkward, but Chip persisted and lightly scribbled those three little words, which gave us all strength and hope.

It was during the night when Chip had a heart-to-heart talk with one of the nurses. Apparently there was no communication gap since they were about the same age.

Chip said, "I woke up and there was this real pretty nurse in my room. We started talking.

"The nurse said, 'Chip, you've got something that's terminal. You are your own person.'

"We talked for a long time. Then she said, If you want to get out of this hospital, tell them, "I'm leaving." She told me, 'At least you'll be doing what you want. Even if you die on your way home, it's what you wanted.'"

That seemed to be just the nudge Chip needed. In optimistic relief he announced, "I did and it worked!

"I summoned the doctor and told her I was going home. She tried to convince me not to go, but I had my mind made up."

I was surprised to receive a phone call at three o'clock in the morning from the nurse, saying Chip wanted to come home, but I was delighted she called and was soon on my way.

Chip was about to be surprised with some real challenges.

He said, "The assholes wouldn't even help me get dressed. I guess they figured, 'Well, if you can't get dressed, you're not going anywhere.'"

Chip chuckled, "I did it. I could barely sit up, but I put on my blue jeans. I put on my socks and shoes. My mobility was poor. It was hard to move my arms and legs so I could get dressed. I called the nurse in and told him to take the catheter out. They took a long time deciding to do it, but finally did and I was ready. I was ready!"

Chip was in good humor while he told this and was excited to be going home. Even if it meant dressing himself, one way or another he would do it.

He said, 'I had everything out. I buzzed the doctor, and said, I am ready to go now. Now!'"

He sighed with a big grin.

He was overwhelmed when he started to step from the bed to the floor, saying, "I couldn't walk! I had to totally learn to walk. They put me in a wheelchair and I guess they figured, 'Well, let him go home and die if that's what he wants.'"

Chip said, "Well, I guess it was the wrong time for me to go home and die because, you know, at home it was 'party down city.'"

With Chip's perseverance, months later on a tape he was all heart telling about those hospital experiences. With Chip's empathetic attitude and being a good sport was unbelievable knowing what he was up against, but that seemed to be the story of his life.

I went after Chip at three o'clock in the morning, but the paperwork took much longer than we anticipated and it was mid morning before we left the hospital. It sure proved to be "lucky 13" for Chip to have insisted upon leaving the hospital on his thirteenth day.

In the hospital Chip hadn't actually gotten any better and was steadily going downhill. If he hadn't come home when he did, chances are he may never have. If it hadn't been for Cram ma he may not have survived the life machine. Love prevailed.

Before we left the hospital, they told me to call the visiting nurses if I wanted them to come to our home. A couple days later I called to ask a question. Their only concern seemed to be how I would feel about Chip's dying at home and whether I could handle it.

I assured them I'd rather he pass away at home than anywhere else, but I didn't understand their questioning that. Now it's more clear. When I talked with them they were evidently expecting my call and already had the idea that Chip wouldn't live long.

I wasn't thinking about Chip's passing on. I brought him home to get well. We weren't talking about death, although we understood there was a possibility. We had always been positive, and Chip had always been determined. So why should we be any different now?

As Chip said, "It wasn't time for me to go home and die."

Still, he made a long, steady series of trips to the hospital every week after he came home, for close follow-up observation. I was beginning to wonder why they were only giving him limited supplies of medicine, causing the trips to be more frequent.

One day I asked Dr. Douglas why he wasn't at least given monthly prescriptions. About the time I asked her it dawned on me, possibly it was because they didn't expect him to live much longer. So then I asked if that was the reason.

Dr. Douglas said they were surprised with his improvement.

Even when I asked her that question, I didn't contemplate the possibility of Chip's dying. He would get well, I was sure. Before he had left the hospital and after he was home, they continued treating him for TB. Dr, Douglas kept telling us they didn't know for sure which kind of TB Chip had, that they were still running tests and weren't able to develop a culture yet. She told us if he had one kind of TB they could treat it, but if he had the kind that was AIDS-related—which was M-Avium Intracellular Tuberculosis, known as M-Avium or MAI—it would be hard to treat.

Still they couldn't seem to get a conclusive culture from the many tests. We were apparently kept in the dark, possibly because there was so much they didn't know at the time.

It's a coincidence that Chip was taken completely off the life machine his eleventh day and went home from the hospital the thirteenth day to continue life, just as I'd been in the hospital years ago and regained consciousness the thirteenth day to continue life. Neither of us was expected to survive. Seems number thirteen meant survival for both of us.

It seemed unfair after all Chip had been through, the devastation and confusion of the past few months, to still not know what to expect. At least he was home where he was surrounded with our love and attention, which was the best medicine for him.

Jerry and I decided I wouldn't work full-time, if at all. I could set my own pace and Chip would come first. I wanted to be home to take care of him.

I had no idea what a lonely, ruthless road lay ahead for Chip. At the time we weren't expecting to come to the end of that road. We knew AIDS could be in the picture, yet I don't believe Chip, Jerry, or I actually focused on AIDS. We were aware that chances were great he might end up with it (or possibly already had it because little was known about this at the time). Still we closed out all negative thoughts and concentrated on Chip's survival.

There was very little literature available on AIDS or ARC because it was all too new. It was up to Chip and me. Chip was a pioneer on his dreadful journey. Together we learned through experience about what might happen at any time, never knowing what lay ahead, but always praying it wouldn't be a repeat or be anything worse. There still didn't seem to be any hope while he continued to suffer and develop complications. We had been told that you can die with ARC or AIDS, yet we weren't consciously letting that sink in.

I would say Chip was possibly facing AIDS and the fear was constantly with me, but I wasn't accepting the fact that my son's life was almost over. Down deep I never really admitted his life was coming to an end, even though the fear was constantly with me. Maybe I never did accept it all the time he was sick. I'm not sure. If I had, I don't believe I could have held myself together. When they said he had "possible AIDS," I held onto the word "possible" and dismissed AIDS. Too, I was believing it was TB—not AIDS-related TB.

Chip assured me, "Mother, you're strong. You'll be strong."

I kept telling myself I was strong, and with Chip, I was. Chip made me strong. Yet I couldn't sleep. I didn't sleep, nor did Jerry. Our sleepless nights turned into months.

The thought of Chip's being gone was devastating beyond belief. I expected to pass away before my son. He had been my life, and I never dreamed he'd go before me. This young man, once my little boy, was what kept my world alive all these years. Then to think. Chip's young life was just beginning to shape up through his perseverance. On earth life can be unfair, and it certainly was a challenge for Chip.

13

Party Down City

As Chip had said, it was "Party Down City" when he came home from the hospital. His twenty-sixth birthday was only one week away. Then the holidays followed in quick succession: first Thanksgiving, then Christmas, New Year's, and Valentine's Day!

Heartily Chip chuckled. "Well, I guess it was the wrong time to come home and die. It was Party Down City and I had no choice but to get well."

Chip's perseverance and good sense of humor prevailed, although the real nagging, deep-down fatigue was always ready to pounce at the least opportunity as a means of defeat.

I was afraid this might be Chip's last birthday and wanted to surprise him with the best party possible. Since partying hadn't entered my mind until he came home, I needed to make some quick arrangements—and for Chip, I somehow would. Although he was in no condition to be partying, I felt he needed something to take his mind off the negative. If he hadn't much time left on this earth, why not let him go enjoying life? Perhaps one might say his life was already over.

His future seemed dim not knowing what he would be going through before the final day or when that would be. If it was AIDS, there was no hope, no cure; it was fatal. Still, we didn't know definitely what he had.

The day of Chip's birthday came, and because this party was a surprise I couldn't decorate ahead of time. So when Ray, his friend from Houston, and another friend. Shannon, arrived they took Chip to Dallas for awhile. I was usually organized, but when the other guests started arriving I still didn't have the house decorated or the punch made. I hadn't planned it, but everything worked out even better when the guests pitched in and the preparation was fun for everyone. This was like the good ol' days with several of Chip's high school friends.

When Chip returned home he was surprised to hear everyone shout, "Happy Birthday, Chip!" Then to see balloons floating everywhere and a "Happy Birthday, Chip" banner made everything a special delight!

The party was going along great. It was getting late and it was apparent Chip was getting tired, when suddenly, there was a knock on the door. The last guest had finally arrived. To Chip's surprise he was a doctor!

Chip was seated in a chair in the middle of the living room and the doctor proceeded to check his heart with his stethoscope. Then the doctor stood Chip up several times, but Chip kept falling back down. I was becoming worried because he did look weak.

Then the doctor personally handed Chip a telegram from Strip-O- Gram! He was the stripper and the show was on! It was hilarious to everyone, including Chip. He livened up and loved it!

On the cake I ordered Rhonda suggested, "Happy Birthday, Chip, 26 and Still Sexy." And naturally, "Welcome Home" was included.

The next day Chip's face was all lit up when he happily said, "That was one of the best parties I've ever had! It was great with Uncle Duane, Ray, and everyone else here."

Chip was continually running a fever, having profuse cold sweats and chills, along with constant diarrhea. I took him to the hospital for routine tests every week, and oftentimes twice a week, that included drawing blood every time. Daily I counted out numerous pills that he was taking on a regular basis.

I was still grasping at the idea he would be okay. Several attempts had been made to develop a culture so they could diagnose what Chip had. They hadn't been able to develop one and so far they hadn't reached any conclusions from the bone marrow biopsy either. I was under the impression that if they couldn't develop a culture, then it must not be AIDS.

I didn't want to believe that the son I loved with all my heart, who had always been a big part of my life, might all of a sudden have AIDS. No, not Chip! I couldn't lose him. I wouldn't. I was prepared to do everything I could to keep him alive. I was most thankful he wanted to come home when he did. Chip was swift and always seemed to be ahead in doing what was right. Now I must make the most of his days on earth. He deserved the best. He deserved even more than the best. If only, without a doubt, he could have been told he was going to be fine.

I talked with God every day, all the time. Now I needed him to help my son get well. If he didn't, I knew there had to be a reason. It's just that Chip was so young and he wanted so much more out of life. Why must it end now? Why?

Then I turned my thoughts to God, Oh, please, God, keep Chip alive. Please don't let him suffer. I don't know much about all the different complications, but I will do all I can to help Chip. He is what I have been living for all these years... him and my husband. You can call it selfish, but I want to keep both of them. I love them both very much. Why must I give Chip up? God, all these questions keep going through my mind and I know I'm not supposed to be questioning at a time like this, but I can't help i I.I only want the best for Chip and maybe the best would be for him to be there with you. He wouldn't be searching for a love anymore if he were with you, God, and it would be all right then. I would understand. I really would. Even if I must give him up, it would be okay if I knew it was going to be better for him. Oh, God, I am so sad, so afraid, so brokenhearted. I know Chip feels that way too. I hate his feeling that way more than anything. To see his face while he lies here suffering is heartbreaking. It is so unfair to him! I can't help but believe that. Why must he suffer like this? Here I go again, asking questions and maybe they're the same ones I've already asked. I don't know. All I know is that I love Chip very much. He is on my mind twenty-four hours a day. I don't sleep. I can't sleep. I keep wondering about him and worrying. God, please don't let him go through any more of the pain, as he has been these past several weeks. He's had some terrible pain and feels miserable. Please, please, God, help him. Please help me to help him. Please help me to make his life a little easier, if at all possible. Even being sick he is still kind and considerate, not wanting anyone to do for him. He's trying not to bother me, but please, God, let him know it's okay, that it's what I want to do. He knows I don't mind. Yet he doesn't want to burden me. How can he be so sick and still so gracious? His attitude isn't any different now that he's sick than it was when he was well. You understand, God, why I'm so thankful you gave me such a fine son. Even if his lifestyle was to be different, it didn't make him any different. He was and still is as decent and respectful as ever. He is such a rare type of person and I'm so proud of him. I can understand why you would want him back so soon. Still, I'm being selfish for the same reason. Forgive me for wanting to keep him. It's just that I love him so much and life would be so different without him, I'm afraid. Thank you, God, for listening to me.

Chip's birthday always marked the start of the cheerful holiday season. We were a close and traditional family that celebrated birthdays and holidays in a special way. After Chip moved out, when he came home we always planned for them to be extra nice. This year Chip's friends from Houston came for the festivities on Thanksgiving Day and again on Christmas, which made it especially meaningful to Chip.

When Chip came home from the hospital he was extremely weak and needed a lot of rest, but had shown a great deal of improvement, which helped to lift everyone's spirits tremendously for Christmas. When Christmas arrived we still had Chip's birthday decorations up, with more Christmas decorations inside and out, and the Christmas tree was cheerfully decorated and brightly lit.

We only had snow one time that year, and it didn't stay on the ground very long. Still, we had "old faithful," Chip's snowman, out front, snow or no snow. Jolly Snowman was like the typical snowman Chip had made in the snow when he was a little boy back home in Indiana, but he had gotten this plastic snowman for our snowless winters in Texas.

Jolly Snowman had button eyes, a carrot nose, black buttons down his belly, a black hat, and a plaid scarf, with a twig for the mouth to make a big smile. The only difference, this was a large, heavy plastic snowman about five feet tall, rather than one made of real snow, which would melt, and there was a light inside to brighten the night.

Chip enjoyed lots of snow before moving to Texas, and even though snow wasn't a sure thing in Texas, Chip could always depend on this particular snowman every year! One of his favorite pictures was taken of the first snow we had in Texas after we had lived here a couple of years. The snow was a couple of inches deep and softly covered our swimming pool almost completely. It was rare for Texas to get that much snow. When I look at that picture I always remember Chip admiring it, then chuckling as he remembered his cousin the winter before in our pool, and saying, "I bet Lisa would agree that is a better picture than the one we have of her last winter in the freezing water. Remember?"

Laughing, I said, "Yes, I'm sure she'd agree. She would much rather see the snow in the water than herself, thanks to you and her husband! Even now I can see her standing by the pool cringing while the soppy, cold water ran off her drenched body and clothes. That was terrible! I felt so sorry for her."

"That was wild!" Chip chuckled.

"It sure was." I laughed, then reminded him, "You all ended up in the pool before the day was over, didn't you?"

"For sure! Lisa caught me off guard later that day!" He laughed. "Then together we treated her husband."

It was apparent from all of Chip's nice gifts for his birthday and Christmas that his friends weren't putting him on a "time limit." I'm sure that made Chip feel better, and their love and concern inspired him. He needed that more than anything to help cope with what he was going through. From Baltimore, he received a large bunch of helium balloons from his cousin Debbie and a lovely bouquet of flowers from his Aunt Mary Lou. These naturally enhanced the mood for his party.

Chip tried to play the piano from time to time, but it was tiring for him to sit very long. Jerry was good at surprising him with the appropriate gift, and he delighted Chip with an electric keyboard. Somehow Chip seemed to finagle me into slipping up, and before I knew it he'd know what I'd gotten him.

Chip enjoyed the keyboard's being light enough to hold on his lap with his bed raised to lean back. Chip wasn't the only one who liked this. His little two* year-old nephew, Aaron, would go into his room, turn on the keyboard, and then with a grin hand it to Chip. Of course, little Aaron had to climb upon the bed to sit on Chip's lap to make beautiful music like a live orchestra to his heart's content. Chip tired quickly, even though he was patient and hung in there as long as he could for little Aaron's entertainment

Chip often took extra time with little kids, the same as he did older people, and came up with super ideas for them. This year, even though weak, he devoted much time to a small, tedious project for Aaron's Christmas. He took a roll of quarters and individually wrapped each one, then laid them in a path like footprints leading to little Aaron's gifts under the tree.

When Dustin, his four-year-old nephew, lived with us, he went everywhere with Chip. Being a little guy, he loved entering and exiting through the sunroof of Chip's sports car. When he wasn't working Chip gave him lots of time and attention, as a father would. It was apparent they thought the world of one another. They were a good team. Chip only wanted what was best for Dustin, and he was especially concerned when Dustin had to leave our home, where he had so much undivided love and care from everyone.

The real kicker came months after Chip's illness when we got a long-distance phone call from Dustin, asking if Chip had gotten bit by a mosquito. I was surprised he asked that question, knowing the latest rumor on the news was about AIDS being obtained from a mosquito bite. At Dustin's young age of seven, he no doubt didn't fully understand what he was talking about.

At an earlier date I had already been alerted when my visiting youngest stepdaughter. Candy, said, "Mom said he probably has AIDS."

This happened in the beginning when Chip was being treated for TB and I wasn't willing to believe his TB was AIDS-related. After Candy's remark, I wasn't about to confirm her comment with the devastating fact of possible AIDS, knowing the animosity she and her sisters were raised with, although when in our home they got along together.

Vaguely I said, "Candy, people die from all sorts of things!"

When Chip and I touched upon the subject of the mosquito, and the apparent animosity and disregard from his (three) stepsisters, Chip said, "They're probably glad I'm dying."

We looked at each other in dismay. Chip shrugged his shoulders and I nodded my head.

I solemnly said, "That's a shame about some people and dying when you're made aware of their attitudes and the apparent control of their surroundings. You're all near the same age, and each of those girls knows how thoughtful you've always been regardless of their circumstances. They couldn't deny that. You've always helped them some way or another." I sighed. "Such a difference in character!"

Chip said, "I understand, with Cindy being back there (in Indiana) and with her mom's influence about my gay lifestyle, how she would feel."

"I know, Chip, but look at all you've done for her over the years! It's never been a problem with her in our home, even though they have a different lifestyle than we do. That derogatory letter she wrote to me speaks for itself. It was unbelievable, with no standards whatsoever. There isn't any way you would ever do such an immoral act to her about her mom or anyone she cared about, by mail or verbally."

I didn't want to perturb Chip further and needed to set the idea aside.

I said, 'I'm just sorry this pathetic memory is what she's left you with, Chip. Where washer common sense?" I questioned, then concluded, "With her animosity it didn't matter."

Chip's only comment was "Consider the source."

I agreed. "That's true, what can we expect? Makes one wonder, maybe in their next life..." Then the subject lay dormant.

We lived separate lives, but when they were in our home they were expected to live according to our standards.

Chip really would have made a great father. It's sad knowing how much he wanted a child, yet he knew he never would have one unless it could be done by artificial insemination, a method Chip had seriously started to contemplate. Of course, he was still young.

Chip and I never had a problem talking about his lifestyle.

Once he commented, "Mother, you always told me I shouldn't get married before I was twenty-six. Maybe..."

I understood what he was saying and I was firm on the idea. I always told him, "You're still young and there's plenty of time. By then, you'll be ready to settle down."

Then we tossed the issues back and forth of what may or may not be, of what could or couldn't have been. Chip was always popular with the girls, so why rush it? Enjoy life!

"I felt you should be at least twenty-six because of what we went through when you were little. Evidently your dad wasn't ready. We should have waited. I'm sure he loved me and we definitely wanted you. Chipper. Even at your young age, you're more responsible. Still, I just didn't want you going through that."

Then we'd get off the subject, giving one another a gesture and smile acknowledging what was meant, but not to dwell on things.

This time, though, during Chip's sickness he said something that surprised me.

"Mother, before you had me, Dad was the one to get all of your attention. Then when I was born you gave attention to me and he wasn't used to that." Chip continued, "When I was little I thought it was my fault you and Dad got a divorce."

Shocked, I exclaimed, "Chipper. No! I had no idea you thought that! I wish you would have told me back then. It certainly wasn't your fault! Your dad was used to having his own way. But you certainly weren't to blame! By all means, you never caused any problems. Chipper, I had no idea you thought that! Actually I shouldn't have listened to his mother in getting married as soon as we did."

I was almost in tears, but kept them back while I assuringly hugged Chip and tried to clear his concealed undue heartache.

When I withdrew. Chip shrugged his shoulders and very sincerely he said, "I've always thought that."

Then he continued, "Maybe I would have married at twenty-six."

He seemed to question that his lifestyle might change after that age. Could I have imposed twenty-six that strongly? Was this a possibility or only a predicament we'd wandered into? Then the topic was open for discussion, which always left a question in the air. I knew Chip thought it would make me happy if he'd many, but I assured him it didn't make any difference. I understood. In a way I felt he was better off single, knowing what life was like out there. He was sharp and we both believed "to each his own."

I said, "You always took care of yourself and never expected something for nothing. At least you didn't end up divorced or have kids that weren't loved and cared for by both parents." I told Chip, "Either life has its obstacles."

Once Chip had discussed marriage with a girl. Whether or not anything could have come of that was questionable also. I felt that whatever happened God was with us and we'd abide.

Years later, after Chip had passed away, Candy commented to me while calling from Indiana, "Now I know what Chip meant when he said. This is something I have no control over.'"

"That's right. He had no way of knowing until it was too late," I assured her.

Candy said, "When I was there you said he had TB and I figured he'd be okay. If I'd known it was more serious or terminal I could have helped you take care of him."

I answered, "At that time I wasn't sure and I was believing he had TB just like I told you. I didn't want to believe he would have anything that was going to end his life. And with the attitude you kids and your mom had I wasn't about to say anything to you. Especially after your comment saying your mom implied he had AIDS."

"I told mom I knew it was TB because I had gone with you and Chip to the TB clinic."

"You did. It's just that I didn't know what was going to happen back then. Not much was known and Chip was suffering so much. Nobody seemed to know anything, nor was much being said by anyone."

Candy commented, "I know he was having those real bad sweats and you had to get up and change his sheets and everything several times. I'd hear you talking to him during the night. That's when Chip and me were having our talks, but I didn't know. He didn't tell me. He probably didn't even know."

I answered, "That's when it was ARC and AIDS wasn't in the picture." Candy said, "I wish I had known. I could have come and helped you. I'm a nurses aide."

I replied, "I didn't know. Or remember then if you had told us."

Candy continued, "I wouldn't have cared what he had. I'm a home health aide, too. I've taken care of AIDS patients. I would have been there knowing it was long term even."

Even though it was during the early stages of Chip's sickness, Candy was the last of her family for Chip to have seen before he passed away. She was two years younger than Chipper and they had always gotten along although they weren't around each other much until she was older. The many miles often make a difference, and too, she was young and had her life.

Like Candy mentioned later, "if only she'd known." Even though things weren't said or done for Chip's sake while he was here, I'm sure Chip appreciates her thoughtful words.

Happy New Year 1986! Chip was still with us, thank God. It was bound to be a good year, even though his moving around was slow and his eating habits fluctuated as usual. But overall, he'd come a long ways since he'd left the hospital. I was content having him home and he was much happier. We were much happier!

"Happy New Year, Chip!"

"Happy New Year, Mother and Jerry!"

"Happy New Year! Are you ready for some more eggnog, Chip?" "Sure, that sounds great! I'll have a full glass!"

"Splendid! Three glasses of eggnog coming up!"

That was how New Year's Day started. Chip, Jerry, and I had been sound asleep when the new year arrived. It was a beautiful morning when we all awoke to enjoy a glass of the New Year drink.

Chip had wanted eggnog for New Year's Eve. I arrived at the market just in time to purchase the last quart they had, which wasn't enough, so I made more before the evening was over, trying to satisfy Chip's appetite. I was glad he had a craving for eggnog because his appetite still wasn't very good and this was a nutritious drink that satisfied him. Then I decided to keep some made up for him at all times. Chip always had a taste for foods that were good for him. Even before he became ill, he couldn't be coaxed into eating when he wasn't hungry, not even his favorite foods. I believe that's why he was always so slim. When he did come down with what we thought was the flu, he was on a good nutrition program designed to help him gain weight. He was up to 137 pounds and really looked great! Then he suddenly lost weight.

At times Chip would get angry with me because I kept coaxing him to eat. The more I tried, the less desire he seemed to have. After awhile I'd back off, thinking he'd come forward, but he didn't. Then I thought he was rebelling against me for forcing the issue. I didn't want to admit it or say anything, but I was afraid he might starve to death. I suggested his favorite foods and kept making things I was sure he'd eat. I thought at times he could eat, but just didn't care to, the same as when he was healthy. I didn't understand how the complications he suffered could affect his appetite as severely or as frequently as they did.

Still, the desire to eat wasn't present, although at other times he ate quite well. I had not been informed about what to do or what to expect, maybe because not much was known about the complications then.

Possibly, if the doctor thought he wouldn't live long, it may not have seemed necessary to say much. Still, Chip and I didn't give up and we learned pretty much on our own through trial and error. We were a strong team.

14

Stress Ventures Unknowingly

I continued driving Chip to the hospital for his weekly and sometimes biweekly checkups as an outpatient. There was always a long wait, which was most uncomfortable, frustrating, and exhausting for Chip in his already extremely weak condition. By the time we arrived at the hospital, he was already worn out from the long ride and still faced many hours of sitting on the hard, uncomfortable, chairs waiting his turn to see the doctor. It was ridiculous and too much to expect of anyone in Chip's condition! Soon we started taking pillows with us to lay on the chairs after we shoved them together to make a bed for Chip to lie on while he waited a minimum of half a day, usually into the midafternoon. Chip didn't feel right lying down while I sat on the hard chairs.

I told him, "Nonsense, honey, you need to be comfortable as we can possibly make you. You're too weak as it is, and tiring yourself out won't help how you already feel. I'm okay."

I hated that conditions at the hospital were so hard on him and silently fumed while we waited.

Even when he had an appointment we had a long wait to see the doctor, then another wait for the medicine and whatever tests they wanted done. Blood was drawn every time. Even more painful than having blood drawn were the attitudes of the nurses who drew the blood.

Chip said, "The nurses always made some sort of tacky comment. I guess it was because I had AIDS and they automatically thought, Oh, he's a fagot. They were pretty rude. Well, they weren't outright rude where they could actually get in trouble for it, but I think they came as close as they could without crossing the line. Really pissed me off!"

I was furious when I learned months later about how hateful the nurses were. Once I had suspected something was wrong when I came into the room because of the way the nurse looked at me, but Chip didn't say anything. If only I'd known then what was going on. In their profession what business did they have being malicious, regardless of the sickness or patient?

Ordinarily Chip wouldn't have a problem because there wasn't any reason to divulge his lifestyle. He was careful not to let me know when this happened, knowing I would have said something, and I'm sure he didn't want to put me through the hassle or what he thought might be an embarrassment.

I wondered if those nurses were as thoughtful with their mothers? At times like that I wish Chip hadn't been so overly protective. My well-being was his main concern, even though he was going through all kinds of torture and hell. I'd get Chip's medicine or do whatever I could to save time while he had his blood drawn, but evidently that's when I should have been there! My trying to save time was a terrible price for Chip to pay.

Finally after many trips to the hospital, which were wearing Chip out, I decided it had to stop. If only I had realized then what I do now, it would have been quite different from the start. When I think back I can't believe the things that I put up with. There was actually no need to have put Chip through the hassle. And to think I thought I was doing good. It was unfair for Chip to endure so much in his already humiliating predicament.

In retrospect I see that so many things could have been different if I'd only known more or maybe if I'd just given things more thought. Under ordinary circumstances I wouldn't need to be told, but I didn't realize that either. I didn't know how much I had been overcome by the perplexity of anxiety and how it was affecting my judgment or what I was doing.

I never could handle people's concern for me, even though I appreciated their thoughtfulness and always said I was fine, which I thought I was, even though I was on a tight string and this made me emotional. Chip was my only concern. I needed to take care of him and I wanted everything to be as good as possible.

Chip and I had been through hard times in the past and worked through them on our own, and we were determined we'd somehow get through this. We weren't about to give up or let things get the best of us. Chip helped me. His remarkable attitude and patience were amazing when it was obvious how exhausted he actually was. Fatigue was his worst enemy, plus loss of appetite; his frozen, numb feet; and of course, the never-ending distress. The procedure at the hospital was causing exactly that—fatigue and undue stress!

I spoke with Dr. Douglas and told her it was too tiring for Chip and it wasn't right to be putting him through so much. If there wasn't a better method for taking care of him, then I would take him to a private doctor where he would not need to wait. I felt it was crucial, with his nagging fatigue, and I didn't want his scheduled appointments prolonged.

I only wish I had confronted Dr. Douglas a lot sooner. I wasn't familiar with the pros and cons of what should be done. Dr. Douglas suggested I take Chip to the doctor who had supervised his care during his stay in the hospital. I had planned to take him back to Dr. Blais, but I lamely followed her recommendation, thinking that since that doctor knew Chip's present condition it might be best not to change. Now I realize we could have and should have gone back to Dr. Blais, whom Chip was seeing before he went into the hospital, the doctor Alyce tried to get me to stay with.

I didn't understand the procedures, but when Chip had to wait so long in emergency we should have changed hospitals and gone where Alyce had suggested. I can't believe I didn't do what I ordinarily would have under normal circumstances, meaning I would have pursued matters and made them right for Chip's sake at the very time I was told. To think Alyce was the only one who had gone the extra mile and tried to help, then I blundered things. She was a remarkable, considerate nurse, concerned about her patient. And she was always pleasant to me.

Chip made the switch. No more going to the hospital, but to the doctor's office. This was much better, but there were some adjustments to make. This doctor seemed to be negative about the overall situation of AIDS. We understood and knew there was no hope if it was AIDS, yet it seems the doctor would have shown some compassion and concern. At the time we still weren't told he had AIDS, only TB.

After leaving the doctor's office Chip would go to the laboratory in the same building for his various tests, and from time to time X-rays were taken.

Soon Chip was started on Lamprene and Ansamysin, which were trial government medicines. We were told everyone received TB medicine from the health department because it was the department's purpose to eradicate TB. This was all new to us and we went there next. They ran different tests and gave Chip some informative literature. He was already taking many pills, but was given an additional average of twenty more to take daily. This all confirmed my belief that Chip had TB, although we still weren't sure which kind.

Soon Chip's eyes became very sensitive to light and he needed to wear sunglasses all the time because daylight hurt his eyes so much. Then he started having dizziness from time to time.

There never was any medicine that could begin to conquer the fever that continually caused Chip problems and was one of his worst and most frustrating rivals. Once in awhile the medicine might start to slowdown the sweat process, but never sufficiently. Chip's bed would become completely soaked, including his pillows. Many times throughout the day and during the night he sat in a chair while I completely changed his bedding and put on dean, fresh, dry sheets, blankets, and pillowcases. Often I turned his mattress over. I don't know which was worse, the chills or the sweats. At times Chip would be helplessly freezing, with his body shaking while I stacked the blankets on him. Then he'd break out into a sweat, quivering and shaking so much he couldn't control the trembling. It was so hard to find a balance and seldom was there any.

Chip had been sleeping in his king-size waterbed, but eventually moved to the front bedroom where there was a trundle bed. This made it somewhat easier to manage with the heavy sweats causing frequent changing of all his bedding and many pillows.

Ever since Chip had come home from the hospital his feet were unbearably cold and numb all the time, causing him chronic, excruciating pain that was often intolerable. Chip had been home only a few days when in the middle of the night I heard a loud pounding on the wall and Chipper scream as he cursed in pain.

Frightened by his painful cry, I jumped out of bed and ran to his end of the house. When I got to his room I rushed to his bedside. He couldn't tolerate the severe pain in his feet, which had woke him. I sat down on his bed close to him and took a tight hold of his hands, feeling the pain that I could see in his face and aching body. I gripped even tighter, holding on until he was eventually able to calm down. Then he took a deep breath and sighed with relief as the pain lessened and became a little more bearable.

This was only the beginning of the pain I was to watch him endure, the beginning of my sitting with him helplessly watching, wishing I could do something to ease the pain and agony. But there was nothing more I could do except be there to wait out the suffering he had to bear while the stress ventured unknowingly.

When Chip wanted to walk he sat on the edge of his bed for a few minutes while he slowly edged his feet into his slippers. It was a horribly painful process. Imagine this being his nerve ends with the ice-cold, numb prickling while he tried to move his feet. Even though Chip was trying not to reveal his pain, I could see and feel the agony he must be going through while he slowly completed an otherwise normal process.

Once he had his feet in the slippers he would slowly rise, holding onto the bed to steady himself while adjusting to the pain. If I was there, he would hold onto me until he got his balance. Then he'd slowly shuffle his feet across the carpet, still trying to hide his expressions of pain and discomfort the best he could, although with each slight movement the torture persisted. There were times that I'd pretend I hadn't noticed how difficult it was so he wouldn't know the hurt I felt or what I was thinking, the same as he apparently was doing. Chip had a lot of pride and didn't want to appear helpless or vulnerable.

When Chip was moving about on his own he held onto the brass rail of his bed for balance. Once he stood and steadied himself, he would inch himself to the wall. Then putting his hands against the wall for support, he slowly shuffled his feet. The first hurdle was cleared; he made it to the doorway. Luckily the bathroom wasn't too far. Then he'd lean on the wall for support when he sometimes lost his balance, steadying his movement each step of the way. When he was coming to the kitchen, oftentimes I didn't realize he was even up until he got to the foyer, then I would hear his feet slowly shuffling the distance across the parquet.

This affliction is very trying and unpredictable. It robs the individual of his pride and dignity at every opportunity. Take the walking. Such a minor thing, but in this case, a horrendous obstacle course for the individual. Once Chip was up and steadied, he did alright as he slowly groped toward his destination and was able to move at a fairly steady pace.

Chip had attended an AIDS support meeting in Dallas. While there he talked with a person who had M-Tuberculosis. This was the first and only person Chip knew with the type of TB he might have. It was known to be a rare type of opportunistic infection. This patient told Chip what they were doing in California for persons with AIDS. He told him about a home he could go to in L.A. to be with AIDS patients. He only had to let them know his Social Security income, and he would qualify to stay there.

A week later Chip confronted me about going to L.A. He said it would be better for everyone because he was causing too much work for me and it was taking almost all my time caring for him.

I lovingly scolded, "Chip, I want to take care of you! When you came home from the hospital, I'd already decided I'd stay home with you. You certainly aren't too much work! How can you say that? I love you and this is where you belong. I like being with you and doing things for you. This is your home."

"I love you, too, and that's why it would be better if I went to L.A. Mother, it isn't fair to you!"

"Chip, it is too!"

I pleaded with him, but he had his mind made up, saying it would be best for everyone.

"When I called about going they told me it would be good for me to be around other patients."

Hesitant, I said, "Maybe. That part might be good, but I'll miss you."

I really wasn't keen on the idea at all, but Chip wasn't about to change his mind. So all I could do was let him think I thought it was okay. I didn't want him to leave hurt or upset with me. I assured him I was ready to take care of him any time.

I dreaded his going to California. At present he appeared somewhat better, yet he wasn't. He tired very quickly. He was able to walk although it was difficult and painful, taking so much of his strength to go only a short distance.

Then I had a horrible fear of his dying at any minute, ever since I'd heard it could happen suddenly or unexpectedly. This was a secret fear that hounded me twenty-four hours a day, every day, ever since I'd heard this actually happened to an AIDS patient who seemed to be doing better, then he suddenly died.

I was so afraid of Chip's passing away and my not being near. I wanted to be with him when his time came. But with him in Los Angeles I wouldn't be near, only talking with him on the telephone. Of course, Jerry and I had already been planning a trip and I would go every so often to see him. We wanted to be close for Chip and for us.

I was concerned as we took Chip to the DFW Airport, but I couldn't let him know because I understood this was something he had to do. He had pride and that determination I admired and respected. Whether or not I agreed, this was his decision.

When Chip arrived in L.A. he was surprised there wasn't anyone to meet him, especially in his condition. He was completely exhausted from his flight, and the long walk in the airport had worn him out more.

He hailed a taxi to take him several miles to a motel, where reservations had been made for him to spend the night.

When Chip arrived he was having respiratory problems. Then the clerks couldn't speak English very well and Chip was in no mood to cope with the lack of communication. When he saw his room at the motel, he was even more disappointed and couldn't believe he had been sent there. The bed was sunken in the middle and extremely uncomfortable. There was a television, but no remote control, and in his condition it was most inconvenient and frustrating having to get up to change channels. Then he needed another blanket because of his chills, but had a terrible time communicating. He didn't sleep too well and had a restless night. He was up early and called the place he was to go to and let them know he wasn't coming. He was going back home!

It hadn't been twenty-four hours when Chip called from L.A. and said he would be home in a few hours. I heard his exhaustion over the telephone and went to the airport early to be there when his plane landed. When I saw him coming down the jet bridge he looked extremely weak and worn out, but it was such a relief having him home.

I hated to learn of the hassle Chip had gone through in such a short time, but knew it was something he had to do. That was one time he decided California wasn't the same. Just like his life wasn't the same and never would be anymore was utterly sad. He was facing the realization of his life and I'm sure the disappointment was difficult.

We arrived home and once we were in the house. Chip went directly to his bedroom. He sat down on his bed and quietly looked around.

Then he graciously said, "Mother, it sure is great to be home! I don't know why I wanted to leave all this. My room is so nice. My bed is the most comfortable I could want, and I have my remote to the TV and VCR right at my fingertips. You and Jerry. Everything I could want!"

Pleased with his happiness I commented, "I'm sorry things weren't any better for you. Chip, but I'm sure happy you're home! I'm just glad you weren't gone any longer. This is where you belong, honey."

Chip was so sweet and looked content while he lay on his bed. I gave him a hug and soon he was sound asleep. I loved him with all my heart and hated that he had to go through that terrible ordeal, but I understood and was thankful he was home again.

One day Chip's dad called and Chip told him how his feet were bothering him. He told Chip he would buy him a certain kind of shoe at a store in Cumberland that would help his feet and make them feel a lot better. That was great of his dad to offer to get Chip something he desperately needed and we hadn't been able to find. But they were never sent, nor mentioned again.

Chip liked his dad's idea and would have appreciated them, but from past experiences he hadn't got his hopes up. Still the shoes his dad had mentioned sounded like they could help or would have been worth a try. Even if he had told Chip he couldn't find them, it would have been the thoughtful gesture that counted rather than a forgotten memory.

At Christmastime Chip had gotten a card from his dad, but the only writing was the family names—no mention about his illness, his birthday, the hospital, or even how he felt now. No, nothing! He hadn't even called on Chip's birthday or any of the holidays. It added a dark cloud to what Chip was already facing, knowing his dad didn't do or say anything, let alone come to see him.

That card was the one thing I regret giving to Chip. I had no idea how it would turn out and it was something from his dad that I could not deny him.

Chip softly said, "Dad didn't even say Hi' or sign it."

No matter how Chip tried to hide his hurt, I could see he was devastated as he lay quietly for the longest time with his eyes sadly wandering afar, not knowing how his dad could still be distant, especially now when he needed him.

Chip still wanted to see his dad, but he would only call on the telephone from work every now and then. Had his dad forgotten those trips Chip had made to see him? Wouldn't it be the logical thing to be with your child whose life was ending? Whether those were or weren't Chip's thoughts, he'd finally had enough when he announced, "I don't want to talk to Dad when he calls!"

"Are you sure?" I asked.

"Yes. He hasn't come to see me." Then he angrily added, "He doesn't need to play the martyr role with me."

I could see how deeply hurt Chip was and I understood. I silently wondered. Was his dad only calling to clear his own conscience? How could he expect his son to feel, doing this to him? I just wanted Chip to be sure, but I could see he meant what he said and shouldn't have questioned him. Chip always thought things through and wouldn't say a word until he was sure of his decision. Then he would hold firm on what he had said. He made it clear and I respected his choice, and his firmness.

When Chip's dad called the next time, I told him what Chip had decided. It was important for Chip to see his dad. I suggested he make the trip, but he said he couldn't take time off work. Where was his dad's benevolence? Still he continued to call every so often. He knew Chip wouldn't talk to him, so I'd listen. I believe he needed someone to talk to. If only he would have come to see his son. That was all

Chip wanted. How could he not know how heartbreaking this was for Chip to be lying there hour after hour, thinking and wondering...

One time when his dad called and we talked, I said, "Its our fault this has happened to Chip."

His dad replied, "Yes. I know it is."

I honestly was surprised he agreed, although down deep I don't know how he could help but feel that way. Knowing his dad I felt sure he realized it. Even now I knew he loved Chip. Still, what powerful hold was keeping him from his son? Why was he only calling from work, or why had he only called when he was away from home over the years? Evidently, just like now.

One time when Chip's dad called, he said, "I would rather be in Chip's place than to have him going through this."

At the time I didn't comment. After I hung up I started thinking about his remark. It was some time later when his dad called again.

During our conversation, I said, "Remember the last time we talked and you said you would rather be in Chip's place than for him to be going through this?" After a pause, I added, "If you really meant that, then why aren't you here? Even if it meant your life, you would be doing what you said you wanted."

He didn't comment and I said, "Even if it's only for five minutes, Chip needs to see you."

He said, "I can't come. Someday I'll tell you."

His coming wasn't going to hurt him because of Chip, he knew that. He knew he had no reason to fear AIDS from Chip. I never pursued his coming anymore. Just like over the years, it was up to Chip and me.

It's just a shame his dad never came forward to know what a proud father he could have been. He never gave himself a chance to know how fortunate he was to have such a fine son. If only he had opened up his heart over the years, there was so much he could have learned from his son and grown with him, the same as I had. Chip certainly made our life richer. I am sure it could have made a world of difference for his dad and Chip.

15

Sentimental Heart

"Happy Valentine's Day, Mother and Jerry!"

Chip was in great spirits, coming into the kitchen while we all exchanged greetings.

"Wow, Chip, you sure look nice! Looks like you're ready to go out on the town all spruced up," I teased, seeing him dressed in jeans and a white shirt, "but I see you still couldn't get your shoes on."

While looking at his feet I added, "I wonder if we got you a size larger if that would help."

"Maybe, Mother. These slippers were all I could get on." He paused, thinking, then said, "But I'm only going to the store. I'll be back in a little while. Need anything?"

"No thanks, Chip. I go t every thing yesterday. Next time I go to the store, I'll get you some Reeboks a size larger. It's worth a try."

"How about you, Jerry?"

"No, Chip. You take it easy."

"Chip, you sure you don't want Jerry or me to go with you?"

"No. I'll be alright. I'm only going down the street. See y'all later."

Chip had been doing pretty well. He wanted to do as much for himself as he could without our help. I had a feeling he was much weaker than he was letting us know. He would go for a ride every so often just for something to do, but he wasn't going to Dallas nearly as often because it was so far and he tired so quickly.

Chip had been gone a couple of hours, and I was becoming concerned. Then I heard him pull in the driveway. Jerry and I both went out to meet him. He handed Jerry a lovely heart-shaped cake with scrumptious-looking white frosting, trimmed with fluffy red roses and hearts.

"Looks good, Chip. We'll have to hide this from your mother," Jerry teased. Chip grinned while reaching for another package.

I asked, "Chip, are you okay? You look exhausted."

While he was getting out of the car, he said, "It did take longer than I planned, but I wanted to get y'all something for Valentine's Day."

"That was really sweet, Chip, but I wish it hadn't been so hard on you. How are your feet?"

"About the same," Chip said.

"Maybe we should have gone with you."

"That's okay. I wanted to go by myself. That's probably the last time I'll go shopping."

"Chip, you'll feel better after you rest. I'll bring you in some Haagen Daz, if you'd like. Yesterday I bought some strawberry, knowing it's your favorite."

Chip smiled and said, "Thanks," as he headed toward his bedroom. He did look like he had overdone that trip, but it was important to him. I'm sure he would have gone, no matter how he felt, especially after hearing him say that no doubt would be his last time to go shopping.

Hearing that remark was frightening, even though we lived daily with the fear of death. And I'm sure with the way he felt, it was a message that it was only a matter of time, because there didn't seem to be any way his tired body could make it another year. He'd already lived much longer than anticipated. And I believe he himself had expected to be gone long before now.

The holidays and birthdays were even more intense. I hadn't realized in the beginning, but I was using them as a crutch to encourage Chip, as something to look forward to. I believe he was also doing this or had an idea I was.

A little later we were enjoying the delicious cake Chip had gotten. Then Chip surprised me by sitting a snow-white "Applause" teddy bear on the table in front of me. It sat ten inches high and had big dark eyes that looked as though it were listening. In its ears and on the bottoms of its feet were velvet red hearts, and in his chest pocket there was a soft, cushiony, red velvet heart attached to a gold strand.

Chip was reaching over to the bear's pocket when he said, "Mother, when I'm gone and you want to talk to me, take this little red heart." He pulled the heart out of the bear's chest pocket and handed it to me, saying sincerely, "Just rub it, and we'll talk."

I looked up at his smiling face as he stood so tall beside me and smiled. I instantly understood his genuine message and my heart fluttered. Several days ago (without thinking) I asked Chip an unfair question, and it must have bothered him just as it had me.

I asked, *"Who will I talk to once you're gone?"*

This is what must have taken him so long. Even with his miserably cold, numb, aching feet, he had to find the perfect gift. The "sentimental heart" truly was perfect! He knew what I meant, how very much I loved him and how I was having a problem about losing him, even though I was trying to conceal it as much as I could. That question had been nagging me for a long time before I blurted it out, and I'm sure that's why Chip's last time to shop was important, regardless. He wanted to assure me I could still rely on him.

Chip was routinely seeing the doctor, and the visits were still dreary and difficult. He was already under enough stress not knowing what to expect, let alone having to endure the doctor's stoic attitude and not being the least bit informative. He hardly spoke, even when asked. Chip was averaging thirty pills a day in medication, sometimes more. Blood was still being drawn every visit, plus various new or repeated lab tests were being done.

Even though we still hadn't been told whether or not he had AIDS, we still feared the likelihood of the diagnosis. Nevertheless, deep inside I wasn't accepting the idea. They had tried several cultures, but still none had developed. And above all I was banking on this being in our favor since they couldn't seem to develop a culture. I believe I knew better, but perhaps I was grasping at straws.

One day Chip let me know he was going to ask the doctor just what he did have when he saw him again. I believe the fear of being "told" (it was AIDS) left me speechless, and I didn't comment.

During the next visit when we were about to leave the doctor's office. Chip asked, "What do I have?"

Impassively the doctor bluntly announced, "You have AIDS."

Chip was devastated, as though his world had dropped out from under him.

In dismay he said, "You mean someone gave this to me?"

"Yes," the doctor replied with not even an ounce of compassion. I was astounded and angry he was so heartless! I didn't say anything, only listened while the hurt and anger intensified.

I snapped, "You haven't got the culture back yet, have you?"

With no apparent sense of feeling, he replied, "No, but we know it's AIDS."

I couldn't believe he could disclose such information and not say another word, to be so callous! Chip opened the door and walked out.

I was furious while I continued to glare at the doctor in disbelief of his cold manner, that he could treat any human being this way. What was this doing to Chip? My anger fought this new pronouncement. He didn't have a culture back yet to be so positive. What was he basing his facts on? Above all, I was angry with his lack of tact. True, we knew the possibilities could culminate in this diagnosis, but to actually hear the words was like a piercing knife. It was disturbing enough without his provocative attitude. This had to have crushed Chip. I opened the door behind me and left. I needed to be with Chip.

I realized it was possible and probable for Chip to have AIDS, although down deep I may not have been accepting the reality of no hope, knowing AIDS did not have a cure. If you had AIDS, death was the only answer and there wasn't any way of knowing when it would happen or what to expect. Not much was known, nor being said about AIDS at the time. We had been told Chip had TB that might be AIDS-related; now without any reasoning or explanation, it was AIDS.

Chip had gone for lab tests to another floor, where I joined him. After a few minutes, he left. He didn't come back. Puzzled by his disappearance, I decided to go looking for him.

He was down the hall and around the corner sitting on the floor, leaning with his back against the wall and his knees hiked up in front of him. I saw a little boy sitting there lost in his thoughts with such a desperate, forlorn look. Bewildered and alone. Oh, God, it was terrible! What could I say? I was at a loss for words while the thought permeated my mind, apparently as it had Chip's.

After a few moments I said, "I wondered where you were."

"I told you I was going out in the hall."

Maybe he had or maybe he thought he had, more than likely he had, but at any rate I guess I hadn't heard him or my mind wasn't thinking.

I apologized, "Oh, I'm sorry. I didn't hear you."

It was as though the world had cascaded down on him. He was devastated and in profound thought.

Moments later he announced, "When I get home, I need to call some people. I need to let them know."

In silence I nodded. Where are words at a time like this?

On our way home we didn't say much. We were stunned and speechless while gravity seemed to be pulling us homeward. To think about the possibility of having AIDS is one thing, but to be told you have AIDS was a death sentence with no recourse, no appeal.

When we arrived home, without hesitation Chip went to the other room to make the calls delivering the reluctant news. How hard that had to have been, to deal with the fact that his life was now limited in all facets now that he had been diagnosed with AIDS. Apparently he was doing fine with the phone calls until he called California, then he seemed to have received a setback.

Chip came into the living room where I was, and in a voice of anger and alarm, he said, "Neil has AIDS! His lover died from it."

I don't remember my comment or if I did, only that I was astounded. Neil was supposed to be a friend! I knew this had struck the same cord with Chip and myself.

Chip had a perplexed look on his face when he went on to say, "He didn't even mention it to me!"

I could imagine the shock that was to find out Neil hadn't complied according to ethics or even as a friend while Chip was in California with him. Where were his scruples? Then to think, that's why Chip called him. The calls Chip was making had to be difficult, but he knew they were necessary.

Jerry didn't believe Chip was going to die. In fact, he never did accept the fact that Chip had AIDS.

In the beginning when Chip had flu symptoms, Jerry was reluctant to accept the fact that Chip was as sick as he appeared.

Chip's being fine one day and sick the next or being tired so often and sleeping for long periods of time was questionable to Jerry, who wondered if Chip really was sick or just wanted to sleep. Of course, at that time we had no inkling of AIDS or what its primary symptoms were, such as this. Jerry knew Chip wasn't lazy, yet he was beginning to question why he was sleeping so much. This caused some conflict between us. Still, Jerry knew Chip wasn't one to cause friction. This illness in itself is deceiving. We didn't know at first, but in time to come learned that with this sickness you may look, and even seem healthy in between setbacks.

Chip was happy with our relationship and admired how well Jerry and I got along. Then when Jerry learned of the seriousness of Chip's condition, it bothered him. Still, he wouldn't believe Chip might have a terminal illness. Chip was his stepson, but Jerry had raised him like he was his own son since he was fourteen.

I'm only sorry we didn't change doctors when we realized what this doctor was like. I couldn't understand his attitude. With what Chip was facing he needed a good, compassionate, caring doctor.

One day Chip and I were sitting in the lobby waiting for the doctor. The only other person waiting was a salesman. Chip was feeling weak and exhausted when the doctor finally arrived. The doctor walked into the lobby, addressed the salesman, and they went into his office.

I couldn't believe my eyes! I was furious! Chip and I looked at each other. I know we were thinking the same thing, What the hell is he doing? Knowing Chip's condition, why on earth would he take a salesman in first and neglect a patient who he knew was in no condition to be kept sitting any longer than necessary? Damn, I was angry! So was Chip, but he wasn't in any condition to say anything.

I waited a few minutes, then went to the receptionist's window and asked in a clear, loud voice, "How much longer is he going to be?"

"He shouldn't be much longer."

Enraged I snapped, "I hope not! I can't believe he took that salesman in first! I'm about ready to walk right in there this very minute! If it's much longer, I will!"

I calmed down for Chip's sake. It was enough disturbance to have happened. Since Chip was already there, he wanted to see the doctor and leave.

At last Chip went in for his brief checkup. The doctor was closely checking Chip's skin, but as usual never said anything. Since I was the only one taking care of Chip, I volunteered information on different things that had happened, hoping I'd get a response. But the doctor didn't say much. I understood that whatever he was doing was normal procedure, but what I didn't understand was why he wouldn't relate things to us, at least what it was he was looking for. Later, I realized he was probably looking for spots. I didn't see any reason for Chip to have spots because he didn't have that kind of an infection, which was Kaposi's sarcoma, KS, a form of cancer. He had TB and I didn't think he'd get spots with it. It was as though the doctor was expecting them, looking for the longest time, and it bothered me although I never mentioned it. I didn't know then that you can go from one kind of infection to another.

Kaposi's sarcoma has existed for over a century. It is one of the commonly seen opportunistic conditions in AIDS. What I've been calling spots are tumors. To me, these often raised spots look like bruises in color and texture or maybe like blood clots surfacing. These lesions may appear anywhere on the body or membranes of the mouth, on the lymph nodes and internal organs. Usually there's no discomfort. Sometimes in final stages it can involve the lungs and other organs.

After I knew more about this I understood what Chip's doctor never explained and why he obviously kept checking as he did. I wouldn't have been so upset or afraid if I'd been told. Chip didn't get those lesions, nor did he ever get KS. He had Military TB (MTB), which was most likely secondary to Mycobacterium Avium-Intracellular (M-Avium or MAI) TB, plus other various complications.

We were only told he had pneumonia while he was in the hospital, but not pneumocystis which is most commonly associated with AIDS patients. There wasn't any evidence of pneumocystis on his lung biopsy. I believe this was also puzzling the doctors. I had the feeling that Chip was striking out on some of the symptoms they were looking for or expecting while he was in the hospital. Still, he was going through continually gruesome measures. Of course, with nothing being in any particular order and not much being known, it would be even more confusing and could only be a wait-and- watch situation. I wondered why we were left in the dark so often, although I understood there was so much they were still learning.

Chip had leukopenia, but I didn't learn that until later on in his hospital report. My Uncle Guy who was a chiropractor had passed away with leukopenia years ago when I was you ng. Too, it was a coincidence that with Chip's complications they were constantly checking his lungs for symptoms, and to know when he was only six weeks old we almost lost him due to lung congestion.

Jerry believed Chip had TB, but not AIDS. Many times I agreed with him. I would take Chip to the doctor, then go home and talk with Jerry about his visit. Before I knew it, with Jerry's reasoning things out it made sense and I'd agree with him. The doctor sure wasn't talking! I was so confused, believing and not believing. Down deep I was afraid it was AIDS, yet at other times I didn't believe it was. It was bad enough to be faced with the likelihood my son was dying, let alone all the other mixed feelings I had. Maybe that is why Chip was all the more devastated when he was told the verdict of AIDS because I may have convinced him the way Jerry had me. Not knowing or understanding, maybe we were not wanting to accept the idea of something with no hope. All these years our positive attitude and persistence had pulled us through many crises. What were we to believe? With AIDS we knew there was only one verdict—death!

In the beginning we were cautioned that it could be most harmful for Chip to catch our germs because his immune system had no way to fight them. Amazingly,

Chip never did catch anything from anyone, not even from me when I had the summer flu two different times. It was things like this that made me question what he really had because he was to have had an immunodeficiency. How could I have had the flu and it didn't bother him either time? It seems he would have gotten my germs if he had AIDS. And too, I remembered the doctor saying we wouldn't need to wear the masks and I related this as a plus for Chip.

The one time I was in bed for three days. I seldom got sick, but I was sick a second time that season. The first time I wouldn't go near Chip. I didn't know what I'd do if I caused problems for him. Yet I was worried about not being able to get out of bed and care for him. It troubled Chip, wondering if I was okay.

Finally he came to my bedroom and stood in the doorway asking, "Mother, are you okay? Can I get you something?"

He knew better than to get too close; still he wanted to help. The second time with the flu I could hardly talk, I was so hoarse. I was trying to keep my distance from Chip, yet there were things I needed to do. While I was in his room one of those mornings he sincerely said, "Mother, I really felt bad last night. I heard you coughing all night long and I couldn't do anything. I couldn't help you. I wanted to do something so much."

He was already suffering, and hearing him, knowing what he meant touched me deeply.

I couldn't restrain my tears and without thinking, I hoarsely cried, "Chipper, now you know how I feel. You're sick and I can't do anything."

Our helplessness was hard to handle and those various tender moments were most frustrating.

Actually if it weren't for what I learned about Chip's ADC symptoms (after Chip passed away), I may still be questioning many things about his complications and passing, even wondering if he wasn't convinced in his weakened condition or if he could have gone into remission.

Chip really helped me. He was weak physically, but his spirit was amazingly strong, especially for what he was facing daily. My instincts told me he wasn't going to let things happen to him mentally as they had in the beginning, if there was any way he could help it.

Not much was made public about AIDS when Chip was first told he might have the complications. If something was televised, it was during late hours and not publicized too openly. Television was Chip's pastime and he kept me abreast of the news.

One day he had seen a show of AIDS patients who told about their experiences with it so far. It really tore Chip up when he saw one girl in particular with AIDS. She was thin and already noticeably atrophied. He felt very sorry for her. He made the comment, "I don't want to live to look like that."

Chip was loving and caring. He loved humanity and never liked seeing the human body decomposed in any way, not even in horror movies. After seeing the girl on TV he wouldn't watch any more shows with patients who had AIDS. He would inform me if he knew one was going to be on, so I could watch it in another room.

He enjoyed talk shows, although the discussions about AIDS were constantly negative with no hope in sight. Therefore, he eventually quit them altogether.

One day Chip asked if I would like to go with him and Rhonda to an AIDS support meeting in Dallas.

"Okay. I'm glad you're going. You need to get out of the house," I said. "You haven't been to one since prior to your going to L.A. Is everything still about the same?"

"Probably. They're still an hour long. When I mentioned to Rhonda I was going she said she'd meet me there."

"Good, I'll fix dinner early. Are you hungry?"

"Not really. While you were gone I fixed some oatmeal."

"Well, if you don't eat any supper, maybe you'll want to stop somewhere on our way home. Want to?"

"Sure, that sounds good."

When we arrived at the AIDS support meeting there were several people there. It was very informal. We each introduced ourselves and some told their reason for coming. Of course, everyone was therefor primarily the same purpose, which was dealing with the AIDS situation. Some had AIDS, some were lovers of those with AIDS, some were friends, one was the spouse of a bisexual who had AIDS, and some were parents.

The importance was the questions and concern about AIDS.

Since AIDS was so new and not much was known, these informative meetings were helpful for everyone involved through actual experiences. At the same time it helped some to let go and share or just to be there, knowing you weren't the only one facing the terrible burden life had handed your loved one or you.

The stigma of AIDS was most unfair and at these meetings we felt unified, and it wasn't as though we were alone. We could speak freely and openly. On the outside we couldn't.

While at the meeting we learned there was another meeting strictly for AIDS individuals and another for grievers. The meeting we attended was mixed.

The following week Chip went to the meeting next door for AIDS patients. I believe it was too heartbreaking for him to have seen other patients with their bodies deteriorating so badly. Chip never discussed others with AIDS. I understood because we never dwelled on the negative. I could imagine how he felt, knowing he might someday be that way. He didn't attend any more meetings, although he encouraged me to continue, knowing they were people who cared.

I was afraid of the complications Chip might be faced with, let alone the idea of AIDS being fatal. I was hearing and seeing different things since we had been made aware of AIDS with Chip and never knowing what might happen or when. My biggest scare again was a person with AIDS suddenly dying without warning or people dying suddenly not even knowing they had AIDS. Others had it and went into remission, then without warning they might pass on. Still others lived for months through all the pain, suffering, and misery until death. There were similarities, but never seemed to be any two cases that were alike.

I was extremely tense and afraid every time I went into Chip's room, not knowing if he would be alive. It was the most terrifying thought, living with the fear he might pass on at any moment.

I'd quietly walk into his room, trying not to wake him if he were asleep, yet fearful, wondering.

I'd whisper, "Chip, are you awake?"

I'd watch him while always looking for some sort of movement to be sure he was only asleep. When I finally saw something move or heard him cough or any slight noise, I'd breathe with relief. In latter months the coughing and clearing of his throat was mostly due to the complications. But long before that I'm sure there were times he'd softly cough or clear his throat just so I would be relieved. Neither of us was saying, but Chip knew.

One time Jerry asked, "Chip, are you asleep?"

Then he teased, "You better not say, 'Yes.'"

Chip laughed.

I was in a nervous turmoil living with the worry and fear of my son's passing, although I tried my best to conceal it. I kept remembering what Chip had said, "Mother, you're going to be strong."

I was surprised how well I conveyed my message to others when they asked how I was. I was strong on the outside, but no one knew the agony and sadness I faced everywhere I went.

How could he be feeling? He was the one going through all the pain and agony with no life to look forward to. That was why I had to be strong, for Chip. He was the one suffering, he was the one who needed peace of mind, love, and care.

Every so often Chip had fast, electrical pains in his lower back and abdomen. These pains wouldn't cease or they moved from one location to another. At times the pain pills helped, but not always. Many times they were unbearable.

I thought of going to a faith healer, but Chip didn't care for the idea. Finally I did go to a psychic. I described Chip's pain and told him Chip had a horrible fear of going through even worse pain before he left this earth. I told the psychic that Chip couldn't take pain. The psychic told me to light a blue candle and on a piece of paper write Chip's full name and place it under the candle, then let the candle bum for three days and the pain would stop.

On my way home I purchased a light blue candle that was six inches high and three inches in diameter, wanting to be sure it was large enough to bum for three days. Chip and Jerry knew I had gone to a psychic, but didn't question me or ask why I was burning the candle. I didn't think to ask the psychic if it would make any difference if I talked about it, but rather than jinx it I kept quiet.

The pretty blue candle burned a full flame for three days and three nights. At times I was afraid it might go out or maybe it wouldn't last that long. But on the third day the candle was still burning and remained an inch high. All the pretty, melted paraffin lay delicately, but brazenly around the brilliant light blue candle which was still aflame in the serene brown sauce dish. It was even more beautiful because Chip's pain ceased. For all the suffering Chip was going through, this was one sure thing that worked. I was grateful and thanked God.

For months I still hadn't told Chip or Jerry why I burned that candle. Once Chip mentioned his fear of future pain.

I wholeheartedly commented, "Chip, I don't think you will have any more pain."

Confidently, I smiled. I prayed he wouldn't ever have that terrible, gruesome pain again.

16

Nothing Anymore, Except Honesty

Chip had a tendency to sleep more during the day, since the daylight bothered his eyes so much, and was awake more during the night In the morning before starting my aerobics at five-thirty. I'd always check on him first thing. He was usually wide awake watching television. Then he'd lie quietly and not bother me until he knew I was done. Whether he was eating or not, the day always started with his large quantity of pills.

Sometimes during the night I'd hear Chip's slippers shuffling across the kitchen floor. It was still too painful for him to lift his mystifyingly cold, numb feet. But as long as he was able to get around he often prepared things for himself. The times he would ask me to make something for him I was frequently having a frustrating battle against time, hurrying as fast as I could to prepare whatever he wanted, knowing that by the time his request was ready he might not be hungry. This bothered Chip to know I'd fixed something special. Wholeheartedly he would apologize, saying he really was hungry when he asked.

I tenderly assured him I understood his appetite played tricks on him, but still I wanted to fix him anything at any time. The times Chip could eat were well worth all attempts, and we both felt better.

Still, Chip fought being taken care of.

Then one day, smiling, he cheerfully said, "It sure is nice to be taken care of. I really appreciate everything you're doing, Mother."

"You're welcome, honey. I like taking care of you," I assured him, adding, "and I could do a lot more if only you'd let me!"

Once a week was our family night out and we took turns treating each other to dinner. Since Chip wasn't able to do much, this was a real treat and something we all looked forward to. Often we went to Chinese or Mexican restaurants, until Chip suddenly couldn't eat beef. Anything with the slightest beef flavor left a terrible, foul taste in his mouth that lingered for hours. Lobster had always been a favorite of Chip's, so we soon enjoyed seafood restaurants more often.

Chip didn't eat beef for six months and said he could tell a big difference; it gave him such a good, clean feeling. Then when his taste for beef returned, I was impressed with his self-discipline in limiting himself.

He continued to routinely see the doctor, with two tubes of blood drawn every time and lab tests done. He was still taking many different pills for the various symptoms. Now though, when Chip knew he was to see the doctor the next day he was apprehensive and couldn't sleep the night before. Not realizing this I'd remind him the day before so he could adjust his sleep, knowing when he needed to be ready. Then I started noticing how much more tired he seemed to be on the days he went. I asked Chip if I should change his appointments until later in the day.

"No, Mother. It's because I don't sleep the night before I know I'm to go."

"No wonder you're so tired! Next time I won't say anything until after you're awake."

While we were at the doctor's office that morning I mentioned what was happening to Chip. The doctor said the visits brought back memories of what Chip had been going through the past months.

That day when Chip was given a refill of Lamprene and Ansamysin, the doctor mentioned giving this same medicine to a hospital patient, but said he was still debating if he would.

Naturally, after hearing what the doctor said during that visit, Chip would question taking the medicine himself, especially since the doctor hadn't sounded too enthused. The way Chip was still feeling after a couple more trips to Fort Worth seemed to support his indecision.

During Chip's next visit to the doctor, he announced, "I don't want any more blood drawn!"

The doctor told Chip it was up to him, but if he continued the government medicine, which was Lamprene and Ansamysin, he would need to continue the blood tests because it was an experimental medicine. But then he went on to say that some doctors in San Francisco weren't even giving it to their patients.

Upon hearing that Chip said, "Then I don't see any reason for me to continue."

That day Chip was taken off the government medicine. He continued his Nizoral, which was for thrush, even though he didn't have any at present. Possibly the medicine was keeping it under control. He continued taking the many TB and fever pills. His high fever seemed to be the predominant ailment and there didn't seem to be any way to prevent, nor keep the fever under control.

At long last Chip was through making his frequent trips to Fort Worth. He would only go once a month for checkups. Feeling as weak as he was that was the wisest decision he could have made.

The human body can only take so much and Chip had been run ragged from the many repeated trips. Then, according to what the doctor said, he was apparently having flashbacks about the rude attitudes of those who had drawn his blood. And by all means his doctor's cool manner didn't help matters. Chip had always been a positive person, but was worn out from all the negativity plus how he felt physically, knowing he was to have been gone long before now. But for some reason he was still here and he didn't understand why.

The doctor still didn't have an answer about Chip's feet. He mentioned sending him to a neurosurgeon, but didn't think that was a likely solution. He said it might be because of the medicine Chip was taking and there wasn't anything he could give him to alleviate that. Chip would need to endure the constant pain and live with it. He still couldn't wear shoes for very long or too often. He tried a size larger, which helped some, but still the comfy slippers felt much better even though his feet remained cold with numbness. He wore ankle sport socks, which were easier to put on and take off. At times I'd massage his feet, trying to help the circulation to make them feel better. One time I started rubbing them real fast, thinking it might cause some warmth.

Chip yelled, "Stop that!"

I was concentrating solely on what I was doing, and his abrupt yell startled me. I instantly stopped and just looked at him.

He exclaimed, "That hurts!"

"Oh, I'm sorry. I thought that would make them feel better."

I really felt awful and almost cried, realizing how I must have hurt him. Then in a split second we were both laughing. That was just one of the many little things we learned by trial and error. All in all, we did pretty well together. Most important, we were good for each other through all this.

One day Chip's teeth started bothering him. He called different dentists to set an appointment. When he told them, he had AIDS they refused to see him. The pain was getting much worse.

Finally I called Chip's doctor, and he said he would call his own personal dentist. The doctor's orthodontist also refused treatment. Chip bore the pain for several more days until miraculously it stopped.

Chip's medicine seemed to be the only definite thing for him, although he was now taking two pills less. He took so much medicine throughout the day that I'd arrange them in pillboxes to make it easier to keep track of what he had or hadn't taken.

I asked Chip's doctor whether Chip should take vitamins and protein, but he didn't think they were necessary. I disagreed, but it was for naught once the doctor had said that. Too, it was understandable why Chip protested, considering the many big pills he was already taking.

Until now Chip had always been surrounded by friends, but I believe he was starting to get lonesome. Our living in a different area so far away made it inconvenient for his friends to visit often and Chip wasn't in any condition to travel far or do much himself. If he had lived in Dallas I'm sure friends would have stopped to see him more.

Every now and then friends wanted to take him to the lake or a movie, anything to get him out of the house, but Chip didn't feel like going anywhere. At first he may have wanted to go, but it seems before the actual time came he was too tired or was out of the mood and changed his mind. The many months he lived like this were sad and heartbreaking with the way this sadness put a damper on things. His friends were understanding and kept in touch, yet dwindled away as the days wore on. These complications seem to thrive on interfering in the patient's life any way possible, including friendships.

Chip's only comment was "They have their lives to live."

He didn't say it, but I'm sure he felt cut off because of the illness. And actually he was, but he understood. He never asked for sympathy, nor felt sorry for himself. He accepted the fact and knew life as it was for himself and others with the same complications. If anything, Chip was too hard on himself. He said he deserved AIDS or it wouldn't have happened. I tried to reason with him, but he wouldn't listen. Still he didn't know what he had done that was so bad to have brought on something as terrible as AIDS. I believe it had to be karma. He wasn't a bad person ever during this life, even though he went through pure hell, it seemed.

It wasn't until years after Chip passed away that I learned from Sonny, a very close friend of Chip's, whom he'd known for years that what I had suspected was truly Chip's doings in cutting himself off from his friends. It was about four or five months before Chip passed away when he told Sonny on the phone, "I don't want you to come and see me because I know it hurts you so bad to see me like I am."

I told Sonny that Chip was probably telling everyone the same thing during that time, when I thought back about it, and Sonny agreed saying he called a couple of times telling him that very thing. I know it was lonesome and sad for Chip, but he had so much pride and it was difficult for him with the way his body was deteriorating.

Chip hadn't driven his car for at least a month, since operating the clutch in his five-speed had become increasingly difficult with his progressive weakness, discouraging his desire to drive. Then one day he decided to drive to Dallas. I suggested he take our car. To be sure everything was okay I rode around the block with him.

Chip's judgment seemed to be off and he had a tendency to drive on the wrong side of the street. The effort of getting the car over to the right was difficult and beyond his control. We lived on a quiet street and Chip remained calm while he drove slowly and carefully. There were a couple of cars parked alongside the curb which weren't any problem as he easily passed. My heart ached, knowing this had to be a blow to his ego to be defeated and deprived of driving. Chip had always thrived on his freedom. His illness mocked him, letting him know that little by little it was going to take everything away.

That was to be Chip's last time to drive. I cried on the inside and he must have too. I told Chip I'd take him to Dallas or anyplace he wanted to go, then explained

I could do other errands while he visited. Unfortunately this was the beginning of things steadily going downhill for him, even more.

As Chip said, "Life is a bitch."

At times like this I had a tendency to agree.

Rhonda visited Chip fairly frequently or they'd talk on the phone. Once in a while they would go out to dinner and sometimes to a movie, depending on how he was feeling.

Chip decided to call the Oak Lawn Counseling Center about their buddy system for AIDS patients. Soon after, a buddy named John called Chip and set a time to come to our home.

Then Chip started having second thoughts. He wasn't sure if he wanted a visitor or to be thought of as a charity case. Chip had a lot of pride and the more he thought about John's coming, the more the idea bothered him. The day John was to come Chip called to cancel his visit, but it was too late. John was on his way.

When John arrived we introduced ourselves and I took him to Chip's room, but Chip was sound asleep. John and I went into the living room and talked. Before we knew it we were conversing quite candidly. John was Chip's age and seemed to be a lot like him. It was almost as though he were a longtime friend of Chip's. John was surprised at how easily I talked and so openly. Chip and I had had similar discussions and I gave him the credit. I understood things on their level and wasn't an authority figure. I listened and liked our sharing.

I knew I was lucky Chip was my son and I would miss these talks someday. We had relied on each other all these years and Chip told things like they were. Even while he was going through all these relentless complications, he was still strong and a great support for me.

After awhile Chip woke up. I checked on him and let him know John was in the living room. I assured him he'd like John and that he was pleasant. A few minutes later Chip Joined us in the living room and I excused myself while they talked.

Chip was impressed with John and his successful career. Yet he wouldn't allow him to visit anymore. John called several times to set another meeting time, but Chip refused. He thanked John, told him he appreciated his time, but they were on two different levels: Chip was sick and dying while John had his life ahead of him.

Nothing like this had ever bothered Chip before these complications. In fact, John and he probably would have been good friends, but not now. Things were different. Chip realized this and that was where the real heartache lay. He knew he would never be the same again, and he had to lay aside all his dreams and goals. It was understandable how discouraging that must be. Still he kept it to himself and accepted life as it was.

I believe this is when Chip unknowingly drew a dividing line between himself and the rest of the world. He was facing reality, knowing it was only a matter of time. Already he had been deprived of being an active person. He knew he couldn't live life to its fullest as he had been used to doing. Also he was having mood swings, which were common with these complications and made things even more ambiguous and depressing.

Slowly, but surely, he would be deprived of all his dignity and self- esteem while he suffered through these complications to the end. If there had been a ray of hope it could have made a world of difference.

One day when Chip woke he said, "I'm lucky, it's another day," then he caught himself and didn't say another word.

Chip encouraged me to go to the support meetings. He felt that they would help me and he knew the people would help in any way they could. More than anything Chip was looking out for me to be sure I was taken care of. At the time I had mixed emotions about going. I felt it was more important to be with Chip, although this would give him and Jerry time together.

Finally I attended the support meetings in Dallas, thinking I'd learn something that would help Chip, or maybe he would change his mind and go with me. But I knew he couldn't sit that length of time, and too, he didn't feel he could handle the meetings. I don't believe Chip wanted to have any more outside dealings with AIDS than necessary. He hadn't said much about the one support meeting he had gone to that was for patients with AIDS, but he didn't care to go again. He had always been such a sensitive person and now he had to deal with the worst things happening to the human body with no mercy to himself or others. I imagine it was pure torture knowing he and his fellowman would be haunted while their bodies withered away with no mercy.

Rhonda went with me to a couple of support meetings, then I continued by myself for awhile. It was a good group, with people from all walks of life. Everybody learned together while they listened and shared. Some attended regularly, some only one time, and others once in awhile. The important thing was that they came and always felt that it helped in some way. We discussed whatever was on our minds or what was bothering us. This time it was my turn to talk.

What still bothered me was Chip's doctor's attitude. I told my story about what had been happening and waited for their feedback.

Everyone chimed out, "You get Chip to a different doctor! There isn't any reason for him to be going to a negative doctor. He needs positive feedback to know that they are continually trying to come up with a drug that will overcome AIDS. He needs a doctor who is compassionate and caring, etc., etc."

Different ones made suggestions and some even volunteered to help in any way they could.

It was as Chip said, "They were very caring, concerned, and would do anything to help." At a time like this that meant a lot. I told them how Chip didn't want to go to another doctor, that his doctor let him know it like it was. Too, the doctor even said there was no reason to change. Then I let them know Chip did not want to start all over again with all the tests, which meant more poking to draw blood. Chip had accepted AIDS for what it was. He wasn't seeing his doctor too often anymore and he felt better about that.

When I returned home that evening I went into Chip's room and we discussed the meeting I had attended. I told him what they had said about his needing to see a different doctor.

They said, "You are not obligated to that doctor. You can change. You don't need to be with a negative doctor! I told them how you accepted things as they were, how what the doctor was telling you and everything you were hearing on TV about it was all the same. They didn't think I should let that stop me. They said it isn't right you aren't seeing a good, caring doctor, and I agreed."

Aggravated, Chip said, "Don't start about that."

In a meek voice I said, "Oh, I'm not. I knew how you'd feel when I told you, and they didn't mean it smart. They want it for your own peace of mind."

Distinctly, he said, "My peace of mind is just fine!"

It got quiet. Chip wasn't saying anything.

After a few minutes I asked, "Chip, aren't you talking to me now?" Clearly Chip stated, "Sure, I'll talk to you. I'm not going to argue with you." "Well, I'm not going to argue either."

Assuringly he said, "I appreciate your help, and I love you. I'd be having a hard time without you, but I'm doing what I decided to do."

I pleaded, "Chip, they feel with these complications and how it is, you need positive feedback."

"Well, it's awfully late in the ball game."

"Chipper, I told them I even questioned your having AIDS, and they said that was why I needed to take you to another doctor."

"I'm not going through all that again!"

"I know. I understand, and told them how you felt. Then they said, 'You're putting the responsibility on yourself and later it may bother you. It may be something you have to live with, wondering if you did the right thing.' I guess I'm all wrong in not doing anything, they said."

"Mother, you've done so much!"

"What?" I asked.

"Don't ask me what," he said in an aggravated tone.

"Yes, it's hard to answer, isn't it?"

"No. You've done more than anyone has done for me!"

"But I need to get you to a good, caring doctor. I really haven't done that much."

Chip said, "Yes, you have. You have talked to me, and basically, in a way, begged and pleaded and I told you no. You respected my wishes."

I started to interrupt, "But..."

Chip went on, "And I consider that doing a lot more than to fight with me, when I'm already not in the mood to fight."

"That's another thing I brought up at the meeting. I said, 'You have lovers. I'm his mother. That's different, lover to lover, than mother and son.' Understand? You've always had a hang-up about being mother's boy. Haven't you?"

"And being tied to mother's apron strings?" Chip chuckled.

I said, "Right."

"You know whose fault that is."

I asked, "Whose? "

"My dad's."

I wasn't thinking and asked, "Why?"

"He's the one who made that comment years ago."

"Oh, I remember. You hadn't told me at the time he said it, not until years later after your trip to New Orleans. He said that when you went to live with him, when you were only fourteen!"

I paused, nodding my head, then continued, "It's too bad he didn't do his part if that's what bothered him... and then to think, you were there to live with him! It's a shame you carried that burden all those years, even though we knew differently. It's the idea of his saying such a thing!"

"Sure, I had to get away from my mother's apron strings." Chip laughed.

"You should have said, 'Sure, if I'd had a father to go to.'"

"Yes, he's the one who said that. And the other time he said he would pay for my trip up there," Chip chuckled, "which he never did pay for, and he promised he would. Or what? That he would give me sixty-five dollars, I think."

"You hadn't told me about that. You sure went through enough hassle because of his neglect, Chip. But still, you've always had a good attitude about him and your stepsisters. It's a shame they can't be like you were to them, mainly now! That's why I don't understand this. It's so unfair, especially when you think about what they do and get away with."

"I know," Chip replied.

We were both silent for a few minutes. Then I encouraged, "Well, you need to go to a positive doctor."

Chip said, "See, that's another good thing. After I die, knowing what I wanted the whole time, and even years before, you tried and did everything possible. And that should make you feel good—to know you did everything possible and more."

"That could be a question right there! If I don't pursue another doctor, will I have failed you? If I listen to you and don't do what I really should have done, because I'm a willing, able person."

"And so am I!" Chip exclaimed.

I said, "But—"

Chip interrupted, "We're adults. We're both adults of sound mind. I'm sick, but my mind is 100 percent!"

"I know. Chip! But your doctor has been very negative to you. You need a positive doctor who can at least talk about the good research being done."

"Mother! Reports keep saying they don't expect a cure for a long time, and we know my doctor doesn't have any faith in the medicines they're now using."

"Chip, there are times I know you're ready to live longer, but you've just accepted it because you've got AIDS and you're told you're not going to live. You get very angry at me when I say that." Pausing, I added, "You know what I'm talking about?"

Chip didn't answer and I continued, "You really want to live and maybe you can. You know? You really go on a rage against me for saying that. Just like, 'What the devil are you talking about? You know darn well I'm dying.' In so many words that's what it amounts to. Right?"

"Yes," Chip replied. "You've done that to me. It's just like, put the knife in and turn."

I asked, "Am I doing that?"

"No, I'm doing that to you with my response... because I'm not agreeing or saying what you want to hear." Chip continued, "I want to be totally honest I have nothing anymore, except honesty," He paused, "And it makes me so mad because I don't want to hurt you, but there's no hope. You know there's no hope."

"Chip, I say that because I really believe... and here we go again and you're really going to get mad at me, but there are times, and there isn't anything wrong with it, for a human being to want to live."

"No, that's not true."

I asked, "Why?"

"That's the way society puts it in human beings' minds, but there are lots and lots of people committing suicide."

I said, "But that's only because of complications of life."

"That's what it's all about, Mother."

"If you didn't have AIDS, you could pull through and be happy again. Going back to when you were depressed and spoke of suicide, I really feel, outside of the depression you've been through, which they say was a breakdown, which I question, and someday we may know differently... if it weren't for those complications, you would be up and like you once were. I think you want to live and be positive because maybe a cure could come, but then you get upset and angry. That's because of AIDS, right?"

"You're right." Then Chip added, "But I want this to be over with. I'm sick of being sick!"

"I didn't think you were depressed now," I commented.

"I don't think a person has to be depressed to realize they want out."

I could understand Chip's wanting this to be over with. I couldn't blame him because of what he was facing. What would it be like not knowing what to expect next, knowing it wasn't going to be good, dreading going through it again and not knowing how long it was going to last? It was as though his world was caving in on him. With this agony, how must he feel? Imagine the distress, day after day. I understood his thinking; he had had enough. I was being the selfish one trying to keep Chip here, also knowing down deep he was right. I couldn't blame him. Why stay here? There was no future with these complications once they pounced in this stage of the sickness. Chip hadn't expected to live this long.

Nightly news about AIDS was just the cold, bare facts with most talk starting to be about the many who were dying from these complications, such as Rock Hudson and Liberace, plus many others, famous and not so famous.

We were soon back to our discussion, which sometimes got heated. This was a typical conversation between us at different times. Apparently I was still denying his dying and trying to persuade him to do the same. I'm sure he had been doing that too until the doctor told him he had AIDS. The attitude toward AIDS during his time was "the day you're diagnosed, you die." Ever since, I'm afraid I hurt him by trying to persuade him to still be positive about living. He did have a good, realistic attitude and did better than could be expected with everything being negative and endlessly hounding him that there was no hope.

As Chip said, *"I have nothing anymore, except honesty."*

Still, what was I doing to him, knowing honesty always was important to him, to us? Because of the stigma on AIDS, I was denying the word "AIDS," although this was only to people whom I didn't know could accept it. I knew I didn't have time for any qualms about it. All that mattered was that my son not be ridiculed. He never had been, and I didn't want it to start now. I never had to defend him because of the person he was, and I wanted it kept that way while he was on earth. I quietly dealt with the situation— just like Chip.

The pioneers, like Chip, were the ones who would weed out the animosity, hopefully. The complications were difficult enough, let alone ill will.

I sat a few minutes, silent, then said, "Chip, let me change your bed for the night. It looks like you've been sweating."

"I have been. It's really wet."

Chip sat in the chair alongside his bed while I changed sheets. I mentioned his seeing a Dr. Wheeler, who was suggested at the meeting. Chip recognized the name and said he was known to be good.

He said, "I don't know, let me think about it for a couple of days."

"I'll call him tomorrow. It will probably take us a few days to get in. Only the doctor and no going to the hospital. Okay, Chip?"

"I don't want to fight with you, and I can understand your doing it after they were all over your case at the meeting, but I don't appreciate it one bit. I'm beginning to wonder if I have AIDS, tuberculosis, or what. You'll need to get all the records. Mother."

"Okay, Chip. I wonder, too. I'll call Dr. Wheeler tomorrow. Your bed's all clean and fresh. I'll get you a glass of Gatorade for the night. Okay?"

"Sure, Mother, that sounds good."

I called Dr. Wheeler's office to schedule an appointment, but he wasn't accepting any more patients at the time. I tried to let the receptionist know the situation, but she said she was sorry. I almost cried before I hung up the telephone. This was one doctor Chip would have gone to, and I couldn't get him in! What was I going to tell Chip? He had finally said okay, and now, another negative. This was tearing me up. I hated to tell Chip, but I had to once I got control. I felt so lost. What was this going to do to him?

A few minutes later I went into Chi p's bed room and sat down on his bed beside him, then proceeded to tell him about the call.

"That's okay, Mother. You tried."

"I'm sorry. Chip. I didn't want to tell you." Then I couldn't stop the overwhelming flood of tears, but managed to continue, "We need to get you to a considerate doctor."

"No, Mother, that's okay. I have a doctor." He reached for my hand and said, "Don't cry, if s okay. It just wasn't meant to be."

Chip was so kind and gentle. I couldn't help but feel he must have been disappointed at not being able to see Dr. Wheeler, and here he was comforting me. I felt awful for him, and to be crying. It was another letdown, but you might know, Chip handled it much better than I. I should have been the one comforting him.

I knew Chip really didn't care to deal with another doctor ever since he was in the hospital the first time, remembering when he locked me in the garage last year and ended up in the hospital. He felt he had been tricked and couldn't get out because of me. I couldn't blame him for being skeptical ever since that happened.

"Chip, I know what you're saying and I'm sorry." I finally calmed down and smiled as I said, "I don't blame you for still being upset after I kept you in the hospital and put you in Wichita Falls when you didn't belong there to begin with. Even Dr. Gravelee said you didn't belong there."

Chip laughed, "I called the police, but didn't mean for them to come. I hadn't said anything, but guess I hung up too late."

Chip and I were talking about the time he had locked me in the garage, thinking I had a gun.

Tickled, I laughed, "You did say you were going to call the police when you ran into the house. I was thinking about calling, but wasn't sure if I could. Then I was surprised when I looked up and there they were, before I had called."

"You didn't need to." Chip chuckled.

"That's true. You beat me to it," I agreed while laughing.

I smiled, "You're taking it well now." We both laughed.

"We still need to get you to another doctor, Chipper."

"I don't care to deal with it—the doctors or the hospitals. I know what I'm up against. I have known what I'm up against and it's lasting too long, in my opinion. Much too long."

"Then are you depressed?"

"No, I'm angry now."

"You're angry at me now?"

"No, I'm not angry with you. My adrenaline's just high. I know what I'm up against. I know that really I should already be underground."

"Why?"

"Because I already died!"

"But they saved you."

"Did they? Think that's what it's called?" he teased.

"Well, they brought you back to life," I laughed, then started coughing.

Chip said, "I call it torture,"

I couldn't stop coughing. I excused myself, saying I'd be back. When I returned. Chip said, "I figure as long as I can get up and walk to the bathroom and to the kitchen, then I'm doing just fine, basically."

"Yes, but like today, you fell."

Chip said, "That was only because the chair turned and if I had to, I could have gotten up by myself. It just scared me, and I needed some help."

Then he laughed while he teasingly said, "I thought it was funny, and I just wanted you to see me."

"You did?" I jokingly asked.

Chip's good sense of humor often helped when we had a controversy. He liked my going to the support meetings, but he didn't like the conflict it sometimes caused when I related it to him. I told him it was only because they wanted things right for him and from what they were hearing, I needed to seek more help.

I said, "Evidently, I'm not doing right with you."

"Yes you are! You're being more than right. You're respecting my last days on earth!"

"Yes, but maybe you could live a lot longer."

"Mother, why do I want to live longer? For what?"

"You might live a couple more years." He didn't comment, then I added, "Do you want to stay like this for a couple more years?"

"That's how I'd stay if I were here a couple more years. No, I don't want to live like this a couple more years."

"Well, if you go see a doctor you may be able to get around and do more."

"Mother, I could never live the kind of life that I lived again."

He paused, then said, "Because of having a dreaded disease. Everybody would run from me, if they were smart."

Chip talked about how he couldn't understand why some people weren't a little more concerned, "I don't know. I don't understand life. Only that I have been..." His voice trailed off, then he added, "I guess I have been handed a rest for the fast life I've lived. Somebody up above says, 'Okay, now is the time for you to rest.'"

I laughed. He really tickled me with his candid, dry sense of humor, and sincerity at the same time.

"Still, I need to do more now. It's not right for you."

"Mother, don't you start feeling guilty. You've done enough for me. You've done a lot. And you know, I'm at the point now where I'm all here mentally and because of what I have (AIDS), I have problems and I'm stuck. I am stuck! There's no way I could commit suicide," he added with a sly grin, "decently."

Then Chip told me about a talk show on TV in which the subject was mercy killing. It was about a mother and daughter, and mercy killing was done, knowing the mother was only suffering and wouldn't get any better. Slowly, but surely they gave her pills until she fell asleep and didn't wake up. Chip said that's how he would like to go, to just go to sleep and that would be it.

Chip said, "I should write down on paper that once I am unconscious, do not put me on oxygen, do not put me on a life machine." Then he told about that topic also being discussed on television.

He said, 'There are people out there who have AIDS and want to live. I'm really happy for them. I'm glad they obviously have something to live for, but I don't feel that way. Maybe it's because of the way I lived. It's also because of the way I've seen other people live, wealthy as well as poor, good as well as bad. I just don't like the dog-eat-dog world. I don't want to put up with it. I've put up with a lot more than most people will put up with in a lifetime. I feel I've had my share."

"I understand what you're saying, Chip, and I really can't argue with that. You've always done more than your share."

I had been making his bed. When finished I said, "There, Chip, your bed's all nice and fresh. Your pillows were soaked, so I'm going to air them out to dry while you use these others."

"Okay, that's fine. Thank you." He slowly moved back into bed and said, "This feels great!"

I started to cover him up when I noticed his feet.

Shocked, I exclaimed, "Chip, what did you do to your feet?"

"I guess I scalded them in the tub. The skin's starting to peel off now."

I checked them closer, saying, "I wish you had told me, and we could have put something on them! In fact, I should have run your water! I hadn't thought about your not being able to judge the temperature, with them being cold and numb."

Chip laughed a little as he said, "I didn't see how red they were until I got out."

I'm sure he was trying to laugh to make me think they weren't all that bad.

"And naturally, you would want the water hotter with them being so cold. Chip, I'm sorry. I hate that!"

Chip said, "I can't handle taking a shower anymore."

I suggested, "If you put on your bikini, I could bathe you."

Chip didn't comment. He was tired and ready to rest. I kissed him good night, saying, "I love you."

He said, "I love you too, Mother."

I turned out his light and went into the kitchen. The night was quiet and lonely.

Chipper continued to do the best he could, bathing himself until it was too hard for him to get out of the tub. He was becoming extremely weak and exhausted. We were both very modest and like most mothers and sons, we were embarrassed about nakedness.

The last few times after Chip was through bathing, I would go into his bathroom with my head turned away holding his towel up for him. I'd wait until Chip had the towel around him, then help as much as I could while he struggled to get out of the tub. Then Chip would slowly shuffle down the hall and into his room, where I would help him back into bed where he could stretch out and relax as much as possible.

17

Where Are My Keys?

Chip was almost out of medicine and it was time to see the doctor again. Even though his visits were still a traumatic ordeal the night before, he decided to stay with the same doctor rather than start over again. He was only seeing him once a month and felt he could deal with that.

"Mother, you may not like this doctor because he is the one who told you I am going to die."

"No, Chip. I thought about that. True, I didn't like hearing it, but still, that didn't make me dislike him. It was before that with his overall attitude. Look what happens to you every time you know you're going to see him. You were never that way before about any doctor, not even when you were a little boy. It's so unfair because of what you're already dealing with. You know you've always gotten along with everyone. It's never been a problem until now."

"Maybe it's because of AIDS and he can't handle it because his patients are dying. That could be hard to take."

"I know. Chip. I thought about that too, and it would be. Sometimes I feel sorry for him. But that's still no excuse."

The last couple of visits I had waited in the lobby, but this time I wanted to hear what the doctor said about Chip's medicine. The examination didn't take long. Chip was sitting upon the gurney when he asked the doctor about his pills and exactly what they were for. The doctor told him the medicine was to treat the symptoms, but they weren't going to prolong his life. That was all that could be done. He repeated how some doctors gave the medicine and other doctors didn't feel it was necessary.

Chip said, "Do you mean I have been doing all this for no apparent reason?"

"No, this was something we needed to do."

"If these pills aren't doing any good, I don't see any reason to continue taking them."

The doctor acknowledged that would be his decision, but he would need to continue the Nizoral which was for the thrush in his mouth. Then whatever pills he needed at different times, the doctor would prescribe. Chip agreed and we didn't go after his TB medicine as usual.

I could imagine how Chip felt when the doctor told him all those pills weren't helping him. I didn't blame him for his decision after being told that! If the doctor had given him a ray of hope or at least shown some concern, I'm sure Chip would have continued them. He had been taking so many pills and we had been making so many extra trips, whenever necessary, to do a certain test. He had quit the Lamprene and Ansamysin and now he was told all the medicine wasn't helping. What was Chip to think or how was he to feel, with all he had gone through all these months since being in the hospital. It would be understandable how he must have felt down and out with no encouragement whatsoever.

A few days later a note was left on our front door. The nurse from the health department came to give Chip his TB medicine since he had failed to pick it up. I must have been in the backyard and didn't hear her. The note asked us to come for Chip's medicine or call her. I called and let her know that Chip was no longer taking his medicine. She was quite concerned and felt it was still necessary. I told her the doctor said the medicine wasn't helping, and therefore Chip stopped.

I asked, "You are familiar with his case, aren't you? You know he has AIDS and M-Avium TB, don't you?"

"Yes," she said. "That's on his record, and it's still important for him to take the TB medicine."

We talked about Chip's situation and I told her he wasn't going to be seeing his doctor much anymore. She suggested I take him to another doctor. I told her about the many calls I had made, but had been unsuccessful in locating another doctor. She gave me the name of a couple of doctors and urged me to call. I was grateful for her empathy. Chip needed that and so did I.

I called the doctor she suggested, but he wasn't in. I had a long talk with the nurse.

She said, "Yes, the doctor is taking care of AIDS patients. Would you like to make an appointment?"

I explained I would need to talk with Chip first. I told her how he felt and that he didn't want to go through the same routine all over again. She understood and said the doctor would still be happy to see him. I told her I'd call back if I could get Chip to change his mind. She was most pleasant and helpful.

I told Chip about the concern and empathy of the two nurses and about calling the doctor's office. I didn't want to push if he didn't want to see another doctor. Still it was important for him to know there were others out there who cared about him. Chip appreciated their concern, but since the doctor had said it wasn't necessary, he didn't want to take the medicine or go to another doctor. But he did comment it seemed strange not taking the pills anymore, saying it was as though a security was gone or there was nothing to fall back on, even if they didn't help.

Physically and mentally, he had enough to do to combat the loss of energy he felt constantly from the illness, never knowing how he was going to feel. Chip didn't understand it himself. He accepted what was happening and knew it was only a matter of time until he would be gone. He had gone through enough experimental research without complaint. He had endured a lot of undue stress, because things could have been handled in a more diplomatic manner ever since he had gone to the hospital. Chip let them probe his body and do whatever was necessary, until his tired body was worn out and exhausted. He had already exceeded his life expectancy, which prolonged his suffering. It had to stop somewhere. The symptoms were enough to cope with, knowing there wasn't anything to help much. There would be a cure eventually, but not for those who had already been infected. It was only a matter of time.

Chip said, "I have no choice. I have to accept it."

All I could do was give Chip all my love and support and pray the suffering would lessen. At dinnertime Chip came to the table while he could still walk that far. When he became too weak to walk the distance, I took dinner to his room. After awhile I ate with Chip, knowing how alone he must feel. When I went to the health club or had errands, Jerry spent time with him. Chip liked our being near, even though he might helplessly fall asleep. Our love and closeness was the most important thing we could give Chip. We had each other and made the best of it, knowing Chip's days were numbered. The loneliness had to have been long and staggering to him. Al! we could do was live each day to its fullest as much as possible.

Chip went through another phase when he didn't want to be bothered by anyone or anything and slept a lot as before. Now though, it seemed to be more often or for longer periods of time. What bothered me most was his insisting that his door be kept shut. It was almost impossible to check on him without disturbing him. I tried to quietly open his door in case he was asleep. He often sensed what I was doing and felt it unnecessary that I check on him so frequent

One time he scared me when he yelled, "I'm alive!"

I was startled and giggled, yelling, "Chipper! You scared me! I didn't want to wake you."

He knew what I was doing and didn't like it. He wouldn't even let his door be cracked a little bit. It was a horrible nightmare, living with the fear of his passing away at any moment.

Another time when he caught me, he yelled, "I'm okay."

In relief, again I laughed and said, "Okay. Don't be upset with me. Hove you."

Chip answered, "I love you, too."

Although Chip was the one going through the different stages of death, we were often on the same wavelength. The first time we noticed it was the day we both woke up angry, for no apparent reason other than the sickness. According to a book written by Elizabeth Kubler-Ross, the five stages of death for terminally ill people are shock and denial, anger, bargaining, depression, and acceptance. They do not go in any particular order or they can happen simultaneously, stop and start again. Once I became aware, I had more of a tendency to notice them as I did his mood swings, which I believe were about the same as the five stages. With this sickness, depression and withdrawal are often common denominators.

I had Chip all tucked in for the night with fresh, dry sheets, provided the severe chills and sweats didn't flare up before morning.

Soon I went to bed. Jerry was already asleep, but when I got into bed he awakened enough to ask how Chip was. After I told him, he gave me a kiss and fell back asleep. I lay thinking. It seemed that was always the saddest time of day, yet there was no predominant time. It's just that now I was all settled down, and it was so dark and quiet.

Before I knew it, my thoughts started wandering. It was hard to fall asleep, not because I was too tired because taking care of Chip didn't seem to tire me. I never thought of it that way; I liked having the time together. It was becoming extremely lonesome for him and I wished I could have done something about it. The tears started falling. I'm glad Jerry was asleep so he wouldn't know I was crying. I tried not to show the tears, but when the faintest thought came to mind of how sad and lonely it must be for Chip, it was almost unbearable and choked me up. I felt melancholy, thinking he must feel that way too. He tried not to make me aware of his emotions and concealed his burdens the best he could because he wanted to keep that protective shield over me. He had always been that way and it didn't change now. The tears flooded my eyes while I tried to keep my sobbing and sniffles quiet. I reached for a Kleenex and softly blew my nose and wiped the tears, hoping I wouldn't wake Jerry.

I sat up in bed and looked down the long, dark hallway to see if I could see a light under Chip's door. Sometimes it was dark, but many times there was a light, or he might be watching TV. If I saw a light, heard a dry cough or any kind of a noise, I felt better because it gave me some assurance in the dark. The quiet usually meant he was sleeping, but I couldn't help listening and looking throughout the night like a sentinel on guard. I awakened often. I'd sit up and look for a light.

We both seemed to keep mixed hours. Sometimes during the night when I'd hear him in the kitchen, I'd join him. At times he couldn't sleep much, then other times he slept a long time. He always woke early. Of course, we never slept straight through nor all that well at any time.

Jerry and I decided we'd better make the funeral arrangements. It was good we did because I don't know how I could have done anything the day Chip passed away, although we did need to verify everything when that day came. Evidently because of my state of mind, I still overlooked a mistake on the gravestone. I thought the birth and death dates were always on the stone, but they weren't, only the years. Therefore the correction would be a double expense. When we chose the caskets and were deciding on the colors, I said, "Since Chip and I have blue eyes and Jerry's are brown, why don't we have silver, and bronze for Jerry?"

I was asking Jerry what he thought when Phil, the funeral director, commented, "It's usually the mouth that people notice at funerals."

As soon as he said that, it dawned on me what he meant. We all smiled and softly laughed.

For a long time, it seemed like every time Chip and I talked, before we knew it we were on the subject of his imminent death. We talked so much about it, one day I said, "Chip, we've got to quit talking about your dying all the time."

Chip said, "I know."

Henceforth, it seemed as though we both clammed up. It was like being so close, yet so far away in silence. Apparently we were having a hard time adjusting and it had helped to talk. We were devastated, with death facing us constantly.

A few minutes later, Chip said, "Mother, we've been through a lot together."

"Yes, I know, honey, I think that's what is making it so hard for us now."

I took hold of his hands and clenched them. Smiling I said,"! don't want to lose you. I love you so much."

Chip smiled, "I love you too. Mother."

These moments were always with us, although neither of us said anything while we let our thoughts silently wander for a few more moments in deep thought. Then I broke the silence, saying, "Chip, it's almost lunchtime. Are you hungry?"

"Yes, Mother. Would you like a chicken sandwich from Wendy's? I'll buy you one."

"No, honey, but I'll get you one. Would you like to go with me?"

Chip thought for a minute, then said, "Yes, maybe that would be a good idea. I haven't been outside for awhile."

It was a pretty day and the fresh air was good for Chip. With his sunglasses, the light didn't bother him. I liked his going with me and it broke the monotony for him. Chip loved Wendy's chicken sandwiches. He always ordered the same way: "Chicken sandwich with mayonnaise, lettuce, and pickle. Hold the mustard and cut it in half, please. With a large order of french fries."

On our way home I said, "Chip, I'm going to Dallas tonight. Do you feel like going to the meeting?"

"No, Mother. I'll probably be awake when you get home and you can tell me about it."

"Okay. I won't be gone long."

The meeting went fairly fast. I hadn't given thought to having help with Chip. At the meeting they said it was too much on me, taking care of him by myself. I told them it hadn't been a problem and everything was going as well as could be expected.

David had been attending the support meetings since I'd started. He said his lover had a nurse come in every couple of days to take care of him. He said he didn't know how he could have done without her help.

I told them Chip wasn't seeing his doctor much anymore or on any regular basis and he had stopped taking most of his medication. David felt I should definitely have a nurse in that case. He told me the name of the person I needed to contact.

When I got home I asked Chip if he would like a nurse to come to our home. He wasn't sure at first. He thought things were going okay at present.

I said, "I don't know how long it would take to get one, so do you care if I try now for later or whenever they could come?"

"Only if they don't take blood!" said Chip.

"I will let them know how you feel. I doubt if they would."

I called his doctor to okay a nurse's attending Chip. He said that was fine. The following week a nurse named Lynn called and set a time for the next day. I told Chip that Lynn would be here tomorrow. Suddenly he wasn't too keen on the idea. I didn't say much and figured I would let everything take care of itself when she arrived.

Chip was up really early the next day. In fact, it was about four o'clock in the morning when he woke up and couldn't go back to sleep. I woke a little later and was in the kitchen fixing breakfast when I heard Chip's feet shuffling on the parquet.

Good, I thought, he's coming out to the kitchen for breakfast this morning.

Chip shuffled on past me to the other end of the counter. He looked all around. After awhile, he said, "Where are my keys? Have you seen them. Mother?"

I said, "I don't know. Aren't they there at the end of the counter?"

"I thought they were, but I don't see them."

"I don't know, Chip. I haven't seen them either."

He seemed real concerned while he looked all around, but didn't say anything else. Then all of a sudden, he hurried back into his bedroom. I was surprised at his obvious haste, but hadn't thought any more about it. I called and reminded him Lynn would be here after awhile. He didn't answer.

Lynn arrived a little later. She and I sat in the living room and talked a few minutes. I let her know about Chip's not wanting to have any more blood drawn. She assured me she would not be doing that. She had been forewarned by his doctor. She said she had come to talk with Chip and do what she could. We went to his room.

Chip was sitting up in bed with his pillows stacked behind his head, facing straight ahead. When we entered his room he didn't acknowledge Lynn's presence or even look at her. I was shocked! I'd never seen him act like this. He was always cordial. Then I was surprised even more when I noticed he had on his jeans and a shirt. I introduced Chip to Lynn.

The first thing she said was, "I'm not going to take any blood. I'm only here to be with you and do whatever I can."

The relief was obvious as Chip eased up a little. I left the room and let them talk. When I went back in she was about to call Chip's doctor to let him know about the exam she had done. She said his pulse rate was extremely low. She added, "From the sound of his chest, he needs to see the doctor."

The receptionist at the doctor's office put Lynn on hold a couple times and when she came back on the line, she told Lynn to get some blood from Chip.

Lynn told her, "No, it was our agreement that I didn't take blood."

Lynn told the receptionist that Chip needed to see the doctor, but he would only come in if they wouldn't draw blood. The doctor agreed and we set an appointment for the next day.

Another suggestion Lynn made was that the doctor prescribe some Reglin and Augmentin for Chip. Hopefully the Reglin would help his appetite and the Augmentin was an antibiotic. She was surprised he wasn't already on an antibiotic and hadn't at least tried the Reglin. She said the Reglin didn't always work, but it was worth a try to get him to eat. I had talked with Chip's doctor in the past about his appetite when I was worried about his not eating. Not once had the doctor mentioned Reglin or anything to help Chip's appetite. That seemed to be one of many things Chip and I were never told. His doctor asked all the questions, yet when I inquired about anything, he didn't seem too concerned. I understood not too much was known about these complications, but I couldn't understand him. There was only one time he communicated with me, which was long after I needed to know. While I was going to the support meetings and the short time Lynn visited was when I learned some things, not from the doctor who was supposed to be taking care of Chip.

Chip said he was impressed with Lynn. Once she reassured him she wouldn't take any blood, he relaxed. Until then he had planned on leaving.

He said, "It may have cost me forty dollars to take a taxi to Dallas, but that's what I planned on doing."

I was shocked, and it tickled me when I realized why he had wan ted his keys. I said, "That's why you were dressed and wanted your car keys."

"It sure was. I thought for sure you had something planned when I couldn't find my keys and you wouldn't tell me where they were."

I laughed, thinking about it. Chip was serious. He was going to leave. Then I could imagine how he must have felt.

I said, "Oh, Chip, I'm sorry! I didn't have any idea why you were looking for your keys and I really didn't know where they were."

I hadn't realized how afraid he was about Lynn's coming to see him. I continued, "You thought that because your keys had been lying on the counter and now, all of a sudden, when you wanted them they were gone." And it dawned on me more as I laughed, apologizing, "Oh, I'm sorry. I know that's not funny to you, but just knowing how it happened, it is."

I went over to Chip and put my arms around him, hugging him, telling him how sorry I was. He definitely had an embedded fear of nurses, which had never been there before.

A couple days later when I was in Chip's room, I started laughing as I thought about him and his keys the day the nurse came and his determination to leave rather than have blood drawn. That struck me as funny because Chip was so cute, searching for those keys and not saying a word. I could recall how he suddenly, silently had rushed to his room. The reason why had never crossed my mind. To think about the taxi, no matter what the cost, made it even funnier. I couldn't stop laughing when I was finally able to tell Chip how it had all struck me.

"Seriously," Chip said, "I though t for sure you had something planned."

Still trying to stop laughing, I said, "Chip, you know better than that. You know I wouldn't do anything like that to you."

Chip said, "Yes, but I wanted to be sure."

I took hold of his hands and, smiling, said, "I love you."

Chip smiled back and said, "I love you too, Mother."

Even though it wasn't funny to Chip at the time, later he laughed.

After Lynn's first visit. Chip had said, "She is special."

He enjoyed her company and she was good and thorough. She checked Chip every time, same as her first visit, but nothing more. It was what Chip needed. He had become more resigned to staying home and was lonesome. Therefore her visits were important.

Lynn had been visiting Chip for one month. Suddenly we learned that Chip would no longer have a nurse visiting him.

I asked Lynn, "Why can't Chip have another nurse if you are going to be taking a different job? Surely there are other nurses"

Lynn said that Chip didn't need medical attention at present. I told her he needed the exact same attention other patients in Dallas were getting with a visiting nurse and exactly what she had been doing for him this past month, but I understood it was out of her hands since she was changing jobs. She said she was sorry too because she did enjoy Chip.

It was heartbreaking for Chip. He didn't say much, but I sensed his sadness and the feeling of being deserted.

Later, when we were away from Chip, Lynn let me know that Chip's doctor had said he couldn't have a nurse since he wouldn't give blood. I was furious and heartbroken. I couldn't let Chip know what that doctor did! Chip wasn't on any medications that required blood analysis. Why was the doctor doing this? The few times the nurse was here, she did more for Chip than the doctor ever did, including her examinations. Lynn was much more thorough and certainly much more pleasant. This was what Chip needed. I almost went to the medical board. In fact, I would have if Chip weren't so sick. I wasn't leaving him alone, so I couldn't do anything. Also, I didn't want Chip to be under any more stress. I felt that his doctor himself was causing a lot of undue stress for Chip because of things such as this.

We had gotten a hospital bed while Lynn was visiting and Jerry rented a hospital table for Chip. After having the bed a month. Chip said he wasn't going to keep it. I asked him why not.

He said, "It's not electric like I thought it would be. It's too hard on you cranking it all the time."

Surprised, I said, "Chip, no it's not!"

He looked at me and nodded his head. "Yes, Mother, I know it is. It's hard on your back bending over like that to crank it."

"Honey, that s sweet of you, but really, my back's okay. Why don't you keep it? It's not hard to crank. Don't you think it's a lot easier going from one bed to the other while I change your sheets? Your king-size bed in the other room is too far away. This way you can lie down and rest without waiting on me."

"Yes, but this doesn't have any thing for me to hang onto like my own bed." I hadn't thought about that when we got it. I checked it and said, "Here, Chip, this rail should come up," I tugged at it and tried to raise it, "and it will help you as you get up."

I wasn't sure how to get the rail up, but finally managed. After putting the back rail up it was just right for him. Then he decided to keep it. Even though it was difficult for him to raise, he still thought it was too hard on my back, and he wouldn't ask. Different times I caught him raising it himself. It was a long time before he let me raise the bed for him, even a little bit.

Chip still ran a fever most all the time, but he wasn't having any pain. His feet were still frozen down to the bone, but he learned to live with it, knowing he hadn't any other choice.

It was getting close to my birthday and Chip said, "Mother, I'm sorry I won't be able to go out and get you a birthday present, but I will give you some money and a card. I want to get you something special."

"It's you I want to be here, that will be my present." I smiled, even though I felt melancholy to say that.

Chip was thinking ahead, knowing I'd treasure pictures. He said, "Mother, we will take some good pictures on your birthday."

I was sure he didn't feel like posing, but he knew what pictures meant to me. On my birthday, after taking some really good poses, we cut the cake and started to take some more pictures when we realized there wasn't any film in the camera! Oh, no! After all those good pictures! It was a disappointment to everyone, but the next day we bought some film and tried again. Chip was definitely worn out from the day before, but he did the best he could even though the second time for something like this wasn't the same. I'm sure Chip was thinking about next year's birthday and how he felt, knowing more than likely he wouldn't be here. Although on my card he had written,

"Mother, I love you so much. You've been the best. See you next year.. I betcha. "Love, Chip 8-14-86."

Our exchange of smiles was a heartwarming, true declaration of love. Leave it to Chip, hanging in there with a positive, happy thought, regardless. Always such a sweetheart.

Chip went the extra mile for Jerry and me both on our birthdays. For the way he was feeling it took a lot of effort for pictures, especially a second time, and Jerry had rated two cakes! When they delivered the first cake Chip was disappointed, so he immediately ordered him another one. Chip said we deserved the best and he wanted things right for us.

I smiled, saying, "That's why we have you. Chipper!"

I went to another support meeting the following week. Afterwards, when I got home I went into Chip's room, but he was sound asleep. I sat down by his bed, thinking he might be waking up. Sure enough.

As he awakened he smiled and said, "Hi. I wondered when you would be home."

I smiled and replied, "I have something for you from the meeting."

I showed him what was left of my birthday cake, telling him David had baked it special for me.

Chipper was delighted. "That's great!"

I told him I was surprised.

Chip was bubbling and said, "That makes me so happy he did that for you."

"David's a lot like you, Chip. You would have done something like this."

I told Chip about David's lover dying last week, how his mother came and David went with her to Ohio for the funeral.

"He's having a memorial service for him at the MCC Church in Dallas." I added, "I think I will go, for David. What do you think?"

Concerned, Chip asked, "Will you be okay?"

"I believe so."

Telling Chip about the funeral and memorial service started Chip and me on the subject again. "Mother, you'll have family and friends with you..."

"I want a nice funeral for you." I couldn't hold the tears back as I said, "I know it's going to happen, but I don't want to think about it."

"Mother, can't you admit, at the same time you just wish it would happen and get it over with?"

I tried to stop crying. "No, I don't feel that way."

Chip said, "You like hanging on like this?"

I couldn't stop crying. "Yes, I worry all the time about when it's going to happen. You keep getting mad at me when I open your door, but I can't help doing that. I really don't want you to go. I don't." I was sobbing my heart out. "How does that make you feel?"

"It makes me feel bad for you. You know, Mother, I don't know what's more of a slap in the face, somebody with an attitude like me who wants to get this over with or all those guys who are building false hope on false promises."

"Well, lean understand both. At the same time, positive thinking comes into focus: 'Live each day to its fullest.' You don't get false hope by positive thinking, you live each day to its fullest. Really, that's what we're supposed to do. You're doing that and facing reality, knowing there isn't a cure. Even though we don't like it, it takes a lot of courage facing it for what it is."

Chip said, "That's what everybody does, I thought."

I said, "Well..." and Chip spoke up, "I mean I can't do much, but I do what I can or want to do."

I said, "Yes, and..."Chip added, "I don't have the energy or effort. I can't handle the heat and bright light."

"Yes, but I think that's where yours is different and not many have your kind that we know of."

Chip said, "I just face it."

"That's good. At least you accept it, knowing it's holding you back. You don't make excuses, and you're doing well."

Chip sighed, "Yes, but you can only watch so much TV."

"Is that why you sleep so much at times?"

Chip said, "That's about all there is to do."

I asked, "Have you rested today?"

"I've been trying to get comfortable, but I'm having a hard time."

Laughing, I said, "Maybe after you eat your cake, you can rest more."

Chip said, "Yes, that does look good."

I was fixing Chip's blankets when he said, "Tonight on television they were talking about giving patients drugs to help them with their appetite."

"Do you mean grass?"

"Uh huh."

"I don't know, but I suppose that would be one way to get patients to eat." I added, "But that would be the worst thing for you because of your lungs."

"I'm not worried about that. They said I could smoke."

"Dr. Douglas said you could smoke a little bit. I think she said that because they didn't expect you to live much longer. That's been quite some time ago. I thought that at the time, did you?"

"Maybe."

"Chip, do you feel like walking to the kitchen? We can check your weight."

We went to the kitchen. The scale registered 115 pounds. I commented, "You've only lost a pound."

"Yes, I weighed 116 a couple of days ago."

"No, that was a week ago since you weighed, I think."

He started walking away, "Are you coming back to my room?" "Well, I don't know. I'm not sure," I teased.

I always tucked him in.

"Well, kiss, kiss, I do love you," he said, walking slowly.

He was funny. I laughed and asked teasingly, "You want me to come and tuck you in? I'll be there in a couple of minutes."

When Chip got almost to the doorway in the living room, he started to fall, but caught himself on the sofa.

I called, "Are you dizzy?" and rushed to his side.

"No, I'm okay."

"Chip, are you sure?" I demanded.

I watched him while he walked to his room. He was a little wobbly, but moved slowly and made it.

I hadn't even given thought to his asking if I was coming to his room. Maybe that was his indirect way of saying he felt dizzy, but I didn't get the message. He was so nonchalant, as usual, when he said it. Too, he still felt that it was up to him to do everything on his own. He hadn't changed since he was a little boy, not even now while sick. He never gave up. I couldn't blame him for wanting to get this life over with. For what reason was there to prolong his life? Ever since he knew he had AIDS life was trying, unfair, and cruel. I wondered why and felt bad for his sake.

A few minutes later I went to Chip's room to tuck him in for the night. Often we talked more late at night than at any other time of the day. When he was a little boy. Gramma always said he seemed to get more hyper at bedtime. So much about Chip hadn't really changed.

"Chip, do you know what makes me really feel bad?"

"What?"

"The way you wait until problems get really bad or they happen several times before you let me know."

"What do you mean, 'problems'?"

It seemed Chip was searching for what to say next. "Well, I don't need to be telling you all my problems."

"Chip, I need to know."

"Well, you need to know. Why?" He frankly asked.

"So I can help you and be more aware of things. You almost fell over that chair the other day and that chair then almost fell on you. You didn't say a word to me. What if that had happened and I didn't know anything about it? The same as a few minutes ago. I think you almost fell down and you caught yourself. You didn't say a word to me. If I hadn't seen you, I probably never would have known. Right?"

"Well, I probably would have lain there and then gotten up. I guess my equilibrium is off."

I sat for a few minutes, thinking, then said, "That's why when I leave the house to go to the health dub, you should try to stay in bed until I return home."

"I do."

"That's why I shouldn't be gone too long at a time, even if Jerry's here, because you never tell either of us if there's a problem."

Chip got up to go to the bathroom, moving slowly from his bed, then bracing himself on the wall. He steadied himself more, moving slowly and carefully until he made it. While Chip was gone I changed his bed and checked his pillbox. I noticed it was empty and refilled it. When Chip came back, I asked, "Have you been taking your thrush medicine?"

"Yes."

"Did you take your temperature today?"

"Yes, it was 102I /2." Chip had been taking his own temperature since we got him a digital thermometer which was easy for him to use by pressing a button, inserting it into his mouth, taking it out in thirty seconds, then reading the numbers it registered.

"Okay, Chip. You've got clean, dry sheets and pillows."

"Good."

Chip hated the darn ol' sweats and chills all the time, but he loved the fresh sheets. He said it made him feel like a baby.

"You are a baby, you're my baby," I teased.

He chuckled and said, "I like being a baby."

We laughed. He was my baby.

It was true. Now my son, this grown young man, was needing the extra time, love, and attention like a baby. Still, he was as good as gold and just as priceless as always.

"Well, Chip, I've got to get to bed. Can I get you anything before I go?" "No, Mother, you've done more than enough. I love you."

"I love you. Call me if you need anything before morning."

I gave Chip a kiss good night on the forehead and touched his cheek as I smiled and again said, "I love you. See you in the morning."

When I started to walk out of his room I felt sad. I stopped in the doorway and looked back at Chip again. Almost choking in tears, I softly repeated, "I love you."

I poked down the hallway, feeling so alone and sad. That was pretty much our nightly routine. I hated to leave Chip. There wasn't anything else I could do, only say, "I love you," which were always our last words to each other every time I left his room. It was sad knowing it might be the last time to say those words. What was more important to say and hear at a time like this?

18

When You Get Old

"Good morning. Chip. May I come in?"

"Sure."

"You didn't sleep much last night, did you?"

"No, not really."

While I was checking his pillbox I said, "I heard you coughing most of the night. I almost came down, but waited and you seemed to be a little better."

Chip couldn't say much as he grabbed a Kleenex to clean the phlegm from his mouth. He had been having a lot of congestion lately with a persistent dry cough.

He cleared his throat and said, "You should have come on down. I didn't sleep."

"I didn't think you did. I should have. Remember your appointment with the doctor today?"

Chip wasn't too enthused when he shrugged his shoulders and nodded his head.

"Well, Chip, after this I can make your trips to the lab and for whatever is needed, except the doctor. Okay? I dread the ride for you today, but it shouldn't take too long. Do you want to stop and get something to eat on our way home?"

"No, I'm not hungry."

I was hoping the Reglin would quickly increase his appetite, although it might take a few days to get into his system. Chip slowly got up and headed for the bathroom, supporting himself on his bed and then the wall. He was becoming much weaker.

"Chip, when you get back I'll have these sheets changed. Do you want the blanket on your bed?"

"Please."

"You didn't change beds during the night, did you? This bed is soaked." "No, I was too cold until a little while ago. I may need another blanket." "Okay, I'll put another one on now. Jerry's going to get you a portable space heater. That way we can keep this room much warmer for you than the rest of the house."

"Good. That's what I need," Chip agreed.

"Jerry thought you would like that. I was afraid that it may be too hot for you."

"At this time, does that really matter? Why not be comfortable in the time I have left?"

I hesitated, then said, "Well, I guess you're right."

In the beginning I'd argue because of his fever, but quit. I was beginning to agree, even though I still worried. It was amazing how my thinking changed. Yet what choice did we really have? If his days were limited, why not let him be as comfortable as possible? Chip was right. Live each day, but face the facts! My son could be gone at any time. Knowing that and living with the thought was a nightmare. All we had to live for was each day, being together and praying it wasn't the last day, even though living was unfair to him too.

When Chip came back to his room, I helped him put on some clean sweats and socks. He still wasn't able to wear shoes, only slippers. He was chilly before even going outdoors, so he slipped on his jacket.

Once Chip was in the car, I leaned the seat way back so he could rest, although I knew he wouldn't be relaxed until we were home again. My driving seemed to make him nervous now.

While we quietly waited in the doctor's office, I observed the other patients. I felt certain another young man had AIDS too. He was very slim, looked fatigued, and had the same dry cough as Chip. I felt sorry and a little guilty to be thinking this, knowing how it was for Chip. I wanted to talk with the young man, to let him know I understood and cared. I realized that would be an intrusion, so I kept quiet and asked God to give him lots of love and care.

I looked at Chip and smiled, then looked down, thinking about this terrible, heartbreaking sickness that was taking my son and so many young men.

Chip had grown to accept things for what they were, thinking he wasn't going to be here much longer since he was having a hard time breathing.

He said, "That's how it was before when I stopped breathing. It was respiratory."

Finally, Chip was checked by the doctor and given his prescriptions for Reglin and Augmentin.

Then Chip asked the doctor for some barbiturates to take when the pain became unbearable again. I believe the doctor understood, although he only looked at Chip.

Chip continued in sincerity, "When the pain gets bad, really bad, I would like to take them."

After talking with friends, Chip had informed me he was going to ask for barbiturates, although he understood it wasn't likely the doctor would comply. Still, it was worth a try. The human body can only take so much, and he was ready to be free from suffering the leisurely unbearable pain.

Next we went to the lab. I had to take another sample of Chip's urine and stool to the doctor's in the morning, so this meant another trip, which happened often. His diarrhea was getting worse again and he was having terrible times making it to the bathroom.

I never questioned the trips, even if I needed to go back the same day, believing it might help with whatever problems Chip was having; I was anxious for his sake. Too, his testing was needed for research.

The next day after I got home from taking Chip's samples to the laboratory, Chip was sound asleep. So I decided to lie in the sun. Noticing how pretty the rose garden looked made me think of how Chip often gave flowers. I smiled and picked a single rose. Chip was still sleeping when I went back into the house, so I put the rose in a small vase, placed it on his table, and sat down next to him, waiting. When Chip woke up and saw the rose, a big smile covered his face.

He glanced at me and softly said, "Thanks, Mother. That's real pretty. Love you, too."

"I was sunbathing. The flowers looked so pretty, and I wanted you to have the prettiest rose of all."

Smiling, I leaned over and kissed his temple. "Have you been asleep since I left to go to the doctor?"

"Uh huh. What time is it?"

"It's almost time for Jerry to come home."

"Good! I slept most of the day."

Chip liked sleeping because time seemed to go much faster and helped cut the boredom.

The telephone rang. It was Chip's gramma calling from Indiana. She and his gramma in Michigan called him frequently and sent him tokens of love through the mail—anything to help build his strength, both mentally and physically. Chip and Gramma had been talking awhile when I picked up the extension.

With Chip being sick he was more tolerant of my being on the extension. Sometimes he'd tire suddenly and need to hang up abruptly, saying, "I'm hanging up. Bye." Then I'd talk. No matter how tired or sick he felt, he somehow always kept up his enthusiasm, at least until the sudden dick, when necessary.

Today Chip and his gramma were talking about the hospital in Wichita Falls when he had gotten sick physically.

Gramma said, "It seems they would have found something on the many tests, doesn't it? They did take tests, didn't they?"

"Yes, all the time. I was so deathly ill while there. They were piling five and six blankets on me, the opposite of the hospital, freezing me to death. My doctor told me I could quit taking all the medicine and I thought, Great, my feet will go back to normal. On the TB papers it said numbness of the hands and feet was common. They're still pretty numb and I haven't been taking that medicine for weeks. I think they're still numb because they froze me so long in the hospital. They kept it so cold and kept that ice blanket on me. You know, they forgot about my poor little feet." He chuckled.

"Yes, yes! It was cool in there," Gramma agreed.

"Oh, sure. You were there!"

"Yes, I came down there and took a look at you, all white and pale and wired up." She laughed.

"Oh, really? And you saw that blanket? Wasn't that a treacherous piece of equipment?"

"Well, the whole room was."

"You know, I think all they wanted me for was, not to get me well, but to run experiments and learn, and I've just about had enough of that. I'm tired of being their guinea pig!"

"Well, when they don't know anything, I guess they have to do some of that."

"Yes," he laughed, "but why am I the victim?"

"It seems like it, doesn't it?"

"It sure does! The only thing that bothers me is that I'm scared there will be pain."

"Well, we're all praying there isn't."

"Well, I'm not going back in the hospital."

Chip told Gramma how he felt about things and Gramma assured him that we all have those days, even when we're not sick. She told him not to let it get him down.

Chip told Gramma he had to hang up, that Jerry would be home any time. Chip was keeping close tabs on Jerry. If Jerry was the least bit late, he'd comment, "You're late, aren't you?"

This tickled Jerry and me. It was a reversal from when Chip was younger, and we'd laugh.

This time when Jerry got home Chip said, "I heard on the news that the freeway will be done soon. Then you'll be home earlier, won't you?"

Jerry said, "That's right." He touched Chip's forehead to check his temperature. "I'm going to get your heater. Be back in a few minutes."

"Great!" Chip said.

When Jerry got back he also had something else for Chip. He took them into Chip's room and said, "I thought this porta potty might save you rushing to the bathroom."

I said, "That's a good idea, Chip. With the diarrhea it's so hard for you to make it to the bathroom sometimes, and this way you won't need to. We can keep it close by your bed. It's real nice and clean, almost like having another handy table near with the lid closed."

Jerry was good at making things easier and handier for Chip.

A little later Chip said, "Mother, will you fix me a cheese omelet with green peppers, tomato and onion?"

"That sounds good, with fresh tomatoes and peppers from the garden. Would you like hot, dry peppers on it too?"

"No, but I would like an English muffin with cream cheese."

"Would you like some protein to drink?"

In an aggravated tone, Chip said, "No, Mother."

I laughed, and said, "Well, I thought maybe..." I really knew better, but I kept trying every now and then to get Chip to drink protein.

A few minutes later Chip called, "I'd like a glass of chocolate milk too."

I thought, I'll put a little protein in the milk, he'll never know.

When I had everything ready, I took it to him and sat it on his bed tray. He was eating very well. A few minutes later he asked, "May I have another glass of milk?"

I don't know how, with one sip, but he must have known I put protein in his milk. He made no comment, but I did get him a glass of milk without the protein and he drank it all.

A couple of days before. Chip had gone to the kitchen to eat. He sat down and after two bites, he wasn't as hungry as he thought. This was happening more often and the walk to the kitchen was exhausting him.

One day Rhonda came for dinner and spent the evening with Chip while I went to the club to swim. When I got home Chip was talking with Grams on the telephone. Rhonda said they had been talking for about forty- five minutes. So I picked up the other telephone and said, "Hi." Chip was telling Grams that Rhonda and I were ganging up on him.

I laughed and said, "Chip, we are not!"

He told Grams that Rhonda and I were trying to get him to see more doctors. Chip said, "And Grams, it's no use."

"Oh, Chip, don't give up hope," Grams said.

"There's no hope. Not for me."

As Grams tried to convince Chip, they were both talking at once.

"Well, I'm just facing life. And I won't talk about it anymore because nobody else can handle it," Chip said.

"But I think you should try to keep yourself on as good a level as you can," encouraged Grams.

"Well, I do."

Grams said, "Huh?"

"We've been doing real good. Mother's working with me and Jerry's working with me real good. He goes out of his way to be real kind and gets me whatever I need."

Grams said, "Jerry's that kind of a guy, isn't he?"

Chip said, "Yes, he sure is!"

"And your Mother's the best."

Chip said, "Yes. Mother is always busy."

Grams said, "So, by golly, I think you should hang in there and keep up all the strength you can. So if something does come up good, you'll have something to work with. And I don't want you to give up hope on it."

"Well, Grams, every time I turn around..." he paused to clear his throat, and Grams said, "Everybody's trying to find another cure for you, huh?"

"Yes, everybody's trying to find a cure and thinking if you go to the doctor, you're going to get well, and that's not true. They can't do anything. They can't do anything!"

Grams said, "That's because they love you and they want the best for you."

Chip said, "Well, yes, that's true. That's true."

After a few more words. Chip told Grams he was glad they had talked, but they'd been on the telephone a long time.

Grams said, "I don't care as long as I get to talk to you. I don't care if it costs a twenty-dollar bill. I'd rather spend a twenty-dollar bill this way than any other way I can think of."

Chip chuckled and said, "Make it a forty-dollar bill, at the rate we're going."

Grams laughed with Chip and said, "That's okay. You take care. I love you a whole bunch!"

Chip said, "Okay, I love you, and you sound fabulous!"

Grams laughed, "So do you. You sound better."

"Yes, I feel good."

"Take real good care of yourself."

Chip hung up, then Mother and I talked a few minutes. After I hung up, I went into Chip's room and found him sound asleep. Rhonda was lying on his other bed asleep. I didn't disturb them. After awhile they woke up and Rhonda went home.

In the hospital an Episcopal minister had visited Chip and then came to our home, but soon after he was transferred to another state. I invited another minister to our home. Since Chip had been baptized as an Episcopalian, I felt this was important. Chip's condition seemed worse and I thought spiritual comfort might help. I had told the father about Chip and his illness, so he knew why I had invited him.

The minister was kind and congenial while talking to Chip and me. But after that I couldn't reach him. I called several times, but my calls were never returned. He was polite at church and I'd call again, but he didn't return my calls. I was surprised and disappointed to finally realize he was avoiding me.

I couldn't believe an Episcopal minister was doing this, especially after being in our home and letting me think all was fine. If he suddenly couldn't accept my son, then I certainly could not accept him as a minister! He didn't even have the audacity to say if that was the reason, but what he had done was enough to let me know I wanted nothing to do with him ever again. I was hurt and I was angry. I expected more of a minister: to naturally be a comfort when there was a need, no matter what.

Chip had been having a trying time with God since this had all taken place. Then for a minister to react as he did, what was Chip to think? He knew there was a higher power, a supreme being, but he wasn't sure what to think anymore. At this time he had mixed feelings. The cult was out of the picture. I'm sure he never would have gotten involved if he hadn't apparently had the confusion of these complications during that time, which no one realized. He knew of cults before, but wasn't interested. Confusion is a terrible experience for any human being and many of these patients go through this. Isn't it easiest to be angry at the one you love the most, knowing they will love you and understand? God is Love.

Chip believed in God, although at this time he had unanswered questions, and he was still searching. His thoughts were understandable, with all he was going through during this crisis and with all he'd already been through throughout this life.

Chip wanted his friend Reverend Jim to give his eulogy.

He said, "He knows me and will give an honest eulogy."

Chip had gone to the Agape Metropolitan Community Church (MCC) in Fort Worth different times. He spoke highly of Jim and his services. When he had first gotten sick, at different times he mentioned going there, but couldn't because of his complications.

I called Jim to let him know about Chip's illness and that Chip would like for him to give his eulogy. Jim came to our home immediately to be with Chip. He was exactly as Chip had said, most pleasant and sincere. Chip definitely would have been happy with the beautiful eulogy that this dear friend would one day give, and to know he was assisted by another friend who was an Episcopal lay minister, Reverend Brooks.

In time we would see what Chip meant by an honest eulogy. It was exactly as he had said, "Jim knows me."

When Jim came out of Chip's room, he said, "He will be going to heaven. We talked awhile and Chip was smiling. His eyes were watery and spoke for themselves."

I understood what Jim was saying and I was happy for Chip. He needed this.

Then Jim said, "His only worry about dying is leaving you. He said, 'I won't be here to take care of my mother when she gets old. I was supposed to take care of her.' This is really tearing him up inside."

"I know, Jim. That's what he told me when he first learned he wouldn't be here much longer. It's been bothering him. He even talked to Jerry about it. I tried to tell him it was okay, but he said, 'I was supposed to take care of you, Mother, when you get old.' He has always looked out for me, actually, ever since he was a little boy. This seemed to be natural for him. I've really been fortunate, Jim."

Chip was pleased that Jim had come to see him, and Jim's presence had done him a world of good. He was content when I tucked him in that night.

The next morning Chip was looking out the window when I went into his room. He said, "The yard looks so nice, Mother."

"Thanks, Chip. Jerry will like hearing that. I want to keep things as pretty as possible," I said, grinning. "I put more flowers out this year since it's a nice view for you."

"I know." Chip smiled. "Yesterday Jerry came in and asked if I was awake. He was going to mow the lawn. That was real thoughtful of him. And you ask me before running the sweeper. I appreciate that, Mother."

"Honey, it's just that we know the noise bothers you, and we want you to rest when you can."

Chip graciously smiled.

"I'm going to the doctor's office pretty soon. Would you like to sit on the porch swing before I go?" I asked.

"No, not now. It was about four o'clock in the morning when I went out there the other night and sat on the porch swing. I swung with the birds while I talked with them." Chip chuckled. "They would go 'chirp, chirp,' and I would say 'chirp, chirp' back."

Still laughing, Chip said, "It was real quiet except for the birds and I chirping up a conversation."

We laughed together at silly, fun times such as this.

"Well, okay. Chip. I'm leaving. See you in a little bit."

"Be careful. Mother."

While driving down the freeway, I was thinking how strange it was without Chip, and I didn't want to be gone too long. I wished he were with me, but knew it was best that he wasn't.

When I arrived I parked the car and hurried into the building and up the elevator to the doctor's office. I waited for the receptionist to get the doctor's signature on the prescription. There were two other young men waiting in the lobby who had familiar coughs like Chip's.

Please, hurry, I was thinking.

I don't know if it was because Chip wasn't with me or what, but this time I could hardly take the coughs. God, if it's this way for me now, what's it going to be like later? I heard another cough. It was difficult to hold back the tears. Finally the receptionist came out. We smiled. She handed me the prescription, and I was on my way, thankful to be out of there.

By now I could hardly bear my thoughts. I couldn't keep from crying any longer as I ran to the elevator, waiting for the door to open, then hurried in and back out again once it stopped on the main floor. I hurried down the hall to the exit door, still sobbing. Then down the steps, thinking how far apart each step was and how awkward they were. What if I missed and fell? I don't care! I don't care! Why's this happening to Chip?

I ran onto the parking lot without looking. A car approached as I ran. What if the car hits me? I don't care!

By now I was crying helplessly. I could hardly see while I ran. *Let the car hit me, I don't care. Why is this happening to Chip? Oh, I can't stand it! What am I going to do once he's gone?*

I was crying, gasping for breath, and my stomach was aching. My mascara was running down my face. I wiped the tears and blew my nose once I was in the car. I've got to pull myself together. But I was getting this terrible, pounding headache.

My eyes ached, my forehead throbbed, my whole head felt as if it weighed a ton. My neck hurt.

God, what am I going to do? Please, please help me.

Sad images ran through my mind. It was starting to be too much. I sat behind the steering wheel with my head leaning back on the headrest. At times like this I couldn't stop the aching in my neck and shoulders, but I knew I had to pull myself together so I could get home to Chip. I loved him so very much. I prayed he was alright. An urgency came over me as I said to myself. Please, God. Please may he be alright

I started the car and headed home. This was just one of those times when I felt as if my thoughts and emotions were all closing in on me. *Still, I must be strong. Chip gives me strength, and I will be strong for Chip just like he is for me.*

19

Mother, I'm Sorry

Chip was becoming restless. Then he saw the advertisement on TV for Meals on Wheels.

He called and said he wanted to do volunteer work helping with the elderly. His face was sad when he thanked them and hung up. He said there wasn't anything he could do to help since he couldn't drive anymore.

I believe this bothered Chip more than he was letting on. I tried to relate how well he was still doing for the condition he was in, the length of time, and all he had already been through. But that was the sad part, knowing it was pure hell and misery all the way. And now this letdown, not being able to help the elderly.

Sometimes I thought that was why he was almost shutting his friends out when they wanted to see him. He had always been a proud person and steadily he was being robbed of his pride and dignity through this relentless disease. He wanted friends to remember him the way he was before this illness.

Still, when anyone came to our home, they commented on how well Chip was doing for being so sick. Jerry's brother John, from Ohio, visited us for a few days.

When we were leaving Chip's bedroom, John said, "He never bothers you. You hardly know he's here."

That is why I always said, "If ever there was such a thing as a star patient, and I know there is, because Chip is one!"

It was hard for me to actually realize how sick Chip was at times because he was such an exception. It was amazing how he took care of himself for as long as he did, not letting me know how miserable he must have felt or what was wrong.

One day I asked if I could get him anything.

Chip answered, "Twenty pounds."

I smiled, saying, "I wish."

Chip still wanted to see his dad before he passed away. He was crushed, but as of yet hadn't given up on his coming.

"You know something that bums me up? I gave my dad the easy way out again." He paused, then said, "Which I guess is better."

I asked, "How's that?"

"By, you know, basically giving him the cold shoulder." "He knew you really wanted to see him and needed to." Downhearted, Chip repeated, "I gave him the easy way out!" "And he took it, didn't he?" I said.

Chip said, "Yes, and that's been p me off, thinking he's always gotten away with everything. And now I'm sick, when I really could use love and support, even though I have such mixed feelings for him, you know. It bums me up that I gave him the easy way out. He didn't deserve it."

"I know, Chip. You sure haven't deserved what he's done. If only he would take the time and come."

As the days wore on it was even more sad seeing Chip lying silent, wondering what he had done to deserve his dad's denial.

Chip and I never talked about his dad anymore, still it hurt to see the added stress and heartache he obviously was having to tolerate. Next thing I knew I was thinking about his dad's Christmas card last year, remembering how it had crushed Chip so bad that the card had only a signature and no word from his dad. And the birthday card from his half sister was the same way. I still couldn't imagine that being done to him. I wondered if they knew ho w sick Chip actually was? II was so unfair to him, and he still wasn't hearing from his dad. I don't know if it was seeing Chip day in and day out getting worse and feeling so sad, or what, but the pressure seemed to be mounting when suddenly I decided to call his dad's home. Chip was in no condition to be hurt again with the holidays nearing. I hadn't called there since Chip was a little boy, but felt I must under the circumstances. I didn't want Chip to be devastated again.

His half sister answered the phone. I introduced myself and asked her if she knew Chip was sick, and she replied she did. Then I asked her if she knew when she sent him a birthday card last year. She replied, "Yes, I was trying to be nice."

About that time her mother took the phone. I told her who I was and again asked, "Did you know that Chip was sick and dying?"

She said, "Yes, we've known since you called last November and told my husband's sister."

I started to tell her that was why I was calling, because I wasn't sure if they knew, but next thing I knew she was yelling, saying something about calling to lay blame. Shocked I then raised my voice, answering, "We know where the blame lies!"

Next thing I heard was a click. Just like years ago, she hung up on me. I sat bewildered. What had I done? I was trying to help Chip's predicament and now I must have made it worse.

"Oh, God, please help," I stammered. "This is unfair for Chip!"

I didn't know what to do. At the time, I couldn't tell Chip because it would only add to his heartache.

Chip looked forward to Rhonda's calls and visits. She was visiting Chip more than calling, but now she had a terrible cold and was afraid of giving it to Chip. Then they talked on the phone almost constantly. The third day Rhonda was going to come out, and Chip said, "No, not until you get rid of that cold."

They talked awhile and I heard Chip say, "Rhonda, with all this I have been having and going through, you're still coming out to see me and calling. Why are you doing all this?"

There was a pause, then I heard Chip say, *"I* love you, too."

When Chip hung up, he happily told me what was said. He truly appreciated Rhonda's loyal friendship.

"Your relationship is ironic considering what Rhonda's dad said years ago. He planned on your taking care of his little girl someday. The beautiful part is that you remained good friends."

Rhonda had been trying to help me get Chip to see another doctor, but he still declined. He told me his mind was made up.

"I have you and Jerry, and I have Rhonda to talk with. That's all I need. That's the way I want it to be."

I quit pushing the idea of his going to another doctor for the time being. I sensed that he may have been going through the anger stage. Being with him all the time and seeing what was happening, I understood and respected his feelings. I agreed with him, whether it be anger or another stage he was going through or Just living with the thought of death all the time. He had a right to feel as he did. He wasn't complaining, but he was worn out.

I heard on the news about the new AZT drug for AIDS patients. I called Chip's doctor, wanting to know more about it and to be sure if it was or wasn't something he needed to try.

His doctor said Chip didn't have pneumocystis and AZT was primarily being experimented with patients who had those complications. He said he didn't know too much about the drug at present and I could call an 800 number to find more out.

I related our conversation about AZT to Chip. I knew Chip's thoughts, Why prolong it? It's bad enough as it is. I didn't want to lose him, yet I couldn't argue he was wrong. Until you live with this or are with someone day in and day out who has it, it's hard to comprehend what it does to the patient The facts during this time were not anything anyone could be happy with or expect much of a future.

Chip's cousin Debbie, in Baltimore, had been great keeping Chip's spirits up by calling and writing every so often.

Chip hadn't heard from Debbie recently when he decided to call. I handed him his telephone. Thinking he wouldn't talk long, I rearranged his bedding, knowing he was ready for a nap.

Chip said, "Hi, are you busy?" There was a pause and he said, "You've been sitting on the porch."

Chip looked tired. I knew that meant he might need to hang up suddenly. So I went to the other room and softly said "Hi" when I picked up the receiver, but I don't believe I was heard in their excitement talking. If Chip weren't sick, I never would have picked up the phone.

"You sound like you're awfully tired," Debbie said.

"Yes, I'm fixing to go to sleep. I was lying here thinking I sure need to talk to you. Give you a shout and say hi."

His voice sounded weak, as though it was ready to give out.

"Oh, I appreciate it," Debbie said. "I started you half a dozen letters and never got them mailed. I'm so glad you called. How about that new drug they have come out with, are you eligible for that or not?"

Chip said, "Oh, I don't know."

"Not sure?"

"No, I'm not even interested."

"No giving up, though."

"I'm not giving up. I'm not interested in what I have to do to take the drug. Some people can deal with IV's and stuff in their arms, but I'm not going to do that. I don't need to. I've had enough of that."

"You haven't gone back in the hospital, have you?"

"There's no way I'll go back in the hospital."

"Now you're going to stay home, huh?"

"Uh huh, yes."

"You're kind of holding your own?"

"Uh huh, I am. I had a visiting nurse once a week. She checked my blood and heart, everything like that."

"That's good, that gives your mother a break, too. Kinda lets her keep tabs on things and she doesn't worry as much."

Chip told Debbie about the nurse and this being her last week.

Chip said, "The pressure's back up and the heartbeat's normal. I'm so sick of this constant phlegm I'm coughing up. It's real disgusting."

"It's better to get it up than let it lie there."

Chip agreed, saying, "Yes. It's real ironic. It's what I had when I was a baby and almost died. Phlegm filled up my chest."

"Oh, no. Is there anything they can give you to help break that down or slow it up?"

"I'm on an antibiotic and Nizoral. I don't know if you're familiar, but have you ever seen a person when they get this white-like cake that develops in their mouth? Do you know what I'm talking about?"

"Yes," Debbie answered.

"That's what they are scared of, if you swallow it and it gets in your lungs. That's how a lot of them have died. And this Nizoral has prevented that. So I take it."

Chip sounded like it was taking a lot of effort to talk.

"It takes good mouth care and all," Debbie said.

Chip said, "I'm having a hard time with personal hygiene."

He had been a fanatic almost. So naturally it wasn't the same and was awkward for him not being able to go to the bathroom to clean up. Debbie told Chip about her cancer patients and how they keep looking forward to holidays or anything to keep going.

Debbie said, "That's what you call buying time until they can find out what to do to get it taken care of."

Chip chuckled, "Well, I would rather sell mine out."

Debbie laughed and said, "No way!"

Chip repeated with a chuckle, "I'd rather sell mine out."

Debbie told Chip he felt that way now, but he needed to find himself a goal and work toward it.

Debbie said, "At least you're on the phone and talking."

Enthusiastically, Chip said, "Yes, I'm sorry I'm so negative."

"No, you're not. Hey, everybody has their negative days. If you'd heard me today, you'd known negative." She laughed and Chip chuckled.

Suddenly Chip sounded like the "real Chip," not the least bit tired, but full of vim and vigor!

"How's your Mother doing?" Debbie asked.

"She's feeling real good. She's going to write a book. She's doing her real estate some, aerobics one day and swimming the next day. And just keeping busy, busy, busy."

"I bet it makes you tired to look at her sometimes," Debbie laughed.

"I know. It does." Chip laughed, "She keeps busy!"

"Have you heard from your dad?"

"He's tried a couple of times and I really don't care to ever talk to him when he calls."

Debbie said, "Ooh, okay," and Chip continued talking, "Cause you know, all I have is, I don't know if hate's the right word, but I don't want anything to do with the man. You know. I don't want anything to do with him! Twenty-seven years and he hasn't messed with me. So, you know, do you think I'm going to give him the pleasure, just because of my situation, of kissing ass? I'm not going to do that."

"No, that's your decision."

"I don't have to do that. So many years I dreamed, 'Oh, please just let us get along.' But, you know, there's no way. Because the only time he calls me is from work. I'm sure it caused trouble when I called up there in the past, so I don't even want to bother his lifestyle."

"Yes," commented Debbie.

Chip continued, "We all pay for what we do, and I guess he's paying for a lot of the things he's done and I'm paying for a lot of the things I've done. I just think he's a real jerk, to be honest." Chip went on to say, "And I won't talk to him because I think I would tell him that, in a lot worse words."

"Well, it's better not to talk then," Debbie agreed.

"Exactly. I have too much resentment built up inside me. It used to be, 'Oh please. I want him to call so bad. I want to talk to my dad.' But now it's changed. I mean, you can only love somebody who slaps you in the face again and again for so long, you know," Chip ended with a slight, dry chuckle.

"Yes, guaranteed. You think after awhile, It's not worth it," commented Debbie.

"That's exactly the way I feel. And it's really too bad because I used to have such respect. I don't know if it's respect, but admiration."

"Oh yes, hero worship. I don't think there was anyone in the family he wasn't number one with while they were growing up. You kind of got everything settled with yourself then."

Chip said, "Yes."

"That's good. Is there anything I can do?"

"No, thank you."

I don't know how he talked as long as he did, as tired as he was. It was times like this, somehow he surprisingly jumped right back and you almost wouldn't have thought he was sick. Before he got sick that's how he always was, and many times, like this, he still was. He was exhausted though and fell asleep almost immediately after he hung up. I was happy I didn't need to intercept his call. It was good he had Debbie to talk with.

At different times it was getting difficult for Chip to form words or maybe it would take a little longer to say something. This slowness came on gradually and didn't get too extreme or happen too often. Still, when this first happened I'd impatiently say, "Come on, Chip, say it." This didn't seem to bother him, and with his persistence the words gradually flowed out.

Later I learned that opportunistic infections that affect the brain or central nervous system may develop slowly and are sometimes accompanied by subtle changes in speech or personality. It's sad to think I didn't understand how this was for him. Only now can I look back and say, "If only I'd known more of what to be aware of or how to have coped with it better." But at that time, there was not any way of knowing or finding out.

I'm sure there had to be others out there going through what Chip and I were, but we didn't know them. Everyone I talked with seemed to have a nurse, was in the hospital frequently, or didn't live too long. Chip and I learned together pretty much on our own, maybe the hard way, and only through experience with my inexperience. But together we were able to deal with whatever was necessary.

Even though Chip was suffering and in constant pain, he gave me strength through a remarkable quality he had always had about himself, even before he was sick. Above all, we always had lots of love. We managed our time together through hard times and good times. Neither of us wanted it any other way. Love definitely pulled us through those trying months of sickness starting soon after Chip was only twenty-five. All my heart was in making him as comfortable as possible...and just to be near.

When I awakened I heard Jerry going into Chip's room. Enthusiastically Chip said, "Good morning. How are you today?"

"Good morning, Chip. I'm fine. How was your night?"

"About the same. Has Mother already left?"

"No, I believe she just woke up."

Chip enthusiastically said, "Would you like to fix those orange Danish rolls for us?"

"Would you like eggs with them? Your Mother's getting up now." Jerry went to the kitchen and fixed the rolls. I went into Chip's room.

I asked, "Do you want to come out to the kitchen or would you like me to bring them in here?"

"I really wanted it to be like a family affair, you know, so we could eat together and I was going to come out there, but would you mind bringing them in here?"

"You can't walk out there?"

"No, I'd really like to eat in here."

Apparently Chip suddenly felt tired, but didn't want to admit it.

"Okay. I will, and we can eat in your room with you."

Chip was becoming weaker and thinner. His legs and arms were very thin, with his knee joints and the bones protruding outward in extreme. Still, it was amazing he got around as well as he did. To see him, you wouldn't think he could walk, let alone move by himself.

For the first time in months, Chip asked me to make him a protein drink. I anxiously made it and sat it beside his bed while I did my aerobics. When I was through, I checked on him.

Opening his door, I softly said, "Chip."

He must have been asleep because he didn't answer, so I went back out.

It wasn't even five minutes until Chip loudly called, "Mother!"

I laughed as I hurried back to his room. He was starting to call me a lot like this every so often.

Laughingly teasing, I said, "Did you think I wasn't here?"

Chip assuringly said, "Just checking."

I noticed Chip's protein glass and said, "Chip, that's great! You drank all of your protein."

"Yes. Thank you."

"You're welcome. Let me know when you want some more. I'm going to take your glass to the kitchen and do some cleaning. Call me if you want me before I come back. Okay?"

"Okay, Mother."

Chip hadn't called so I decided to check on him. When I got to his room, he had his heater turned all the way up.

"Aren't you hot, Chip?"

"I am. I was going to buzz you to tum the heater down."

As I lowered it, I said, "I will put it on medium low. Okay?"

"That's fine."

"That's a pretty nice heater," I commented. "Jerry sure is spoiling you, isn't he?"

Chip grinned and nodded his head yes.

Jerry heard me and called, "He needs the heat when we don't."

"Yes. That was a wise buy," I replied."

A few days later Chip asked for a glass of chocolate milk. He was lying in bed when I took the milk in to him. Something caught my attention on television while I was standing at the head of his bed behind him, holding his glass while he drank it from a straw. Chip wasn't quite finished when he said, "Why can't I..."

I looked down at him, and not quite hearing what he'd said, I went around to the side of his bed and asked, "Why can't you hold your glass? Is that what you said?"

Chip apparently repeated, "Why can't I live?"

I was stunned. I dropped down to my knees at the side of his bed. My eyes watered and I was choked up, at a loss for words. I said, "Ooh, Chip, if only..." I leaned over and hugged him, saying, "I love you. I love you so very much, baby."

These were moments when words weren't there.

Chip's friend Mike had been over earlier in the week. That was my first time to meet him, although I had heard Chip mention his name over the years at different times and knew they were good friends. It was as though we'd been friends for years, too. Chip had told me Mike was Mr. Dallas one year and it was apparent why he'd had the honor. He was a tall, good-looking, pleasant young man.

Several days later I heard Chip talking on the telephone to him. "Mike, Mother really likes you. Are you going to be there?"

I'm sure Chip must have been talking about the funeral. Then Chip said, "You take real good care of her cause she's really going to need somebody."

Of course, Chip knew Jerry would be there for me, but he was being extra cautious, which didn't surprise me. The tears stung my eyes and rolled down my cheeks. Sometimes I thought Chip was hanging on longer for me, wanting to make sure I was ready. Today when I lookback, I'm sure he was.

Then I heard him telling Mike all the things Jerry had been getting him and doing for him. Chip was telling how we were so good about not trying to make him eat when he couldn't or didn't have an appetite.

He said, "Mother understands now that I can't eat at times, and they are really great."

Chip was listening, then said, "It's just a shame that she doesn't have somebody else for all her love, always caring and always being there and always listening to whatever it is. She sure saved my ass different times."

Chip listened and replied, "Yes. Uh huh."

Then he said, "It really makes me mad that there's nobody here to take advantage of my mother's wonderfulness." After a pause, he added, "I mean, she really is the greatest and neatest lady I know. It's really shortchanging some kid who can't have her to love him and take care of him."

Chip waited, then said, "Nobody does the job that she does. I know, you may think I'm saying this just because she's my mother, but really, Mike, I know a lot of other mothers and none of them care about their kids the way my mother has cared about me." After a pause, Chip said, "She's just a real good lady."

Mike and Chip talked awhile longer, and then I went into Chip's room. I told him I'd overheard what he was saying.

"That's okay, Mother, that's how you are."

I smiled, gave Chip a hug, and said, "You are so thoughtful and appreciative, even with what you're going through!"

I kept thinking more about what Chip had said to Mike.

Then I said, "Chip, you have the biggest heart Here you are about to die, and you're thinking of some other person getting all the love that is yours. How can you feel that way? You have always been so generous and kind. Ohh, I'm sorry," and I started to cry, "I don't want to lose you."

I went on to say, "From the beginning, I have been the lucky one to have a son like you."

"Mother, I just wish you hadn't put all your eggs in one basket."

"Chip, how can you say that? I mainly wanted another child for you at one time, but it's just as well I didn't."

"Mother, I'm sorry I was gay"

I was crushed and the tears gushed out, knowing what Chip was saying and how it had been for him all these years, and now this. "I know. Chip. I never loved you any less. If anything, I wanted to love you more. I felt I was much to blame, your dad and I. And that is what really hurt me more than anything, knowing it was something that happened and wasn't your fault. It wasn't what you wanted. Yet you've had to live with it."

"Mother, it wasn't your fault."

I was sobbing and interrupted Chip, *"I* hated it that life wasn't like it should have been for you ever since your dad and I separated."

Chip wasn't saying much while I continued, "I'm so sorry he kept hurting you. If only his wife knew what it was like to have step kids who tried to do nothing but cause trouble, just the opposite of you. Then maybe she would have appreciated how lucky she was. And your attitude was always so good about their daughter. I really don't know how you were always so understanding, especially with the way they were unfair and selfish with you. Yet you never said a word against them or anyone else! You were even the same way with Jerry's kids and always went out of your way to help them when you could, especially Cindy!"

Looking away, I sighed in dismay while I shook my head, "Such a difference in attitude and appreciation." Then I looked back at Chip as I smiled through the tears and said, "At least I could always be proud of you and your attitude, and the way you were."

Chip didn't comment. We more or less considered the source and accepted things for what they were, never d welling on the negative. His dad was the only one he mentioned and not much anymore.

We didn't say anything for a few minutes and I pulled myself together, saying, "You look like you are about to fall asleep. Do you want anything before I go to bed?"

"No, Mother. I love you."

"Good night, honey. I love you, too." I leaned over, giving Chip a kiss, then started to leave his room. At the doorway I turned around and again softly whispered, "I love you."

Then I quietly poked along to the kitchen and on into our bedroom. I don't know if it was all these recent happenings or the talks Chip and I were having or exactly what. But for whichever of the reasons, it seemed to be even more quiet and lonely in the still of the night.

20

Last Letters

Would Halloween always be a day that would haunt me? Remembering that not only had Chip entered the hospital on that day last year, but twenty-two years before at that time was when I learned Chip and I would be on our own without his dad. The first event changed Chip's life, the second event was the beginning of the end of his life. During those thirteen days in the hospital, we came to realize that Chip's life was destined to be lived out in much pain and suffering, completely different from his previous twenty-five years. Still I couldn't seem to accept this even while I watched Chip's body deteriorating and wasting away day by day. He couldn't walk far without assistance and was semi-bedfast. His thin, precious body looked as though he should have been bedfast long before; still Chip hadn't given in.

He buzzed and I called, "I'll be there in a minute, honey."

Jerry had gotten the intercom for Chip because often in his weakened condition it had become hard to hear him when he called. We put the control on his bed where he could reach it easily.

When I got to Chip's room, he announced, "Mother, I want to go to Gramma's for Christmas."

I didn't reply right away and Chip lay waiting for my response.

I cautiously asked, "Do you feel up to making the trip?"

Then I hastily said, "it has been a long time since you've been back there, and I know Gramma would love having you." Smiling, I continued, "Christmas would be the best time with all the family."

"That's what I thought. There's always so much going on at Grams' and it's been a long time since I've heard her play the piano."

He lay seriously thinking, then smiled and said, "Sure, I'd like to go."

We both were quiet for a few moments, contemplating, when Chip asked, "You wouldn't mind, would you, if I go there for Christmas? I don't want you to feel bad."

"No, Chip. I think that would be good if that's what you want."

"It is. I'd like to go by myself."

"You mean fly back?"

"Would that be okay with you?'

"Well, yes. Chipper. Do you want to call Gramma and talk with her?" "Sure!"

While I was getting Chip's telephone, he said, "Mother, you know what? The other day I was dreaming about going back. When I got there, I didn't know if I should go to Gramma's in Michigan or Gramma's in Indiana. So I decided to go to a hotel. Then I woke up."

"Well, I'm sure, by no means, would either of your grammas let you stay at a hotel!"

We laughed as I handed him the phone.

"Hello, Gramma!"

Grams exclaimed, "Chipper! Hello, how are you? It's so good to hear your voice!"

Chip and his gramma talked awhile, then Chip mentioned coming for Christmas. Grams was real excited and thought that would be a great idea, and it wasn't long until Chip was almost there by the way she was talking. Grams said, "I could be right there at the airport waiting."

I picked up the other telephone and talked with them.

"But, Mother, he really doesn't have much strength."

"We could have a wheelchair ready," Mother anxiously said.

"That would be good. He loses his balance so easily sometimes."

Chip added, "And I can't figure out why."

Grams commented, "Well, you've got to have strength, honey, to perambulate."

"I don't know, uuh," clearing his throat, "it's real strange. I'm only taking three medications now besides the fever pills. The thrush, an antibiotic, and Reglin to make me eat. I have been eating a lot lately."

"He's been doing much better. Mother."

"Mother's been so good. She cooks everything, anything I ask for."

Grams exclaimed, "Oh boy. That's good!"

"Mother, I don't think he weighs a hundred pounds."

"Oh my goodness, Chip, and as tall as you are, that's pretty much a willow." She paused, then asked, "Did you share your cashews with your mother and Jerry that I sent?"

Chip chuckled, "For sure! Jerry loves them."

"Well, good," Grams said.

Chip assuringly said, "I said, 'Eat them, eat them! Help me eat them!'" "Just so you don't get any bad aftereffects."

I heard the scare in Chip's voice, and knowing what Grams meant made me giggle softly. Grams had no idea of Chip's fear of things happening to him unexpectedly.

Grams said, "I hope not, sometimes they constipate you or something dumb like that."

"Ooh, I'm having such a horrible problem now, only the opposite! I go, but, uumm," he cleared his throat, "sometimes I don't make it to the toilet, and I go in my underwear right as I get to the toilet."

Grams laughed, "Well, join the crowd, Chip! You're not the only one. Bless your heart"

Mother was tickled to hear Chip sincerely telling about his helplessness. She understood because she'd been taking care of her elderly sister and had taken care of her deceased husband, who had similar problems to those Chip mentioned.

Grams said, "Well, you can't help that. You'll have to try a little faster the next time."

"Mother, when he goes in his underwear, he washes them out. Then he calls me! I tell him to call me first and I will take care of them, but he still thinks he should do it himself. Really, as weak as he is, I know this is hard for him. He does well to make it to the bathroom, walking as he does with his nagging feet."

"Well, Jerry bought me a porta potty, and it's right here in my room."

Grams said, "That's good, that will help."

"But I thought if I could make it to the bathroom, I could save my mother from having to clean up the porta potty."

Grams said, "Yes, but shoot, use it. That's what it's there for."

"That's what Mother says, Use it, I don't mind.'"

Mother told Chip about all the different plans already being made for Christmas and that everyone was coming to her place.

Grams said, "And I'm going to invite your grandparents from Indiana. Chip, you should be calling and getting your plane reservations made."

"I will. I was going to call after we talked to you."

"Are you and Jerry planning on coming too, Kitty?"

"Oh, I don't know. I kind of doubt it Yet I wouldn't want Chipper to be by himself, except during the flight, if he comes alone. Still, I'm not sure."

I was hesitant at the time because I knew Chip wanted to *go* alone, yet I was concerned and didn't know how to respond.

"Well, I would take care of that at this end. Gee, that would be wonderful, if that would work out. Having you here, Chip, would be beyond all my expectations."

Mother talked about all the young great-grandkids being there and Chip was becoming a little concerned, knowing he couldn't take the noise. Grams assured him it would all work out okay.

Chip asked, "Do you think maybe it's not a good idea for me to come?"

"No way! We want you to come. If you feel up to it at all, I think it would be wonderful."

Chip commented, "I've been thinking about it. They're all going to come down here when I die and, you know, not party, but have a feast and everything. Basically party, and I won't be able to have any part of it!"

Grams and I broke out in laughter while Chip went on to say, "So, uhh," clearing his throat, "you know, I thought, 'I'd better get in the Christmas spirit." Chip chuckled. "And this will probably be my last Christmas."

Grams said, "Well, my golly, let's not talk like that, 'cause we're going to pray for more Christmases, lots of them."

"Graammaa, you try and lie around all day long."

"Oh, Chip, I'd hate it, I know."

"Actually, do you want me to be honest with you?"

"Yes."

"I just love it! I just dig the shit out of it." Chip chuckled.

Grams laughed and said, "You what?"

Chip said, "I just love not having to do anything."

Grams gasped, "Really?"

Chip laughed. "And having Mother help me all the time."

I chimed in, "Yes, he likes being waited on hand and foot."

Grams laughed, saying, "Sure, just like a rich kid!"

Grams and I chuckled as Chip cheerfully commented, "Sure."

Chip changed the subject back to all the noisy little kids. Mother and I laughed, but he was definitely worried.

Teasingly I said, "He's like a little ol' man, very candid. And he's used to the peace and quiet."

Grams said, "That's alright, he's entitled."

We laughed some more. Chip was just the opposite of this before his illness, but now he had enough to cope with.

I said, "I'm sure we would come down. We would drive, probably, so we could get Chip on his flight and be there shortly after."

Grams talked about taking Chip out in the country to his aunts' and uncles' homes and I said, "Chip can't go too much."

"No, we don't want Chi p to be in the cold much either," she said. "Chip, if you can think of anything else you'd like, let me know."

Chip quickly spoke up. "Can you guarantee snow?"

Grams laughed. "No, I can't guarantee snow, but if you'd like it, then I would say, 'Let's have some snow for Chip,'" and Mother heartily laughed some more.

In a pleading, weakening voice, Chip said, "Okay, yes, please. It will be the last snow I'll ever see. I'm sure."

Chip was obviously getting tired when he said, "I'm going to hang up. I love you. Gramma."

"I love you, Chip, and look forward to seeing you at Christmas."

Chip hung up and I said, "Mother, don't make any definite plans yet. For Chip, I hope he can make this trip, but he's awfully weak and I'm not sure how much longer, you know what I mean? That's almost three months away."

I was using the phone in the other room away from Chip, but needed to due Mother in, now that he had hung up. Mother and I talked a little longer, then hung up.

I could never handle it when I talked about Chip's "time" approaching, nor could Mother. I was concerned about Chip's being able to make the trip, but I didn't want to concern him. More than anything it worried me about his going alone. What if something were to happen on the flight? The more I thought about it, the more worried I became, but I didn't say anything. Still I was happy about Chip's going to Michigan for Christmas because he was going from love to more love, and this was what he needed. He was getting lonely more and more every day and I knew the family would be great with him. Again, we were buying time, bargaining.

A little later, I asked Chip, "Are you sure you don't want me to fly to Michigan with you?"

"No, I want to go by myself. I think it would do us good to get away from each other. We're starting to get on each other's nerves and we need our own space."

"Well, not really, Chipper. It's just that we're around each other almost twenty-four hours a day, and that's natural."

I paused, thinking, then asked, "Are you talking about the other day when I yelled at you about the carpet? I'm really sorry I acted that way when you couldn't make it to the bathroom. That was so wrong of me! It wasn't that bad and I knew you were trying to help me. I know I should have bit my tongue." My voice was weakening and I had to catch myself. Then I said, "And that's really been bothering me, too."

Chip was just too good beyond words. I was almost in tears thinking of my first reaction when I saw what he had done trying to make it to the bathroom. Then I felt even worse seeing him so helpless and feeling bad already (before my yelling), but I'd already yelled. He was only trying to keep me from having more work. I was so wrong and he was so good. I was fighting the tears.

"No, Mother, if s just that we need our own space. I love you and I don't blame you for getting tired of taking care of me."

I scolded, "Chip! You know better than that! I want to take care of you!"

I was becoming choked up, fighting the tears while I continued, "You're really doing more than necessary trying to help me, and if s unfair to you. I can do it. Honey, I understand how you feel, and I know if s hard for you to make it to the bathroom. You know I don't expect you to. I'm not complaining. Only at times, you know how riled I get. Honey, that's not your fault! And I'm sorry. You know I love you and you're all that matters! I really didn't think I yelled that much, although I know I did that one time in particular."

Chip replied, "No, Mother, you've really been doing great. And you don't yell much. You just need to calm down."

Chip was trying his best to do things even though it was almost impossible. It seemed we were trying doubly hard to be good to each other and both felt bad because of what was happening when there was a mishap. Actually those times were few. The last person we ever wanted to hurt was each other.

Even though I was skeptical of his making the trip home for Christmas, I was hoping he could. With Chip living so far away from his friends and what he was used to, it was even more sad. In Dallas everything was much more open and it was like a community within a community, whereas in the Fort Worth area gay lifestyle was kept quiet more.

It was most unfair to Chip that I couldn't share what he was going through with more people. He was my only concern and I was skeptical of other's reactions. This hurt and caused a withdrawal for both of us, I believe.

It was so crushing, so heartbreaking, and so unfair. I'm sure some people would have come to see him if they had known he wasn't going to be here much longer. Yet ho w could I tell them and chance it? If only people could have handled AIDS. If only I could have told them. If only the stigma hadn't gotten out of proportion. Many times I wanted to and almost did. If only, if only. What is this world coming to? I was so confused.

One minute I thought he had AIDS, the next minute I questioned it. Chip wasn't having some of the symptoms I kept hearing many patients were having. Still the fear was there that they might happen. His TB kept him down, along with his other complications. He was suffering, miserable, and having difficulty breathing. He wasn't eating, or very little when he did. There wasn't any way he could relax and be comfortable. He still had the frustrating, constant, nagging high fever with the horrible, profuse sweats and chills. His feet had been cursed! And the diarrhea was most aggravating. What more could be expected?

Jerry still hadn't accepted Chip's AIDS. He believed Chip was going to be okay. I knew Chip was getting worse, yet I kept trying to convince him that he could get well, if only he would believe it. At times he got angry and I couldn't blame him. Still I persisted. Chip would like to have lived, but he knew better. He knew how he felt and ALL reports about AIDS were negative. For a long time I was even thinking he had been convinced he had AIDS, so he quit eating. I was afraid he would die from starvation, even though they were saying AIDS caused loss of appetite. I was petrified. Yet I had to be strong.

I'd discuss it with Jerry, and next thing I knew, Jerry convinced me that Chip didn't have AIDS. I was constantly pulled back and forth. And of course, I didn't want to believe my son's life was coming to an end. So how could I tell anyone he had AIDS? Down deep, I knew I was losing him. Then I wondered what I would do without him.

Actually, I wasn't sure it was AIDS until after he was gone. It was when I learned my suspicion made sense, which I had mentioned to Chip, about his not having a nervous breakdown. It was from *physical* causes that Chip had confusion and complications in the beginning. The doctor never did give us any concrete reason or explanation for saying Chip had AIDS. And the way he acted was enough to discourage Chip from what little hope he may have had. Even if the doctor had said it was because they didn't know very much yet, it would have helped and made more sense than the way he was treating Chip.

I honestly believe Chip could possibly have gone into remission if the doctor hadn't been so negative. Chip had always been a fighter and never let past complications get the best of him. Still, faith prevailed and Chip did better than expected, even without the doctor's encouragement. He had come a long way primarily on his own, even though he had expected to be gone long ago.

Eventually Chip had no control whatsoever over the diarrhea. The doctor did a couple of tests, but never suggested what I should do for Chip's comfort. Mother had mentioned diapers and finally I realized they were the only alternative.

Jerry went to the drug store to buy adult diapers. It was strange how at times like that I didn't think of the logical, such as when we got the diapers, I would need to put them on Chip. There wasn't any way he could have done it himself. Although later there was a time or two he tried, but didn't quite acquire the knack. As usual he was trying to lessen my work load and help.

We were both quite modest and at first putting the diapers on was a bit awkward for us I suppose if I had been a nurse it may have helped the situation some, but I wasn't. I was his mother and I hadn't done anything like this since Chip was a baby. It was enough when I had to hold the towel up for him when he got out of the tub a while back. Now we both had to make some adjustments. At first, my reaction was to turn my head. Soon I realized that was ridiculous. We were adults and with these complications there were many things we needed to learn to overcome. This was just another one of them.

Chip made flight reservations to leave DFW Airport a few days before Christmas and return January 7. He wanted to stay long enough to hopefully see snow. His excitement and enthusiasm were overwhelming. He sure deserved and needed this.

Within a few days Chip received a letter from his Aunt Susie and cousin Jeanine who lived near Gramma. They were excited he was coming and had already made arrangements and plans for how everything would be taken care of with Chip. He was going to be treated like royalty, no doubt about that Jeanine called Chip to tell him her plans. She was in high school and working part-time, but while Chip was there she wouldn't work. After school she would go to Gramma's to take care of him. Chip had been Jeanine's idol ever since her visit to Texas when she was fourteen. She was a cute young lady with a great personality, well mannered and a sharp dresser. These traits in Chip's opinion were a big plus, and she could expect the best when it came to being shown off and living it up with him. Chip had taken her to the most exquisite places, such as shopping at the Galleria Mall and sightseeing in Dallas and Los Colinas. The high point was taking her to the top of the Reunion Tower, fifty stories high. At this great height they dined at the famous Antares restaurant while it gently revolved, giving them a panoramic view of Dallas.

I called to let Mother know Chip had made reservations. Also to make sure his being in diapers wouldn't be a problem.

Mother said, "No, no problem at all."

She was happy that Chip was coming; this was all that mattered. She said that her only worry was his traveling alone, which was my concern too, but that's the way Chip wanted it. I told Mother that Jerry had suggested I fly and he would drive, but we were waiting, hoping Chip might say something first.

It wasn't long after that when Chip called me into his room and said, "Mother, if you want to go to Michigan with me, that's okay. I shouldn't have been that way. I know this will probably be my last Christmas and I'd like to be with you and Jerry too."

Grateful, I smiled and said, "Thank you, Chipper, I've been hoping you'd change your mind. I will call and make reservations before it's too late."

I felt much better, although still not sure if Chip was going to be able to make the trip. It scared me, but I didn't say anything and made plans to go.

Different times Chip wanted to write family and friends, but his many difficult complications interfered.

One day he had been very quiet and preoccupied all day. Late afternoon, he buzzed. When I entered his room, he handed me a letter and I realized the importance of his time. My heart ached and I was deeply touched, knowing the phenomenal task he had accomplished in this stage of his life with his weakened, bony hand when I read his floundering writing—beautiful words that were such a wonderful blessing from his heart:

October 27, 1986

Dear Mother,

It's so hard for me to put things in writing. I want you to know that I love you more than anything or anyone and thank you for loving me so much. I think many times you've gone beyond the call of duty. And yes I'm glad you're coming to Michigan. I guess I am getting into being tied to my mother's apron strings. Be watching for a quiet vacuum. I want to get one for you. I don't blame you, and I am sorry that I put you thru some of the crap I have. I could go on and on, but someday you'll realize how much I respect and love you. I am beginning to wonder what kind of sickness I really do have. I'd almost really love that final chance to become somebody respected and admired by family, friends, and professionals, and mainly my dad, Jerry Williamson. Well, Happy Halloween. Think you'll be able to put up with me next Halloween? Love, Chip Happy Holidays.

I love you all so much. We will have great holidays.

This was just like Chip to do something special! I was numb and speechless. I sat down beside him on his bed, giving him a hug.

In retrospect, it was as though I were in a stupor, and today I realize it had to be stress, which we didn't talk about, let alone acknowledge at any time. I gently clasped Chip's strong, bony hand. It was as though he knew time was closing in and he wanted to leave this one last treasure. He wrote in such a positive manner, although a little later he told me how hard it was to collect his thoughts and write at the same time. I could imagine the challenge it was with what little strength he could muster, being both physically and mentally worn out. I remembered how busy he'd been all afternoon while he grasped his pen, and I hadn't disturbed him. This was another toll due to the complications and no doubt the heavy, added burden of anxiety. Still, no matter what, Chip didn't let that stop him.

It was especially sad reading, "I'd almost love that final chance..." I was thinking. Of all times for these complications to settle in and attack, at his young age of only twenty-five when he was well on his way toward a successful career, and now this. Ooh, honey, I am so sorry and I love you so very much. You've always been respected and admired by many throughout your life, ever since you were a little boy. Even so, with the pit fail he was in, his feelings were understandable, although the pressure and guilt he was putting himself under was most unfair. Still, down deep he knew he'd always had love, respect, and admiration. Yet that one void in his heart ever since he was a little boy must have left him quietly crying on the inside over the years, while the subject for the most part lay dormant.

He lay quiet and neither of us spoke. He mentioned not being sure of his complications. This was sad, yet he hadn't given up and wrote of the "hope." We may have convinced each other over the months, desiring that his life wasn't ending as we'd been led to believe. He hadn't put me through any crap. We'd had some trying times, but no real problems. He had always worked hard and played hard, living life to its fullest. And I'm especially glad now, since his life was so short. He matured quickly and had a good grip on life starting at an early age. He started traveling and doing a lot in his young years and this never changed. It was a tough, promiscuous generation to grow up in. Still, he kept his grip. He was a proud person and gave me every reason to be proud of him, even during his sickness. He helped me tremendously with his remarkable attitude, always.

Above all I trusted my son, knowing he had good common sense. He was never a violent person, nor a problem. Nor did he cause problems. I truly believe if karma had anything to do with what happened to Chip, he paid his dues in full with these disastrous complications in this lifetime.

He wrote, "You' begone beyond the call of duty." Not really. Even now, he was the same genuine, thoughtful person. He still had the same good, caring attitude, knowing his time was near—no doubt, in the worst way possible to mankind at present. It was so sweet of him to mention Jerry as his "dad" and wanting to make Jerry proud of him. Truly, we were proud of Chip. He had always given both of us reason to be proud. Yes, his life was changing and the love between them was like Chip had wanted from a father who cared and was always there when needed, especially during this sickness. Apparently he conquered his rejection. Then, how more diplomatic could he be about my noisy Kirby vacuum? How more positive and considerate could he be, writing, "We will have great holidays." He truly was our holiday blessing.

A little later, Chip asked if I'd mind getting him a strawberry slush from the Sonic Drive-In. He didn't feel like going with me, so I rushed to get it. He liked certain things from certain places and getting them in a hurry was still important because he was losing so much weight, and too, I didn't like being away from him.

When I arrived back home and gave Chip his Slurpee, he handed me another letter. I looked at it. He said, "You can read it."

It was a letter to his dad. It read:

"Hi, Just one last time to say, please figure out a time. I'm coming to Michigan Dec. 11-Jan. 7 and staying w/Gramma. All I can say is there best be snow!!

Even if it's a flight in and out the same day, I need to talk w/ you. Last chance it might be. It's the best you could do. It will have been 27 years. And if it's your physical problems you're embarrassed for me to see, wait until you see me.

Please call me when you get this letter.

Chip

Chip said he didn't know how to start his dad's letter, so he just said "Hi." It was understandable with his torturous memories of his dad and with how his relationship with his dad hadn't gotten any better. Still, this late, with his devastating sickness he tried. He apparently wanted both of them to have peace of mind before he was gone. Again Chip was thinking of his dad, relating what his dad had told him years ago about his accident. Chip conveyed the message to me that maybe because of his dad's accident and how it had left him physically he didn't want Chip to see him, that things such as this sometimes bothered people. Chip was assuring him he understood. That he, himself, didn't look too good. It seemed Chip was sincerely trying to give his dad an excuse for not coming to see him yet, but still Chip wanted to reassure him it was okay, he was his dad and nothing else mattered. Chip was going more than halfway, not even knowing if he would survive the trip. He was willing.

Chip had given his dad plenty of time to plan for the holidays. The next few days were tense while Chip lay in bed, not saying a word, wondering, hoping, and praying the telephone would ring and it would be his dad. Surely he wouldn't repress his love and responsibility as a father, not at this late date. All Chip asked for was a fraction of his dad's time, ONE LAST TIME. Was this too much to expect from his dad? To know his son had given in and would talk. Hadn't he realized that this no doubt was Chip's *last letter.*

Chip waited. Chip didn't say a word. I didn't say a word, and neither did a word come from his dad. Why? His son's life was ending—not possibly, but definitely—at any time, any moment. Was this a repeat of when Chip was only ten years old? Only a telephone call away.

21

Living Overtime

Again Chip was having a hard time sleeping. He was wide awake both day and night most of the time. I asked the doctor to prescribe some stronger medicine. When I got his prescription I was shocked to see that it was Valium, ten milligrams! And he was to take one pill three times a day. I was skeptical from my own experience years ago after my car accident that critically injured my back and neck. Once I learned more about Valium, I immediately stopped taking it and learned to bear the pain. Again I was skeptical, but that's what the doctor prescribed.

The first Valium knocked Chip out totally. When he finally awoke I was shocked and frightened to see the effect the Valium had on him. He was groggy and in a terrifying state of weakness, hardly able to wake up.

Later when Chip's friend Mike called, I told him the strength of the Valium prescribed for Chip. He, too, was surprised. After Mike had talked with Chip, we talked again and he said, "Thirty milligrams is too much for Chip! Take that bottle away from him."

Mike had advised Chip not to overdo it and take too much Valium, warning him it would make him vomit. With Chip's strong will he never vomited, even though in the beginning of his sickness he felt nauseated different times. He wouldn't vomit.

I assured Mike I kept the pills and was only giving Chip half a Valium now and had a call in to the doctor. "When I called the doctor I told him I wanted something strong, but not like this. They're too powerful!"

Mike agreed. "No, he doesn't need that."

"Thanks, Mike, for talking to Chip. He trusts your judgment, and he sure doesn't like the way they make him feel. Talk with you later."

Then we hung up.

The next day I continued to break the pills in half, only giving him half a Valium. After that and seeing the ravaging effect they had on Chip, it was too much.

I didn't trust Valium and I quit giving them to him altogether. Chip agreed he didn't like what they did to him and felt better without an added drag, saying he needed all the strength and energy possible.

One day I was in Chip's room cleaning and changing sheets while he was brushing his teeth. When I was done, I sat down beside him. We were talking when he suddenly became a little vague and somewhat confused. What he was trying to say wasn't coming out quite right. He asked for an ashtray, but pointed to his cigarette lighter lying beside the television. At first I wasn't sure what he meant, then realized he must want his cigarette lighter as I reached for it. Sure enough, that's what he wanted. I didn't think any more about it and figured he had just said the wrong thing by mistake.

A little later, Chip and I were watching television. Momentarily I reached over and touched him. "Chip, take your temperature. You're burning up."

I handed him his thermometer. He put it in his mouth, waited thirty seconds, then read the digits 104.5.

Anxiously I said, "We've got to get some Tylenol in you."

"No!" Chip audibly said.

He didn't like taking Tylenol because it broke his fever, causing horrible, cold sweats that usually drenched his body and bed, leaving him freezing with chills. These were both becoming so monstrous that Chip decided he would rather deal with the fever as best he could than the aggravating sweats. I understood his reasoning and didn't say much, remembering a male nurse had forewarned me about Chip's high temperature and said he could deal with it, provided it didn't go too high. Dealing with these complications was a daily, frustrating battle. His fever being that high frightened me, and I handed him two tablets, insisting, "Chip, will you take this Tylenol?"

"I will take some Bufferin," he decidedly said.

I checked. Usually I had Bufferin, but was out. I nervously persisted, "Take this Tylenol. I need to get some Bufferin."

Chip gave in, saying, "Okay."

I stayed with him a little longer. When I started to leave his room, in a short, determined tone, Chip said, "Over there. I want over there," as he pointed to his other bed across the room.

Wanting to do something else, I said, "Wait, Chip. Not yet, okay? I need to go to the kitchen. When I come back I will help you change beds. Okay? You can wait that long, can't you?"

He only looked at me as though he didn't want to wait. I walked on toward the door. Apparently his fatigue was draining him and oftentimes he was expressing himself using short phrases.

"Chip, if you need me, ring your buzzer or call me. I'm going to be right in the other room," and I left him.

I had only been in the kitchen a few minutes when I heard some loud crashing noises and Chip frantically yelling, "Help!"

I rushed to his room. All toppled on the floor was Chip, pinned down with his heavy television across his feeble legs. The Gatorade and water glasses had broken and lay on the floor with his scattered pills and other items that had tumbled off the also-broken glass shelf surrounding his lamp pole, and his turned-over ashtray stand. He was lying near his brass-and- glass case from where his television had fallen on top of him!

He lay stunned and speechless while I ran over to him, hurrying to move the monstrous television off him, then checking all over his body to make sure he was okay. Thank heavens, he didn't have any broken bones or cuts! I was astounded, and relieved he wasn't any worse.

Chip said, "Give me a boost," while reaching his arms up toward his bed. I lifted on his rump, boosting him back into bed.

"Chip, I'm going to put the other rail upon this side of your bed for you. Okay?" I said while checking to see what I needed to do to raise it.

Bewildered, Chip shook his head and said, "Uh huh, please."

Finally I figured it out and raised the rail.

Chip agreeably said, "That's better."

From then on he kept the rails raised when I wasn't with him. If I started to walk away and they were down. Chip would motion, saying, "Put up, up. Please."

And I'd hurry back and raise them. He never forgot that fall. It definitely scared him, and me too.

Shaken, I said, "Chipper, why didn't you call me? I don't care what it is, you call me. Anything you need or want or have to do! You call me to help you!"

Apparently I should have helped him before I left the room, knowing how persistent he always was.

Bewildered, Chip said, "Well, I thought I could make it. All I had to do was jump over to there."

"Where?" I quizzed.

"Over there to the other bed," he said, "to the brass post on the bed."

I was flabbergasted at what he was saying and had tried to do. I said, "Chipper, you can't do that!"

Chipper said, "I know I can't now."

It seems Chip thought be could jump from one bed to the other across the room and go on into the bathroom. He had attempted to do this on his own, apparently because I hadn't helped him.

"Chipper, you are disoriented, aren't you?"

"Yes, I am. That scared me!"

I repeated, "Chip, please call me!"

Then I giggled, relieved that the scare was over and touched by his genuine honesty. I gave him a big hug and again made sure he was okay. I loved him so much. It was times like this I just wanted to hug him like a baby. He was so thin and fragile, and such a sweetheart. Seeing how helpless he was, like an innocent little boy trapped on the floor in bewilderment, was even more sad. I didn't want to see him hurting or feeling bad in any way, especially unnecessarily. He was already going through enough pain.

A little later I walked into Chip's room while he was lighting a cigarette. He took a couple of puffs and put it out.

"I'm glad you're not smoking in bed too much," I said with a smile, and he smiled back.

A couple of nights before he had fallen asleep smoking and burnt a hole in his sweatpants. That's when he resorted to only a couple of puffs at a time, not wanting to chance it again. After awhile he lost most of his desire to smoke.

"Here, Chip, you got another card from Gramma today."

He held the letter with his hand stretched out in front of him at arm's length while he read. Chip's reaction spoke louder than words when his arm limply dropped to his side while he lay grasping the letter, staring afar... thinking. No doubt Chip was thinking of Gramma's love and concern, of all the good fun times they always had together... And now this, to think how his life was. A sad, empty feeling swept over me. I hurried out and rushed into his bathroom as the tears stormed beyond control, trying not to let him hear me.

When I returned Chip was hot again. I opened the door a little for a slight breeze and turned the heater down. He took his temperature; it was 102, which meant he'd soon be sweating.

After Chip's first time in the hospital when we were told he'd had a breakdown, Jerry had remodeled his end of the house so he would have his own private entrance once he returned home. We wanted to ease whatever discomforts he may have had, thinking his move back home may have put undue pressure on him because of his pride, after being on his own for so long. His two bedrooms were now a nice efficiency apartment with the closet a kitchen with double stainless sinks, disposal, cupboards, and all necessities. To ensure complete privacy, Jerry moved the bedroom door to the hall to separate our living quarters, and built Chip his own private entrance to the outside.

Chip appreciated all Jerry had done, but then felt bad for all his work after realizing he wouldn't be living to use it. We assured Chip we weren't sorry and with his being sick it all came in handy and helped even now.

Chip's eyes looked heavy, as though he would doze off, until assuredly his sweating would wake him. Then I'd change him and help him to the other bed. It was hard for him to go from one bed to the other by himself, but together we managed. Chip wore sweatpants and sweatshirts that were comfortable and ideal for him to get on and off fairly easily since we were changing both him and his bedding several times a day.

One day Chip had been talking to his friend Mike on the telephone. A little later he asked me to pick up the other phone, saying Mike wanted to talk to me. Mike said he was telling Chip about talking to his friend who was a doctor and relating Chip's condition to him. The doctor said he'd gladly see Chip.

I asked, "Chip, would that be alright with you?"

"Sure. Mike said he was good."

I was so glad Mike had taken care of this with both Chip and the doctor. Chip must have thought I'd hung up the phone, and I started to, until I heard him telling Mike his leg was hurting from the television falling on him. Chip said he couldn't walk on it, then clarified his statement. "Well, I can, but I feel it."

Maybe I should have hung up, but that alerted me and I stayed on the line since Chip hadn't said a word to me about how his leg still bothered him. He told Mike that Jerry had made him a cane to use for a little support.

Mike asked, "Who made the cane for you?"

Chip proudly said, "My dad."

Mike commented, "He's good to you, isn't he?"

Chip replied, "Yes, he's the finest." Then he repeated, "He's the finest. This past year we've really become friends. I used to resent him. But I love him so much. I do. And I love my mother so much too."

Chip told Mike he was totally bedridden and had an intercom system. He said, "I have to bother Mother and Jerry to get me whatever I need."

I hated hearing him use the word "bother." Chip wasn't any bother, but he finally realized he had to swallow his pride and surrender to our help at long last. Doing this really bothered Chip, not us.

Hearing Chip say he had resented Jerry surprised me. All these years he sure hadn't shown this. Too, Chip wouldn't let anyone get too close to him because of his dad. He had been hurt deeply and tom apart by their non-relationship. Still, there were times every now and then when he called Jerry "dad," and he always related to him as his dad. Jerry was the kind of dad he would have liked his biological dad to have been.

I hung up the telephone while Chip and Mike continued to talk. Then later I called to set an appointment for Chip to see the doctor in Dallas. I didn't expect to get in very soon, but the nurse said they were expecting my call and scheduled his appointment for the next day.

I thought, If only I had talked with Mike a long time ago, things could have been different for Chip.

Still, I was thankful Mike had set this up for Chip.

The next day it was nippy outside when it was time to go to Dallas. Chip hadn't been outside in a long time, so I bundled him up real well in his sweats with an extra heavy jacket, wool socks, and his still-like-new tennis shoes. Yes! A miracle at last!! Chip was able to wear his tennis shoes in comfort! Real comfort! His feet were back to normal and he had feeling in them! Finally, after thirteen months, Chip's feet weren't miserably cold and numb with die steady, excruciating, painful discomfort.

Chip excitedly chuckled, saying, "A couple of new feet!"

His feet being back to normal was quite an accomplishment; the only difference now was that he wasn't walking much anymore. He was practically bedfast.

I situated Chip in the car and leaned the seat back so he could relax as much as possible. This was the first time he had actually slept the night before and was looking forward to seeing the doctor. I was concerned about the twenty-mile ride with his being much weaker and exhausted. Still, I knew his going to a good, compassionate doctor would be worth it. He needed and definitely deserved this.

When we arrived, the nurse was quite cordial. She saw how weak and tired Chip was, so she immediately put him in a room to lie down until the doctor came. The nurse was very compassionate and spent a lot of time talking with Chip. Seeing and hearing them almost broke my heart, knowing how things had been the extreme opposite with his other doctor. This was more like what Chip had always teen used to when it came to other people and himself. Even though he was worn out, he somehow managed to be himself, almost as he was before the sickness. Such an inspiration and a joy to hear! It was over a year later since he had come home from the hospital, and he wasn't expected to even make it home. This late in the sickness he was amazing.

The office was crowded with patients, but the doctor didn't keep Chip waiting long. There were two doctors. The first doctor came in and talked with Chip while he examined him. Then a short time later, the other doctor checked Chip too.

One doctor continued with Chip while I went into the other doctor's office to talk about Chip's complications. The doctor and I both knew there wasn't much they could do at this late date, but it was their response and attitudes that made the difference. Chip and I both felt these doctors cared, regardless, and that naturally made us feel better.

The doctor I talked with was actually amazed Chip was still alive because of how thin and atrophied his body was. When we talked about Chip's eating habits, I told him I was trying to encourage Chip to drink protein and take vitamins, but it was in vain since his other doctor didn't think they were necessary, even though he had been taking vitamins and drinking protein before he became sick. I also related the many pills he had taken, how he'd quit them when eventually they were sometimes hard to swallow; even those he was still taking sometimes gagged him. The protein he'd only drunk a couple of times after that.

A little later the other doctor joined us. Both doctors felt it was important for Chip to be taking protein and vitamins. I was happy to hear this, knowing Chip would listen with their encouragement, which he did. From that day forward Chip drank protein daily. In fact, in days to come that was primarily all he had and he felt much better and could tell a big difference. At last Chip had gotten the quality medical support he needed.

I mentioned to the doctor that Chip was going to Michigan for Christmas and wanted his opinion about Chip's making the trip. The doctor didn't say Chip wouldn't be able to make the trip, but in so many words he said Chip was *living overtime.*

He said, "If he feels up to traveling, it would be good."

I sensed the doctor was saying he didn't think Chip would live that long. He was surprised, with Chip's weight loss and his body deteriorated as much as it was, that he was still alive. He said he'd only seen one other patient (but in the hospital) who had lived to be in the extreme condition Chip presently was in.

I hadn't realized how Chip looked to others. I knew he was steadily losing weight and was extremely weak, yet his inner strength and determination were amazing. He still looked good to me, considering all he had been through the past and prior years. Always being with him, I apparently hadn't realized or wouldn't see what others were seeing. And too. Chip had an inner strength about him that I believe gave us both endurance.

To think the doctors were amazed he had lived this long; still, he was to live a substantial time longer.

Chip's trip to Dallas was the best thing for him, even though it was rough for him getting in and out of the car. Then the moving and maneuvering he entailed while there was difficult and tiring. Still, it proved to be a blessing.

On the way home Chip was content and told me he was pleased with the doctors. Their encouragement and moral support was what Chip needed. This was extraordinarily crucial at present with all he was facing during his loathsome days.

The next day Chip called Mike to let him know how grateful he was for setting everything up with the doctors.

Chip was becoming extremely tired, and again he was wanting to be alone more as time progressed. At times when I was sitting with him talking, all at once without saying a word, he'd turn over on his side facing the wall. At first this caught me by surprise, then I realized he apparently wanted his own space. Too, I believe he was too drained to even say a word.

I'd say, "You must want me to shut up, don't you?"

Chip would murmur, "Uh huh," and not another word. Other times he wouldn't even murmur, and I'd instantly be quiet He was completely exhausted. At times like this. I'm sure we both felt empty.

Oftentimes he seemed to be in deep thought. I believe I sensed what he might be feeling and often felt it with him. We were devastated and alone. I saw the sadness in his pretty blue eyes that spoke louder than words while he silently stared, as though he were all alone, helpless, silently pleading: What can I say or do? Oh please, take me. Let me go. Why am I still here? I don't understand. I had no control over this happening. If I had known in time that the virus existed, I could have had control. There's no reason for keeping me here. Please do something. I can't stand this. It's been a long time. Look at Mother. She's trying, but I can't even talk with her, I'm so worn out. This is so unfair to Mother, and to me. I love her so and it isn't fair hurting her this way. Let me go and keep her strong.

At the same time while I saw Chip lying there, not speaking, only thinking, I too let my thoughts wander: Oh, Chipper, if only you could get better, if only I could give you some hope. I can't; we know there isn't any. Until now you always had control. You always took care of yourself. This factor alone must be most devastating to you. If only you had known about the virus before it was too late. Why, why is this happening to you? If only I could do something. I don't want to lose you. Am I prolonging your life because of this? Are you holding on for me, to get me ready? Oh, Chip, I love you. I'm being so selfish. I know how miserable you are, yet I don't want to lose you. I will miss you. I do now. The thought of your being gone is so wrong it tears me up. Already we can't talk like we used to because you are becoming so weak. Still, we are holding on.

I know this is hard on you. Chip, as much as it is for me, knowing it can't be forever. We had so many good times together. You have really been my world all these years. I know I'm losing you, my son. Why? Why? I know I'm not supposed to ask why, but I do. I can't help it.

Chip, you have been so good and I know this is why God must be taking you. God needs you up there with him to be his "right-hand man." That's where God knows you belong. God wants to take you away from all this heartache you have been going through. I'm so sorry things weren't better for you with respect to your father. I will never understand how your dad could have treated you as he did, no more than you can. All you ever wanted from him was love. I am sorry he rejected you. You are everything a father could want in a son, plus much more. Still you did not let this void in your heart affect your character in any way. I am thankful you love Jerry and he loves you. You said you wished Jerry had been your real dad because he is the kind of dad you wanted. Yet because he wasn't, he couldn't get as close to you as he or you wanted, until recently. Still, you've had a mutual respect. You have gotten that love from a dad you had been wanting. I believe we are now united as a family. Maybe this is why God brought you back to life at the hospital, which was hard to understand then, knowing what you would be facing with your complications and your search for love.

Definitely, Chip, you have been a man, your own man, from the time you were quite young, maybe too young. You and I always had a lot of pride. We learned early how to take care of ourselves and each other. And we did. We understood each other. We respected each other. Our influence over each other was only intended with the other's best interests in mind. You had a mind of your own. You cared, you shared, and you listened. Yet you did your own thing. Always. You were never tied to my apron strings, even though you later wrote that it was okay, you wanted to be. Maybe that's because you didn't want to let go. If you were tied to my apron strings, maybe, just maybe you could be here a little bit longer.

You wanted happiness. You were a true glow of love and happiness all during your young years, and into your adult life and the present.

I know you are wanting to live, the same as I am wanting you to. We can't seem to speak the words we ordinarily would. I don't understand. Our love shines through. Still, these wordless moments are unfair while you lie sick. Why is this? I love you so very much just as you do me. Oh, God, please help us. I must stop this wandering while! sit here with Chip. It is so sad and lonely. If I feel this way, how must Chipper feel? He is the one doing all the suffering and not knowing...

22

27ᵗʰ...How 'Bout That?

It had been over two weeks and Chip still hadn't heard from his dad about the holidays. He hadn't said a word, but I sensed his heartache. It seems Chip's dad couldn't help but know how important that letter was, how hard it must have been for Chip to write it, and how hard he had been making it for his son... all these years.

Couldn't his dad see what his son was saying, "I need to see you, to be touched by you, to know you love me. I'm sick and I may not look like I used to, but I'm still the same person. Are you? I'm worth your time. I am your son, you're my dad. What is keeping you away? I'm only asking for a few minutes."

As a rule I wouldn't involve other people, but for Chip, it was time I did something he couldn't do anymore. The unanswered letter had taken all his strength, but he had tried. I called his friend Mike and told him about the letter Chip had written.

"Mike, I'm sure it's gnawing at him, but he won't say anything."

At that point, Mike said, "Yes, I can relate to that when it comes to his dad. He doesn't talk about him much."

"I know, and this is tearing him apart. He's already under enough distress, let alone this adding to it."

Mike suggested that he call Chip's dad. I thought it would be worth a try—anything, at this time, for Chip's peace of mind.

That evening Mike called Chip's dad, then Mike updated me about their conversation since I was concerned for Chip's sake.

Mike said Chip's dad's wife had answered the telephone. She sounded skeptical of his calling and didn't seem to want him to talk with Chip's dad. Mike asked if it would be better for him to wait and call his job tomorrow. Then she was willing to call her husband to the telephone.

Mike introduced himself and said he was calling about his son, Chip. Mike asked him if he was aware of the seriousness of Chip's condition, that he was getting weaker day by day and it was only a matter of time until Chip would be gone. Chip's dad said he was aware. Mike told him that Chip wanted very much to see him, but Chip felt that his dad didn't want to see him.

It seems Chip's dad became defensive and made excuses about not being able to get time off work and said that he didn't want to chance catching Chip's disease. Mike assured him it wasn't likely he'd catch it from Chip. The only way he could catch it was through sexual relations or blood contact. Then Mike asked him if his mother was still alive. He said she was.

Mike said, "I'd hate to hear her saying that she didn't want to see you on your dying bed because she was afraid of catching something from you."

Chip's dad didn't say much and Mike said, "If there comes a day when we have to stand forces and you stand up and give excuses about your son, I feel sorry for you."

Then Chip's dad said that his doctor had told him it wouldn't be safe to see Chip because of his disease. Mike offered to give him the names of doctors in Dallas who would be glad to talk with him and let him know the facts, if he still had questions. Mike asked if he couldn't come because of finances. If that was the reason, Mike would make arrangements and send him the money, assuring him that that wouldn't be a problem. He said Chip's dad had changed the subject, making remarks about me. Mike told him that he didn't know what had happened in the past, but he was sorry his heart was so hard that he couldn't even get over it and come to see his boy who was dying. He didn't understand how he could be so cold.

Mike said, "I know if it were one of my children or anybody I loved, I would be there no matter what it was. I talk to Chip a lot, and the sad part is, I talk to him more than you do. And I care more about him more than you do, and he's not my kid."

Chip's dad told Mike he had another family now and that was his concern. Then he said he had already been told by twenty doctors that he would catch the disease from his son if he visited him.

Mike said, "In other words, you don't really want to see the boy? Am I to tell your son, 'Chip, you call your father. He doesn't want to come and see you because he's afraid he'll catch the disease.' And that's supposed to be enough for a kid who's only got a short time to live? Chip's wanting to come and see you. Now how can he do that? The boy's too weak to even walk across the room, and he's talking about getting on a plane to come and see his dad because he won't come here."

He said Chip's dad started talking about me again. Mike told him he needed to bury the hatchet because he had a kid here that belonged to both of us. "Not just one of you, both of you."

Click! Mike said the line had gone dead.

'I'm sorry, Mike. That's exactly what happened tome when I called. It's a shame, for Chip's sake."

I told Mike about calling not too long ago. "I'm afraid I wasn't thinking, and I apparently played right into her hands and made things worse for Chip. I no doubt gave her ammunition, and as usual. Chip was the innocent one being fired at. It isn't right with Chip's condition and our distressful frames of mind. Chip doesn't seem to stand a chance with his dad," I sadly added, "not even now."

Mike said, "If his dad has any kind of concern or any love, that would win over. If it doesn't, then Chip's better off not to see the man."

I agreed. I only wanted what was best for Chip. I'd never bothered Chip's dad before because Chip wouldn't allow it. But why another silent rejection? Why wouldn't he at least call, knowing Chip was ready to talk? If Chip hadn't been terminally ill I wouldn't have pursued the matter.

A few days had gone by when Chip buzzed me to come to his room. Almost expressionless, he said, "Mother, I need to cancel our flight to Grams'. I want to stay home for Christmas."

Chip didn't make any other comment. Nor did he mention his dad...ever again.

I smiled bleakly and said, "Okay, Chip, I will call and cancel. Do you want to call and let Grams know we're not coming?"

Chip said he would and quietly added, while looking out the window, "If only we could have snow."

"We never know in Texas, we might get some," I cheerfully said.

Chip said, "That would be nice."

Chip wasn't a quitter; he would continue to search for this one thing called *love* to the very end. And he did! Somewhere, somehow, he would find the love he needed. Down deep he must have believed and known this.

Later that day I walked into Chip's room and he was sound asleep. I sat alongside his bed a long time, not wanting to disturb him, but to be near. He looked peaceful. After awhile he woke up, gave a slight smile, and lay quietly without moving. While I sat there, not a word was spoken. We liked being together, even in silence.

At times when I was talking and Chip was listening, suddenly, without saying a word, he would turn over on his side facing the wall. This wasn't like Chip, and it bothered me at first, but I came to realize he needed his own space to think, to comprehend what was happening. He was so worn out and it was taking all his strength to deal with what must have become holiday stress with the disappointment he was concealing. He was ready to go. He didn't like being in limbo, knowing it had to cease sooner or later, so why not sooner? He wanted this to be over with, to end. Why was he being kept here so immobile and bedfast with nothing to do but think?

It was sad seeing the solemn look on his face. But I kept quiet while I cried on the inside.

After awhile Chip started getting the chills. He asked me to turn the heater on high. His frail body was trembling and his lips were quivering. I put another blanket on him. A few minutes had gone by and the room was starting to get hot.

I could hear the quiver in his voice when he asked, "Will you put those other two blankets on me. Mother?"

"You mean the two blankets off your other bed?"

Still quivering, Chip answered, "Yes, please."

"Honey, I know you're cold, but don't you think that will be too much? You have two blankets on now," I felt Chip's forehead, "and you're starting to feel hot."

Chip raised his voice, "Mother, I am cold! Please get me those blankets!" "Okay!" I put the other blankets on Chip, and said, "You know they kept you cold in the hospital to keep your fever down."

Chip interrupted, "I'm not going to be here that much longer anyhow. So what difference does it make? I may as well be comfortable for what time I have left, or as much as possible."

"I know what you're saying, and maybe you're right, but..." I was almost at a loss for words while I was trying to answer and think at the same time. "Well, that does make sense."

The blankets were all heaped on Chip with his little head sticking out, still shaking. I bent over and kissed him, saying, "Let me know when you want the heater turned down. I love you, honey."

"I love you too, Mother."

I sat down and waited. This was always the most aggravating, dreadful part—having to watch the misery Chip was going through and not being able to do a thing about it, knowing it was going to get worse before it got better. It was almost like clockwork the way this happened so often. The only change there might be about the sweats and chills was that you didn't know which one was going to be first. Now, in addition to those two complications, Chip was having miserable hot flashes quite frequently. It could only make you wonder. What's next?

Chip wasn't expected to be here for his last birthday and it was almost a miracle to be celebrating his twenty-seventh year. But Chip was a survivor and there must be a reason.

It was early morning when I walked into his room and said, "Happy Birthday, Chip! How you doing?"

Chip smiled, "Good morning, Mother. *I am here for my twenty-seventh year! How 'bout that?*"

I smiled while I walked over, gave him a big hug, and said, "You sure are, honey! And I love you very much."

Chip hugged me back, saying, "I love you too, Mother."

My eyes watered while I tried to keep the choking out of my voice. I replied, 'You're a real sweetheart." Then I asked, "Chip, were you awake most of the night?"

"I woke up at one o'clock and couldn't get back to sleep until about four." "I know. I looked down here and saw your light on."

"You should have come down and we could have talked."

"I almost did, but since it was your birthday today, even though we didn't plan anything, I wanted it to be special and had things to do. Of course, Rhonda is coming for dinner. Remember?"

Chip smiled and said, "Yes. I called her when I woke up and we talked for awhile."

I laughed, "You called her at that time?"

"Yes. Sometimes she can't sleep either, so we talk."

It was good for both him and Rhonda. I believe Rhonda was like me when it came to Chip. Whenever he felt like talking, we wanted to, knowing many times he didn't feel like talking or we weren't sure if it would be our last time.

After going to bed at about eleven-thirty, I routinely woke up at one and three o'clock during the night and was up early, by five-thirty. We kept our bedroom door open and I'd sit up and look down the long, dark hallway to see if Chip's light was on. Usually it was and I'd feel better for some reason. Maybe it was because I always turned it out for the night and then, strange as it may seem, seeing it on seemed to tell me he was okay and I could rest awhile longer.

After I bathed Chip I helped him into his other bed, which was all clean and fresh. While I was busy changing sheets on the bed he'd slept in, Chip fell sound asleep, but not for long. He was wide awake the rest of the day. No matter how sick Chip was, he had that willfulness that saw him through.

When Jerry got home, he went into Chip's room with a cake.

He cheerfully said, "Happy Birthday, Chip!"

Chip chuckled when he saw the snowman on his cake and said, "Well, that's better than no snow at all!"

Earlier that day, on the spur of the moment, I called his friend Mike and invited him over for some birthday cake. Then between Mike and me, we called a few friends for a small party. Rhonda came early for dinner and brought Chip some red heart shaped balloons, imprinted with "I LOVE YOU" and a red toy Mercedes 380SL with movable parts inside and out. Chip had planned on this being his next car, but now this 380SL was to go with him on his journey.

Chip had a nice birthday celebration, but since he had stayed awake all day he couldn't seem to stay awake that evening. He was happy his friends had come, but was worn to a frazzle.

Later Chip apologized, "I didn't mean to be rude, but I couldn't stay awake."

I assured him they understood. If anything, that was one time when his friends left sad, seeing how atrophied Chip was. Some of them almost couldn't handle it. Maybe it was because I was around him all the time, but I really thought he looked fine, considering all he was going through. I was proud of the pictures we took that day and sent some for Christmas to family.

There was another surprise on Chip's birthday, which I told him about the next day since he was asleep. His dad called.

When I answered the telephone, his dad said, "Is Chip up?"

"No, he just went to sleep. Let me check, though, but I'm sure he's asleep. Some friends just left and he fell asleep before they went. He stayed awake all day and was tired, besides being awake during the night, just a minute, let me check to be certain."

I started to lay the phone down when I thought about the letter Chip had written him. I picked the phone back up and asked, "Did you ever get that letter Chip wrote you?"

He answered, "No."

Surprised, I asked, "You didn't?"

He vaguely said, "No, not that I know of."

"Well, just a minute. I have a copy." I laid the phone on the counter and went to my office to try to find it While I was looking, I asked Jerry if he would check on Chip and see if he was awake to talk with his dad. I couldn't locate the letter, maybe because I was hurrying. I went back and picked up the telephone, "Are you there?"

"Yes."

I asked again, "You did not get a letter from Chip about—"

He interrupted, saying, "In fact, I did get a letter from him. He's going to Michigan at Christmastime."

"Right! Why did you say you didn't get it?"

Haughtily, he said, "Well, I just forgot. Is Chip up?"

I called to Jerry in the next room, "Is Chip awake, honey?"

"No, he's sound asleep," Jerry answered.

"No, he's sound asleep," I told Chip's dad.

"Oh, well, okay, I just wanted to wish him happy birthday. So I'll try and get ahold of him tomorrow."

"Well...uh...what about that letter he sent you? He never heard back from you."

"Well...I...uh...I don't know what to make of it. But I'll try and get ahold of him tomorrow. And uh..."

I boldly asked, "Well, what do you mean, you don't know what to make of it?"

In a smart tone, he answered, "Well, just what I said."

I snapped, 'Isn't it obvious that he would like to see you?"

"Oh, from one of his..." he paused a bit and added, "gay friends, I guess it was, and I just, uh..."

I instantly interrupted, and distinctly said, "From one of his *what* kind of friends?"

"Just forget it! Anyhow, just tell him I will call him tomorrow."

Now we were both snapping.

"What did one of his friends have to do with that letter?"

"Well, nothing. Look, I'll call him tomorrow."

While I was calling his name he hung up the telephone. I banged down the receiver and yelled, loud and clear, "You S.O.B!"

I shocked myself. Ordinarily I didn't talk that way. I only wanted him to realize the value of Chip's letter. It seemed he was trying to misconstrue the letter and the telephone call. I didn't want Chip to be blamed for something he knew nothing about, and too, all was only done for love. I really felt bad for Chip, knowing what that letter meant to him and the time he took to write it. It's a shame his dad didn't know his son any better; he definitely would have known Chip wouldn't have a friend help him, ever. Even though it was strenuous for his son, there again was his determination. If his dad was having such dubious thoughts, why hadn't he called and gotten them resolved?

Chip said, "He did?"

"Yes, but you were asleep. I told him you'd been awake all day and hadn't slept much the night before."

I didn't mention the letter conversation to Chip. Maybe I shouldn't have told him his dad had called because he never called back. Possibly that is why Chip stayed awake all day, hoping he'd call. If that was the reason, Chip didn't say, and I understood. I also buried the heartache deep down inside over the whole outcome.

Over the years his dad always seemed to do this to Chip. Every so often, out of the blue he might call. One time he was almost next door to our home, at the DFW Airport, when he called Chip. It was as though he were teasing Chip with a little encouragement. Then he would never carry through with what he had started. This was rare, yet enough to rekindle the fire, with the love Chip carried all those years. Now, at long last, I believe the fire was smothered, leaving a gray mist of smoke that might someday singe his dad's heart.

Nothing more was said. Chip somberly rolled over on his side. No matter which way he turned, it seemed as though he was still being crushed one way or another by his dad's silence or his impulsive actions.

Still, in all respects, Chip was the one with the broad shoulders who bore the brunt!

23

The Heartache of Unnecessary Fear

"Good morning, Chip. How you doing?" I cheerfully asked asl walked into his room. I knew the answer as soon as I saw him. He had all his covers shoved off and his sweatshirt pulled up above his skinny little belly as high as it would go without taking it off.

"Ohh, Mother, would you please turn down the heater?" Chip asked with a sigh of relief that I had finally come into his room, rather than to have "bothered" me before now.

"Sure, honey," I replied, while I was bending down to lower the dial.

"How 'bout medium low? Then it won't get too cold."

"Sure, Mother," Chip said. He was exasperated with the hot flashes that wouldn't seem to stop. It had always been the aggravating cold chills and soaking sweats, which still hadn't let up, and now the frustrating hot flashes were leisurely on the attack.

"Chip, do you want me to take your sweatshirt off?"

"No thanks. Mother. I believe I'll be okay in a few minutes. Then I'll probably need it to keep warm."

"Yes, I suppose that's about right. You're sure doing a lot better than I could!"

I sensed that Chip was starting to feel a little better when he answered with a bit of a smile, "I don't know about that."

I kissed him on the forehead and smiled. "I'm sure you are."

While I was rearranging his covers, I asked, "Chip, do you need changing now, or would you like some protein first?"

"No, Mother. I believe I can wait on both until after you do your aerobics. Maybe then I'll be okay. You know, in case I start sweating."

"Okay, honey. But you let me know if you want something. You know I'll be doing aerobics for an hour."

"Okay, Mother."

Leaving his room, I turned in the doorway to look back. He had such a sweet, wholesome look. I smiled, "I love you, Chip."

He replied, "I love you, Mother."

As soon as I had finished aerobics I went into his room to see how he was. When I got there, I saw him gasping for breath. I hurried over, asking, "Are you alright?"

Chip took another deep, slow breath as he replied, "Yes, Mother. I'm fine." "Are you sure?" I watched him a few minutes. He was trying to conceal his shortness of breath again. I didn't comment, only waited and watched for him to say something. Instead he calmly lay there, then flipped on the television with his remote.

"Mother, there's an aerobic show on at eleven. It's filmed in Hawaii with a guy called Gil. You might like to watch it."

"Okay, honey, thanks. Remind me when it comes on."

Chip's care and concern never altered. Ever since he was a little boy, he'd let me know when I looked especially nice or he liked my outfit. Just like now, knowing my interest and how good aerobics was for me. Watching television was about all he could do. It kept us abreast of AIDS as it surfaced, but eventually, with only negative talk, we stopped watching it. As Chip said, "I was cursed!" Even though he was destined to the worst possible death for a young man his age, he abided with his complications and continued to help me with his usual love and concern.

I bathed Chip, then he sat up in the chair beside his bed while I changed his sheets, covers, and many pillows. Once I had him situated back in his fresh bed, he asked, "Mother, do you mind getting me an English muffin with cream cheese and a glass of strawberry protein?"

"Sure, honey, would you like an egg with it?"

"No, not now, thanks."

"Okay, give me a few minutes and it'll be ready."

I still tried to fix whatever he wanted as quickly as possible for fear of his sudden loss of appetite. I'd make it as enticing as possible, knowing he enjoyed a pretty plate. When I took it in to him, he said, "Ummm, that looks good."

"Great! Let me know if you'd like some more."

At times Chip was starting to have a good appetite, and at other times, the same as before, he couldn't eat anything.

"Your Aunt Ruth and cousin Lisa will be here with her family in a couple of days."

Chip smiled, yet he was apprehensive when he said, "I sure hope they aren't noisy!"

I laughed and said, "No, Chip. I don't believe they'll be any problem. They're older now. Remember, Michelle was born on your sixteenth birthday."

Chip smiled and said, "Yes. That's right. It will be good seeing them." I cheerfully said, "Yes, and the girls will fight over who will get to rub your feet the most." I smiled and added, "Lisa said the girls can hardly wait to see you."

Chip smiled, then chuckled, "Lisa has her hands full with those kids, I'm sure, but she seems to have her act together!"

Chip and I reminisced about his cousins from California.

I said, "Chip, when your Aunt Ruth and I were little she'd look up in the sky and say, 'Kitty, there's where our sister, Mary Lou, is. Right up there on that prettiest little cloud.' I'd look up and see right where Mary Lou must be. Now, Chip, I'll be looking up to find the prettiest cloud where both you and your Aunt Mary Lou will be."

My eyes started to get watery, so I bent over hoping he hadn't noticed, giving him a hug, saying, "I'll really miss you, Chip."

Trying to change the subject, I said, "Lisa told me to tell you not to do anything funny because they all want to see you."

Chip said, "That's what she told me when I talked with her awhile back." He chuckled. "We've sure had some good times."

"Yes. you always did with all of Ruth's kids."

They would only be in our home a couple of days, so I didn't think there would be too much commotion for Chip.

When they arrived Chip was sound asleep and I didn't wake him.

Later, I was in my bedroom combing my hair. My sister Ruth came in and started apologizing. At first I was confused when she said, "Kitty, I am sorry. I can't believe I did this."

I looked at her, wondering what she was talking about. She went on, "The minute I walked in and saw Chip, I knew there wasn't any reason to be afraid. He's fine."

Ruth continued apologizing and finally she said, "I had told the kids on our way coming, 'Don't go near Chip.' I was afraid for them."

Until now I had kept combing my hair and hadn't really looked at her. Now I did! I looked right at her, surprised and not knowing what to say. I was overwhelmed with what I was hearing from my own sister, in our own home—my sister whom I had talked to frequently all these months about Chip! Frequently and openly! Now I was hearing this! I couldn't believe my ears!

This was the sister who had been trying to help me get help for Chip in California about eighteen months ago. She had no fear of him then. Why now? Was it because of AIDS? All these months we talked on the phone about Chip and I had no idea of her fear. I couldn't believe she was afraid or still questioned this. She knew I was the only one taking care of him and I wasn't having any problems. Why? Why was she worried and why didn't she talk to me about it before they came? I could have set her mind at ease then. I realized this was a problem with the general public because they didn't understand the true facts about AIDS, but my own sister? I was at a loss for words.

Ruth continued, "The minute I saw Chip, I felt bad, knowing there wasn't anything to be worried about. Now it's too late. I've already told the kids not to go near him."

What was I to say or do? I kept looking at her, thinking of Chip all the while. I know how she must have felt because she knew how wrong she was. She hadn't meant to hurt Chip, but she had! I was sure. There I stood, crushed and torn, hearing this. If I was feeling this way, how must Chip have felt? Why, why? Why was this happening to him? She knew he would never hurt them! My emotions were so torn and mixed. I loved my sister and couldn't be rude to her. Yet what about Chip? I loved him and things were bad enough, let alone something like this! This particular cruelty I didn't want to happen to Chip and I never thought it would. Not in his own home! I knew it was only because people didn't understand and know the true facts about AIDS. People are afraid of the unknown. And maybe this fear was because people only hear what they want to hear. *If only Ruth had talked to me about this, then there wouldn't have been this heartache of unnecessary fear.* There honestly wasn't any reason for this to have happened. If only I'd known! I thought she understood and knew the true facts, which are: you can only get AIDS through blood or sexual fluids that have the virus. No other way!

"That's okay, Ruth. I'll talk to Chip. He will understand."

I hurried down to the other end of the house as fast as I could, knowing how Chip must be feeling. My heart was aching. These were the kids that Chip was looking forward to rubbing his feet. At least his feet were okay now and that wasn't necessary.

Sure, he was concerned about the noise, but really, he was anxious to see them and share good times. These were the kids who could hardly wait to see him.

"Don't die on us, we want to see you, Chip." is what they'd said.

When I got to Chip's room, there were Michelle and Melisa, nine and eleven years old—not in his room, but in the hall outside, leaning over the door frame looking in at Chip from the farthest distance, but so they could see him and talk.

When I walked up, they didn't budge an inch to go any closer. They weren't about to get near him. This was so obvious! I thought, Oh Chip, I am sorry, so sorry. How could your Aunt Ruth have done this to you? And now, Chipper, how can this ever be made right for you? I felt terrible. I couldn't be mean to Ruth. But yet there lay my son, obviously crushed. He didn't say a word. The girls walked away.

I walked in and sat down on Chip's bed beside him. This was hard. I was almost in tears, seeing his sad, solemn face. He was trying to look as though everything was okay, as though it didn't make any difference, but I knew better. *This was the heartache of unnecessary fear.*

I touched his hand and squeezed it. "Chip, I'm sorry. I know how you feel. Its just that they don't understand."

Chip calmly said, "That's okay."

"Chip, I will talk to them, and it will be alright."

I was on the brink of tears.

Chip angrily raised his voice, "No! Don't say anything!"

Then I cried and tried to talk and plead with him, knowing how hurt he must be. Right in his own home! He was getting the message: Don't go near him, don't touch him.

This had to have torn him up. This was exactly why I didn't tell others about his illness. Most people just didn't understand. And I hadn't ever wanted anything like this to happen to Chipper. Never!

The next day Chip came into the living room and lay down on the sofa. I'm sure this was his way of letting them know there wasn't a problem. The kids were all playing and the adults were sitting around talking. Chip was observing and I was sitting on the sofa with him.

Lisa came over and while she was talking to Chip, she touched his forehead as though to push his hair back. I'm sure she was wanting Chip to know that she understood and she wasn't afraid to touch him.

Angrily, Chip yelled, "Get your hands off me!"

Lisa immediately stopped, and softly laughed.

I yelled, "Chipper!"

Then I felt wrong that I had yelled. He was hurt and had a right to the anger that was no doubt boiling inside him.

Lisa said, "That's okay," as she sat on the sofa with us.

Chip thought for a few seconds, then looked at Lisa and said, "I'm sorry." Lisa smiled and said, "That's okay, Chip. I don't blame you. I understand." Michelle was sitting across the room looking at Chip. I asked if she'd seen his new birthday ring. She glanced over and nonchalantly said, "Oh, that's nice."

Invitingly, I said, "You can come over and look at it. It's a gold nugget ring with his initial in diamonds. For his pinky finger!"

Michelle came over and bent down saying, "I love you, Chip," and gave him a hug, and Chip hugged her back, saying, "I love you, too."

Once they were around Chip, they loosened up and knew there wasn't anything to be afraid of, but the fear had been planted when they were forewarned. And too, they weren't with us long enough to completely dissolve the damper.

Lisa had disagreed with her mother about the kids touching Chip and her husband, Orin, was neutral, although Orin was hesitant to take a part of Chip's sandwich that Chip hadn't bitten into. Chip only offered it to be polite, but understood. We knew it wouldn't hurt. Still, Chip never encouraged eating or drinking of the same food, even before these complications. Of course, Lisa understood because she was a doctor's assistant and had taken care of patients with AIDS. Besides that, Lisa and Chip had always been close cousins over the years, even with the miles often between them.

We had a good visit, despite the heartache. Chip and I understood, although we had never expected anything like this.

Ruth and her other grandson, Joshua, were here a few days longer. During that time Chip told me he was going to tell Ruth to leave, but I didn't think any more about it. It wasn't until later that I learned he did tell her. I was sorry Ruth was apparently hurt, but it seems she should have understood and apologized after what she had done to Chip. And possibly she did. I don't know. She knew how sick he was and what all he was going through, let alone *the unnecessary heartache* she had caused. She knew Chip had a tender heart, but surely she remembered how hurt he had been. This alone would be cause for an upset. It wasn't often, but there were times when Chip let you know the score. Apparently this just happened to be one of those times.

If only I'd known Ruth's fears, I could have prevented the negative attitude, which left scars on both hers and Chip's hearts.

Before Joshua went back to California, he and Chip were buddies again. Isn't it understandable why I had not told some people about Chip's having AIDS when they asked? For this very reason, I said nothing. This was most humiliating to both Chip and me. I only wanted to surround him with all the love possible. At the time, though, I didn't realize how unfair my avoiding the subject was and how it may have made him feel. Today I do, and I don't know if I will ever be able to live this down. It is heartbreaking, sad. Chip never wanted to shame me in any way—and he never did, ever. It was my own doing because of the stigma on AIDS. Still, in his heart he knew how I loved him and he meant the most to me.

In Chip's last days, at times I wondered if he wasn't putting himself on guilt trips while he lay idle only able to think, day in and day out. It was wrong, and it hurt knowing this might be happening.

I commented, "Chip, you haven't done anything any different from anyone else. Nothing was known when you came in contact with the wrong person."

I tried to reason with him that he shouldn't be putting himself on guilt trips, but Chip was past the talking stage. He was miserably fatigued while the days lingered on. And apparently the stress was unknowingly overpowering us both from speaking needed words. Things were bad enough with his physical discomfort, let alone the emotional and mental anguish.

A few days later we had another visitor in our home who was like family. Aaron, who was about Chip's age, had visited incur home different times when Chip first started having his complications. At the time Chip was being treated for TB, and we weren't talking about possible AIDS. That was when I truly was thinking he might be alright. Today I realize this could have been the denial stage, and I can also see the added pressure I was putting us under in denying the word "AIDS", but I could only accept TB.

Chip, Aaron, and I were sitting in the living room talking. The comment was made about how much weight Chip had lost and how he was still able to walk fairly well,

I said, "Yes, it's been a little over thirteen months since he came home from the hospital. And at that time he wasn't expected to live another week"

There was silence.

Then I said, "You do know what's wrong with him, don't you?"

Aaron said, "Well..."

Chip glanced at me and then at Aaron. His face was serene when he announced, "I have AIDS."

Chip was respectful, but saying what I hadn't. As Chipper had said, "Honesty is all that I have left."

I admired Chip, and I could see how good he felt by speaking up. This made me feel good too. If only Chip's life wasn't ending. I believe together we could have conquered the terrible stigma he and many others were unfairly having to endure.

I felt like Chipper, that Aaron had a right to know, and I was sure it wouldn't be a problem, which it wasn't. As I mentioned earlier, Aaron was the same as family and a good friend.

24

Bright Lights

Chip was sound asleep lying on his side facing the window while I was quietly sitting beside him. It was important he know I was near while he lived with the wonder of death, even though he had accepted it. I still seemed to be harboring my thoughts of reality in the depth of quietness while the time drifted.

It wasn't long until Chip turned over. I smiled and told him I'd been waiting for him to awaken. He tried to smile, but it seemed his energy was drained. He lay quietly, then slowly raised his long, skinny, limp arm up and stared at his hand in despair, seeing that it was almost all bone snuggled in his slight, firm layer of flesh. Through his bewilderment I saw the forlorn look in his eyes and felt his distress while a twinge of pain pierced through my heart. Suddenly, helplessly his hand dropped to his side; his lips clenched.

"Can I get you anything. Chip?"

"No, thank you, Mother."

After moments of silence, he said, "I've got to get well, physically and emotionally."

"You've been doing pretty well, Chipper," I hastened to say.

He didn't comment and slowly turned back on his side, asking me to turn out the light. I leaned over and kissed him, telling him I loved him and to let me know when he needed something.

Chip earnestly said, "I love you so very much."

"I love you very much too, Chipper."

I turned the light out and walked down the long, dark hall, the tears streaming down my cheeks. These grim, silent moments I kept to myself... so sad and alone, all alone.

"Oh, God, please help," I cried. "I love Chip with all my heart."

I was all choked up with emptiness and tears that wouldn't stop. All I could think about was how Chip must feel, if this was how I felt. Oh God, please, please help him, I silently prayed. If only I could do something. To see his body so frail and going down to nothing is almost unbearable for him. Why must all his self-esteem be taken from him? He never asked for much, nothing that he wasn't willing to give in return.

I slipped into bed and quietly sobbed my heart out, not wanting to wake Jerry. Soon my pillow was sopping wet and I tossed it aside. It was like a nightmare, yet I was wide awake. I couldn't sleep. Then I saw daybreak coming through the window and there wasn't any reason to lie there any longer. I was about to get up when I heard Chip's buzzer.

As I went into his room, he joyfully said, "Good morning, Mother. How are you today?"

I smiled and said, "Okay, honey. You seem to be in good spirits."

Chip smiled.

I said, "You must have slept well last night."

"I did," he replied.

"That's good. You were almost asleep when I left your room."

"I was, wasn't I?" he replied. Then he asked, "Would you get me some strawberry protein?"

"Okay, I'll fix you some and be right back," I said as I left his room.

Chip placidly replied, "I'll be here."

I grinned to myself thinking. That's Chip! Such a sport.

When evening neared I noticed the neighbor's Christmas lights. I walked outside into the cool, brisk air, surprised to see that almost everyone already had their homes decora ted. Time seemed to be slipping by, but Jerry planned on putting our lights outside, along with Chip's snowman, this weekend. I prayed for snow, just for Chip since he wasn't going to Michigan to enjoy it.

This holiday season was different from last year, when Chip came home from the hospital. With a strong will he had endured so much for almost two years with the steady nagging at his body. It was only recently that he seemed to drastically slow down, It was apparent how he felt physically and emotionally, with it being more difficult to move his worn-out body, and when he did it took a diligent effort. The talks Chip and I often had seemed to be slipping into silence while he lay in deep thought hour after hour.

It was understandable how he felt and why he was shutting everything and everyone out at times, especially with the way his holidays seemed to have started, or stopped before they even got started. No doubt the memories of his first birthday without his dad when Chip was three years old, and now at twenty-seven, were haunting him since his dad hadn't even as much as answered his letter about the holidays. Imagine the added stress he was having to endure during this holiday season.

When I look back on Chip's life, it makes me wonder if he wasn't being prepared since the time he was a youngster for this terrible time he would be facing before he left this earth.

Chip said, "I had a good life. I probably did more in my short lifetime than a lot of people who live a long life."

"That's true. You've done most anything you've wanted and have always had nice things. You've taken care of yourself and never let anything get the best of you or hold you back, starting when you were a little boy."

I paused, then continued, "Life wasn't always easy, but to know you, no one would ever guess differently. You've always been the kind of person people want to be around. You're always so much fun and liven things up, ever since you were little! You've never changed."

Once he was talking about the year his complications began. Chip chuckled, "That was one hell of a year I don't remember."

"That was quite a year for everyone! It's almost unbelievable the things that happened. But then, you've always had a full, adventurous life." I laughed.

Christmas was nearing and for some reason, neither Jerry nor I could bring ourselves to put up a Christmas tree. I remember Chip and I talking about a tree before it was time to put it up, but I can't remember who said what first. I don't know if he didn't want a tree because he heard me say I didn't feel like decorating one, or if I didn't want to put one up because Chip said he didn't want a tree. Yet at one time he wanted a real tree.

In retrospect, it's confusing and sad. I can't believe I didn't put up a tree his last Christmas! For what reason couldn't we put up a tree? The thought was there about a tree, but still we didn't seem to have the initiative, let alone the strength or energy, to get a tree out of the attic. Why? For what reason had we lost our desire to put up a tree? I remember being apprehensive about a tree with bright lights. I couldn't accept the idea of a tree representing happiness and a time of celebration. Maybe it was hearing the doctors say they couldn't believe Chip was still alive. If so, it had to be subconsciously because consciously I wasn't aware of it. I just couldn't bring myself to put up a tree with sparkling lights.

A couple of times I stopped the car when I came to a place where they were selling real trees. I'd wander around trying to decide if I would like a tall tree, a big tree, or a small one. Before I gave it much more thought, I was walking away empty-minded—and empty-handed.

The year before I had even bought more decorations to make the tree extra special for Chip. And we had two small and two large trees in the attic and all these hours in a day. Still for some reason we couldn't put up a tree.

Again I asked Chip if he would like a tree and he said, "No."

I thought of putting a tree up in the living room, but that didn't seem right either since Chip wasn't getting up much anymore. Then the thought crossed my mind to put a small Christmas tree in his room, but the thought of an accident if he was to get up entered my mind and phased that thought out Why, why was I left with these fears? Where was my usual motivation? If he couldn't enjoy the tree, I didn't see any reason to have one.

— 251 —

Now the real heartbreak is remembering the day I saw Chip quietly maneuvering his way down the hall, peeking around the comer into the living room, then slowly turning around and going back to his room.,.never saying a word.

Today I can't believe I did that to him. He was looking to see a Christmas tree, I'm sure. Why didn't I then put up a tree? I don't know. I honestly cannot give a logical explanation and it leaves me feeling nothing but deep regret and sorrow each Christmas now that he's gone. To remember that was his last Christmas!

I did decorate a Christmas table for him with homemade cookies and candies. Even though he didn't have an appetite for sweets, it somehow created a Christmas atmosphere with the holiday decorations complementing his entire room, along with lots of Christmas decorations throughout the rest of our home. *But no tree with bright lights!*

From Chip's front window he could see the neighbors' homes all lit up with Christmas decorations. I asked if he'd like to ride around the block to see all the other houses. He wanted to, yet he couldn't seem to bring himself to do this. I believe he felt about those lights the same way I did about the Christmas tree. For some reason, we couldn't bring ourselves to deal with the bright lights, the shine and glistening. Possibly because deep down we didn't feel that way and were unaware of our concealing this, only wanting a good holiday season for each other.

One day while shopping, I saw an adorable, soft, cuddly, wrinkly toy pup, Kris Krinkles. Seeing Kris made me think of Chip, and then I read the story about Kris on his tag. That did it! I bought Kris and took him home to Chip. Kris's tag told of an important lesson. It all started somewhere on the other side of the world. Santa found the pup one cold Christmas Eve, shivering, lost, and alone. When Santa took him to the North Pole, the elves laughed at all his wrinkles. After Santa told them it wasn't how you looked that counted, but what was in your heart that mattered, the elves were very sorry.

Chip smiled when he read what Santa had said. I knew he was tom apart and humiliated with his uncontrollable weight loss, with his whole body wasting away. I'm sure Chip knew I was saying: I know your appearance is bothering you. But honey, you know I understand and my eyes are blinded. All I see is our love, which is all that matters to me. Like Kris, you have a heart of gold even though yours isn't tumbled in with the wrinkles, but is snuggled secure inside with your tightly stretched skin covering your bones causing you to look differently than you ever wanted or expected. But, like Kris, we all love you. Above all, Chip, you know I do love you with all my heart.

Chip didn't have any desire to watch television anymore. For hours he would quietly lay thinking until he dozed off.

Then Chip was wanting to hear Christmas music and for some reason that year I couldn't seem to find any Christmas music on the radio every time I tried. Finally, on a cassette tape I put together a variety of religious and popular Christmas songs from old records and tapes for Chip to listen to. For days he was content listening to that one Christmas tape repeatedly, over and over, day and night.

One day while I was in his room, "Blue Christmas" started to play. Knowing it was a pretty, but sad song, I moved the control on his recorder to fast forward. Chip said, "Mother, I like that song."

I was stunned and said, "Oh, I'm sorry. I'll reset it for you."

I was almost in tears listening to the words and thinking how he must feel, but kept my poise.

Still there was the joy of Christmas with Rhonda joining us for the traditional Christmas dinner and exchange of gifts. Above all, we had a Christmas with lots of love.

One day I was making Chip some eggnog when he excitedly called, "Mother, come quick. It's snowing!"

I stopped what I was doing and hurried into his room.

"Look, Mother! Isn't it beautiful?"

"Yes, Chipper, it is and just what you wanted! Looks like we didn't need to go to Michigan to see snow after all. Someone must be looking out for you." I smiled.

Chip smiled back. Then he joyfully spent the entire afternoon watching the snowflakes gently fall.

One day the Oak Lawn Counseling Center called. Chip was asleep, so I took the call and spoke with a Roger. He was the person who coordinated visitors for those with AIDS. Roger told me that Chip had called him about eight to ten weeks prior, while I was gone. He was lonesome and wanted someone to visit. Roger was calling to let Chip know he could be expecting calls from hospice individuals who would set a time to visit. I thanked Roger and let him know I would relay the message to Chip when he woke up.

When I told Chip that Roger had called, he was pleased and looking forward to having company.

Chip said, "Mother, I hope this doesn't make you feel bad, but I know there are times you must go away."

"No, Chip. I wish I had known sooner and I would have checked on it for you. Roger said you were lonesome and that was some time ago, a long time ago! I didn't think I was leaving you alone that much. You should have told me."

"No. You're not now."

"No, I never leave you alone now. One of us is always with you. Of course, it's been awhile since you made that call. At that time I was leaving you sometimes just before Jerry arrived home, so you weren't alone for long even then."

Chip questionably insinuated, "Mother," as though to say, Are you sure?

"Chip, you know I never left you alone for too long."

Jerry arrived home while Chip and I were talking about my leaving the house.

Jerry chimed in, grinning, as he teasingly said, "I used to come home, and Chip told me how you'd been gone all day."

"Chip knew better than that, didn't you, Chip?"

Then Jerry and I teased him, but Chip was serious. He didn't like it when I wasn't with him. When I'd go to the health dub or to get his medicine and Jerry would be with him, Chip would say, "Mother's been gone a long time."

When I got home and Jerry would tell me what Chip had said. I'd say to Chip, "I haven't been gone long."

Chip quizzed, "Are you sure?"

I'm sure time must have seemed a lot longer to Chip, or it was just the idea I wasn't with him. Months before at the support meetings, they talked about the possessiveness that happened with this sickness. I never felt Chip was possessive, although I could understand his not wanting to be left alone and how lonely it was with no one around but Jerry and me. I was with him most all the time, even though there were times I may have been gone longer, knowing Jerry was with him. I hadn't related our conversations to that, and Chip was always on my mind wherever I was. Only a couple of times was I longer than usual.

A few days later, a couple of hospice men set a visiting time. At this early date everything to do with AIDS was fairly new to everyone. In our area not as much was being done as in Dallas, and even Dallas was just starting. Apparently Chip's call got caught up in red tape between different organizations trying to get organized. The Oak Lawn Counseling Center and Hospice in Fort Worth came to the rescue at last.

Once I learned about Chip's call, I felt it was unfortunate he had waited almost two months before his call was returned. If only I'd known or thought about doing this myself. His loneliness must have felt like it was over exceeding itself and no doubt he didn't have the stamina to make more calls, even though he was lonely and desired company. It was sad seeing him day in and day out while he lay idle with nothing more to do...or nothing he was able to do.

Chip wasn't telling me how lonely he was and evidently wanted to take care of it himself with people he felt he could be confident with, who would help him. He patiently waited. He knew I was keeping quiet to the public. If only I'd known and hadn't let the stigma interfere as it had. This was most unfair to Chip! If only I'd known more, as I do today. This was my son and he didn't deserve the added, undue pressures that resulted with AIDS! His life had taken a complete turnabout. Still he was the same decent, respectable young man he'd always been, with a great attitude.

I'm sure the loneliness and agony of despair was just as bad as the physical side of these complications. Still, Chip was thankful and looked forward to visitors coming once a week starting in January.

25

"Special Son, Chip"

Happy New Year, Chip!!

The New Year of 1987 was here...and so was Chip!

It was incredible how Chip was living beyond all expectations. He had always lived life to its fullest and apparently his journey wasn't over yet. Could this be because his life hadn't yet been fulfilled?

We brought the new year in with eggnog, a good standby drink for Chip. Between that and his protein, he was well satisfied and in great spirits. It was a great new year for all of us.

Chip's cousin Lisa called to wish everyone a happy new year. She asked if Chip had heard from his dad, and I told her no, not for some time.

About a week later Lisa called to let me know she had called Chip's dad, but was not able to talk with him. She said she had left her name and number for him to call her. She didn't know if he'd remember her, so said she was Chip's cousin and it was most important that he call as soon as possible. Before calling me, she tried again since she hadn't heard from him. Still, she wasn't able to talk with him.

I said, "If he got the message, it seems he would have called, in case Chip had passed away."

Lisa said, "I know. I can't believe he's ignoring Chip."

"Well, Chip's not mentioning him now. He's been through enough, but doing as well as can be expected—I'd say, a far sight better than his dad. Tell everyone in Michigan hi, and I'll talk with you later. Thanks for your concern and for calling."

"Okay, you take care and give Chip my love. Bye."

Ever since we had seen the doctor in Dallas, Chip was drinking about a quart of eggnog and several glasses of protein every day. Always it had to be strawberry protein, which he loved. Every so often he would have a cheese omelet with fresh vegetables and an English muffin with cream cheese.

Until now Chipper hadn't had a problem with thrush. But this chalky paste-like substance had finally pounced on his mouth, and the buildup on his gums and tongue was becoming almost uncontrollable. I called the doctor to ask if Chip should take two thrush pills a day instead of one. I was afraid this thick substance might choke Chip in his sleep, but his doctor said one pill was enough. This worried me, and eventually I gave Chip a washcloth and he'd reach way back in his mouth and around his teeth, wiping out as much as possible. After that he would brush his teeth, then I'd try to wipe out some more for him. Of course, there wasn't any way we could ever get all the thrush. It seemed like the more we tried, the more it clung to his gums, which was most frustrating.

After a couple days, I called the doctor again and insisted I talk with him. I let him know how bad the thrush was and told him something had to be done. Then he told me to give Chip two Nizoral pills. This did help, but still we continued wiping out the thrush.

Then I decided to mash up the Nizoral, maybe that would help. I thought it was worth a try. Sure enough. From that day on, I mashed his Nizoral pills and one a day was sufficient. At last, his mouth was clear of that nasty ol' thrush!

One day I asked Chip if he would like his hospital bed moved into the living room. Chip agreed that would be fine.

That evening Jerry dismantled Chip's bed, then put it back together in the corner of the living room. Chip was content and I was happy he was closer.

Chip looked forward to his hospice visitors each week. I only wish I had given thought and had known who to call a lot sooner.

One day, John with hospice, stopped to see Chip. It was a cool, nippy day outside and the three of us enjoyed hot tea with Chip's favorite, almond cookies.

While John kept Chip company, I slipped away briefly to get a gift I had ordered special.

Valentine's Day was over a month away, so that evening Jerry and I decided to give Chip his gift early. Chip's eyes brightened and he gave a beautiful big smile when he saw his unique pillow inscribed with the words *Special Son, Chip*. This small decorative pillow had a beige linen cover with ruffled trim in dark brown lace over white lace and a pair of Texas longhorns beneath his name.

Chip treasured this pillow and kept it near all the time, either on his chest or at his side, snuggling it close. If he ever turned over and misplaced it, he immediately called me to find it.

One day Jerry came into the kitchen while I was preparing dinner, wearing a big grin. He took my arm and led me into the living room. Chip was sound asleep lying on his back, with that little pillow slightly under his head. It was sticking out like the edge of a postage stamp, Jerry and I softly laughed.

For Valentine's Day Jerry made Chip a planter resembling a dog, with the dog's face being the face of the clock at one end. Then in the planter we planted a prayer plant.

Chip was becoming extremely thin. Three months ago he stepped on the scales until the digital light came on—seventy pounds! We were shocked as we looked at each other in dismay. That was the last time for Chip to weigh himself.

Even though he wasn't able to get up and walk by himself anymore, Chip still hadn't given up. He was staying in bed until Jerry arrived home. Then with Jerry on one side and me on the other side of him. Chip would position his feet on the floor and put one arm around Jerry and his other arm around my shoulder. Chip would steady himself while we walked to the other side of the living room to the chair he liked, where he could rest. The strength in Chip's feet and legs was amazing while he walked with us. It seems like it would have been hard or awkward, but he was determined and kept moving.

Chip always looked forward to Jerry's coming home so he could walk, and then he walked several times back and forth during the evening with us. He never seemed to wear out during the walks, but it was difficult for him to sit in the chair very long.

One time Chip was wearing only his diaper while we walked him back to bed. I glanced at him when he happened to see himself in a full-length mirror, which was sitting against the wall. He didn't say anything and neither did I, but I could see he was as crushed as I was for him to see that his body had gone down to almost nothing. His once beautiful, slim, muscular body and handsome facial features were now to the point where he appeared to have aged beyond his young years. He never wanted to live to look like he was seeing himself! And now he was even much, much slimmer than we'd ever seen anyone. It was phenomenal he was still walking!

Rhonda hadn't seen Chip for a couple of weeks when she came to visit. She had only been with him a few minutes when she joined me in the kitchen.

She looked faint and astounded, crying, "I never noticed how thin Chip was! He looks like he has lost so much more weight since I last saw him."

I told her he wasn't weighing himself anymore, but I was sure he was losing steadily, even though he was drinking lots of protein. Until now I hadn't given much thought to the difference in his looks, maybe because I was around him all the time and his appearance didn't seem to be as extreme to me as it may have seemed to others. It truly hadn't bothered me until the day Chip saw himself in the mirror.

One day while Jerry was at work Chip wanted to lie on the sofa, so I told him I'd help him if he thought we could manage. We tried. My height was about right for him to put his arm around my shoulder and lean on me while we walked together, then I helped to hold him up. We walked like this a few times. Then I suggested that he let me carry him. Chip was tall and lanky, which made it a little awkward for both of us at first, but with a little persistence we seemed to do okay. He wasn't the least bit heavy; I imagine he may have weighed fifty pounds, at the most.

One time I told Chip, "This is how I used to carry you when you were a baby, but that was so long ago, I've sort of forgotten how."

Chip smiled and I laughed, saying, "But we seem to be doing pretty well, don't you think?"

Chip murmured, "Umm huh."

Chip got to the point where he really enjoyed my carrying him back and forth. Then one day I laid a blanket and some pillows on the floor for him to lie on. After that it was our general routine to spend time together on the floor, where we'd talk and Chip could rest. I'm sure this helped with his boredom of lying still at length. It wasn't long until this was happening several times a day—from his bed to the sofa, then to the floor and back again.

A couple of times I had to say, "Let's wait awhile. Okay?"

Chip said, "Uh huh."

Then in a few minutes he'd say, "Up, up. Okay now."

I'd laugh and carry him again. I believe he loved the attention and we were making this fun and games, almost like when he was a little boy full of bliss.

One time when I started to lay him on the sofa, somehow I lost my balance as I was lowering him down and wham! His head hit hard against the sofa table that was behind the sofa. I could actually hear it and felt the pain as he hit. It scared me! I grabbed Chip, apologizing over and over. Jerry rushed over and took him in his arms, telling me he would take him back to bed. Then while Jerry was trying to set Chip on his bed, it was awkward. It was then that it suddenly dawned on me why Chip wasn't able to sit.

"He can't sit! He doesn't have a butt," I exclaimed.

Then Jerry hid him back comfortably in bed. Chip didn't say anything, but the terrible bump on the back of his head bothered me every time I saw or felt it, knowing how it must have hurt. Chip never said a word, but I was extra careful after that.

After awhile there were times when Chip would be lying on the sofa and he would yell, "I'm falling!"

I would stop whatever I was doing and rush to him. It didn't look as if he had budged, so I would go back to whatever I had been doing.

Again Chip would yell, "Help, I'm falling."

I'd hurry to him, but still he was okay. Sometimes he had his arm down toward the floor as if he was about to catch himself. I thought he did this because he remembered the bad fall he had in his bedroom before we kept the rails up. Now he was on the sofa and there weren't any rails. The floor may have seemed farther away to him than it actually was. After his calling a few times, I was beginning to think he was teasing and just wanting my attention.

I would laughingly tease, "No, Chipper, you're not falling. I can see you."

Sometimes he'd shake his head and disagreeably say, "Yes, I am." Other times he would just look at me as though he were surprised I was teasing and couldn't imagine my questioning it.

Jerry didn't think Chip was joking about falling and I only wondered after awhile, but I did know he was terrified from his fall. The few times I teased, he remained serious and wasn't joking.

At a later date I learned Jerry and Chip were right. Dr. Gravelee, who had become a good friend, said his equilibrium may have been off from an ear infection and he was correct in thinking the floor seemed farther away than it actually was. Fortunately this had worked itself out and Chip's getting my attention was assuring for him, to know I was always there, teasing or serious.

One day Chip said, "Mother, do you want to take my picture?"

If Chip ever surprised me, he did with that question.

I said, "Well sure, Chip! Let me go get the camera. I'll be right back."

I didn't waste any time because I didn't want him to change his mind. When I came back, he was proudly holding his *Special Son, Chip* pillow on his chest, ready to have his picture taken. He was so proud of his pillow. I knew Chip was doing this just for me, knowing I would cherish this proud picture forever.

A little later Chip and I were having some Haagen Daz, which was a real treat because almost all he had been consuming lately was his protein and eggnog.

Chip's bowl was almost empty when I said, "Grams would sure be proud seeing you eating all this ice cream, wouldn't she?"

Chip smiled and nodded his head, saying, "Uh huh."

I asked, "Would you like me to call Grams and ask her to come to Texas to see you?"

Chip said, "That would be nice."

I said, "Okay, I'll go call right now."

Mother answered, and I told her I was calling because Chip wanted her to come to Texas. We talked for a few minutes, making plans for her to come in two weeks, then hung up.

"Chip, Grams will be here in two weeks. Can you wait that long?"

Chip solemnly shook his head and said, "Yes."

I assured him she was coming. It was much later when I realized what I had done. I was bargaining with Chip for another two weeks, knowing he wanted to see Grams.

26

"Mother, Jerry, Help"

Chipper's body was weary and he was becoming almost completely incapacitated as the days wore on. He was sleeping most of the time, but he hadn't given up. The horrible afflictions he had gone through in the beginning I prayed were not going to curse him again.

I was primarily concerned for the first time in months about the spasms of pain in his lower back. Once again they were becoming so severe that he could hardly bear the piercing agony.

"Chipper, I really hate to leave you, but "I was hesitant, then asked, "but do you want me to call the doctor and get you some pain medicine?"

I hadn't left Chip alone for months and was hesitant, but he definitely needed something to stop the relentless pain.

Hearing his painful plea frightened me even more. "Yes, please, Mother. I want you to."

I called the doctor for a prescription, then rushed to the drugstore near our home. I wasn't gone long, although it seemed like forever until the medicine was ready. I was afraid being away from Chip, but tried to remain calm while I nervously waited, praying he would be alright. When I returned, the pain had started to ease, but to be sure he took a pill. Fortunately the pain eventually ceased altogether.

On Tuesday evenings I had recently started going to support meetings in Fort Worth, thinking it would be good to get acquainted in our area. When I received the call, I went to the last meeting of the first six-week session. I rode with Barbara, who was in charge of the meetings. Several months ago I had stopped attending the support meetings in Dallas, not wanting to be away from Chip. I still wasn't sure if I should be leaving him, even though Jerry was with him.

This support group had a few more women than men. There were a few men with AIDS and a young woman with AIDS who had already lost a baby and would be losing another son, as well as her own life, all due to a blood transfusion. There also were a grandmother, several mothers, and friends.

Chip liked hearing about these meetings, so I'd tell him about them usually while he drank his protein.

Chip said, "Mother, you have made a lot of nice, new friends at these meetings, haven't you?"

"Yes, Chip, I have. People from all walks of life. In Dallas, even the parents of a doctor who would have graduated this year. Thanks to you, honey, for encouraging me to go."

Chip solemnly listened, then gave an agreeable smile. After a brief pause, he sighed, "That's a shame, the doctor in his last year."

I rambled on, "Julie is a good Christian and she lost her son a few months ago. He only lived eleven days. You'd like her, the same as Barb, I'm sure,"

Chip smiled.

Then I tiptoed onto another subject. "Chip, one thing I want you to know is that I now know of other patients who went to the same doctor as you, and they all feel the same way. It isn't only us! In fact, one of them changed doctors. I won't say any more because I know how you feel, but I just wanted you to know."

Chip didn't comment. I only wanted to reassure him, but took his cue. Too, he was tired, so I didn't talk much longer.

I believe that was one of the traits I admired most about Chip. He had a distinct way about him and he handled matters with control. We never dwelled on the negative. So much could be said, and that was it. You knew when to stop and felt good with his intelligent manner.

A few days later Chip was lying on the sofa when he gave me a terrible scare. I happened to look at him and his mouth was wide open, his eyes stationary, staring straight up to ward the ceiling. Not a muscle was moving. My own eyes widened and my mouth dropped open. Frightened, my heart stood still. I hesitantly moved toward him, watching all the time for a sign, any sign that he was okay. Then, thank heavens! I saw his sweatshirt slightly move. I gasped and hastened to him. What a relief that slight move was to my heart! I stood watching Chip for a few moments, not knowing for sure what to do. He appeared to be sound asleep, so after awhile I slowly backed away, continuing to watch him.

I lived in constant fear of what to do or what to expect when his time came. Until now I wasn't familiar with a fatal sickness, or the transpiring. Would I be near? When, where, how? I didn't want him to be alone. To know his time was nearing and the idea of my not being with him was almost unbearable. Chip had told me he wanted to die in my arms. I, too, wanted this, but secretly feared that final moment.

He had already suffered enough and I worried about him suffering even more. If these thoughts were always on my mind, then I could only imagine what Chip was going through mentally, let alone physically, while he lay quietly day in and day out with his exhausted, helpless body withering away, little by little with no mercy.

After calling and talking with Julie and Lydia, who were in the support group, I agreed Chip was apparently in a coma when he scared me the time I didn't think he was breathing. This crossed my mind that was what was happening since it wasn't the first time. He had been briefly, silently staring in that same manner every so often the past couple of weeks. This time though, it had been much longer and scared me more because I couldn't see him breathing. I wasn't sure what to do.

Then I called the doctor, but he wasn't at his office, so I mentioned to the receptionist what was happening to Chip. She said she would tell the doctor to call, but he never did. Therefore, I figured Chip must be going into comas and there was nothing I could do or the doctor would have called. I believe it was embedded in my mind that there wasn't anything I could really do at different times. I constantly lived with this helpless fear of such as what was happening now. This was a part of what could be expected to happen to the son I loved dearly.

It was some time later when it dawned on me why the doctor may not have returned my call. Possibly he had thought Chip's time was near, which was expected long over a year ago. And too, Chip had told the doctor he was ready and didn't want his life prolonged again. Still I was concerned, not knowing anything for sure. All I cared about was soothing Chip and making him as comfortable as possible. I told Jerry I didn't like Chip's being sick, but I liked taking care of him.

Jerry replied, "I know. It's like when he was little."

Jerry knew. I smiled and agreed, knowing in my heart I felt good being home with him. Only now it was sad knowing he wouldn't be growing strong anymore.

That week I was especially attentive to Chip. In retrospect it was as though Chip subconsciously knew his time was near and in different ways he may have been trying to let me know. Yet for some reason I couldn't (or maybe wouldn't) grasp his messages. Apparently I wasn't ready, but Chip still tried, knowing I would someday understand. His death was overdue; still it was phenomenal how he was his last six days. As usual, right up to the end he was watching out for me.

For hours I sat with Chip. Nothing else seemed to matter except for the special closeness, as we'd always had over the years. We'd talk some, and other times we didn't say much. He'd quietly watch me until he fell into a slumber. I'd wait. When he opened his eyes, I would smile, touch his hand, or gently brush his hair back with my hand. He'd somehow force a bit of a smile with what little strength he had.

Every so often his speech was brief, slow, and hesitant, coming in short phrases. Still other times when we'd be talking, his words flowed smoothly without complications. His dry, irritating cough hadn't subsided, nor the shortness of breath every so often. He was still drinking lots of strawberry protein and sometimes chocolate milk too. I was still lifting and carrying him from his hospital bed to the sofa and then to the floor. Often I'd lie on the floor talking with him, as I had when he was a little boy, until he fell asleep. During these tender moments there were many times I had to turn my head away to get hold of myself, to keep the tears from falling.

One time I said, "Honey, you have really helped to make me strong, but there are times when the tears are there to let you know how much I am going to miss you because I love you so very much."

Chip smiled while his firm, bony fingers reached over and touched my hand.

He said, "I know. Mother, that's okay. It makes me feel good. I love you so very much too."

When I think back about the fifth Tuesday night, I remember telling Barbara on our way home from the meeting that I was having a hard time leaving Chip. I told her I wanted to attend the meetings, but was having second thoughts. I assured her I'd call if I couldn't go. Barbara said to do what I felt was best.

That night as usual, I told Chip about the meeting while he drank his protein. Then I tucked him in, making sure he was comfortable.

I started to turn off the light, but he said, "No, leave it on."

That surprised me, but I let it on.

Jerry always went to bed early since he had to rise early for work. By the time I was ready it always seemed to be later, after I had gotten Chipper all tucked in for the night. It was usually about eleven-thirty. The days were fairly routine with Chip, and the more traumatic times came during the next six nights.

I hadn't been in bed long when Chip called, "Mother! Mother!"

His voice sounded desperate and distant, as though something was wrong. It scared me and I scrambled out of bed and rushed to his bedside. Apparently he was having a hot flash and wanted his blankets off. I pulled them away, then resituated him and his covers. He asked for a cigarette and I moved his ashtray stand over to his bed where he could reach it and handed him a cigarette. Then I waited, watching him while he smoked, not saying much. He looked at me with a warm, gentle smile. I smiled back, thinking how sweet and refined he was. He was still only taking a couple of puffs. When he finished he handed me his cigarette and I put it out for him, which had been the general routine lately. I hadn't thought about his not having the strength to put it out, only that he may have liked my doing it for him. Whichever, I enjoyed doing this for Chip. I then moved his ashtray stand away from the bed. Ever since he burnt a hole in his sweatpants his fear remained. So I kept the cigarettes at a distance, and he'd tell me when he wanted them.

I kissed him good night and went back to bed, saying, "I love you, Chip." "I love you too," he said softly.

I hadn't been in bed long when Chip called in the same distant, desperate voice, "Mother! Mother!"

I went back out and asked what he wanted.

"Nothing." He looked at me with a puzzled expression as though he was wondering what I meant.

"You called me. Do you need to be changed?"

"No." He tilted his head, looking at me with his eyes squinted as though he didn't understand why I had asked.

I said, "Okay, I'm going back to bed."

I kissed him good night and left. I was hardly covered up when he called, "Mother, Mother."

The same distant, desperate sound in his voice. I waited.

Then Chip called, "Jerry! Jerry!"

That same desperate voice, but Jerry didn't answer. After calling Jerry and not getting a response, he yelled, "Help! Help!"

Hearing that desperate sound and the word "help" scared me and I hurried to his bedside. I checked if he needed to be changed or if there were other complications. He seemed to be alright. So I fluffed his pillows, fixed his blankets, gave him a kiss, and went back to bed.

It wasn't long until he started again. After awhile I quit rushing out to him every time. He'd repeat the pattern, first calling for me, then Jerry, and finally he'd call, "Help! Help!"

This continued, always the same and with the same clear, but distant, desperate sound in his voice. He'd only stop when I'd go to him. At times he might want or need something. But other times he might not say anything, only look as though he wondered what I was talking about. He continued calling like this until three-thirty in the morning and I kept checking to be sure he was all right.

Chip and I woke early the next morning, at six o'clock. We had a good day, moving him many times to the sofa, the floor, and back to bed.

That night after I had Chip tucked in bed at eleven-thirty and started to leave the room, he wanted to go with me. I told him I was going to bed.

He called, "Take me with you!"

Startled, I asked, "You want to go to bed with me?"

In an aggravated tone, implying "you know better," he said, "No!"

My voice was apologetic as I tried to clarify what he meant. "You mean you just want to be near, in our room."

He nodded his head and said, "Uh huh."

In a loving, sweet voice I said, "Honey, I'm not too far away. Call if you need me and I'll come right out. Okay?"

Looking back, I believe he may have sensed his time was near, and he didn't want to be alone. If only I had realized this.

No sooner had I pulled the covers over me when Chip started calling. Again our night was the same as the night before with him calling, "Mother! Mother!"..."Jerry! Jerry!"...then "Help! Help!"

Again he continued with the same distant, desperate sound in his voice. As soon as I'd get back to bed, he'd start again. By now I was becoming frustrated and tired. While getting out of bed I quietly moaned to myself (which wasn't like me). By the time I was up and to him again, I was calm and ashamed I'd moaned, certainly not wanting him to hear. I sensed he needed me near, although I didn't understand. I knew he wouldn't be doing this intentionally. This continued the same every fifteen minutes until three- thirty, stopping only when I went to his bedside.

The next night we seemed to go through the same routine again.

One time I firmly said, "Chip, do you remember the story about the little boy who kept hollering for help all the time? Remember? He didn't always need help. One time he did need help and he didn't get it, because no one knew if he really needed it. Remember, I'm here with you and I'm in the next room, but if you keep calling me for no reason, then what am I to do?"

Chip looked at me as though he didn't understand why I was saying that. Then I really felt terrible talking to him like that. I wasn't thinking about the whys and whats. I knew this wasn't like Chipper and there had to be a reason for his repeating the same words every fifteen minutes. Evidently he needed me, and as Chip had said before, I needed to stay calm. It seems he was right.

That day David, with hospice, would be visiting Chip. Usually I still stayed home. But today there was a luncheon for million-dollar producers in real estate, which I primarily earned the first quarter of '86, even though I declined pursuing real estate to be with Chip. Chip encouraged me to go and after much debate I decided I'd make it brief. I heard the doorbell and told Chip it must be David as I went to answer.

"Hi, David, come on in. I'll be leaving in a few minutes."

David walked over to Chip, who raised his frail, thin arm and hand to welcome him. David firmly clasped Chip's hand in his hands, and said, "Hi, Chip, I'll be here until your dad comes home."

Chip happily smiled and replied, "Good."

A few minutes later Chip asked David if he would get him some strawberry protein. David hurried to the kitchen and fixed Chip's favorite drink.

I said, "Chip sure likes you, David. He asked me earlier when you were coming. He looks forward to your visits."

David pleasantly said, "I like Chip, too. He's a good young man. I enjoy visiting with him."

I smiled saying, "Thank you. Your coming helps him and eases his loneliness a lot."

When I started to leave, I walked over to Chip, softly squeezed his hand and said, "I love you. I won't be gone long."

"I love you. Be careful," Chip replied.

Chip was always on my mind and it was hard being away from him. I hadn't gone far when the tears flooded my eyes. I felt empty and my thoughts were rambling. *This isn't right. Why is this happening to him? Oh, God, please,* I pleaded while I gasped for breath, desperately crying and wondering why. I *don't understand. What will I do? What am I going to do? It isn't right!* I kept sniffling and the tears wouldn't stop. *Cod, oh, God. What will I do?* I couldn't stop crying. *I love Chip so much. He's all I think about. I know he will be better off and in a better place. I am being selfish.*

I blew my nose and tried to pull myself together. It wasn't easy. I was so sad and frustrated. My neck and shoulders were tense. I reached back and pulled on them, trying to loosen some of the muscles. The tension always seemed to be there. I'd be fine, but what about Chip? Then I'd start again. The tears kept coming, along with the sniffles. Chip still hadn't cried, although I'm sure he must have been crying on the inside. He wanted to cry, but couldn't.

When I arrived at the Amfac Hotel where the luncheon was, at the DFW Airport, I waited a few minutes while pulling myself together before joining the other realtors.

As soon as the luncheon was over and awards were given I hurried home.

Jerry said, "Chip's been wondering when you'd be home."

Chip replied, "For sure. How was your luncheon, Mother?"

It always seemed like forever to Chip. Even though it wasn't, I could imagine how it seemed longer while he lay sick.

"It was nice. How was your visit with David?"

Jerry said, "David said Chip kept him running today."

"He did? Chipper surprised me, asking David to make him some protein before I was out the door. Chip, did you drink it all?"

Chip was shaking his head yes and Jerry said, "He must have. David had to make him some more. Then I made him some when I got home. He's drinking his fourth glass now."

"Chip, that's good! Did you sleep today?"

"Not much."

"Well, maybe you will sleep well tonight." I smiled.

John and David had been great company for Chip the past six weeks and so had another hospice man named Stan a couple of times 'til his vacation.

At a later date, John and David joined us for some homestyle Chinese cooking. We talked about Chip and his care. They knew I had been the only one taking care of him all these months and were complimentary about the attention it was evident that I'd given him. They were especially surprised to notice he didn't have any bedsores. I told them only one time were we afraid he was going to get them, so I put Vaseline on him as I often did when he was a baby. Never again were there any signs of them. Also, Chip walked with our help up until the last week, and then I carried him right up to his last day.

Then I told them the sad part was to think that all of Chip's primary complications were those known to require rest and keep one down. They did challenge him tremendously, yet he did extremely well for what could be expected with everything else happening to him. He had always been active, and I'm sure the movement must have helped.

I commented, "I wanted everything to be as nice as possible for him. Many things we learned the hard way, but didn't give up. There's so much I've learned since then that I wish I'd known. It would have been much better for Chip."

After dinner we talked more. Eventually the evening concluded and I earnestly said, "John and David, both of you were great at spending time with Chip. He was so lonely long before and greatly enjoyed your spending time with him."

That evening after tucking Chipper in, he started his desperate calling at eleven-thirty, "Mother! Mother!" "Jerry! Jerry!" and "Help! Help!"

I repeated the same routine every fifteen minutes, making sure he was alright after he called. Apparently I was tireder than I realized. The last time I had gone out to him the grandfather clock chimed three times when I returned to bed. I must have fallen asleep because I suddenly woke from a deep sleep. The clock said four o'clock! Chip was calling.

Startled, I jerked up in bed. "Oh no, I must have fallen asleep. I wonder if Chip slept."

Jerry said, "No, he hasn't stopped calling."

Jerry was always aware of the slightest sound Chip made. Again I was going back and forth while Chip continually called, this time until daybreak! Then he fell back asleep for a couple of hours. When he awakened he was hoarse and could hardly talk. I mentioned his apparent hoarseness from calling all night. Chip looked puzzled as though he wasn't sure what I meant.

During the day we were wide awake except for Chip who slept briefly. I'd rest ten minutes, then feel refreshed the rest of the day. I didn't understand what was happening to Chip. Apparently we were both in bewildered states of mind from the shock and hadn't comprehended this during the entire crisis, going from our positive concept to the most negative ordeal life could offer.

At first I hadn't even given thought to Chip going in and out of comas during the night. Then when it crossed my mind, and after talking with Lydia, that seemed to be the only explanation. At a much later date there was the thought that he was possibly having near-death experiences and he kept trying to give me clues. Apparently he wasn't quite ready to go yet. I understand this now, the same as I now realize how much stress we were apparently under. Chip was my only concern and I never analyzed or thought of the detriment stress was causing us. Even when people would mention my stress, it actually didn't faze me and I never thought any more about it.

Chip's good attitude, determination, and telling me I was strong saw me through everything. He was what kept me going, along with my aerobics every day. This evidently was a good combat for the stress.

On the fourth night at eleven-thirty. Chip was right on cue the same as the past nights since Tuesday, desperately calling, "Mother! Mother!" "Jerry! Jerry!" and "Help! Help!"

It was the same pattern, although this time he sounded faint and even more distant when he called with the same desperate note, "Mother! Mother!"

"What, Chip?"

"I need help."

When I got out of bed and went to Chip, I asked, "What kind of help do you need?"

"My legs."

I was shocked when I saw him with his legs all twisted around each other. I didn't understand how he could possibly have gotten into such an awkward position. The gouging of his bony knees and feet into each other had to have been most painful and uncomfortable.

Chip said, "Spread them."

I turned him over, separating his legs, saying, "Okay, is that better?" Chip didn't say anything, so I took it as a "yes."

"Chip, I'm going to turn your light out, and I will lie on the sofa. Okay? Will my lying out here with you make you feel better?"

"Uh huh."

Then he called me to come over to him. Just as I got there, he said, 'Pull my arms apart."

"Why? What do you mean?"

No sooner had I asked when I saw his limp, bony arms tightly pressed together and somehow twisted around each other while he lay on his side. His body had to be aching from the prickling of his joints and bone rubbing against bone.

I pulled them apart, asking, "Are your arms okay now, honey?"

He nodded. He was having difficulty with his speech every so often, mostly because he was so tired and worn out, I believe. Still he couldn't stop talking. His persistence was overwhelming!

"Are you comfortable? Now, try not to call me back over here to pull your legs apart in a few minutes. Okay?"

I watched him, trying to figure out how his legs were getting wrapped around each other. It looked almost impossible. Suddenly, somehow during the night, they repeatedly became entwined as though he didn't have any muscle control. He'd helplessly lie still, apparently until the aching became unbearable. Then he'd call me for help.

I asked, "Chipper, are you comfortable? Your legs look okay with you lying on your side. Are they?"

Chipper didn't answer, and I must have been wearing out to have raised my voice, "Chipper, answer me!"

He said, "Uh huh," in a weak voice.

"Okay, I'm going to lie down. I'm turning the light out. Okay? Let's go to sleep. Alright?"

"Uh huh."

"Okay, I'll be right here."

Usually I left a light on for him, but with me lying on the sofa, he seemed to be comfortable with it out.

Chip was slower answering me or didn't respond at times. It was as though he were drained of all his energy as the night wore on. Then he'd somehow start again.

After awhile, Chip sincerely asked, "Is that all?"

I hardly understood him. "What?"

He repeated, "Is that all?"

"All what? What do you mean?" I questioned.

He was slow to answer, then he softly groaned.

I asked him, "What are you doing?"

"I'm falling," he yelled with a gasp.

"No, you're not falling."

"Uuh! Uuh!" Those were serious moans and groans, I believe, yet I knew he wasn't falling.

"You're not falling. You have the rails up on your bed, don't you?"

He may have seemed contrary, but I knew that wasn't like him. His routine calling and all the constant commotion only happened during the night; during the day he was always okay.

Very firmly, he said, "Yes."

"Okay, go to sleep."

"I can't."

"Why not? I am." I paused, then told him good night.

Again Chip firmly said, "No, I can't."

"You can't what?" I asked.

"I can't roll over."

I called, "I heard you, I think you did roll over. I think you're on your back, aren't you?"

I was getting tired and aggravated, yet hying to be nice.

Chip moaned and I asked, "What are you doing?"

"Nothing," he said.

I yelled, "Chipper, do you want to go to the hospital?"

Chip didn't hesitate and distinctly said, "Yes!"

I wasn't thinking when I yelled that! I wish I'd bit my tongue. I knew Chip never wanted to go back to the hospital, ever again! It was so wrong of me to say that to him. I'm sure he answered thinking that was what I wanted and that we were starting to get on each other's nerves. Knowing Chip, he would go to the hospital if he thought he was bothering me or because we were arguing. His quick response bothered me because I knew better.

I asked, "Why?"

He defiantly answered, "I don't want to be here."

"Why not?"

Chip said, "I don't know."

"I won't be there with you."

"I know."

"That's okay?"

Very determined, he said, "Yes."

"Who is going to take care of you?" I paused and added, "Did you think about that?"

"Uh huh." He paused and said, "I want to go."

"Well, if you still feel that way in the morning. I'll take you."

Raising his voice, he insisted, "I want to go now!"

Argumentatively, I said, "No, not now. It's in the middle of the night." I needed to get out of that terrible remark to him.

Chip gave a disgusted sigh, then he yelled, "I'm falling."

I asked, "Falling from where?"

"The bed."

"How can you fall?"

"Mother! Mother!"

Chip was tired and each word sounded as though it took a great effort when he tried to call out. Still he persisted.

"What? I thought if I lay out here you would quiet down and go to sleep."

"Hunh uh."

"Well, if you're not going to sleep, I'm going back to my own bed." Chip defiantly said, "Go back to your own bed!"

I argued, "Then you keep calling me."

"Umph hhuu!" he moaned.

"Yes, you have been for over an hour now!"

"Ummm, umm huuu!" he moaned.

"I've been coming to you every fifteen minutes."

Chip moaned, "Uumm, roll me over."

I asked, "Do you want a sleeping pill?"

He hadn't had a sleeping pill for days.

I added, "Let me see if you have any sleeping pills," while I went into the kitchen to find him one.

I came back to his bedside and said, "Here, Chipper, take this," and handed him a pill with a glass of water.

I asked, 'Is it going down?" I paused, then asked, "Did it go down, Chip?" He said, "Hunh uh," and he kept trying. Finally, the pill went down. While I stood waiting I asked Chip why he thought he was falling. He looked at me and shrugged his shoulders. While I talked I was fixing his covers and making sure he was okay.

"Honey, are you going to sleep? Why don't you lie on your back?"

I asked, "Are your legs okay? Are you warm enough?"

Chip shook his head yes and I said, "Good night. I love you."

I felt melancholy and ashamed of the way I had talked earlier about the hospital. I was really trying to be extra nice to Chip. We were always nice to each other, except when we were tired, which wasn't often. Those were the times I knew he wanted me to calm down.

Chip called, "Mother."

I looked back while I was walking toward the sofa and said, "What, Chip?" "Nothing."

"I'm going to be lying on the sofa, okay?"

"Uh huh."

While I was lying on the sofa I asked Chip if he was going to stay home, and he said he was. I told him that made me happy.

Chip was quiet for a few minutes. Then he wanted some chocolate milk.

I asked, "Why didn't you tell me that before? Are you just saying that so I'll get back up again?"

In a very apologetic, earnest tone, Chip said, "No."

Then I asked Chip why he wanted it now. I had never questioned him when he asked for anything to eat or drink, no matter when or what time of day or night it was. I had to be getting worn out, or I never would have talked to him that way. He was being so sweet, and it made me feel even worse.

After a long pause, Chip softly asked, "No way?"

Still I hadn't answered when he tenderly repeated, "No way?"

I asked Chip, "No way what?"

Softly he replied, "No way I can have it?"

Chip sounded so sweet and sincere, so much like a little boy, and I was giving him such a hard time. Suddenly all these tense moments tickled me.

I laughed and said teasingly, "Yes, I'll get you some chocolate milk. Will you go to sleep then?"

"Alright," Chip agreeably replied.

Goodness, that was terrible of me to be bargaining with him like that, but I needed some rest. This was the first time I had ever been tired since his emergency at the hospital a year ago Halloween, but Chip never seemed to be tired the way I was at present. I didn't understand how he was able to keep this up. He was the sick one, not I, and he wasn't sleeping much, day or night, and hadn't for almost a week.

Tired or not, no matter how I sounded, I would get Chip whatever he wanted. I got him his fourth glass of milk, which was unusual for him to drink that much before going to the doctor in Dallas. He took a swallow, coughed, then drank a little more. I watched Chip closely while holding his glass for him. He looked adorable lying in bed, snugly holding his special pillow against his chest. Then he proudly held his pillow up, apparently to show me how pleased and devoted he was, knowing what it meant to him— and to us.

I happily laughed and said, "What does that say?"

Smiling, I assured him, "It says, Special Son, Chip.' That's what you are."

I stayed with him talking and laughing awhile longer. Chip wasn't saying much, but his precious facial expressions spoke.

I believe Chip was slowing down when he asked, "Would you turn me over?"

I felt at peace, happy and relaxed with Chip. It had to be his sweet, amiable manner that calmed me down. No matter how I was, he was still mastering things while lying calmly and helplessly.

Every so often he tried to give me a sweet, comforting smile as though to say, "Mother, I can't say much to you now because of how I'm feeling, but you know how much l really do love you, and I'm sorry I'm giving you a hard time."

I could read this in his face. Isn't it understandable how I would adore him so much and already be missing him, knowing he wouldn't be here one day soon? True, I was being selfish, but there aren't many like him in this big, wide world, it seems. I was definitely blessed with Chip.

"You're starting to calm down. I think that sleeping pill is starting to take effect. You think so?"

"I hope so!" Chip firmly stated.

Then he coughed, trying to stop and to catch his breath from the persistent coughing.

A few minutes had passed when Chip called, "Mother."

I could hardly understand when he continued, "Where are you?"

I was feeling sad when I answered, "I'm on the sofa, honey."

Chip didn't say any more, and I asked, "Are you okay. Chipper?"

"Uum huu," and he coughed more.

We talked briefly every now and then throughout the rest of the night. I had been so tired and nervous, but with Chip it passed.

Now I felt sad thinking, What will I do without him? He's always been a big help all these years. He's been gone and on his own, still I knew I would be seeing him. Once he's gone, what will I do?

Jerry was up early and after checking Chip he left for work. A little later I went to Chip's bedside.

"Good morning. Chipper. How you doing?"

He had such a pleasant, sweet look and I gently touched his face and started apologizing, "Chipper, I'm sorry. I'm sorry I yelled at you last night. I'm not taking you to the hospital! You know that, you know better. I would never take you back there. I know you don't want logo, and honey, I don't want you to go! I love you and I'm going to keep you right here with me."

I started to cry. I felt terrible for mentioning the hospital. I talked while I made sure everything was alright with him and his bedding.

A few minutes later I said, "Chip, I'm going to lie back down. Okay? I'll get up with you in a little bit. Will you try to sleep? We both need some rest, don't we?"

Chip nodded his head and said, "Uh huh."

I slept until eight-thirty, which was unusual. I checked to see how Chip was doing and he was wide awake, lying quietly. I asked him if he'd been awake long and he nodded his head yes.

Smiling, I asked, "Were you waiting for me to wake up?"

His eyes had a little twinkle in them as he nodded again. Still smiling, I said, "Honey, that was so sweet of you to let me sleep. May I get you some protein?"

Chip again nodded.

After he drank his protein, I changed his bed and rearranged his table. Then I bathed him and put lotion all over his body. His eyes looked heavy, and he was almost asleep before I finished. Then he slept for awhile.

When he woke up, I asked, "Are you going to sleep all day?"

Chip murmured a little and started motioning with his hand.

I asked him, "Do you want your legs up?"

"Uh huh."

I hiked his knees up in front of him while he lay on his back with his many pillows behind him.

"Is that more comfortable? Are you more comfortable on your back?"

Chip nodded his head that he was.

It was amazing how he could hold his legs hiked up in front of him with his knees bent for the longest times. He seemed to have more strength, although it had been becoming drastically harder for him over the past couple of months. It wasn't until after he was gone that I realized the proper wording would have been "how uncomfortable he had to have been no matter what position he was in, including lying down, because of his being almost all bone with no padding whatsoever to cushion his frail, atrophied body."

In retrospect, I can recall this going back at least three months when he didn't sit in the chair too long. I hadn't given thought to his returning to bed quickly because of the discomfort on his tailbone. Chip wasn't one to complain and never said a word. To now realize this must have been an act of stress, for me not to have modified this is heartbreaking.

My thoughts were interrupted by Chip's cough, which didn't seem to want to stop.

After his cough did finally cease, I said, "Chip, I got you a new pink sweatshirt. Would you like to put it on?"

Chip smiled and attempted to answer yes, but he could only nod his head as his annoying cough tackled him again.

Pink was the "in" color for men this year and Chip loved it

I said, "Let me move these for you," as I shifted his pillows, then added, "Gramma will be here in another week. Okay?"

Chip said, "Uh huh," while he nodded his head and smiled.

I said, "Do you want her to come before that or will a week be okay?"

Chip said, "Uh huh," as he somehow raised only one eyebrow. This tickled me and I laughed.

"Chipper, would you like me to wash your hair today?"

"Uh huh."

Chip was exhausted, but he remained awake.

I was resituating his legs, turning him every which way, and he worked right along with me. This time, though, his knees were weak and wobbly. He sort of grunted and moaned every so often.

Even though his body was almost all bone snuggled in a tight, thin layer of skin, he still seemed to have a strong spine and an amazingly strong neck and chest. To have lost his muscle control all at once during the night seemed strange because during the day when I carried him, he could put his arms around my neck and hold on securely.

While Chip was sleeping, I called Mother to make sure she had made her flight reservations to come the following week.

"Hi, Mother."

"Kitty, I was going to call you today."

"Did you get your reservations made?"

"Kitty, I'm not coming yet. I want to remember Chip the way he was before. I've been looking at a lot of his pictures and I want to remember him this way."

I felt sad and was almost in tears while I listened. I could tell Mother was trying to be strong. I understood and knew what she meant. It would tear her up to see Chip now. Yet what about Chip? With his whole life ebbing away, he needed the people he loved to be with him. He was never alone as much as he had been the past months. His life had taken a complete turnabout.

How was I going to tell Chip Gramma wasn't coming? I could imagine how he would feel. This was all I could think about while she continued. I don't believe I was hearing anything she was saying. I didn't care to hear her reasons, although I understood, but this was awful news for Chip. I loved him so much and I knew Mother loved him with all her heart. Yet I had to tell him she wasn't coming! By now I was in tears, and of course Mother was too, but she kept talking, trying to cover up her sobbing. She could never talk about Chip without crying.

She tried to get control of herself and said, "I also have a bad cold and I wouldn't want to give it to Chip. You give him a big hug and kiss for me and tell him I love him. Will you?"

Crying, I said, "Okay, Mother, I will. It may not be long until you will be coming here anyway. Chip is getting much weaker, even though I'm still carrying him to the sofa and laying him on the floor every so often, the way he likes. In fact, when I hang up the phone, I told him I'd lie on the floor with him after he wakes up. It's like when he was a little boy, remember? We had gotten him a playpen but he never used it much because he liked his dad and me on the floor playing with him or just lying alongside him until he dozed off."

I rambled on, "And Mother, now that we moved his bed into the living room, he watches while I do aerobics. Remember when he was a baby, and we had that big, cushiony chair with the wide arms that tilted back? I'd sit him in it while I did housework, then I'd talk to him every time I passed by. He was such a content, happy baby, like now, he's still so tenderhearted and sweet."

Mother gleefully answered, "Yes, I remember. He was like a little king, watching you, all spruced up in his outfits."

Then I told her about his pillow and how it meant so much to him.

"You know. Mother, he's always been special and I believe that pillow was the best thing we could have gotten him. He sure does treasure it! We didn't want to wait until Valentine's Day. It's amazing he's been doing as well as he is. Of course, the holidays were always special, just like when we used to come home and celebrate together. Chip hasn't forgotten. He's been hanging in there."

"Yes, I know. I have lots of good memories of Chip."

I briefed Mother more about Chip, and before I knew it I was crying and telling her about yelling at him last night.

"Mother, I even told him I was taking him to the hospital! I can't believe I said that. That's the last place he wants to go and I'd never take him back there! He's really so good, and he didn't deserve that."

I was crying my heart out.

Mother said, "Kitty, just talk nice to him and tell him you are sorry. He'll understand. He knows how good you are to him."

I couldn't stop crying.

"I know. I already did, first thing this morning. But if s so unfair. We always get along well together, and I don't want to yell at him. I only want things nice for him; it's bad enough what he's going through."

I was starting to pull myself together when I said, "Mother, I believe Chip is going in and out of comas. I'm not sure, but it seems like he must be He will lie with his eyes wide open and not respond. One time when he was doing this and Tasked him if he knew who I was, he said, 'Moth...' and didn't finish. I called Lydia, then another friend, Julie, who had a son who passed away with these complications. He had been in a coma eleven days and never came out of it. She told me to put a damp washcloth over Chip's eyes to keep them from drying out, but Chip's eyes are the opposite. They are real watery and have been for a couple weeks.

"Well, Mother, I'm going to hang up and check on Chip. You take care of your cold. We love you, and I'm sorry I cried so much. I'll be talking with you later."

Mother and I were both in tears when we hung up the phone.

Chip wasn't awake yet, so I called my sister Ruth in San Diego. When I told Ruth that Mother wasn't coming next week she wasn't surprised. I didn't understand her comment.

Ruth continued talking, saying that while she was visiting Mother, at different times Mother had gotten sick and vomited when the subject of Chip came up. She said Mother couldn't bear the thought of what Chip was going through, with how his little body was going down to nothing. I told Ruth she should have told me and I never would have suggested that she come. Now I felt bad for both Mother and Chip. I had no idea she was as upset as that about Chip. I didn't talk to Ruth much longer, and then Chip woke up.

Smiling, I went in to Chip saying, "Hi honey, how you doing?"

Chip looked at me and sort of nodded his head as though to say, "Okay." No matter what, he was still polite.

"Chip, I talked to your Gramma in Michigan and your Aunt Ruth a few minutes ago. They both said to give you their love, along with a big hug and kiss." Then I bent over, hugging and kissing him.

I added, "And here's one from me, honey."

Smiling, I commented, "How's that? You're getting all kinds of love."

Chip smiled, nodding his head yes.

"See, we all love you." I hesitated, then said, "Chipper, Gramma has a terrible cold and doesn't want to give it to you. Will that be okay with you if she doesn't come yet?"

I was sitting on Chip's bed and sensed his relief. I imagine he was thinking, Now I don't need to wait another week. I'm ready and I can go sooner. Otherwise, I truly believe he would have waited for Gramma. It was a miracle that he had survived this long. Even though he looked weak and was weak, in his mind I'm sure he felt he had to be strong, and miraculously he was.

Chip's eyes were watery, then I saw a tear falling down his cheek.

Teasing, I said, "Chipper, you have a big tear on your cheek."

I reached for a Kleenex and wiped his tear, saying, "Are you crying?" Chip nodded his head and said, "Yes."

I asked, "Why, what's wrong, honey?"

"'Cause I can't get up," he solemnly answered.

I laughed and said, "No, you're not crying 'cause of that" and gave him a big hug.

His seriousness tickled me; he was such a sweetheart, keeping his composure. He wanted to get up and go over to the sofa as I had told him we would. So I lifted him up into my arms and carried him over. We made several trips back and forth, from his bed to the sofa, and to the floor before Jerry arrived home. Then Jerry carried him a couple of times to the sofa to rest. For added support we were now putting a cushion behind his back while he lay on his side.

This Saturday evening things were a little quieter, that is, until eleven-thirty after we had all gone to bed. Even though Chip was still a little hoarse he persisted with his routine calling of "Mother, Jerry and Help" in pairs.

Again he was being challenged with the puzzling flexibility of his muscles. I believe this sometimes happened when Chip tried to hike his knees up in front of him, as he'd been doing for months without any difficulty. This seemed to be a natural, comfortable position, but now it was no doubt devastating to him the way his legs and arms repeatedly became mingled together beyond control.

I would suggest he lie on his back or I'd help him to get situated, but somehow whether he was lying on his back or his side he was having a terrible time with his limbs. When he would lie on his side, he couldn't seem to turn without his legs and feet tangling. Other times, while on his back hiking his knees up, they'd fall over to the side. He wasn't able to get control or didn't have the strength to move them the way he wanted. This kept happening, for almost two hours straight this time. It was unfair I didn't understand what was happening. If only I'd known professionally how to take care of these frustrating events. His patience was better than mine under these trying circumstances and he did amazingly well.

I unraveled Chip's legs again, and he said, "Okay, that's what I want. Can I roll over?"

I was getting tired and said, "Go ahead," I watched him try. He wanted to, but there wasn't any way he could budge on his own.

In a soft, sweet voice, Chip asked, "Will you help me?"

I asked, "Which way? Come on, Chip, I'm pulling on your shoulders and your rump. Come on."

After I got him situated, I asked, "Is that okay?"

"Uh huh."

I asked, "How can that be comfortable, honey? Is it?"

"Hunh uh."

I asked, "Why don't you lie on your back? Do you want me to cover you up?"

"Uh huh."

While I covered Chip and tried to make him comfortable, I said, "I love you, honey."

"Love you." Then he started coughing.

I walked over to the sofa to lie down again.

Before long Chip called, "Mother, Mother."

I went back to his bedside and seeing he needed to be repositioned, I asked, "Do you want to turn this way or that way?"

He pointed toward the side and I asked, "Will you be able to sleep?" Chip nodded his head yes.

I asked, "Do you want me to stay out here or do you want me to go back to my bedroom? I came out here because I thought you would sleep better. Every time I get covered up, you start calling me again. Why do you do that?"

Chip sweetly said, "I don't know."

I asked, "Do you know how often you're doing it?"

Chip's lips weren't moving too much as he said, "Hunh uh."

He couldn't move and looked uncomfortable.

I asked, "Do you want me to turn you over this way, honey? Come on," I encouraged.

I tried to imagine how I'd be situated if it were I and then fixed Chip's legs and arms in that position.

Then I asked Chip, "Is that comfortable?"

He shook his head yes while his annoying cough persisted. Once his cough subsided, I tenderly smiled and sat down in the chair alongside his bed, saying, "Chip, I love you."

"Love you. Mother."

Chip was lying calmly while I was sitting beside him looking at some papers. Then momentarily I looked up when I heard Chip say, *"Mother, God is reaching for me. He wants my hand."*

I was startled, and a remarkable feeling swept over me seeing Chip earnestly raising his weakened, feeble arm up high—as high and as far as his hand would reach. It was as though a surge swept over him while he was reaching and fervently stretching with all his might! I wouldn't have thought he had the strength to hold his fragile hand up that high and for as long as he was.

His face was so calm, so peaceful and serene, as though he must have heard God saying, *"Come my child. I love you."*

I stood up and leaned over the bedrail to give him a hug, saying, "Yes, Chip, that's where you'll be going. Will you save a place for us?"

Chip's serene expression didn't change. He was looking upward, and he nodded his head, sincerely saying, "Yes."

I kissed Chip and slowly sat down while he lay calmly gazing upward. I must have gone into shock after that, or maybe I was too tired and hadn't thought of how soon it might be or of all the messages Chip had attempted to deliver since Tuesday night.

A little later I said, "Chip, when you want me, I will be on the sofa. Okay? I'm going to lie down. I love you."

"I love you. Mother."

It was Sunday morning when we awoke bright and early after having only a couple of hours of sound sleep. I believe Chip stayed awake knowing Rhonda was coming today, even though it wouldn't be until later on. Somehow he still seemed to have that knack for hospitality. When Rhonda and a friend arrived. Chip and I were on the floor lying on his blanket with a bunch of pillows. Spontaneously they joined us. Then after awhile I got up, deciding I'd go to the health club while they were with Chipper. This would give them time together they hadn't had for awhile.

When I returned home they were still on the floor talking.

I laughed and said, "It looks like y'all haven't moved since I last saw you. You're still on the floor!"

Rhonda laughed and said, "Chip hasn't moved, but he sure has had me hopping! I've fixed him three glasses of protein and two glasses of chocolate milk since you left!"

"Great! I know Chip likes his protein. That's about all he wants anymore. He did surprise me, wanting a cup of coffee the other night. He hadn't had coffee in months."

Rhonda said, "I forgot to put the strawberry in one time and he wouldn't drink it until I added some."

"Yes, it must be strawberry! I believe he likes his strawberry protein as much as he did his banana splits. Remember?"

Rhonda laughed, saying, "Yes, I remember. He always had room for a banana split!"

They were still on the floor when dinner was ready. When Rhonda and her friend started to get up, Chip apparently thought they were leaving and hastily said, "Wait, don't go."

"I'm not. We're going to have some spaghetti and meatballs. Then I'll be back and talk with you," Rhonda assured Chip.

Chip nodded his head, saying, "Okay."

A little later they left. Chip still remained awake with Jerry and me until Jerry retired for the evening, which was a little later than usual since tomorrow was his day off.

It was almost eleven-thirty when Chip started calling for Rhonda.

After awhile I asked, "Would you like me to call Rhonda so you can talk?"

I remember when Chip called her at all hours, which was fine for them, yet I was hesitant. Although this time, for some reason it seemed especially important that he talk with her even though she had been with him all day and all evening.

When Rhonda answered the phone I apologized for waking her if I had, then told her Chip wanted very much to talk with her.

Rhonda said, "No, that's okay. I had just gone to bed. This is really strange because I thought about Chip calling me when the phone rang."

I handed the phone to Chip. Hearing this end of the conversation, I surmised Rhonda told Chip she loved him and he told her he loved her. Then Chip was talking about going to the movies tomorrow if he wasn't tired.

After he hung up, the three of us talked awhile.

Jerry was about to go to bed and I told him I thought I'd sleep on the sofa so I would be near Chip.

Jerry agreed that was a good idea, saying, "He wants you near."

Chip was still wide awake. I don't know how he kept going, although it was understandable, being surrounded by those he loved and getting their undivided attention all day. He sure had everyone busy making protein and enjoyed every minute.

Chip and I talked awhile longer, then he fell sound asleep after his busy day. Before lying down I was breezing through the newspaper, but my thoughts were not on what I was looking at. Then I walked over to the sofa to lie down. Instead I picked up a pen to write. I was thinking how quiet it was and that I'd rather be hearing Chip.

I wrote, "I'm not ready to let go," when my thoughts were interrupted by Chip calling, "Mother, Mother."

I went over to him and he reached his hand up to me. I took his hand in mine. Through his hoarseness he started talking deliriously. With all that had been happening to him spiritually, possibly he may have been speaking in tongues. I'm not familiar with that, but it was a thought. He was very abrupt and serious.

Then Chip motioned his hand and said, "Pencil," and apparently wanted a piece of paper. After I got him a pencil and a sheet of paper, he leaned the paper against his knee, which he had hiked up in front of him while he lay on his back with the head of the bed raised. Chip tried to write, but his strength only allowed some light scribbling. He tenderly looked at me with a disappointed, hopeless expression. Then he raised his shoulders up and dropped them back down, as though to say, "I'm sorry," and moved the paper toward me.

My heart ached.

Holding the paper I glanced at it, then smiled saying, "That's okay, honey. I understand. I love you too."

Chip assuringly nodded his head. "Yes."

I assured him I'd be near on the sofa tonight. He smiled, then closed his eyes. I sat quietly, admiring what a fine son I had.

Then a little later, while walking toward the sofa, I continued to grasp the paper Chip had so desperately attempted to write on, making out some of the vague, fine scribblings: *To my Mother. Thank you. Just wanted...* Then they faded away.

After awhile, Chip called, "Mother, Mother."

I answered, "Yes, honey, I'm right here."

Chip didn't say any more. Then we both fell back asleep.

About an hour later, Chip called, "Mother, Mother."

I went to his bedside and we talked awhile. This night was more restful than the previous five nights of continual calling until three-thirty and the one night, almost all night. Chip only called me five or six times during this night. If he needed my attention or wanted something, I was content to take care of whatever it was. Otherwise, we'd say a few words, which seemed to soothe him and be all he needed. Then he'd fall back asleep and so would I.

Chip's voice was tranquil, rather than desperately calling, knowing I was near. This was the assurance he needed. With our being together there was a peacefulness that saw us through the night.

We all slept later than usual, until seven-thirty.

Jerry talked to Chip while I fixed his protein. Then I joined them, holding Chip's glass while he attempted to drink, but this time he couldn't seem to bring the protein up through the straw.

All the time while he tried, Chip's beautiful, piercing blue eyes were fixed upon me, filled with such heavenly love. His gaze was so strong and intense that I, too, couldn't take my eyes from him during those endless moments. In his weakened condition there were no words, only his magnetic gaze, conveying the divine love that was so brilliantly glowing from the depth of his warm heart.

Consequently after a couple more tries I excused myself, telling Chip I would be right back. I went to the kitchen to get a teaspoon. Then Chip tried to sip from the spoon, but it was still too difficult. His efforts were futile. With an understanding smile I quietly sat the glass and spoon down.

Then Chip motioned toward his room saying, "Take me..."

I cheerfully said, "Okay, honey. Let me get cleaned up first. Then I'll come right back and take you there. Okay?"

Chip knowingly nodded his head yes while Jerry stayed with him. When I returned to Chip's bedside, Jerry didn't say anything. He was fervently, quietly watching Chip. I quickly looked at Chipper. He was having a hard time breathing. This was different from the times before when he had a shortness of breath. Now his breathing was erratic, in short, heavy spurts that seemed to be difficult.

We quietly continued to watch. I don't believe Chip was aware of our presence. This scared me. I asked Jerry how long he'd been this way. He said he had just started. I thought Chip was probably worn out from the past six nights of calling, and he hadn't slept much during the day either.

We continued watching him for the longest time, softly talking about how he was and how he'd been doing.

I asked Jerry if he thought his time was near and he said, 'No. He'll be okay. He's scared us before, then he'd come right back and be fine."

"Yes, that's true, but he's so worn out," I emphasized.

After awhile we agreed he seemed to be doing better. We felt sure he'd be alright after he rested.

Jerry was going to the health club, but still he lingered. A little later I encouraged him to go ahead and go, saying Chip would probably be awake when he got back. Jerry waited a little longer, then agreed Chip needed to rest and would probably be asleep until he returned.

I continued to watch Chip, thinking he'd be okay. Before long the fear intensified, seeing he still wasn't aware or responding. If his time had come, *I* knew he was prepared. I must let him go if it was time. He didn't want his life prolonged again. What should I do? I didn't want to leave Chip's side. Yet I felt I must call a doctor if his time was near. I was nervous and wanted to do what was right. Chip couldn't talk to me; maybe that's what scared me. I believe for the first time ever I may have panicked. I hurried to the phone while watching him all the time. I wasn't sure who to call.

Before I realized it, I seemed to automatically call Dr. Gravelee, knowing how she admired Chip. All the time I was on the phone I kept watching him a few feet away. I told her I was afraid Chip's time was here. I wanted to go back over to him, yet I couldn't suddenly hang up. I don't believe he was aware or could hear, yet if he could he knew I was afraid. She said she was sorry, then talked about what a fine person Chip was.

She said, "Chip was one of those special patients that I adored from the start. I loved him. He was so sharp, with such a sense of humor. He was so charming, utterly charming! He was so special. You know, Kitty, psychologically, he's a pretty healthy person."

I agreed, "Yes, that's what I think. I'm sure he didn't have a breakdown. He was real busy in real estate at that time also, and that's the sad part, to think how well things were going and this had to come about."

She commented, "I'm sure the illness itself was there before we were aware and I'm sure that a lot of what he was feeling, the depression and some of the upsetting confusion, was because he was ill. But it wasn't anything anyone could put a finger on, and I'm quite certain that is what was working even then. But we weren't able to identify it, and of course, we know a lot more now and I'm sure they'll identify it sooner. But, it's just... Bless his heart that he had to go through this so long. He must be exhausted."

I replied, "Yes, and you know, that's what's so sad now. He has had hardly any sleep since Tuesday night. I don't know how he's doing it. He's wearing himself out...."

I was quietly sobbing, trying to remain calm. I wanted to hang up. I needed to hang up, but wasn't sure of any thing or what to do. I didn't want to believe his time was actually near.

Dr. Gravelee said, "God, I wish I could fix it. I'd give anything if I could fix it."

"I need to hang up." I was afraid and felt numb.

She said, "Thank you so much for calling. I think about you all often. I can't help but worry about you."

I didn't want her to know I was crying.

Dr. Gravelee continued, "Please, please call me when you need to. Don't ever hesitate."

Trying to clear my voice, I said, "I needed to call you."

I was afraid all the time while I watched Chip.

I don't know why I called her at this time, yet I believe I do. I knew Chip didn't want his life prolonged, but I felt I must call a doctor. It had to be her because I knew how much she loved Chip. She was always understanding. She really knew and cared about him and that was what I needed to hear. I listened while I continued to watch Chip.

She said, "Think of me as a friend and call me whenever you want to talk. I think Chip is adorable and you are a delightful person. If Chipper's awake enough, tell him I said hello, will you? Thanks for calling, Kitty. Bye-bye."

I answered, "Okay, bye."

I hung up the phone and hurried to Chip. I was terrified and didn't know what to do. Surely he would be alright, the same as he had always been before after the many scares when we thought we were losing him. This had to be another one of those times. I watched while he gasped for breath.

Motionlessly, I prayed, "Chip, you will be alright. You will be!"

The moments were tense while I sat helplessly. I was too petrified to move. I couldn't take my eyes off Chip. I couldn't believe he would stop breathing. I couldn't. No, I wouldn't. The fear was intensifying and I felt desperate while I watched my precious son gasping for breath. I couldn't move. I couldn't speak out. I was petrified.

No! Chipper, no! You're not going to die! I silently pleaded.

Then he suddenly stopped breathing! I saw my son take his last breath.... silent, quiet, no movement. I sat motionless. The very moment I was afraid of!

Oh, God! My son is gone!

"Chipper," I called while I hastened to my feet and quickly lowered the bedrails. I was too afraid of his passing on. I didn't want to believe his time was now.

I was deliriously thinking, *Oh, no! Chip wanted to be in my arms when his time came! What happened? Oh, God, why didn't I take Chip in my arms, and hold him while he passed on?* I couldn't believe his time was here. *Noo! Noo, not yet!*

I took Chip into my arms. I held him tightly. I didn't want to let go. This was the moment I had been afraid of... all these days.

I should have known. He wanted to go to his end of the house, *to go home.* And to think I'd left, assuring him I'd be back to take him. Had he known, and meant home to the *kingdom of love?*

Only a few hours ago Chip was trying to tell me, assuring me right up to the very end, letting me know he was going to be with God.

I immediately looked at Chip's clock with the prayer plant. It was 9:40 A.M. and my son was gone. I had the fleeting thought of how I had looked at the dock when Chip was born—it was 12:25 P.M. He came into the world crying like a newborn will and now was peaceful. His longing for his earthly father was never fulfilled, but a much greater longing was fulfilled by his heavenly Father.

Chip's search ended. He, Jerry, and I gave each other all the love we could find here during this illness. Now he would never need to search again. In Chip's search for love, he now was gone to the *"ultimate love,"* completing *a life of soul and searching.*

27

The Essence of Balloons

It was early Friday morning, February 27,1987, and my son, Chip, was 27 years old. We would be having his funeral services today, even though his soul had been gone now five days and was already in heaven.

It wasn't even daylight yet. I couldn't sleep, nor did I want to move. I had been lying in bed wideawake. My eyelids felt heavy and my eyes were tired. Still my mind was alert and kept wandering. In my depth of thought, this was the day. Then from that thought, different perceptions kept drifting in and out of my mind—not any precise thoughts, but more like idle musings of today, of Chipper.

I had been most concerned about this day. I wanted everything to be perfect for Chip. This was my last time to do for him. *Most parents plan for a beautiful wedding. I planned for a beautiful funeral.*

Chip had some significant requests for this day, and I wanted to fulfill his wishes, which I knew would make for a funeral to be remembered. I wanted this for Chip, for us.

I lay in bed for a few more minutes, then I had to get up. My body couldn't lie still any longer. I raised myself into a sitting position on the bed while I looked out of our bedroom and down the long, dark hallway to Chip's room, mostly out of habit. He hadn't been in that room for weeks, not since we'd moved him into the living room to be closer to us. I still had a tendency to look in that direction to see if his lights were on or if I could hear any noise or a cough. But there was no need for that, not anymore... no more lights and no more sounds. In the dark quietness I leaned over and kissed my husband, telling him I would be back in a couple of hours. I quietly rose and tiptoed out the door so I wouldn't wake the family.

Last night I had talked with Jerry and Mother about going to the health club. I had wondered if it would be proper to work out on this particular day. I thought that it might be alright since I would be going out in the early morning before many had awakened. Still I was having second thoughts about it's not being respectful to Chip. Jerry and Mother assured me it would be fine, saying Chip would want me to go. When they said that, I knew they were right and I felt better. That was all I needed to hear.

"You need to go, Kitty," Mother said. "It would do you good. I will take care of things here. You go ahead and don't worry about anything."

Jerry assuringly said, "We'll go see Chip when you return home and then go after the balloons."

"Okay, sweetheart. I'm going to stop and see him on my way home too."

I had always gone to the club early, although lately I'd waited until Jerry got home to be with Chip. The early hours were quiet and it seemed strange since it had been awhile.

While I swam my laps it always gave me time to collect my thoughts. Like now, trying to gather my thoughts about Chip and count the laps while my thoughts flowed into the water with each stroke and I turned into another lap, trying to drown my sorrow. It didn't seem right he wouldn't be home waiting for my return. It gave me an empty, futile feeling. I knew for Chip it was best that God had finally taken him. And for Chip I was happy. He never, ever was a burden and I felt fortunate we had the time together, even though circumstances were devastating.

The week prior to Chip's leaving us was challenging for him and me. Looking back I believe it was meant to be a blessing and comfort to us in the end. It was just like Chip to assure Jerry and me that we were in his heart and on his mind, which was a blessing. At long last he was content and going to be with God. What could be more perfect than giving him back to God? I'm sure it must have been perplexing for Chip lying there all that time, going in and out of comas, not really knowing what was happening at times.

Chip knew his passing on would be particularly hard on me, but when the time eventually came he wanted to be sure I was taken care of. It was as though he knew, with Jerry being home, he could pass on. That's what was so crushing, knowing how tenderhearted he'd always been, and now he was gone. I was numb; I was just going with the flow.

I felt much better. A mile swim was what I needed, and I'd feel even better once I saw Chip. I wanted to be alone with him one last time, to tell him I would remember he was saving a place for Jerry and me so we could join him someday.

While I drove toward the funeral home it was cloudy, dreary, and gloomy. The dismal weather seemed to have fit the mood ever since Chip had left us. My thoughts were of yesterday's conversation with Mary, the mother of Chip's friend Steve. She had mentioned how polite Chip always was over the years, especially with the little extra gestures that weren't always common for a young man. Such as when Chip and Steve would be playing backgammon and she'd enter the room, Chip would always rise to acknowledge her presence, no matter how engrossed he was in the game.

Mary said, "He always had that special brightness."

Then I told her an elderly neighbor lady had said the same thing. Whenever she was walking past and Chip was mowing the lawn, he'd always stop long enough to greet her and say something pleasant.

I continued, "Chip was raised with good manners and they always seemed to come naturally with him. When he was only eleven, I remember noticing amongst his schoolbooks was a handy pocket-size book on etiquette. He matured early in life and was always wanting to learn more and please more."

I ended our talk, saying, "That's what makes me wonder why he had to go so young. But I don't suppose I'll ever know."

While driving into the parking lot at the funeral home, I saw only one other car. I'm sure that was due to the early morning hour. After sitting for several moments, still in deep thought, I opened the car door and slowly walked to the entrance.

Opening the heavy door, I entered and quietly walked down the wide corridor into the stateroom where Chip's body rested. By now the tears were flooding through my thoughts as I walked over to Chip's casket. I stood quietly looking at him, knowing I wouldn't be seeing him after today. I clenched my lips, took a deep breath and slowly exhaled, it was hard, but I needed to be poised for Chip, and myself. All these months I had been trying to prepare for this day. And now, this was the day. I felt numb, lost, and alone.

It had been a long, hard struggle for Chip. Too long. He looked peaceful now, and I knew he was at peace with God. I had no idea when he reached his hand to God that it wouldn't be long until he would be going to be with him. Looking back, I should have known. As usual, this was Chip's thoughtful, considerate way. What more could I ask? Isn't it understandable why I always said, "Chip spoiled me more as a mother than I ever did him as a child?" Right up to the end he was assuring me, letting me know God wanted his hand. *God welcomed him into his kingdom of love.*

It was only yesterday when I asked Mother to play the two songs Chip wanted at his funeral. While she was playing his piano and I was standing beside her, I started reading the words, knowing this had been a favorite of Chip's that he often played. It was then that I realized the significant words in "Memory." Until now I had only listened to the beautiful music while Chip played. But then asl read the words I understood why this song meant so much to him. If only I'd read this before! These words seemed perfect when it came to Chip's life. Telling of the beauty and happiness he remembered... his younger days, and how wonderful it was to look back... if only the memories could be revived. If only... Still he knew he had a new life, and life goes on... knowing with each night, whichever it is to be, there would be a memory.

In the depths of my grief I cried, saying, "I didn't realize those were the words! I understand why Chip liked that song so much!"

My tears came unrestrained and I cried my heart out. Mother got up from the piano and put her arms around me. We both wept while trying to comfort each other.

Mother said, "Those words seemed to express Chip's feelings of what he wanted to leave with us."

"Yes, I'm sure they are," I replied.

I reached to hold Chip's hand while I was with him in deep thought. I would never have thought of holding a deceased person's hand, but this was Chip. Sure he was cold and he couldn't respond to me, but this was all of him I had left, this was my baby.

The words in Sue's recent letter to me came to mind.

She wrote, "He was a very close friend and I'll never forget that. A close enough friend to stay in my heart forever and those kind are hard to find. The last thing Chip said to me was, *'Take care of your babies,'* and that thought really stays with me."

I knew what Sue meant. My baby had grown into a wonderful young man and here he lay. *Chipper, I love you and you are my baby. Throughout the years you left so many beautiful memories. You'll never be forgotten. We all love you so very much.*

I squeezed Chip's cold hand, knowing how warm his heart always was, and the tears struggled within my heart. Sue lived in Fort Wayne, Indiana. She and Chip had been friends since elementary school days and occasionally talked long distance. That was their last conversation shortly before he passed away.

Covering the bottom half of Chip's open casket was a gorgeous spray of red anthiriums with a deep-red satin ribbon imprinted with "Beloved Son." At the head of the casket was another beautiful bouquet of red anthiriums with baby's breath lightly enhancing them.

Chip had wanted these lovely Hawaiian tropical flowers in all white. I'd called the florist first thing to be sure it wouldn't be a problem to get the quantity we wanted. The red anthiriums were a second choice, also a favorite color of Chip's.

Even though Chip had mentioned things to me from time to time about his funeral, we hadn't made definite plans. If only the silent stress hadn't hindered our planning it together, then he could have known how beautiful everything was going to be. Chip always had clever, original ideas throughout his life. His wit and charm were with him to the very end.

I had added only a few final touches to his casket, sentimental tokens from family and friends for Chip. We placed his pillow, *"Special Son, Chip,"* in the cupola. Fletch was a little, ornamental, furry clip-on character that Rhonda and Darlene had gotten Chip. Fletch was clipped onto the lace trim of his pillow just as he had been clipped to Chip's robe in the hospital when he joined him almost two years before and had been with him throughout his long, hard struggle. His red, toy Mercedes 380SL was placed with him. Grams special ordered a silver bracelet to go with Chip. The jeweler had engraved, "Love, Grams II-19-59." My sister Susie told me how sad it was for Mother to watch this being engraved. While Susie was telling me, I could imagine it and hearing the story brought tears to my eyes too.

Mother was almost in tears again when she spoke up and said, *"I* wanted to do that for Chip."

On Chip's pinky finger was his gold nugget ring. In loving memory I now wear it on my pinky finger, knowing how proud he was.

Chip's choice of dress was his blue jeans and a white, tailored T-shirt imprinted in small black calligraphy: *"I'm in No Shape to Exercise."*

I laughed, saying, "That's about right, isn't it?"

Chip smiled. The T-shirt was a gift from Rhonda while he was sick. It was unique.

Phil, the funeral director, said people wore all kinds of things and with different sayings on them, and Chip's choice would be fine. Phil added with a laugh, "The other day we dressed a man in a Superman outfit. That's what his kids wanted."

I was surprised, although glad to hear this. I had been thinking of more traditional dress, like a suit and tie. I knew Chip and if he thought this was okay, then it must be.

Earlier Chip had said, "Mother, if my wearing jeans and a T-shirt bothers you, I will wear a sport coat. Jeans with a sport coat are the style. I'll wear the sport coat for you. Okay?"

I smiled saying, "It's up to you, honey. Whatever you want." Then I added, "If you wear a sport coat. I'll make sure the calligraphy print on your T-shirt shows."

Chip enjoyed good music. I was pleased with the songs he had chosen, although they weren't what you might ordinarily expect at a funeral. Well, maybe...at Chip's funeral you would. They were perfect! "Memory," and "That's What Friends Are For."

I wanted these songs to be done especially well for Chip. They were to be accompanied with lovely sound track music and sung by our Broker's daughter and Mike, a fellow agent and good friend of Chip's and mine. Before the funeral and during the procession, there was to be the traditional funeral music on the organ, with one special request, "The Old Rugged Cross," a favorite of Chip's grampa, my dad.

I was still holding onto the casket, bracing myself while these thoughts ran through my mind. I reached my hand to Chip's and held tight.

Softly, I said, "If only you could talk to me, Chip. No more."

This was the thought I could hardly bear and the tears flooded my eyes while I kept thinking, "No more." I squeezed my eyes shut and a couple of tears escaped down my cheeks. Somberly I reached over and took two anthiriums from his floral arrangement. I placed them in Chip's hand that I had been holding. I moved my hands away, but his hand moved and the anthiriums fell. I placed them back in Chip's hand. Again they fell. After trying a couple more times without success, I finally said in a quiet, half-teasing voice, "Chipper, you've got to hold these flowers. I want them to go with you. Okay?"

Somehow, after awhile, I did get the anthiriums to stay in his hand. Perhaps this was my nervous pretense.

I gravely smiled when I pulled away, saying, "There, Chip, I knew you could do it."

Aaron, one of the pallbearers, suggested I put a picture of Jerry and me in Chip's chest pocket. So I placed our picture right next to his heart on the inside pocket of his sport coat. Sentimentalist that I am, I was most thankful Aaron had mentioned that gesture.

I told Chip, "This picture is for you and we'll always be with you." I kissed him and whispered, "I love you."

I stepped back and looked at Chip, then reached my hand to his forehead to wipe off some light lipstick, saying with a giggle, "Sorry, Chip. Mustn't mess you up." Then I gave him a big smile while I stepped back, looking around the room at all the pretty flowers; I glanced at Chip and slowly backed out of the room.

I wandered back down the corridor and out through the heavy door. This time the door seemed to weigh a ton when I opened it. It didn't matter. I felt empty as I got into my car and slowly drove down the back roads, out through what was almost like country.

While I was driving down the quiet, lonely road, my thoughts drifted to a letter I'd received from Lydia. In it she had written, "I know how very deeply the loss of a son hurts. We did not have as many memories with our son as you did with yours. The years have given you a great love for your child. Chipper is free now. You will remember him in everything that surrounds you. You will miss him and long for him. In dark hours you may even wish to have him back, but in the sunshine you will know that his freedom is so much more." Then Lydia wrote, "Dwell on this: Chip left knowing how much he was loved by you, thru the devotion you showed. I did not know Chip, but I know from talking to you how much you loved him. If I can feel that love, how much more can a son?"

I was choked up with tears and could hardly see the road, remembering those words. So meaningful, so touching and true. My heart was breaking and I wanted to stop the car, but I needed to get home. After a few more minutes I pulled myself together.

(Lydia has since passed away, the same as her infant son had at an earlier date—due to the complications of AIDS from a blood transfusion Lydia received. The Bryan House in Dallas was named after her son, Bryan. This is a home established in 1988 for children with AIDS.)

Shortly after I arrived home, Jerry and I went after the balloons filled with helium and secured tightly with red streamers, Galloons always had significant meaning to Chip. Therefore, for Chip, this was a natural request. Prior to the funeral, Reverend Jim had told Jerry and me that Chip had said he wanted balloons at his funeral. Smiling, Jerry and I acknowledged the same desire.

I said, "Yes, Chip mentioned them to us and we wanted to work them in, yet we weren't sure how. Balloons played a distinct role in his life on many special occasions."

Above all, he didn't want a gloomy funeral. Chip wanted everyone to be happy and to remember him as he was before: happy and healthy with a great sense of humor and wit.

Reverend Jim understood, and knowing Chip he came up with a splendid idea of how to incorporate the balloons into the funeral. I'm sure Chip would have been delighted indeed. Right after Jerry and I had gotten the balloons, we went to the funeral home to be with Chip one last time... the three of us. We would always have many treasured memories with Chip.

Jerry and I were standing at Chip's casket loo king at him and not saying anything, just thinking. Then I softly spoke, "There are so many beautiful flowers. I know he would be pleased, and to know of all the other lovely plants that keep coming to our home."

Jerry didn't respond, so I kept on rambling, "The neighbors, co-agents, friends, relatives, and everyone have been so gracious with food, flowers, plants, everything. Caring means a lot. Chip's friends have been calling too. They have been kind and thoughtful, ft was great to be hearing from them. Many we hadn't seen for awhile. Some will be coming to his funeral."

Still Jerry was quiet, just listening and thinking.

I said, "I forgot to tell you, Julie called, the lady who lost her son about four months ago to these complications. She said they made a contribution in memory of Chip to a family so they could fly to see their son who also has this sickness. Don't you think that was a nice gesture?" Apparently I was more tense than I realized. Without giving Jerry a chance to answer, I continued talking, 'II was nice that your company made the contribution in Chip's memory too, as well as a couple of Chip's friends."

I paused, thinking for a few minutes while I was holding Chip's hand. "He sure had a lot of friends to remember him. He would be happy, with all he's been through and having been out of touch." I paused, thinking, and then added, "There are so many I wasn't able to contact. Maybe someday."

I knew our being present with Chip was hard on Jerry. He hadn't accepted Chip's sickness, let alone his passing on, until it happened. Even earlier the morning it took place, Jerry and I thought that he would pull through. Jerry never would have left Chip's bedside if he hadn't thought he would be fine. I knew Chip was at peace now. He had really been quite lonesome, especially toward the end. ft was a long time for him, a long time.

Jerry nodded in agreement. We stood holding hands and I was also holding Chip's hand. Neither of us said any more while we looked at the body of the son we loved so very much. Chip had known how difficult it would be for me, but look how he suffered all those months. It was so much better now that the agony had finally ended for him.

Chip had waited and waited while he grew weaker and weaker. It seems that he hadn't wanted to accept the possibility that his dad could be influenced never to see him again, even in the face of death. He had held onto the belief that his dad would come to see him before he passed away. In Chip's last months he lay quietly in profound thought, hour after hour. At last he had found peace within himself. During the last six nights, the words "Mother, Jerry, and help" seemed to convey the message he wanted to leave with us that we were on his mind and in his heart. How more significantly could he have let us know he had accepted Jerry as the dad he had wanted and dismissed the dad who had so cruelly rejected him so many times when he was a little boy, and now. For years Chip had wanted to accept Jerry, but couldn't because he was still waiting for his dad. Apparently he had overcome his rejection. God had reached for Chip's hand and in his search for love he had found the *ultimate love*.

The time was nearing as we slowly walked away, hand in hand. Soon we would be returning to the chapel.

I was in a daze when I slowly opened the closet door to gather the apparel I would be wearing to the funeral. There hung the black dress Chip wanted me to wear. I slowly reached for it, thinking asl touched it how Chip had wanted to go shopping with me to pick this dress out. It seems some things are desired at one time, then left to rest, the same as Chip's countless days were. He had wanted me to wear a black dress, a wide-brimmed black hat, black shoes, and long black gloves.

One day Chip asked, "Mother, do they still dress like that for funerals today, with everything in black?"

"Yes, Chipper," I replied, "they do. Sometimes they go for more color today. But still, all black is fine and that is what I planned to wear too."

I was getting all choked up. I must stop thinking about these things and finish getting dressed. I was actually dreading this, and I don't believe I had fully accepted everything. Really, I'm sure I didn't, but I was as ready as I would ever be. The limousine would soon be here to take us to the chapel. I know I didn't want to go, yet I needed to.

Soon we were all seated in the limousine and the chauffeur slowly drove down the back roads to the chapel. My mind just seemed to be in neutral and I felt numb.

When we arrived at the chapel, we got out of the limo and entered through the family entrance. Jerry was being unusually attentive with me as we walked up to the casket. We stood there a few minutes while the organ played softly. I silently spoke to my son:

"I love you. Chip. I don't know what I will do without you, but for you I will be strong, just as you have been. Honey, I'm so sorry things have been the way they were for you. You have been so dam good and still, look at all you've been through. It's unbelievable, both the good and the bad. Like you said, you had a good life. Honey, that's only because you made it that way, no matter what. You didn't give up and always made the best of things. I'm so very proud of you. I truly am. I must go to the pew, but you will always be with me. I love you so very much. You have been my life. I will miss you. I will come to see you often, or talk with you wherever you are. You have been so good all your life and I have been most fortunate."

I looked at Jerry while he stood solemnly beside me looking at our son. I didn't really want to walk away, yet I felt I must sit down. I bent over and kissed Chip, whispering, "Chip, I love you."

I felt weak, as if I was in a trance. Holding onto Jerry's arm I slowly walked to the pew. I seemed to have arrived just in time to grab the comer for support, then I slowly moved on over. That truly was the first time I had ever felt weak, as if I was about to fall. I was sad and empty sitting in the silence: waiting, listening, wondering. All was calm and quiet with the soft, tranquil music. That must mean the time was near. It was the last time I would be able to touch Chip.

I was dismal and felt lifeless. There were no tears, even though I was crying profusely on the inside. I wasn't going to do this. Chip didn't want a sad funeral. Yet he knew how I would be and he knew I couldn't help it. I know he had dreaded how this day would be for me. I knew this was probably why he lived as long as he did. He knew I was having a trying time, that I didn't really want to let go. He knew. How could I have been so selfish? Why didn't I tell him to go? I wanted to go on taking care of him. I didn't like to see him suffering. Even though he was, he was gallant, and he was surviving. If only his life could have been more like he wanted it to be while on earth. I didn't mind carrying him back and forth. I didn't mind anything I was doing for Chip. He was trying hard and doing the best he could. Chip was one of a kind and I was the fortunate mother. I would only have one more time to see him, only one more time.

Chip's friend Darlene walked over and handed me a long-stemmed red rose, saying, "Kitty, this is for Chip. Will you put it in the casket to go with him, for me?"

Rhonda had a red rose for Chip too. At that time Chip's grammas from Indiana and Michigan, Rhonda and I walked up front to give the roses to Chip. I'm sure he was touched. These *two red roses of love* tied together to perfection all the beautiful flowers that were so lovely and beautifully arranged in the chapel. In the comer of the chapel there was a splendid assortment of lovely sprays, unique and precisely arrayed all the way to the ceiling.

Moments later the soft music stopped. All was calm and quiet when Reverend Jim arose from his seat and proceeded to the podium to deliver his beautiful, specially chosen words. The power in his purposeful voice was brilliantly strong as his loving, heartfelt words rang out to family and friends. He was assisted by Reverend Brooks.

"Lay Your Burden Down"

Psalm 55:22

"Cast your burden upon the Lord, and he will sustain you..." "This is the challenge to us today from our great God... to lay our burden down... for today... we celebrate the homegoing from this life of our dear friend Chip.

"Brandon (Chip) Williamson was born November I9,I959, in Orange, California. Passed from this life February 23,I987, at his home. Surviving are his parents, Jerry and Kitty Williamson; his grandparents, Dorothy Mathews, Dale and Marjorie Caley... a host of friends throughout this land. We celebrate today the homegoing of our friend."

Then came the lovely voices of our friends, accompanied by sound track music that made the beautiful sound of a live band.

"Memory"

Reverend Jim:

"The great psalmist, David, gave us a challenge for this type of an hour as he wrote in the most favorite psalm of all psalms—the 23rd Psalm—and though in the King James version it only contains 118 words, it is one of the most powerful Christian writings in existence today. For it sings with those who have a note of joy in their hearts, and it conveys a message greatly needed by those who have sorrow and anxiety and fears. Its power lies in the fact that it presents a positive, hopeful, faith approach to life and death. Hear it now from the amplified version: The Lord is my shepherd—to lead, guide, and shield me; I shall not lack. He makes me lie down in fresh, tender, green pastures. He leads me beside the still and restful waters—he refreshes and restores my life. He leads me in the paths of righteousness—not for my earning it, but for his name's sake. Yes, though I walk through the deep, sunless valley of the shadow of death, I will fear or dread no evil, for you are with me, your rod to protect and your staff to guide. They comfort me. You prepare a table before me in the presence of my enemies; you anoint my head with oil. My cup runneth over. Surely only goodness, mercy, and unfailing love shall follow me all the days of my life, and through the length of days, the house of the Lord and his presence shall be my dwelling place for ever and ever.

"Let us pray.

"Our eternal and loving God in heaven, in whose love is our hope, in whose wisdom is our life. In your infinite wisdom bring our imperfections to perfection, our marred lives to true completion, and in this midnight hour of our lives, bring the spirit of your sweet comfort to us. We offer you gratitude for the goodness of our departed friend, Chipper. Help us to fix our minds upon whatever things were true, whatever things were honest, whatever things were just, whatever things were pure, whatever things lovely, whatever things were of good report, wherein there is virtue. We offer praise and thanks to you our God. For we who remain, we pray deep faith, renewed confidence, and courage to face this day and all the tomorrows of life that remain for us. May we all experience the comradeship of him who has carried our griefs and on whom the applications of us all have been laid in this eternal fellowship. Keep us until the morning eternal dawns and all the shadows have fled away and we see more clearly in the blessed name of Jesus Our Lord. Amen.

"On this occasion we come to pay tribute to our beloved friend in Clirist, Chipper.

"It is not our purpose to eulogize, though many good, wonderful, commendable things could be spoken about our departed loved one, who certainly touched the lives of all of us and many who are not here today. Nor is it our purpose to pronounce any ecclesiastical judgment, for such is the prerogative of our eternal God who alone shall determine

the destinies of all of us according to our acceptance and the following of Christ, the life that we live. It is rather our purpose today to speak words of comfort, faith, and understanding to us who mourn this passing. For not until we look at death as victorious can we learn to live victoriously. One's life and faith according to God's word determine their destiny. And today, though we stand in the valley of the shadow of death, yet we stand in the light of the greatest hope in our world. Though the darkness has enveloped us, the rays of a glorious dawn are shining through. For though we stand in the presence of death, yet we stand on the threshold of life eternal.

"There is a bronze statue outside the hall of archives in Washington, D.C., that has a young woman sitting on a chair, leafing through a book. The girl is turning the last page of the book and on the inscription beneath the statue are these words: *All that is past is prologue.* That composes our faith this day for our departed loved one, who last August called me to his bedside to make plans for this day in our lives, and in that time together said to me: *'Jim, I don't understand why I'm still here. I suffer so much. But it is as if something has to be done before I can leave this life...'* It was at that time that I was privileged to lead our brother to come to know Christ as his savior. He said he had tried several times in his life to live the life that we should live, and he had failed. But at that moment he made peace with God and we prayed. I looked at his face and on his face came a shine and a smile. He said, 'I understand now. I'm ready to go, because I feel a peace in my soul.'*

"Then the night before he parted this life to go to be with his maker, *he called his sweet and caring mother to his bedside. As he held up his weakened hand and arm, he said to her, 'God is reaching for me now, Mother.'* Oh, to know when that moment comes in our life that we're reaching, God is holding our hand. In the last year he came to love his mother and dad deeply! *Though our departed friend was always smiling, was a loving and caring person who was not selfish or pretentious, his life was just a prologue to something great and wonderful that he enjoys this day as he walks those streets of gold with his maker.* But, in this life, let us say with St. Francis of Assisi: God, make us instruments of thy peace. Where there is hatred, let us show love; where there is injury, pardon; where there is discord, union; where there is doubt, faith; where there is despair, hope; where there is darkness, light; where there is sadness, joy. Grant that we may not so much seek to be consoled as to console; to be understood as to understand; to be loved as to love. For it is in giving that we receive; it is in pardoning that we are pardoned; and it is in dying that we are born to eternal life.

"My friends, God's protection along the way of life and God's direction toward the proper destination are strong evidence of God's wonderful care for us. As we learned from the 23rd Psalm, what need we fear if the Lord is our guide? Because God's word teaches us that Christ's word is the way out—out of the wilderness of sin and out of hell. Christ is our way through the trials of life, the sorrows of life. Christ is the way up—to heaven, to God, to our parted loved ones. In this place that our loved one enjoys today, he will travel for thousands and thousands of miles of gold and never see a cemetery or meet a funeral procession. No clouds will ever darken those skies that he sees. Those doors have no locks and those windows have no bars, for thieves and robbers are not known there. Christ said, 'I go and prepare a place for you and I will come again and receive you unto myself.' *Today I submit to you the message of the contemporary gospel songwriter Chuck Girard, which in some way I feel this day would be the challenge to us from our departed friend, in his struggle io understand life. Chuck Girard wrote:*

"'Lay your burden down,/Lay your burden down./Take your troubled soul,/ Your tired mind,/And lay your burden down./You've been tryin' hard/To make it on your own./ And the strength you once were feeling/ Isn't there no more./And you think the wrong you've done/Is just too much to be forgiven./But you know that isn't true./Just lay your burden down,/Lay your burden down,/Lay your burden down./ Take your worries,/Failures,/Burdens to God's cross/And lay them down./Lay your burden down.'

"Let us pray. O thou who are nigh unto the afflicted, and with tender compassion you heal the brokenhearted. We pray this day that you will hear our prayer. And though, God, we do not understand tire mysteries of death, nor all that happens in our journey toward you and eternity, yet we know without a doubt that you are the all-wise God. We pray, God, that none will become bitter and hardened by this experience that we do not understand. Rather, fill our minds with love and goodwill. *God, we thank you for sharing with us this beautiful life, making this person a part of our lives with the sweet and kind life that he lived— true and genuine, and courteous and thoughtful, and sincere and radiant of love, day by day. Help us, God, to feel assured that the departed is at this moment, without a doubt, in a better life with you.* And, almighty God, may this visitation of death at this moment quicken to each of us a truer and a holy life in our souls, to show love to those we touch in this life. In the name of your son, Jesus, we pray. Amen.

"At this time we hear a song that Chip loved dearly."

Again the beautiful sound track music with the voices of friends.

"That's What Friends Are For"

Reverend Brooks announced, "The family wanted Jim and I to announce that all of Chip's friends are welcome to their home following the graveside services."

While the organ played softly, the long, solemn funeral procession began. I felt numb and lifeless while I sat waiting.

The mood was somber. I could hear an occasional sob among the sniffles, coughing, and clearing of throats while people filed slowly past the casket to view Chip. I was apprehensive for my moment to come, knowing it would be the last time I would see and touch Chip. I still couldn't believe my final moments with him had come. I didn't want this; I didn't want this to be the last time. My mind raced. *What am I going to do?* His last night I wrote, "I'm not ready, not yet," but now I must be. *Please, God, help me, please.*

Everyone else had already passed by to view his body. I lamely raised myself up while Jerry helped me to my feet.

We've been through so much together. The past two years have been so difficult and unfair to Chip.

Feeling numb and in a bit of a daze, I asked, *Please, God, please give me the strength to complete this as Chip would want. What will I do without him? Why was his life so short?*

My emotions were mixed when I slowly approached the casket. I felt as though I were heavily sedated, lifeless. Chip looked peaceful. I knew he was already in heaven and knowing this gave me a wonderful feeling. But this was the last time. Before, I knew I'd see him again. Now those days were gone.

I didn't want to leave him. I kissed him, saying, "I love you, Chip."

Then leaning heavily on Jerry, I walked out to the limousine and joined the family. It was quiet while we waited for the pallbearers to bring the casket out of the chapel and place it in the hearse.

I looked up. The sun was shining! This was the first time there had been sun all week. It was still gray and dismal, but truly, the sun was shining bright! *How wonderful,* I thought, *and just for Chip!* The weather seemed to have fit the mood all week, cold and desolate with no sunshine. *Thank you, God, for the sunlight on this dreary day and just at the perfect moment.*

People were seated in their cars. They slowly followed the hearse out into the graveyard. It wasn't far to the gravesite. Under the tent were chairs for the family. All was quiet and calm, and *the lovely white balloons were awaiting their destiny— the balloons Chip had requested to be at his funeral.*

Reverend Jim announced the interment would be now:

"In the fourteenth chapter of John, the Lord says to us, 'Let not your heart be troubled. If you believe in God, believe also in me. In my Father's house are many mansions, and if it were not so I would have told you. I go to prepare a place for you. And if I go and prepare a place for you, I will come again and receive you unto myself; that where I am, there ye may be also. And whither I go ye know, and the way ye know...But the Comforter, which is the Holy Ghost, whom the Father will send in my name, he shall teach you all things, and bring all things to your remembrance, whatsoever I have said unto you. Peace I leave with you, my peace I give unto you: not as the world giveth, give I unto you. Let not your heart be troubled, neither let it be afraid.'

"The book of Psalms 90, Verse 10: God said to us, The days of our years are soon cut off, and we fly away. *Chipper requested that there be balloons at his funeral. Today we will release into the atmosphere, as we release his spirit to God, three balloons representing the Trinity: God the Father, God the Son, God the Holy Spirit.*"

Reverend Brooks stepped out from under the tent and released the balloons while Reverend Jim announced, *"We release these three balloons to represent the three persons of the godhead, as we release the spirit of our brother Chip into the heavens above us this day."*

People were overwhelmed as they stepped out from under the tent to watch the balloons gently rise... going up, up, up... graciously ascending into heaven, representing Chip's spirit.

"Let us pray. *Almighty and most precious God, we come to you this afternoon in a joyous occasion that Chipper is now with the Lord.* We ask that you descend thy Holy Spirit on this family. Be with them. Guide them. Strengthen, give them spiritual stability to carry out their day. Lord, you gave your word that you would leave us with a comforter until you come back to claim your church. I ask now that this comforter, the same comforter yesterday, today, and forever more be with this family. Bless us and keep us. Guide us, oh Lord, in Jesus' mighty name we pray. Amen."

The pallbearers—Uncle Duane, Aaron, David J., David D., Steve, and Mark—passed by the casket where they lay their boutonnieres. Then friends passed by, offering their condolences.

Jerry clasped my hand softly, then whispered, "Chip's dad is here."

I was stunned! Overwhelmed! When what he just said hit me, I blankly stared at him.

He asked, "Are you going to be alright? We felt it would be better not to tell you until now."

I still didn't say anything.

Jerry continued, "We didn't want to upset you. He and his wife are here." Suddenly I was infuriated! The nerve, after Chip was gone! How absurd! I must have been in shock as I walked out from under the tent. The idea!

Phil, the funeral director, was standing beside the tent. Appalled by what I had been told, I blurted out, "Is he here?"

Obviously, Phil knew who I meant for he replied, "Yes, he's been here since early morning."

I exclaimed, "It's about time!"

Phil smiled knowingly. He understood, and later I learned he had been the one to tell Jerry. I walked on past. At about that time, several yards ahead I saw whom Chip's dad apparently was with. It was his sister who resided in Houston. She was pleasantly looking at me, smiling. I smiled while I walked toward her, and we grasped hands.

She said, "I hope you didn't think I wouldn't come."

I told her, "You're welcome to come to our home if you'd like."

We exchanged a few words, then I walked on to the limousine. I sat looking out the window. Seeing Chip's dad I thought, How pathetic! Chip's dad had finally come. How ironic, after Chip was gone. Reverend Jim had asked if he were coming. I told him Chip hadn't heard from him in months and hadn't seen him all the while he'd been sick. No, I wasn't expecting him. I truly had not. And now, to think I'd stepped aside again, not realizing it until too late.

Why had I gone on to the limo instead of spending time with my son, family, and friends as I would have, as I should have?

I suppose we could chalk his dad's coming as par for the course. Why now? Why not when Chip was alive, during the many long months while he suffered as he faced the end? Or when his son was willing to chance his own life to travel more than halfway to meet him, why not then? Or should I be asking, what? What possessed him to come now? What purpose did it serve? For whose comfort? Could he now say, "I'm sorry that we never had a real father-son relationship, but I do love you."

His dad was contacted the day Chip passed away and he hadn't responded. I wonder... was it because his son's name appeared in the obituary column in his hometown? It wasn't until then when the lovely flowers were received from his fellow workers. Did he finally have a change of heart to "save face"?

They both could have benefited while Chip was still alive! Instead, all the while Chip was suffering, he was forced to accept his dad's rejection as in the past. Whatever the reason, it almost made the funeral complete.

Many months before. Chip had said, "I would like my dad to be at my funeral."

That was long before Chip's last birthday, before his dad hadn't called in answer to his last letter.

I wasn't to realize how total Chip's dad's rejection was until a couple months after the funeral when I called him about one of Chip's requests, the only one not fulfilled: that his dad pay for his funeral. It could have been a final, thoughtful gesture and could have given him his own peace of mind.

When I finally called his dad, our conversation was brief.

Hesitantly, I said, "I have been procrastinating, but months before Chipper passed away, he spoke with me about your paying for his funeral expenses. Would you do this?"

His dad said, "I don't even have enough to take care of my own."

"Well, that's fine. I didn't really expect it. Chip thought it would only be right." I added, "That was the last thing you could have done for him. But that's fine if you don't want to," I paused, then said, "Okay? That's all. I just wanted to ask you because I told Chip I would. Thank you. Bye."

All was quiet the next day. It was mid afternoon and everyone was gone, except my sister Ruth, who would be going back to California in a couple of days.

I picked up the telephone and called the hospital in Dallas. "Hello, I would like to speak to someone about bringing flowers to the AIDS patients."

Soon a woman's voice said, "Hello, this is the chaplain."

"Yes, I'm calling about bringing some flowers to the AIDS patients today."

"How nice," she said and gave me instructions. Then she said, "When you get here, ask for me and I will come down to meet you. We can take care of the flowers together if you would like."

"Fine, we'll be there as soon as we load the flowers into the truck."

We loaded the pickup with all the flowers that they had brought to our home from Chip's funeral. There were so many and I didn't want them to go to waste. I thought that the patients would no doubt like knowing someone was thinking about them and cared. Possibly this would help relieve some of their loneliness. I know how it had been for Chip and he would have liked our doing this.

When we arrived at the hospital, there were some carts waiting for us to put the flowers on, but only three. So while they were getting some more, Jerry called the chaplain. She joined us while we were busy loading the carts. Then we each pushed one cart and pulled another to save time. We got these loaded on the elevators and went up to the floor where the patients were.

In the first room we came to, there was a young man who had just arrived that day. There were three friends with him who were very pleased for him to be receiving flowers.

I said, "These are from my son. We lost him this week."

I smiled, then left the room. I went into each room, delivering the flowers while Jerry and Ruth pushed the carts and waited in the hall. We went from room to room. When we came to the first room where we needed to put on masks, gloves, and gowns, the chaplain said I might not want to go in, that she would take care of those particular patients.

I smiled and said, "That's fine. I understand. I want to."

Suddenly memories came flooding back of when Chip was in the hospital in ICU. Of course, the mask was mainly so the patient wouldn't catch any of our germs. Most of the patients were sleeping and many looked utterly exhausted. I understood how they were feeling. That was the really sad part. I tried to work fast to keep my mind off the pain and suffering. If they were awake, I'd stop and talk. Only a few more flowers and we would be done.

The chaplain said, "The patients will be pleased with the flowers."

Jerry said, "This was something my wife wanted to do since we lost our son."

Ruth added, "She's been planning this ever since she saw how many flowers there were."

I replied, "I'm sure Chip would be happy. I didn't see any reason for them to go to waste."

The chaplain looked surprised, commenting, "How nice of you."

I explained, "He passed away Monday and his funeral was Friday due to these complications. That's why I wanted the flowers to go to these patients first, then to the other patients. I understand what it's like for them. It's important they have love and compassion."

She said, "This must be difficult for you, so soon and to see..."

Smiling, I added, "My son suffered a long time. Still, he helped me. He always said, *'Mother, you're strong. You'll be strong.'* And too, my aerobics and swimming daily helped me through it all. Chipper had a tender heart and a remarkable attitude right up to the end. Of course, he'd been this way all his life. He truly was a rare type of person, always giving me reason to be proud."

The chaplain was attentive while I continued.

"I believe that's why he lived much longer than expected while his precious body gradually withered away. He was suffering and the sheer loneliness was heartbreaking. Still, he hung in there much longer than he should have, knowing I was having a hard time letting go. Chip's tenderness was always so genuine. It was the story of his life right up to the end."

Shaking my head, I smiled. "I'm just thankful I was blessed with Chip. He always was grateful, even of the least little things. Goodness, I mustn't get started. It's just that while he was growing up, and as a young adult, I needn't say anything because of how people always marveled about him and his great character."

I paused and smiled, "But listen to me now."

Then I confided, "It always seemed that Chip, and in all truth, that most gay guys possess a unique quality about themselves. It's a special sensitivity that is strongly felt by those who know them. I'm repeatedly hearing this comment or something of a similar nature about their lifestyle, especially by those who work with them or have at some time or another, and of course, us mothers. Our sons give us reason to be proud." I smiled, then added, "It truly is a rare commodity and a blessing that makes them outstanding."

Smiling, the chaplain took hold of my hands.

Nodding my head, I smiled and proudly said, "Chip truly was a beautiful person, such style and character—always! And the greatest gift he gave and left behind was love."

I took a deep breath, then calmly repeated, "Yes, Chip was a wonderful blessing. He was the major part of my life! For him I am strong. Chip made me strong."

I smiled and squeezed the chaplain's hands while looking deep into her eyes. I then shared with her how Chip had made his peace with God and how he had humbly reached his weakened hand and arm up to God. "I'm sure we both felt the same peacefulness, knowing God was calling him home.

"Yes, I love Chip with all my heart, and the last time we were together it was wonderful how his beautiful, piercing blue eyes spoke those very words of love. There were no words, but I truly felt his love sincerely coming from the depths of his heart."

I smiled, then proudly gazed afar, feeling Chip's beautiful, piercing blue eyes upon me that very moment, just like the last time, enhancing his divine love.

Yes, in all truth he has now gone to *"THE ULTIMATE LOVE "*

www.ingramcontent.com/pod-product-compliance
Lightning Source LLC
Chambersburg PA
CBHW070906120626
46546CB00001B/151